BLACK INTERNET EFFECT

SHAVONE CHARLES

PENGUIN WORKSHOP

**I dedicate this book to the next generation of minds
who will shape our world for the better—SC**

PENGUIN WORKSHOP
An imprint of Penguin Random House LLC, New York

First published in the United States of America by Penguin Workshop,
an imprint of Penguin Random House LLC, New York, 2022

Text copyright © 2022 by Shavone Charles
Illustrations copyright © 2022 by Penguin Random House LLC

Visit us online at penguinrandomhouse.com.

Library of Congress Cataloging-in-Publication Data is available.

Manufactured in China

ISBN 9780593387535   10 9 8 7 6 5 4 3 2 1 HH

Design by Julia Rosenfeld

PROLOGUE

I was sixteen years old when I stood in the living room with my dad at my house in Southeast San Diego and watched a TV special that would change my life forever.

It was a hot Saturday morning in 2007, and I rushed through the house, toothbrush in one hand, flute case in the other, scrambling to get dressed for a scorching day of marching band practice at Helix Charter High School. I was flute section leader in band and had to show up an hour early, so I was in a crazy hurry when my dad called me into the living room. "Aye, Shavone! Where you at? Come on in here! You need to see this."

I scurried over. "Look at this! Look at these people,

can you believe they're at work?" my dad touted. I looked at the TV to see clips of twenty- to thirty-something-year-old adults napping in lime-green pods, eating ice-cream sundaes, and riding down bright red, forty-foot slides. For the first few seconds, it looked like I was watching a scene from *Willy Wonka & the Chocolate Factory* (one of my all-time favorite movies!). I stood there with my mouth open, in awe of this pictured utopia. A few seconds later, Google's colorful, bright logo flashed on the screen and my dad said, "Have you ever seen this? They work for Google! You should look up working for a place like *that* one day."

I was bewildered by the thought. Me? Work for a search engine website? Up until that point, I hadn't thought once about a career path in the technology industry. I was enrolled in every AP class I could get into in high school because I knew I wanted to go to a university and be a writer. That was it. I had dreams of working on music and poetry. I even flirted with the idea of going to law school or being a college professor one day. Working in tech hadn't ever really crossed my mind until that day in the living room.

Band practice would have to wait. I felt so drawn to the idea of this food heaven full of genius people who could nap throughout the day and wear Nikes and jeans to work. My eyes scoured the TV screen in search of a person of color, a Black person, anyone that could give me a sense of familiarity and otherwise convince me that this utopia was a welcoming, real-life possibility for someone who looked like me. Even then, it was hard for me to fathom the idea of seeing a Black woman, a person like me, working at a place like Google.

Thirty minutes passed, the episode ended, and that bright feeling of hope and curiosity was quickly followed by an overwhelming sense of anxiety as I sat in the living room with no blueprint or knowledge of how to pursue a career that would ever lead me to a company like Google. Around that time, my high school counselors were laser-focused on college and more traditional careers. Technology wasn't often brought up as a possible professional path for me or any other Black students. At the time, the popular social media site Myspace was killing the game, and that was the main social platform of choice for me and my friends. We didn't view technology as a standalone concept or industry—it was simply interwoven into our everyday lives as the main way to forge community and stay connected to one another. The only reason I was ever introduced to HTML coding in the first place was because I wanted to customize the color and template of my Myspace profile.

I also grew up in a household with parents who were Black small-business owners and always preached about the importance of me going to college to get a "good job." Every day, I watched my mother and father wake up to work from sunrise to sundown, and they answered to no one. They ran their own mom-and-pop businesses: our family restaurant and a hair salon. They didn't have a 401(k) or a cushy corporate benefits plan, and always urged me to go to a university so I could one day get a high-paying job and avoid having to work as hard as they do. To all of us, that meant being a lawyer, a corporate CEO, or a doctor of some kind. I remember feeling so much anxiety, pressure, and fear whenever I thought about choosing "the right"

career path after high school. I didn't envision myself in a pantsuit, working in an office cubicle anywhere. If there was an industry for me, I thought, it would have to be in media, music, or fashion, where I could really express myself.

Fast forward and here I am, neck-deep as a young Black millennial in Silicon Valley, navigating the world of tech and social media. Currently, I am at TikTok, where I was hired in a newly created role as the company's first-ever head of Diversity & Inclusion Communications. I officially started my career in the technology industry at twenty-one years old with my first full-time job at Twitter, where I led the company's global music and culture communications out of their San Francisco headquarters as the youngest and first-ever Black woman to be hired onto their public relations team. After Twitter, I worked at Instagram, where I launched their Los Angeles office and managed all of the app's global music, teen, and youth culture communications, again, as the youngest and first-ever Black woman to be hired onto their marketing and communications team. At both Twitter and Instagram,

I personally carved out my professional roles, and since then, I strive to bring my advocacy for voices of color into every room I'm in. I am the founder of my very own creative group, Future of Creatives, and I started Magic in Her Melanin, a community organization created with the mission to elevate the stories of women of color and drive equitable career development for next-generation creatives and people of color across the tech industry. I am a multihyphenate creative, classically trained musician, and activist who happened to find her way into the wonky world of the tech industry. My path has led me in many directions and down so many winding roads—all with the hope that in the spaces in which I am the first, I won't be the last.

The right balance of curiosity and nerve have always pushed me toward good directions in my life. During the darkest, most discouraging times, I can lean on those two parts of myself. I credit the majority of my resilient, self-starter demeanor to my two parents, Bonnie and Darryl. I often think about that wide-eyed teenager who dreamed of just being able to *be* and unapologetically exist as a Black girl in every space she occupied. From childhood through early adulthood, I struggled to be accepted and welcomed anywhere, all because of what I looked like and what I represented as "the only Black girl in the room."

So where there wasn't space for me, I had to create it. Where I wasn't welcomed, I had to invite myself. When the room wanted me to stay small and invisible, I had to make myself seen. Against all odds, I had to value myself enough to know that my voice and perspective mattered. I've carried these survival tactics throughout my life, and it's all thanks to the superhero Black women who raised me. Through them, I figured out that I'd have to forge my own path and dare to write my own story—even if I was left out of the fairy tales altogether.

# # #

BLACK INTERNET EFFECT

Truth be told, I applied to Google's BOLD (Building Opportunities in Leadership and Development) internship program on a pipe dream. I mean, who the hell was I kidding?

I was a sophomore at the University of California Merced, and that semester I was living in Washington, DC, as part of a highly competitive campus-wide academic program that allowed students to continue their college coursework remotely and gain on-the-job experience. I'd landed an internship with a San Diego congressman on Capitol Hill, where I was a professional letter reader. I had strict orders to fix the printer often—and I wrote up responses to San Diegan constituents from time to time.

Jokes aside, I learned a lot during my time on the Hill, interning in Washington, DC. I was an English literature major with a double minor in writing and sociology, and had a real passion for civic engagement and public service. This was also my chance to get an unfiltered look at the dicey and difficult world of politics and US government. I spent an unthinkable number of hours interning for free on the Hill while completing a full load of coursework.

One night, exhausted from a day of work, I sat in my dorm room and did some googling on the top internships in the world, searching "the best companies to intern for." As much respect as I had for all the incredible, passionate people I had met in DC, one thing was for certain: The majority of them were underpaid and emotionally run-down by the demands of politics. Not only that, I also found that as a young woman of color, so much of the uniform and attire that I had to wear on Capitol Hill was truly another means of erasing who I was. There was underlying pressure to wear your hair straightened and flat. No braids, no dreadlocks, no natural hair—

you wanted to look smart and well put together. Like you belonged there. You were urged *to want* to blend in and fade into the background like the old paintings that draped the long, cold, white marble hallways in the Capitol. I couldn't see myself thriving anywhere that required me to shrink or become a shell of who I am. I had to go back to the drawing board to figure out my next move.

Along my search, my mind had already been racing about the idea of possibly working in tech. By that time, companies like Amazon, Google, Apple, and Facebook were on the rise and gaining popularity with Ivy League undergraduates who studied computer science and engineering. In the bubble of Silicon Valley, among the tech industry's tight circles, these companies were known as "the big four." Often, each company would handpick candidates for their engineering departments from the most prestigious universities in the country. You rarely saw any of the big four recruiters in person and if you did, you most likely attended an Ivy League school. Their recruiters certainly hadn't made it to UC Merced yet.

 15

To top it all off, I wasn't a computer science major and had no technical knowledge when it came to computer engineering. But my past internships gave me a solid, big-picture perspective on the many different job functions and nontechnical career tracks I could pursue within technology companies. From marketing to public relations, human resources to sales, my internship experiences gave me a solid understanding of other possible paths into tech.

In high school and throughout my early college years, there was no information readily available about the technical and nontechnical careers I could pursue *within* the field of technology. Black and minority youth were particularly in the dark when it came to career resources and the larger privilege of even believing we had "options" outside of the harsh realities and low-paying jobs that were consistently advertised to us. Many of us couldn't afford computers, and weren't provided access to information about how to get into the tech industry or pursue computer science as a career path. I remember having friends in my neighborhood who had to sneak into the library's computer lab just to do their homework and access an internet connection.

I was fortunate enough to have a computer and internet access at home because my parents worked 24/7 to make sure my brothers and I didn't have to do without. While they worked around the clock, I would tinker around on my dad's Microsoft Windows PC and familiarize myself with using the internet, along with all the popular '90s software programs and PC games. That computer became a safe space for my brothers and I to retreat to, a portal into different worlds—worlds a lot happier than the sound of nonstop police sirens wailing outside our window at home. My interest in technology blossomed from computers to gaming consoles like Xbox and PlayStation. As a young woman, I took to all the things society told girls not to do: I played sports; I played video games; I only wore pants and sneakers; I watched anime with my brothers (*Dragon Ball Z* was my favorite); and of course, I worked on computers.

Back then and even now, there's a negative societal stigma that says women and girls aren't supposed to code or be interested in technology or

 17

computer science. According to a 2020 study done by the United Nations, women hold only 25 percent of computing jobs in the United States, with women and girls making up just 19 percent of students who receive degrees in computing, and represent just 23 percent of high school students sitting for advanced placement exams in computer science.[1] Factor in race, and people of color, especially Black women, have even lower representation in the technology industry at every level. For instance, in 2014, Google publicly released their first diversity workforce report, which revealed Black employees made up less than 4 percent of their staff. Fast forward to 2021, Black people still made up less than 4.4 percent of Google's entire 135,000-plus person company.[2]

All of these things were doing somersaults in my head like a relentless anxiety Olympics, as I combed the internet that night. If I wanted to work in the tech

1. Saujani, Reshma, "Closing the Gender Gap in Science and Technology," *UN Chronicle*, February 10, 2020, https://www.un.org/en/un-chronicle/closing-gender-gap-science-and-technology-0.
2. "Representation at Google," Diversity Report, Google, accessed October 25, 2021, https://diversity.google/annual-report/representation/.

industry, I had to stomach the fact that the odds were quite literally stacked against me. While researching, I read an article about the highly esteemed Google internship and the near-impossible applicant acceptance rate, which was somewhere lower than 1 percent. There were so many rumors floating around about Google's internship program and their difficult interview process, but the most discouraging one was that people of color rarely ever got accepted into the program at all.

Any rational person would've probably read all of that and moved on from the idea of applying without a second thought. But what did I have to lose? My dad's favorite motto echoed in my mind: "The worst thing anyone can tell you is no." So I kept on digging, this time searching for application deadlines and more details on all of the programs that were available. Digging and digging, and then—aha! I found an opening for their Google BOLD internship program, and the deadline to submit the application was literally in one hour. So I took action—I quickly wrote a personal statement about myself and fired it off into the Googleverse,

 19

thinking I would never hear from them again.

A couple of weeks later, I was back in central California at UC Merced when my cell phone rang with a number that started off with a 650 area code and read "Mountain View"—where Google's headquarters are located. At that time, I lived next door to my college campus in a huge house with my close friend Tatiana. I was busy microwaving a cup of noodles (the finest of decadent meals for a broke college student!) when Google called. As soon as I read "Mountain View," my gut dropped to my knees. It was *them*, and *they* were actually calling *me*!

I gathered my senses and slid the answer call bar and answered in the shakiest, most high-pitched, fake professional voice ever. "Hello, this is Shavone." The caller then responded with a cheery, "Hey, Shavone, this is Whitney from Google!" At that time, my grip on reality had dissolved and I straight up couldn't believe what I was hearing. Screw the noodles; my hunger immediately disappeared as I sat down on the carpet, legs crisscrossed, propping my back against the wall, and grinning like a candy-hyped toddler on Christmas morning. It was really them. Whitney from Google then went on to tell me that her team loved my application and asked if I was still interested in being a candidate for Google's Global Communications & Public Affairs team that summer. I was elated, and in a matter of days, I became a Google expert. I felt consumed by the possibility, scouring the internet between lectures and work to learn all I could about the company, their sea of products, their work culture, their lawsuits, their blog, and everything in between.

I was also completely nerve-racked by the entire two-week interview process. As a first-generation undergrad and the only person in my family to go to college, a voice in the back of my mind constantly crept up to undermine my self-confidence and question everything I had worked so hard to attain. Being overqualified and overprepared wasn't enough. I had to be twice as good as anyone else that interviewer would ever have a chance to talk to. With tremendous prayer, discipline, and a flawless Wi-Fi connection, I weathered three grilling forty-five-minute interview calls that stretched my brain and imagination to its farthest points. One of my most memorable interviewers, Sandra, asked me to walk her through a step-by-step process of how to do an activity, any activity that I could verbally describe in a simple how-to format. She said the goal was for me to effectively teach her how to do "something" in less than eight clear instructional steps. From all of my online sleuth work and tedious research on Google's interview process, I immediately realized that my answers to their mind-bending questions would need to focus less on responding with the "correct answer" and more on clearly explaining my creative approach to problem-solving. So, I chose something I knew a lot about: basketball. I confidently responded to Sandra's curveball question with a simple eight-step guide on how to shoot the perfect jump shot.

A week or so after my last interview round, I got a call from a Googler (Google employee) named Brian. He called completely unannounced and told me I was accepted into the internship program and that I'd need to start my housing hunt as soon as possible. That fast, a pipe dream materialized into something real.

That June in 2011, I moved to Mountain View. My dad took the time to drive seven hours with me from San Diego up north and help me get comfortable in my new world of unknowns. I became the roommate of a pleasant full-time Googler named David, who I was introduced to through Google's University Programs team. Before my first orientation day at Google's enormous 3.1-million-square-foot Googleplex headquarters, I wanted to get a look at the grounds to ease my nerves and see where I'd be commuting to every day.

The first day visiting the Google campus was completely mind-blowing. My dad and I arrived on site and immediately felt like we were at an amusement park for grown-ups. There we were, at the very place my dad and I marveled at way back when on that fateful day before band practice. Surrounded by the giant life-size Google logos and ten-foot-tall lime-green Android characters, I took a long look around outside the security check-in building to see if there were any other students—or anyone—who looked like me. No luck. I didn't think much of it; it was more of a mental bookmark that I would end up having to come back to much later.

My dad and I met a lovely Google rep and wandered through the campus as if we were the Willy Wonka kids who had found golden tickets. We ate blondie bars and ice-cream sundaes, we rode bikes, we raved about their heated toilet seats, we took a million pictures, and we basked in the sun to reflect on the fact that I had beat every statistic simply by being here. That wide-eyed Black girl from San Diego, who dared to dream bigger than what the world had once shown her, made it to Google.

One of the many bigger adjustments for me when I started my internship was learning to get comfortable with the idea of the unknown and not having all of the answers. Before I actually got to Google, like the rest of the world, I expected every Googler to be all about having the answers and knowing everything. I mean, it's Google, the number one information source and search engine we all go to for answers.

When I arrived, that idea was quickly dispelled. I had no idea what to expect on my first day. The orientation was jam-packed with company speakers from every corner of their organization, giving the Google pep talk. There were so many nuances about Google's work culture; I loved the majority of it—especially one of their infamous company culture mottos at the time, "Don't be evil."[3] The key to succeeding at the company was actually all about your ability to problem-solve and think on your own with a collective goal in mind. It wasn't at all about having the answers—it was about your journey to creating solutions.

I sat there during first-day orientation with that year's summer internship class. The students were a diverse group. Most were from Ivy League schools and prestigious HBCUs (Historically Black Colleges and Universities). It was clear that Google's BOLD program was a prime pipeline for some the most elite underrepresented talent around the world. The program receives a whopping forty-thousand-plus applications every year and only about fifteen

3. Conger, Kate, "Google Removes 'Don't Be Evil' Clause from Its Code of Conduct," *Gizmodo*, May 18, 2018, https://gizmodo.com/google-removes-nearly-all-mentions-of-dont-be-evil-from-1826153393.

hundred applicants are chosen. Now we just had to figure out how to actually *succeed* as Googlers.

For most of us there who were Black interns or interns of color, there was this inherent and ongoing personal obstacle that never moved or shifted: We had to figure out how to fit into a space that clearly wasn't designed with us in mind. Our identities, our unique battles and differences, were all of what made us who we were, but also all of what made the world a harder place for us to thrive in. We were out of the loop when it came to using tech jargon like "ping me," "TL;DR," "burn rate," and other larger social commonalities that most tech workers shared and could relate to together. There was an entire layer of fluent tech speak present in every part of communication on campus at Google, from the emails, to every in-person exchange and lunch conversation held across every corner of the company. From day one of the internship, I was thrown into the deep end, along with my fellow classmates turned colleagues. The intro to this new world brought on a flood of mixed emotions. I felt excitement and suspended terror all at once. You're taught to work so hard for these kinds of opportunities, to be in these coveted, competitive spaces. But nobody ever really coaches you on how to successfully make it through and survive the spaces once you're actually there.

Orientation at Google was about a week long and full of interactive group activities and team-building moments with the other interns. In the process of getting acclimated, I met some of the most amazing students from around the way and also met some pretty interesting characters. Many of them came from extremely competitive universities, so there was this constant air of cliquiness among a lot of the interns. Nobody in Mountain View, let alone my intern class, had ever heard anything about UC Merced until the day I showed up at the Googleplex. When they'd ask me where I went to school, there was always a puzzled look that followed and a bit of an awkward "Oh, that's nice." I found myself in the underdog position again. Only this time, I thought that I had actually found other Black people to talk to and socialize with; some folks I could relate to, right?

Wrong. I assumed we'd all have so much in common, but it turned out many of us were incredibly different, all with different values and different lived experiences, with quite the spectrum of personality differences as well.

I was on a real high heading into the middle of orientation week, but as the week progressed, I realized that making it at Google might be harder than I would have ever imagined. Everyone's goal coming out of the BOLD internship program was to get "converted" and land a full-time job offer after college graduation. It was the holy grail and ultimate stress relief for any undergraduate student who feared entering the job market. I was that summer's only Global Communications & Public Affairs intern and later found out that it was nearly impossible for an intern on that team to receive a full-time job offer. Due to the competitive nature of working in communications, public relations, and marketing, there are seasoned professionals competing for any and every entry-level communications role at the company, and Google would be more likely to hire someone with on-the-job experience than an intern. I knew I had to figure out how to make the best of everything I had in front of me—while I was still in the position to do so.

My first week after orientation, I made it a point to find older Black women to connect with at Google. There weren't very many, but I was able to get connected to Google's small and tight-knit Black community by reaching out to their internal employee resource group, Black Googler Network (BGN). I decided to become the official BOLD intern rep for BGN throughout my whole summer at Google. I took on three times the work that was required of me and my internship, with the goal to truly stretch myself in ways that would help drive impactful and inclusive change during my time there. I also knew that working with BGN would help expose me to more senior Black leaders and Googlers, as I started to really evaluate whether or not this place could be a positive place for me. Thankfully, I met some of the most incredible, hardworking, loving human beings through this program. Two women in particular, Aly and Charlaé, have become my lifelong friends and sister figures. Two other women, Ada and Nava, who took the time to help guide me when I arrived at Google, are my forever mentors and sheroes. They helped advise me on everything from résumé formatting and how to best position myself to apply for tech jobs to tactics on how to navigate the world of Google as an intern and make a noticeable impact with my work projects at the company. These women were living, breathing examples of what could be possible for me. They inspired me by simply existing, moving and shaking in full force as Black women leaders. Seeing them thrive allowed me to see myself and actually believe I had a real fighting chance to make a positive impression and impact as well.

Funny thing is, I found more support, connection, and community in my relationships with full-timers than many of my peers. During the after-hours intern hangouts and social activities, I felt pretty isolated at times by many of my fellow Black interns. I didn't go to Spelman College, Howard University, Hampton University, or any of the other prestigious HBCUs, so I guess they didn't see a lot of value in befriending me or socializing with me. A little piece of me was really hurt by that because for so long before Google or college, I was alone. I was always the only Black person in the room and had longed to have the opportunity to be around people who looked like me, who had my same skin tone, hair texture, and interests. People I could relate to and also help support and empower. I have always believed there's more power in unity and uplifting those around you, regardless of how they look or what their background might be.

My nana, Cookie (my grandmother on my mom's side), always taught me to "go where you're celebrated and accepted. Don't shrink for nobody." So I put my blinders on and moved accordingly. My internship on the communications team quickly became one of the most memorable and rewarding experiences of my life. My team worked on constant, large-scale global problem-solving, never-ending news deadlines, and through the roller coaster of challenges that come along with being a publicist for one of the biggest technology platforms in the world. My experience at Google became less about fitting in and more about the journey of self-growth. It became about leaning in to the best sides of myself and deciding to stand tall in my own skin, regardless of which room I sat in.

As my internship and time there wrapped up, I was proactive about finding ways to keep working with Google beyond that summer. I learned about the Google Student Ambassador Program, where students would be able to go back to their campuses and educate their classmates about Google's career opportunities, applications, and products for education. Through the program, I'd be able to bring a bit of their resources back to all of the first-generation students of color at UC Merced. I wanted to leave the door wide open for others to walk through and get exposed to the world of technology. I was the first person from my university to intern at Google, and I made sure I wouldn't be the last.

Too often, the BIPOC community is an afterthought or quota fulfillment in the corporate world's hiring processes, and yet, these job titles and companies are coached into our psyche as a measure of self-worth. Even as an intern at Google, I saw just how much our "new" identities were now wrapped up in being Googlers. So many of us are coached to validate ourselves with the jobs that we do versus the value we ourselves bring to said job. I realized, then and there, that it is a radical act to stand in my truth and cling to the most authentic parts of myself. Because change starts with me and the resources I have to do something, and continues with any of us who decide to be that spark that inspires others to take action and pay it forward.

Throughout my first two years in college, I didn't have a solid idea of which industry I wanted to work in full-time—and I knew I had a short amount of time to figure it out. Whether it was school clubs, university jobs, or internships, I went with my gut and stayed closely tuned in to what inspired me. If I didn't have a passion for it or enjoy doing it, even through the challenging moments, I stopped and pivoted to something new.

Internships, preparation, and proactive initiative aside, the onset of my senior year of college brought with it a serious sense of panic and anxiety. That panic and anxiety had a name, and it was called "the First." Coming back to campus as the first-ever Google intern from my school and then later the first UC Merced student to intern at BET Networks, the first person to go to college in my family, the first, the first, the first—it all created an immeasurable amount of pressure. And as amazing as those opportunities were, I still hadn't gotten a job offer secured. Here I was, heading into college graduation with no guarantee of my future or being able to feed myself after June.

So, again, I took to the internet and embarked on my next search. I did some digging online for other jobs in tech and applied for a community support job at Facebook. I ended up getting a call back from the recruiter months after I applied. *Thank God! I might actually not be unemployed after graduation,* I thought. After a few chats with the recruiter, Facebook flew me all the way out to Austin, Texas, for an interview. The interview was for a user support role that I had zero background experience in, but I didn't have any other leads, so I flew out for the interview without hesitation.

The day of my interview at the Facebook Austin office, I sat alongside about six other job applicants in a stuffy and crowded lobby, nervous as all outside. I found it odd that we were all sitting there next to each other, sweating bullets. After we started talking to one another, we eventually realized that we were there for the same job (fun). I completed my interviews and they went horribly. It turned out that the job I applied for required coding experience, which I 100 percent didn't have. That weeded me right on out, but during my last talk with the manager of the team, he mentioned I'd be great for a communications job there. "Yes, exactly," I immediately replied. I would be perfect for a job like that. But there was one major factor that stained my impression of Facebook: I didn't see one Black person or person of color during my time on site. Even after the interviews, no one.

My recruiter was kind enough to feed me some of their delicious free food (the tech company standard) and give me a tour of their offices. I looked forward to that and thought, *Hey, maybe I'll see some diversity before I head out today.* As we walked through the open-floor layout, passing desks left and right, we made it to a mini kitchen full of snacks and drinks.

While I took a snack break, one of the recruiting team employees stopped to talk to us and tell me about how amazing the work culture is at Facebook Austin. I just so happened to ask, "What does diversity look like at this office? Do you all have any community projects you're working on here in Austin?" The employee (a white male) cheerfully answered, "Yes, loads of diversity stuff happening here. We are all so close here at this office, like one big family. It's rad."

I crunched on my popcorn and nodded with raised eyebrows. A few minutes later, we were back on the move and being ushered toward the elevator door headed back to the lobby. Before passing the last row of desks, my eyes lit up—I had spotted a Black woman in the office! I stalled behind the recruiter to get the woman's attention. But she wouldn't look at me. She was sitting in the loneliest corner all by herself, with the most exhausted, miserable expression on her face, typing with just her right hand. I was about to go over to her and say hello, but she looked like she had the weight of the world on her shoulders. I made eye contact with her for a split second and smiled.

Her glazed eyes met mine and went right back to her laptop screen. I walked to the lobby with that picture frozen in my memory.

As soon as I made it back to California, I got a call from Facebook telling me I wasn't the right person for the job. But they mentioned they'd share my résumé with the communications team and would reach out if any opportunities came up. Even though I knew the role I interviewed for wasn't the right fit, that swift and immediate feedback still hurt. That fast, I was back right where I had started. No job offer, no leads, yet another failed mission. But perhaps it was a blessing in disguise, after all.

I started at Twitter as an intern in 2012, less than a month after my college graduation, when the app was a small San Francisco–based start-up. I was the second Black intern to ever work at the company and the first-ever Black woman to intern there. I mostly knew of Twitter through word of mouth and within the budding tech industry circles I had managed to start cultivating after my Google internship. In 2012, Twitter was the emerging breakout social media platform and talk of the town in Silicon Valley. My decision to go to Twitter and work some of the longest, mentally grueling days ever was absolutely driven by my passion for the platform and the possible promise of being part of a historical public company that could financially change the trajectory of my entire life.

My first interview with Twitter was one of the most important days of my life and set the tone for how I would choose to show up as a Black woman in tech for the decade to come. For my interview, I actively made the decision to show up to Twitter HQ in downtown San Francisco (the heart of Silicon Valley) with my natural coily 4C hair. My afro was out and proud, in full effect. Arriving in San Francisco, smack-dab in the middle of tech's predominantly white, male workforce, was an intimidating culture shock until I thought more about just how valuable my background and perspective would be in a sea of people who more than likely shared the same outlook and backstory. I chose to proudly lean in to my own identity, tapping into everything that made me different, with a mission to normalize the concept of a Black woman unapologetically existing and thriving in that environment.

Before the interview, I felt a wave of confidence wash over me the very moment I decided to present the truest version of myself. I figured if I showed up as my Blackest, most authentic self from day one, that'd give me all the wiggle room in the world to just be me, day in and day out. If I got the job, I'd then be able to pull up in an afro, or a wig, or braids, or a hat—I had set the bar. The fact that this sort of construct and anxiety lives within the minds of Black women who show up to job interviews and wake up to go to work every day is a whole other tragedy and unfortunate truth in itself. With my 4C crown on, I went to my interview and *slayed*.

A week later, I found out I had been selected for the paid three-month internship, under the condition that if I did well, there was a strong likelihood I'd be hired into a full-time role. Given I had just graduated from college and needed to find a full-time job right away, accepting the internship at Twitter and betting on the startup was a huge risk for me.

At the start of my Twitter internship, a mentor of mine introduced me to one of the few Black employees at Twitter at the time—a recruiter named Scott, who ultimately came to be another dear friend, ally, and professional mentor. Scott was the first friendly face of color I met at Twitter. His warm smile and bright soul lit up the room when I ran into him in the lobby on my first day. He later introduced me to Bakari, who was Twitter's head of legal. Bakari was rumored to be the first-ever Black man to be hired full-time at Twitter. We joked about this to make light of his historic arrival, but in all honesty, we knew the lack of diversity at Twitter, more specifically the absence of Black employees, was a major problem that we wanted to help change.

After meeting Bakari, I sought out more information on employee resource groups and the presence of employees of color at Twitter. I started to ask questions about ways to get involved with the surrounding community and felt compelled to figure out how I could help diversify Twitter's work environment, create a funnel for Black interns to get hired, and improve the experience for Black employees who were there full-time. Weeks after meeting Bakari, he introduced me to a powerhouse Black woman named Erin, who had just gotten hired full-time. From there, we routinely got together for

 44

lunch and impromptu coffee meetups with the other few Black employees. Bakari and Erin were a lot busier than I was in their full-time roles, and they empowered me to offer a helping hand and contribute time toward officially starting Blackbirds—Twitter's first-ever employee resource group for Black employees. With their support, I worked after hours for months to help draft the statement of purpose and develop the official charter for Blackbirds. With any free time I could find, I set up internal gatherings, community service projects, and recruiting events and initiatives that served to ramp up the organization. By the time I was hired full-time, I was the president of Blackbirds and had worked alongside a collective of other Black Twitter employees based in San Francisco and New York to bring the organization to life.

Within my first few months at Twitter, I became a lot more aware of the global impact the platform had on so many lives, particularly the role Twitter played in the lives of underrepresented communities. Some describe Twitter as a microblogging and social networking site where people communicate in short

 45

messages. The truth is, Twitter takes on a different use and meaning for every individual that joins the platform. Whether you're a journalist, a celebrity, or an activist live-tweeting a protest from the front lines in your home country, Twitter serves as a global stage for your voice and story. The app itself was a true and raw manifestation of global online community and connectedness. Twitter the workplace, on the other hand, wasn't yet this diverse melting pot that the platform ultimately was. There was this clear tension between what Twitter represented to the outside world and the alternate reality that existed internally. Fundamentally, what set Twitter apart from other tech companies and social media services was the app's deeply rooted connection to Black users and Black online communities. Somehow, in the midst of Twitter's rise as a global tech powerhouse, the forum became a beacon of light and massive influence for Black culture and communities of color. In fact, much of Twitter's rise to popularity should be credited to Black people and Black online communities.

There I was, one of the only Black women at

the company, this platform that was evidently so intertwined with the Black community online but not so much in real life. I noticed and felt this disconnect immediately. As I navigated Twitter and met hundreds of new faces, I quickly picked up on the mountain of potential and talent Twitter housed as a company. Every day, I met some of the most passionate, inspiring people who truly cared about the work they were doing, as well as the importance of making Twitter a safe and accessible platform for everyone online. But it was clear to me that this dissonance was mostly organic and symptomatic of larger hiring gaps and biases that dominated Silicon Valley as an industry. Many of the engineers and product-focused leaders at the company were just blissfully unaware of the gaps that were glaringly obvious to me. The reality was (and still is) that I had the advantage of having this dual lens as a Black woman who worked for Twitter and also as a Black user of Twitter. Even as an intern, I realized my responsibility and privilege of foresight and access. I knew that trying to convince others of these gaps and growth opportunities wouldn't be a simple task, especially when it came to shaking seasoned, extremely successful professionals out of their biases to embrace diversity and inclusivity—but I also knew that if we (the Black employees at Twitter) didn't speak up for ourselves and our communities, no one else would.

The summer I started at Twitter full-time also happened to be right in the middle of the trial of George Zimmerman, who was being tried for the wrongful shooting and killing of seventeen-year-old Black Florida teen Trayvon Martin. Public outcry following the murder of Trayvon Martin consumed every major news outlet and dominated global social conversation on Twitter. Zimmerman's trial and Martin's unjust killing became a pivotal moment for online communities who used Twitter as a means of information sharing, activism, and community mobilizing for social causes. During my early months at Twitter, I noticed how the concept of hashtag activism swelled into a highly visible and global vehicle of influence that drove impact online and in the real world. An important part of my evolving role at

48

Twitter involved liaising and working with the service's most-followed celebrities and public figures on social marketing strategy and public relations campaigns that amplified their use of Twitter. I watched as celebrities and public figures like Spike Lee, LeBron James, Sean "Diddy" Combs, and others flocked to Twitter to express their outrage around the killing of Trayvon Martin. Thanks to Twitter's platform and its Black users, community petitions, charitable-donation resources, and overall visibility in support of Trayvon Martin circulated around the web, with Black organizations and nonprofits mobilizing national IRL protests.

While the website was ablaze, the hallways of Twitter remained eerily silent. Every Black employee was still required to go in to work. On one hand, we took pride in the small part we played to help ensure the world had a place to be heard. But at the same time, our pain and grief were invisible to everyone around us at work. My role in leading all of the company's global music and culture communications, with a lens on how underrepresented communities were using Twitter, required me to be fully dialed in to every news cycle and cultural happening on the platform. I spent days and nights engulfed in global trends, hashtags, and real-time news updates that dominated the site. Working in social media, I've had to put my job first in spite of battling emotional and mental trauma brought on by real-life events and visibly seeing the never-ending unjust murdering of Black lives. Too many times, I realized that in those moments, my job should have put *me* first. Many of my hardest, most emotionally daunting days as a Black woman in tech coexist with the biggest news moments in history that have unfolded, play-by-play, in real time on the very social media companies I've worked for. The duality of that existence can be so painful and numbing all at once.

In one version of my experience at Twitter, I was thriving in my first real job in tech. I leaned in to every aspect of my expertise as a community advocate, musician, writer, and pop-culture wonk and had the opportunity to personally carve out my own professional role and job title, all based around my skillset, passions, and interests. In the other version of my life, my first tech job (and my first job, period!)

 50

felt extremely isolating and defeating. Most of the women I worked with in my role weren't women of color, and from what I could gather, most of the new hires and people who came to Twitter after me were transplants from other tech companies like Google, Facebook, Salesforce, and so forth. The gaps and differences in our respective real-world experiences and overall societal outlooks were painfully obvious during any and every happy-hour gathering, work lunch, or small talk at our desks. I slowly began to realize that I, myself—my hair, my heritage, my skin color, the way I walked, the way I talked, everything— was a culture shock to my colleagues. And despite the support I received from a number of mentors and allies at Twitter, the challenges felt never-ending.

In July of 2014, an unarmed Black man named Eric Garner died in Staten Island, New York, at the hands of law enforcement after police officers put him in a choke hold. Garner's last words, "I can't breathe," were spoken eleven times as his oxygen left his body. It was recorded and captured on a cell phone video that would later go viral on Twitter and spark one of the platform's most tweeted hashtags, ever. A month later, the police shooting and killing of Michael Brown, an unarmed eighteen-year-old Black teenager in Ferguson, Missouri, reignited national outrage. As images of Brown's lifeless body lying on the street of a St. Louis suburb began to surface online and rapidly spread on Twitter, the hashtag #BlackLivesMatter climbed to over a million mentions from users across the globe and became a rallying cry for resistance. Grassroots activists organized protests in Ferguson and around the United States. Twitter once again was the conduit of all conversation, with protesters and journalists leveraging the platform to shed a true light on Michael Brown's and Eric Garner's stories, along with the ongoing unjust murders of Black people at the hands of law enforcement. For the first time in history, decades-worth of stories about police brutality were now on the world stage for the rest of society to see and notice Black pain, in real time.

That year stands out as one of my most difficult years of being a Black person in America, as well as a Black woman working at Twitter. The images and

 52

videos of innocent lives being brutally snatched away have stained my memory forever, and when journalists reached out for data on the top-trending hashtags and real-time information surrounding the volume of conversation and content being posted about these horrific happenings, I was the company's go-to person, on call to provide insights on how activists, journalists, and communities were using Twitter to mobilize and control the news narrative.

By December of 2014, online conversation had climbed to an all-time high, with more than eighteen million tweets mentioning the Michael Brown case, Ferguson protests, and Eric Garner.[4] Internally, both Jack Dorsey (Twitter's cofounder) and Dick Costolo (Twitter's CEO at the time) had addressed and acknowledged the events and the crucial role Twitter as a platform played for so many marginalized voices. As the current president of Blackbirds, I held space for Black employees to privately meet at their own

4. Rooney, Ben, "Top Twitter Moments of 2014: Celebrities, Social Activism, Sports," CNN Money, December 10, 2014, https://money.cnn.com/2014/12/10/news/twitter-biggest-moments-2014/index.html.

will and comfort levels to vent about and discuss what was happening. We were all exhausted, emotionally broken, and enraged—and yet, we still had to wear a smile and show up at our desks while the world witnessed a small snapshot of our everyday reality.

On December 3, a grand jury decided not to indict the main police officer who caused the death of Eric Garner. Like the rest of the world on Twitter and offline, I was full of hurt, pain, and a rage that words could never quite explain. That particular week, there were no smiles, no small talk at my desk, no cordial moments of passive tech-office etiquette. I was surrounded by food, with no appetite to eat. I was sick to my stomach with grief, tears of rage welling in my eyes every time I opened my computer to log on to Twitter. What could I do? What could any of us really do in that moment? Not even our court system did a damn thing. After all our tweets, hashtagging, online petitions, news articles, trending topics, and protests, justice wasn't served and these innocent people were snatched away from their families, gone forever.

I went through a roller coaster of emotions that week,

all of which drove me to think of a way Twitter the company could stand in solidarity with its own Black employees. I thought about our giant hashtag wall on display in the center of the main floor of Twitter's headquarters. This blue wall stretched about twenty feet wide, and Twitter's leadership team would routinely paint different trending hashtags on it. The wall typically had fun, pop-culture hashtags—phrases like #WorldCup and so on. As soon as I thought of that wall, the idea came to me. I decided to reach out to Dick Costolo and request that the hashtag #BlackLivesMatter be freshly painted on the wall as a signal of solidarity and support for the Black lives that existed in and outside of Twitter HQ. Dick immediately agreed to the plan, and my heart smiles every time I remember the impact of the small gesture. That day, so many of us Blackbirds exhaled and cried tears of release. A painted wall would never soothe our pain or take away from the injustice that plagued our communities. But, for maybe the first time ever at Twitter, we felt truly seen and supported.

There are two sides to the internet, and there's a silent, powerful trade-off when we decide to set up our usernames and "free" social media accounts. On one side, we get to connect with friends, family, and a world of fascinating strangers. Strangers who somehow end up blossoming into the equivalent of family and best friends we couldn't imagine living without. Social media and the internet have also given us the visibility and means to make our unique voices and ideas heard, particularly for young people of color. Underrepresented communities are among the most active and technologically savvy users on social media (and on the internet at large), and the next generation of youths are deemed to be the most creative, advanced, and thoughtful people on the internet right now. We're in a day and age when next-generation content creators and hobbyists are reshaping industries with their ability to make a lucrative living off of social media and cultivate communities online.

The trade-off is often our time, attention, and in some cases, overall wellness, in exchange for thriving as our online, connected selves. For years, there have been studies published about the many ways social media impacts our mental health and perception of self, linking the use of social media to increased anxiety, depression, antisocial behavior, body-image issues, and so on. These problems persist even further for those who work and thrive within the tech industry. The giant gyms, on-site doctor's offices, cafeterias, chefs, and nap pods that come as benefits with the job make people never want to leave work. And before you know it, said company or social app is now your life. The idea of work-life balance, self-care, mental health, and general boundaries between your work and your real life become harder to juggle.

The polarizing role of social media (and the internet) in our lives isn't changing anytime soon. What can evolve is our perspective on the impact these tools have on our lives, along with our ability to positively shape and fine-tune the function we'd like technology to serve within our communities and everyday existence. My time in tech has shown me the many worlds and doorways to opportunity—and, more importantly, the larger role people can have in building safer, more inclusive platforms that make room and access for diverse voices. It's not enough to be the loudest voice or most-followed account on Twitter or Instagram. Our role in shaping the communities we want to be a part of, online and offline, begins with our access to technology and our inclusive use of the digital social spaces we all occupy.

For too long, Black voices and identities have been an afterthought or left out of the equation altogether by the technology industry and developers of our favorite services. But time and time again, Black Twitter trends and social data have proven that Black and minority online communities are the beating pulse of Twitter, Instagram, TikTok, Snapchat, Clubhouse, and many other leading social platforms. As users, creators, and thinkers, underrepresented communities have an indispensable point of view and role in the progress of technology and social media. There are roles for us online as users and there are even bigger career roles out there for us, within the very walls of our everyday apps and go-to social media outlets we use. The belief that you need to be a white male engineer or computer science major is bogus—I am living, walking proof that affirms there's room (and demand) in the technology industry for diverse, creative thinkers who don't have traditional technical backgrounds or educations.

Think about where you spend most of your time, mentally and emotionally—think about self-expression and where your identity lives, according to the perception of the outside world. Our apps and social media profiles aren't just extensions of who we are, they are ultimately *us*. The tech industry has now become a core part of the food industry, politics, music, fashion, the automobile industry, health care, and more. The very fabric of every professional field or career path somehow involves technology and the common thread of online community. Each and every one of us has a point of access to influence through our voice and output on the internet. Working in tech opened my eyes to the prospect of positively influencing the platforms that shape and define our very lives and state of existence. And in the process, I came to realize the significance of my perspective as a Black woman and individual who had very different experiences from 90 percent of the people running our favorite social media apps. Even if the space wasn't designed *for* me, in a way, the tech space was designed *by* me, by us, by our communities.

My hope is that we continue to break down the doors and institutional ceilings that keep people of color out of the technology industry, with the mission to lift as we climb and leave the door open for future generations. I want to help equip underrepresented creatives and communities with the tools and professional network to explore careers in tech and professional advancement in a way that's equitable and rooted in real, long-term systemic shifts toward a more inclusive industry. Shared accountability and collective action is the only way we accomplish more inclusivity and visibility within tech and across the social spaces we occupy.

Because in order to be seen, we have to see each other first.

ABOUT US

Pocket Change Collective was born out of a need for space. Space to think. Space to connect. Space to be yourself. And this is your invitation to join us.

These books are small, but they are mighty. They ask big questions and propose even bigger solutions. They show us that no matter where we come from or where we're going, we can all take part in changing the communities around us. Because the possibilities of how we can use our space for good are endless.

So thank you. Thank you for picking this book up. Thank you for reading. Thank you for being a part of the Pocket Change Collective.

Praise for the
Jane Yellowrock Novels

"A lot of series seek to emulate Hunter's work, but few come close to capturing the essence of urban fantasy: the perfect blend of intriguing heroine, suspense, [and] fantasy with just enough romance." —SF Site

"Jane is a fully realized, complicated woman; her power, humanity, and vulnerability make her a compelling heroine. The fight scenes are exciting and the New Orleans setting is absorbing, but it's the ever-evolving bond between Jane and her Beast personality that keeps this fun series fresh." —*Publishers Weekly*

"Jane Yellowrock is smart, sexy, and ruthless." —#1 *New York Times* bestselling Kim Harrison

"Readers eager for the next book in Patricia Briggs's Mercy Thompson series may want to give Faith Hunter a try." —*Library Journal*

"Hunter's very professionally executed, tasty blend of dark fantasy, mystery, and romance should please fans of all three genres." —*Booklist*

"In a genre flooded with strong, sexy females, Jane Yellowrock is unique. . . . Her bold first-person narrative shows that she's one tough cookie but with a likable vulnerability." —*RT Book Reviews*

"Seriously. Best urban fantasy I've read in years, possibly ever." —C. E. Murphy, author of *Magic and Manners*

"The story is fantastic, the action is intense, the romance sweet, and the characters seep into your soul." —Vampire Book Club

"An action-packed thriller. . . Betrayal, deception, and heartbreak all lead the way in this roller-coaster ride of infinite proportions." —Smexy Books

COLD REIGN

A Jane Yellowrock Novel

Faith Hunter

ACE
New York

ACE
Published by Berkley
An imprint of Penguin Random House LLC
375 Hudson Street, New York, New York 10014

Copyright © 2017 by Faith Hunter
Excerpt from *Blood of the Earth* copyright © 2016 by Faith Hunter
Penguin Random House supports copyright. Copyright fuels creativity, encourages
diverse voices, promotes free speech, and creates a vibrant culture. Thank you for buying
an authorized edition of this book and for complying with copyright laws by not
reproducing, scanning, or distributing any part of it in any form without permission.
You are supporting writers and allowing Penguin Random House to continue to
publish books for every reader.

ACE is a registered trademark and the A colophon is a trademark of
Penguin Random House LLC.

Lyrics to the song "Where's The Fire" (as performed by Roddy Rockwell) by Bill Blakley,
used with permission.

ISBN: 9781101991404

First Edition: May 2017

Printed in the United States of America
1 3 5 7 9 10 8 6 4 2

Cover art by Cliff Nielsen

To the Hubs,
my Renaissance Man,
Always and Forever.

In Memory of my father,
Bobby B. Prater,
who taught me to be analytical.

Those debate lessons around the dinner table
have stood me in good stead.

ACKNOWLEDGMENTS

Many thanks to Bill Blakley for granting me use of the lyrics to the song "Where's the Fire", as performed by Roddy Rockwell.

Melissa McArthur for help with characters and histories.

Sarah Spieth and MG Brown for info on New Orleans port.

Margot Dacunha for French translations.

Kayleigh Webb at ACE, for all your wonderful PR work to make this book fly off the shelves.

Lucienne Diver of The Knight Agency for guiding my career through the hard times of the last twenty-four months. I survived it because I knew I had you in my corner.

Let's Talk Promotions at http://www.ltpromos.com for excellent PR help and for managing my fan pages. You ROCK!

Cliff Nielsen . . . for all the work and talent that goes into the covers.

Mindy Mymudes for beta reading. For being a font of knowledge and a great friend.

Beast Claws fan club. You ROAR!

Lee Williams Watts for being the best travel companion and PA a girl can have.

Jessica Wade of Ace / Penguin Random House. You make me a much better writer than I am capable of alone. I don't know how you keep the high quality up, book after book. You are extraordinary.

CHAPTER 1

Holy Necrophilia, Batman

I slid across the slick gym floor in the lightweight boots, a fourteen-inch, silver-plated vamp-killer in one hand, the other hand back in a fist. I slammed the fist into the vamp's head, deflecting the fang-strike away from the boy's throat. Caught the collar of the fanghead's jacket and spun him after me. Around me. His rotting jacket ripped. I stuck out my boot. Shoved him across my foot.

He crashed to the floor. As he fell, I raised the pommel of the blade and brought it down onto the top of his head. It connected with a satisfying *bonk*. The vamp's eyes rolled back, yellowed sclera exposed.

I stomped his chest to make sure he was staying down. Brought the vamp-killer across his throat and took off his head except for an inch of spine and a few stringy tendons. The stink of sweat and fear and blood hit me when I took a breath, my first good one in the last ten minutes. I registered the screams of the teenagers and adults in the gym but discounted them as panic, and the stink in their sweat as terror. There was no smell of death, so the rev hadn't gotten to them. I took another breath. And a couple more to restore the oxygen levels and throw off some carbon dioxide from my full-out sprint.

Eli Younger stepped close, weapons pointed at the floor, his matte-black fighting leathers a faint gleam in the overheads. He wasn't even breathing hard. "Silver didn't stop him," he said. "Six shots."

"Maybe you missed," I said.

Eli snorted. He flipped the vamp's jacket open with the barrel of his weapon. I counted the holes in the vamp's chest, all but one centered or slightly to the left. The last shot was placed slightly to the right of the chest. Not that my business partner had missed. Eli had aimed there in case the vamp's heart was on the wrong side of the body. It's a rare medical phenomenon but it happens. My partner was nothing if not thorough and efficient.

The fingers of the dead vamp's left hand twitched. Twitched again. The tendons on his neck regrew right before my eyes. His jaws snapped. Eyes opened and glared at me.

I raised the vamp-killer over my head. Eli leaped back, out of the way. The vamp-killer swished through the air as I brought it down with every bit of my skinwalker strength, the steel edge and silver-plated flat of the blade flashing with the overhead gymnasium lights. A clean downward cut severed the bloodsucker's head from his cervical spine. The blade thunked into the floor. The head rolled. The fingers quit twitching. In my peripheral vision, I saw a man hit the floor.

I toed the body. It was dead. He was dead. Again. Davide Berkins had died the first time in 1512. The second time in 1825. And the third time, today. Or tonight. At the moment his head was gone, so maybe he'd stay down. Revenants were vamps who died a second time and came back again, usually on the third day after they were buried, and usually because they hadn't been properly interred. They were mindless, hungry killing machines and hard as heck to put down.

There were a lot of questions, but most important was, how had he come back after almost two hundred years in the grave? How had he clawed his way out of his grave in St. Louis Cemetery Number One—in clear view of half a dozen partying Tulane frat brothers—while escaping, and managed to drain and eat three sailors before vanishing two nights past? Why hadn't silver worked against him? And last, how did I keep something similar from happening again?

Leo Pellissier, the Master of the City of New Orleans and surrounding territories, had sent me to the neighborhood of Belle Chasse to deal with a rash of rogue-vampire sightings and the deaths of three U.S. sailors in port. It wasn't an old-fashioned NOLA Navy Week, when U.S. warships from everywhere docked and the sailors took leave in the streets, but there were three military ships from the 4th Fleet in port in advance of a multinational maritime exercise operation in the Caribbean. Or that was the scuttlebutt. By the end of the week there would be multinational cruisers, frigates, and supply ships as part of the seagoing maneuvers and war games. Not that they called it that anymore. It was now referred to as a "cooperative effort," and this one involved Brazil, Peru, and three other South American nations, and the U.S. Navy boats—ships?—had gotten into port only three days past.

The Navy personnel had been granted twelve-hour liberty, and three sailors hadn't made it back by midnight the first night. NCIS-NOLA had discovered the bodies twenty-four hours later, drained and dead, in the woods just off Yorktown Street. I hadn't seen the bodies, but I'd read the reports. One kid was eighteen and so green he still didn't shave. Davide Berkins was the cause. Davide was dead. I'd give myself a back-pat, except that it had taken me twenty-four hours and an attack in a school gym to track him. The rev had been active for well over forty-eight hours. I had to believe that we'd find more bodies.

Taking down the old rogue wasn't technically part of my job as the Enforcer of the MOC, but as the nation's foremost expert on rogue vamps—vampires who went nutso and started killing their dinners—I had agreed to go, at speed. The younger Younger, my other business partner, was still negotiating my contract for the hunt, and though I'd never have told Alex this, I'd have done the job for free. Suckheads who kill humans go down. Period. Suckheads who kill kids, like the kid sailor, go down with extreme prejudice.

"Leo will be pissed," Eli said, about me killing the rogue.

I showed teeth. It wasn't exactly a smile. Leo had wanted the vamp alive, to question, claiming his own blood was strong enough to bring the rev's brain back online. Leo wanted a lot of stuff and it was my greatest—okay, second-greatest—pleasure in life to frustrate him.

From the site where the sailors' bodies had been found, I'd tracked the rogue through neighborhoods to his daytime lair, and from there to the Belle Chasse high school. This guy had been a killer, pedophile, and Naturaleza blood-sucker in his vampire life, and so I hadn't given him a chance despite Leo's demands. The six chest shots and the behead-ing had seen to that.

Oddly, there wasn't a lot of blood, which was peculiar for a vamp who had drained three young men two nights before, though I wasn't complaining. But . . . I leaned over and took a sniff. The blood smelled wrong. Though what the blood of a thrice-dead vamp should smell like I didn't know. I remembered his eyes. The pupils had been wide and black, but the sclera hadn't been scarlet with blood, but yellowed and sick-looking. Also odd.

I wiped my vamp-killer on the dead guy's clothes and looked around the gym. The teenagers had been screaming at the top of their lungs when I dashed inside. They had fallen strangely silent when I whacked off the vamp's head. There was a scent of shock and horror in the air, not sur-prising since a bloodsucker had walked into high school basketball and cheerleading practice and attacked. I looked around at the floor. Three humans down, counting the teen-ager Eli was helping to sit. The boy was nursing a badly broken right arm and was sweating and pale with shock, but his throat was intact. Eli checked the pulse of the male adult wearing street clothes, probably a parent. He was out like a light, but the nod Eli gave me assured that he had only fainted. The man in a high school polo shirt was also alive, though bleeding from the nose and mouth, uncon-scious. Probably a concussion. We'd gotten here before the rogue did more than break the kid's arm and knock out the assistant coach who tried to intervene.

"You kids okay?" I asked the gymnasium at large.

"You're Jane Yellowrock," a scrawny boy in shorts and practice jersey said.

"Yeah."

"You killed him," a girl in a short skirt and cross-training sport shoes said.

"More or less. Yeah."

"Thank you," a tall, balding man said. He was weaving carefully through the players and I took him to be the head coach. He might have played B-ball himself once, before the years gave him a paunch and limpworthy bad knees. He stopped just beyond the body. "I've called police and an ambulance, but what do we do about"—he gestured to the trickle of blood and body—"the mess?"

"I'll take the body and the head. The mess is yours."

"Call a cleanup service," the teenager suggested. "The kind that does crime scene cleaning. I saw it on a *CSI* rerun last night. It was cool!"

The coach's mouth opened and closed, and he stared at the kid, who was clearly thinking that beheading a vamp was cool too. "Okay. I guess."

I looked at Eli, the elder Younger. "Got a body bag?"

"We used the last one. New batch hasn't arrived."

"Got a shower curtain?"

"Three," he said, pulling flat packages from a backpack-style gear bag that hung across his shoulders.

"Mr. Prepared."

Eli sliced through the packaging and unfolded the shower curtains on the floor. They must have been running low at Walmart, because the shower curtains weren't clear or white but brightly colored with tropical fish on them. "Cute. Nemo," I said. Eli didn't respond. I started to make another crack and Eli said, "Don't." So I didn't. But I did snicker slightly.

Together we rolled the body onto the first Nemo curtain, the stink of long-dead vamp not quite as horrible as I expected, as if the decomposition had been halted during the two hundred years in the ground and the stench had slowed with it. The body's shoulders and elbows thumped on the plastic, and that was when I focused on his clothes. Davide

Berkins had been buried in his butler's suit: dove-gray pants and jacket, white shirt, and black tie. He was still wearing the tattered remains. But . . . They were Clan Pellissier colors.

With my toes I pushed aside the torn shirt, exposing a poorly executed anchor tattooed on the vamp's chest, marred by bullet holes. I met my partner's dark eyes and he gave me a fraction of a nod. Everything about this situation was hinky. We both knew it.

His dark skin catching the light of the overheads, Eli secured the vamp's limbs with duct tape and then we wrapped the body in the second shower curtain. And then a third. And duct-taped it all once again. The plastic shroud still leaked, but it was better than nothing. And the tape hid some of the embarrassing fish.

Grasping the head by the hair, I extended it over the white plastic garbage bag Eli held open. With the fingers of my other hand, I flipped Davide's fangs down from the roof of his mouth to inspect them. Over two inches long, strong and thick, but curved more than a regular vamp's. Even more odd, the vamp had overlarge canines on the bottom teeth too. The teeth were more like an attack dog's than a vampire's. The vamp-tooth pattern on the throats of the sailors who had died had been curving, with bottom teeth punctures, confirming this was the killer. The bite pattern and the uniform explained how the MOC had known the name of the rogue we hunted. Davide had been a scion of Leo's uncle when Amaury Pellissier was the blood master in charge of New Orleans.

I let the teeth go, but the hinge in Davide's mouth didn't fold back up and the fangs stayed down. I tilted the head to get a better look and his hair ripped through his scalp, sending the head swinging, throwing bloody spatter. I dropped the head and it landed in the bag with a plasticized *squish*. Eli tied the orange bag-ties in a knot. I tossed my hip-length hair out of the way, hefted the shower-curtained body over my shoulder, and stood. As a skinwalker-no-longer-in-hiding, I could let my true strength show, and I'm a good bit stronger than a human.

Body hanging behind me, bloody fluid splatting softly on the wood floor and the back of my boots, I looked around the gym and realized I was being filmed by a couple dozen cells. *Just ducky*. The sounds of multiple sirens echoed through the night, drawing nearer. I wanted to be long gone by the time the cops arrived. "Ummm . . . Thank you for your forbearance," I said to the room, and skedaddled, Eli right behind me.

Out in the damp night air, Eli beeped open the back of the armored SUV and said, "Forbearance? Babe."

"I know. I had a brain fart."

He was almost smiling, which, for the former Army Ranger, was tantamount to a belly laugh. "Forbearance," he muttered.

Together we tossed the body into the back, put the head beside it, and hopped in the cab. We drove away only moments before the first cop car turned in to the school parking lot. If we got stopped now, with a dead body in back, this could get messy. I was licensed to kill rogue vamps, but not all local law officials knew that or respected that. If they stopped us, the paperwork would be a pain in the butt. But we made it out and started east on 23 back toward home. Without my needing to ask, Eli turned on the heat and the seat warmers, which were a little bit of heaven as far as I was concerned.

On the other side of the windows, the damp air of very early evening turned quickly into a mist, and then into a heavy fog, obscuring the roadway. The streetlights were halos of light in the night haze. Eli slowed, the wipers not much help in the dense vapor that so often passed as air in New Orleans. But it was almost pleasant, driving in the ground cloud, isolated from everything around us. Eli and I had never needed to fill the space between us with chatter or radio hosts or music. We were comfortable in the silence. Well, as comfortable as we could be with a dead vamp in back. And with my stomach growling. I needed calories to make up for the shift from Beast to human, and Eli had promised me steak. Rare. With double-stuffed baked potatoes full of sour cream and bacon. I was starving but didn't want to compromise and get fast food. Not when I had a feast waiting back home.

We were halfway back to vamp HQ when the SUV's system

dinged and the Kid said over the speaker, "Turn around and head back to Belle Chasse. Sending you the coordinates now. We got more DBs, one fangy, and these are weird."

DBs meant dead bodies. "Weirder than a vamp who's been buried for two hundred years rising revenant and killing people?" I asked.

"Pretty much. We got a human tangled in the arms and hair of a vamp, pulled from the river."

"Any of our people missing?" I asked.

"No one," he said.

I had been hunting the location on my cell and said, "That's less than half a mile from the high school. And not far, as the crow flies, from where the sailors' bodies were found."

"There's Navy housing in Belle Chasse," Alex said, his tone saying he was thinking that might be significant.

"Naval reserves use it now," Eli said, making a legal U-turn. "That's two attacks on or near U.S. Navy property. A rev with a seafaring tattoo. Maybe someone or something is targeting the Navy." Ditto on the serious tone. Eli kept in touch with military types in New Orleans and surrounding areas and he wasn't averse to talking to grunts, jarheads, missile sponges, squids, coasties, zoomies, and any other insulting name he could think of when conversing with them. The Army Ranger considered himself the best of the best, even better than a SEAL, though there had been intense (physical) discussions (fights) of that subject among members of the military and former military in the past. Insults and physical altercations seemed to be a bonding experience with former and active military alike.

I remembered the anchor tattoo. Had Berkins been a seaman? We needed to see if he had other tattoos. "We'll check the fangy DBs out," Eli said to Alex. "Tell Leo to send a car for the remains of the old pervert Berkins. We can meet somewhere near the juncture of Business Ninety and Highway Twenty-Three."

"There's a Popeye's at Lafayette and Westbank Expressway," Alex said. "You can feed Jane and dump the body at the same time."

"There's something distinctly disgusting about that statement, especially when I was promised steak, but Popeye's'll do," I said as I crawled into the backseat and zipped open my larger gear bag. I pulled out better clothes than I had carried strapped around my neck in my Beast gobag.

Brevity itself, Eli ended the call with, "Later." He glanced once at me in the rearview and I gave him a slight dip of my head. Leo's uncle's butler had risen revenant and attacked and killed sailors. Now two more strange DBs, one fangy, pulled from the Mississippi River. Another revenant? We couldn't talk about it, not with the cells and the SUV's com system rigged to share every syllable with Leo. But soon. After dawn for sure.

Eli tilted the rearview mirror up to give me privacy and I started stripping. The lightweight clothing I had dressed in when I shifted from Beast to human during the final moments of chasing Berkins wouldn't do for long. I was cold. My arms and legs and the back of my neck were pebbled and tight with the chill. My gold nugget necklace swung on its chain as I contorted my body in the confined space.

I went back to Eli's last statements. "And the Navy reserves housed near the attacks means what?" I asked.

"No idea," Eli said. "But the attack on the sailors and the gunpowder tattoos on the butler bothered me. Now we have another vamp DB on or near an old naval port. Did you see the skull and crossbones with sword? On Berkins' other arm?"

"No," I grunted, zipping my jeans and weaponing up. My fighting leathers would have been nice, but they were back at the house. "Wait." I looked up at the back of his head. "Gunpowder?"

Eli made breathy laughing sounds and said, "Back in the day, sailors didn't have ink. They made do with what they had, like gunpowder mixed with urine. Tattoos had significance and more than a little superstition in them. I think there might have been a name inked in as part of the tattoo, but it was blurred by time and scarring. He might have more, and they might lead us to whatever made him rise revenant. Alex, make sure whoever picks up the body gets photos, front and back and the soles of the feet."

"Copy," Alex said, over coms.

Tattoos. Naval history. Back in the day, vamps had crossed the oceans the same way humans had, via ships, so seafaring blood-servants were likely to have been a thing back then. Confluence of thought processes was becoming more and more common the longer my partners and I worked together, though it seemed like a stretch to think this was an attack on the Navy based on such scant evidence. Not that I was saying that to Eli. I finished dressing and crawled back up front. I didn't get cold, as a rule, but this weather was abnormally cold for the Deep South. I buckled in and braided my black hair by feel.

We pulled through the Popeye's and I ordered a sixteen-piece, spicy, "Bonafide Family Meal." The fried chicken smell overpowered the dead-vamp stink—intensifying because the heater was on—and the food was fabo. I had tracked the thrice-dead fanghead in Beast form, and the shift back to human had left me hungry. Shifting used energy, and skin-walkers used calories to shift. As we waited for the body pickup, I ate fourteen chicken pieces, the mashed potatoes, and all the biscuits, leaving the slaw, the green beans, and two bird legs for my healthy-eating partner. While we waited, parked in the shadows, he inhaled the veggies and peeled the fried layer off the chicken before munching down.

"Heathern," I accused in my best Appalachian mountain accent, lifting the skin from the box he'd tossed it in. "I'll rescue the poor, cast-aside crispy bits. Yes, my precious, I'll eat you," I cooed to the fried flesh. Biting down.

Eli didn't even look my way, but he did let the faintest sound of a sigh escape. Long-suffering, that's Eli. As I licked my fingers clean, he got out and unwrapped the body, took a few dozen photos, and then transferred the remains to the back of an armored Lincoln that pulled up beside us. Visible inside the tinted glass were Wrassler and Jodi, who were interrupting a date to run a fanghead errand. Neither looked happy at the interruption. Jodi was a cop. Dating Wrassler, head of operations at vamp HQ, had to be some kind of conflict of interest. Having a dead body in the back had to be some other kind of conflict of interest. I fluttered my fingers at her and held up thumb and pinkie, telling her I'd call. She frowned at me but pointed at her nails. She wanted mani-pedis, which was a waste of time and money for me since every time I shifted into animal form, the paint peeled off. Being a skinwalker is tough on the girly part of life.

As they pulled away, Eli closed the hatch and took a private call, standing at the back of the vehicle, and I deliberately didn't listen in, figuring it was his girlfriend, Syl. When he got back inside, his mouth was tight, and he wore what I called his battle face. Utterly expressionless, utterly focused.

"Problem?"

"Personal."

I shrugged. Eli and his snuggle-buns were on the outs because he refused to go on a cruise with her. I didn't know the particulars and didn't want to. "Good. I'm not a marriage counselor."

Eli shrugged back. It was the action of a man pretending not to care but who cared very badly. I had seen the same expression and body language on him when my own honey-bunch had dropped by for the game. Eli on the couch, pretending to ignore when Bruiser's feet and mine intertwined in a wool-sock-footed twiddling match. It hadn't been romantic. It had been playful and silly. But Eli had turned to stone. Yeah. Things were bad between Eli and Syl.

Not long after, we turned off Highway 23 onto Avenue G, passing Plaquemines Parish government buildings, one-story structures constructed of white metal siding and stained clapboards, and various flags flying overhead. In the parking lot there were two cop cars, government cars, and parking for the parish levee, the manmade hill constructed by the Army Corps of Engineers to keep the Mississippi within its banks. At the top of the levee, blue lights flashed into the night.

We crested the levee's artificial hill, pulled over, braked, and watched. Multiple law enforcement agencies were present, some of them crime scene techs wearing white hazmat-type suits, complete with masks, gloves, and booties. And there was a stink of dead fish I could smell even in human form, even inside the SUV. "This is not what I expected for a vamp and a human pulled from the water."

"Yeah, me neither." Eli said. He handed me a coms set

and I put on the gear, clipping the cell-phone-sized unit to my belt and inserting the earbud. Eli did the same and tested the connections to Alex. We were live.

We sat in the dark for all of five minutes before a uniformed officer approached, and we put our hands up where they could be seen. She knocked on the window and Eli let it down. Before I could offer to get out an ID, the woman said, "Younger and Yellowrock?"

"That's us," Eli said, turning off the SUV.

She shined a flashlight inside and blinded us. I squinted against the glare. "Leave your vehicle. This way, please," she said.

Still blinking, I got out of the car and trailed the cop down to the ferry landing, closer and closer to the fish stink. The mist thickened and swirled, coiling and dancing on the altering air temps, moving with the river breeze.

The Belle Chasse Ferry Landing was a narrow two-lane road on a sturdy pier over the water. Well off the shore, the road met a wide wharf where two ferries were moored at a dock or a jetty or something. A late news crew from WGNO, the ABC station in NOLA, were milling around at the end of the road, held back by local cops and crime scene tape. The African-American woman talking into the camera spotted us as we boarded and I heard her whisper, "Jane Yellowrock. Get the shot. Is that the MOC? No. Has to be that hunky partner of hers."

A cop waved us onto the ferry and out of sight, but I could hear the reporter saying, "Put this with the basketball players' cell footage from the gym and we are golden."

Eli breathed a laugh.

"Shut up," I griped.

He laughed louder.

The chuckles stopped when we reached the end of the boat. Stern? Bow? I wasn't sure, since both ends were straight, without the curving bow on, say, the cruise ship Eli refused to get on. The ferry was rusted, the red paint missing in many places, and the sidewalls dented. The white structure where the driver stood was in need of a good coat of marine paint. I later figured out it might be called the wheelhouse, and saying the driver steered the boat would have proven me to be woefully lacking in nautical terms. Fortunately I kept my mouth shut.

I leaped to the top of the wide sidewall to get a better view, the rubberized bottoms of my boots gripping the rubberized railing with ease. A small crowd of parish and state dignitaries and uniformed officers from various interconnected agencies policing the river were standing well back of two bodies, which were lying on the deck in a tangle of ropes and netting. There was a buoy of some kind, a few dead fish trapped in the netting, and what looked like a midsized tree. Everything was wet and trails of river water ran off, as if the mess had been pulled from the water and dropped. I didn't ask how everything got here, didn't ask permission; I just stepped down to the boat deck and walked in as if I belonged there, then across the mess to the bodies.

From the comment about the human, *tangled in the arms and hair of a vamp*, I had expected to find a human man with a female vamp, which proved how stilted my own social and sexual expectations were. It was two males, both dressed in the ruins of gray uniforms and leather shoes, one with very long brown hair. Gray uniforms meant a Pellissier Clan blood-servant and scion, the ones who worked in the clan home itself, the ones most trusted. The rotted cloth suggested they too were from the reign of Leo's uncle, Amaury.

The human was in an advanced stage of decomp. The vamp, however, was far less rotten. He had flesh on his torso and long bones, and his joints were still attached with connective tissue. He had no eyelids or lips, as if something had eaten them away. But his eyes were still intact and his jaws were still working at the long-missing flesh of his human partner. Little *snap, snap, snap* sounds of jaws clicking, his upper and lower canines tapping. Canines like Berkins'. *Well, ducky.* We had two connections, dog fangs and uniforms.

Over the coms, I heard Alex say, "Holy necrophilia, Batman."

Eli was sending live video. The vid would be a help if we needed to go over the scene again. Eli muttered, as if to me but really to Alex, "Silence is golden." Louder he added, "Other than the bodies, looks like fishing line, maybe some shrimping nets, buoys, and a waterlogged tree."

I made an *mmmm* sound, drew a vamp-killer, holding it at my side, and squatted over the vamp.

"Don't get too close, lady," a Plaquemines deputy said from ten feet away. "It bites."

The vamp stopped snapping and his head turned slowly toward the deputy. The sclera of the vamp's eyes were liver-disease yellow and his irises were bright blue. He'd once had a narrow mustache and high cheekbones, a dimpled chin. I had a feeling he had been a very pretty man in his undead state, despite the notch in his left ear, one that had never regrown, suggesting it had been given to him in a prevamp state and never healed properly. His mouth opened, revealing the dog-style upper and lower fangs and his back molars.

Vamp-fast, he lunged at the deputy. Even from ten feet out, the vamp caught the man's sleeve in his jaws. Everyone screamed. Humans jumped back. Service weapons were drawn.

My vamp-killer shot up almost on its own. Pierced through the vamp's throat and out the back of his neck. But my aim wasn't perfect, or the vamp dodged the thrust. The edge slid into the spine at the wrong angle. Sliced along the spinal processes with a skittering force. The bone trapped the edge. I hated when that happened. The vamp's head slid to the side as the tendons on the right snapped in two. The vamp's head lolled and the deputy's sleeve came free as I cut backhand. Jerked the weapon free. The vamp focused on me.

There was no blood in the huge wound. The vamp hadn't fed on the living since it rose. But the eyes didn't look away and the thing's jaws were again snapping fast. Even blood-less, the vampire was healing. I finished the job with a cut that completely severed the head.

"Oh," the deputy squeaked, backpedaling to the far side. He sounded surprised, but really, what else was gonna happen? That's the advantage of lots of blade practice and really sharp blades—steel versus flesh wins every time.

The head rolled off. Bounced and landed on the tree. A broken branch speared into the neck and held the head in place like a warning on a castle wall, but low down. I wanted to laugh, but it probably wouldn't be seemly in front of all the officers.

To Alex I said, "What do you know about this pair?"

"I've been cross-checking police reports. Apparently since the rising of Davide Berkins, keeping watch in graveyards is suddenly chic among the NOLA fraternities, and this rising was witnessed," the Kid said into my earbud. "According to eyewitness reports of the risings, it looks like they crawled out of the coffin together. We now have names and prelim histories. Oliver Estridge is the human and the vamp is Mitchel Hopkins. Histories say the cause of death was a murder-suicide, a lovers' tiff between vamp and human. They were buried together in 1909."

"Who made the COD ruling?" I asked.

"Amaury Pellissier."

"We wanted to question him," a self-important voice said.

I looked over a shoulder and spotted the owner of the voice. She was the sheriff of Plaquemines Parish, and her photo had been plastered over half the parish for months, on billboards that promised to get supernats out of her parish. She had won reelection, but clearly not for brains.

I raised my eyebrows and wiped my blade on the soaked and stinking cloth of the vamp's jacket. The blade wasn't bloody, but it was gooey. I stood, focused on the politician. Keeping my voice toneless, I said, "You wanted to question a rogue vampire." Sheriff Pansy Knight was a tall woman and clearly wasn't accustomed to looking up at another woman, but in my combat boots, I was six foot two to three, a good four inches taller than her. I could play nice-nice or I could go for pain-in-the-butt. I was going for PITB but Eli intervened.

"Eli Younger, ma'am, of Yellowrock Securities." He put out his hand. "Unless you prefer *sir*. Some sheriffs do. And we aim to be courteous."

I slid my partner a look but he was focused on the sheriff. I had seen that look before, when he met Sylvia. Maybe things were worse than I thought. Maybe I should have tried to be a marriage counselor. Or romantic relationships counselor. Or cracked their heads together. Whatever.

Pansy narrowed her eyes but took Eli's hand. "*Ma'am* is fine."

To me she added, "We needed to question him."

My partner might want to be nice. I didn't, and I laughed. "He'd been dead for a hundred years, Pansy." She had a girly name. No way was I not gonna use it. "He had nothing left to chat about, not without a master vamp to feed him and try to bring his brain back online. He was an old rogue killing machine."

"You like killing rogues, don't you? Makes you feel special?"

Eli dropped her hand fast and the interested look vanished. I just chuckled and sheathed my vamp-killer. "Don't try to bait me, Pansy. I'm not that easy."

"I don't like your kind in my parish."

My kind? Cherokee? More likely it was the fact that I was a supernat and had been outed slowly over the last few months. Or someone had told her personally. "Oh? So the next time someone tries to eat your high school basketball team, you want me to let the rogue kill kids? And announce to the world that it was your call?" I stepped to Eli, my back to her, an insult when delivered by skinwalkers, and finished over my shoulder with, "The Master of the City will be calling. Have a nice convo."

"I won't talk to his kind."

I chuckled again. "Yeah? Kid," I said to my other partner, "send this entire thing to the reporter from WGNO. That should make great late-night news, combined with us saving that kid from another rogue. An hour later, post it up on the website and anywhere else you want. When the sheriff apologizes, it can come down. Eli?"

"Got your six," he muttered. And he sounded pissed. Good. We walked away.

CHAPTER 2

That's Pure Politics, Babe

The wind whipped in, bringing vamp scents, pepper and lily and papyrus, more acerbic scents like turmeric and sage. And human blood. And sex. Always that. Always together. I leaped over the railing—gunwale? side?—and came face-to-face with Leo Pellissier, the Master of the City of New Orleans, and the two minor-level vamps and three human-dinners-on-two-legs who were fanned out behind him. I glanced at each and drew in the air in little bursts of breath, taking in their faces and scents to remember and catalog later. Leo's territory had grown and there were a lot of newbies I hadn't gotten to know yet. Worse, we had fangheads visiting from distant U.S. cities who had sworn to Leo, back when an epidemic threatened the U.S. vamps. There were too many newbies to make anyone safe.

I opened my mouth to say hi to the chief suckhead but caught myself. "Pellissier," I said, much more politely and only a beat too late.

"Enforcer," Leo said.

"Sir," Eli said to him. "You heard?"

"I did," Leo said. "So did the lovely reporter. She has

one of the new directional microphones developed by the military."

"Was it a gift from the MOC?" Eli asked.

"Such is always a possibility." Leo smiled, the professional smile, the one he shared with the public, one that never reached his eyes. "She was incensed. I am certain the footage will make its way onto the television newscast tonight.

"However, we have a greater problem. Wait for me at my limo." He stepped gracefully over the side of the boat and dropped to the deck, landing with the poise and balance of a ballet dancer. Or a swordsman. Leo was dressed casually, for him, in a black suit and white shirt. Black shoes, no tie. His shoulder-length black hair was tied back with a black ribbon in a loose queue, and it gleamed in the harsh lights as he strode toward the bodies and the law officers. The MOC was ticked off, his magic pulsing out in a series of waves that raised the hair on my arms.

I glanced back at the reporter and her cameraman, who was working with a mic on a long arm, one that had an inverted umbrella-shaped top. The umbrella part was a clear material that waved slightly in the breeze.

"Jane?" Eli asked.

"Wait," I muttered. "I want to see this."

Leo walked to the sheriff and looked up at her. Leo had been well fed as a human and was tall for his time but not for this era. He focused on her eyes and smiled. I felt his power shift and wrap around the woman. She extended a hand. All by herself. Or so it would look to the reporter and her cameraman. Leo accepted it. And his smile intensified, that beguiling, electrifying, terrifying smile of the mesmerizing predator, the stare of the viper, the gaze of the raptor, the snare of the lover, intense and penetrating. His magic whispered along my face and neck and throat, teased through my hair.

"Pansy," Leo said. "It's been years."

"What?" she whispered, her eyes too wide, bewitched. Or bevamped.

"You are as lovely as ever, my darling," Leo said, lifting her hand to his lips.

My eyebrows went up.

Eli laughed softly, the tone pure evil. "Smart bastard."

Pansy shook herself like a dog shakes off cold water. "What are you talking about?" she demanded.

"Now, now, you must forgive me for not keeping you close. You were destined for much better things than one of my playthings."

"What?" Pansy said, disconcerted and with a dawning anger.

But Leo took Pansy's hand and tucked it into the crook of his arm. Inexorably, he turned her to the side, vamp strength overpowering the human musculature. Pansy's body language indicated that she was trying to decide what to do: scream, deny, resist. But the half second of indecision sealed her fate as she again met the eyes of the MOC. Her body relaxed and she followed him to the side. Pansy was clearly one of those humans easily mesmerized. Leo's vamp crew shook the hands of the other law enforcement officers while his humans knelt on the deck, where they began the process of tucking the bodies into body bags. Two of the deputies started to argue, but the vamps did . . . something. And the complaints stopped.

For Leo and the vamps to be using this much power, they surely had fed from the body of the Son of Darkness hanging in the lowest basement at vamp HQ. The blood of that thing was addicting. I really needed to find a way to kill it. I'd tried silver poisoning and cutting out its heart, and so far it hadn't begun to decompose. Scuttlebutt said it seemed to be healing. Maybe burning the SOD in a kiln or a cremation retort would work.

"Come on," Eli said. "We need to talk."

"Okay." I frowned but followed my partner back along the pier to the limo.

Over the earbuds Alex said, "So Leo used to date Pansy. But he dropped her? And her paranormal-hating is really woman-scorned stuff?" I could hear keys clicking and soft tapping in the background as he checked into Pansy's past.

"I doubt it," Eli said. "Though it doesn't really matter what happened, if anything, between them. That's how the press and her constituents will read it. With that one line,

Leo put doubt on her entire paranormal-hating campaign strategy. Spin. Spin is everything."

"That's Uncle Sam's training, isn't it?" I asked

Eli slanted a look my way. "That's pure politics, Babe."

The chauffeur opened the limo door and Eli and I got in. The privacy panel was up, and Eli turned off his cell. I glanced at mine, hoping for a text from Bruiser, but there was nothing. I turned it off and gave the cell to Eli, and he tucked them both into his gear bag. He turned on a little electronic buzzer inside and zipped the bag shut. The white noise kept anyone from using the cells as listening devices. The limo was swept every day to remove possible bugs. Leo did business in here, and he wanted total confidentiality. Now we could talk freely.

"Leo just ruined her career, didn't he?" I said.

"Hatred is its own reward."

"Who said that? Sun Tzu?" Eli was reading *The Art of War* for the hundredth time.

"Eli Younger. Reworked from some kitty cartoon."

"So why did we go black?" I asked, talking about the cells.

"Because the Kid sent me a text before we got here. It's about the vamps' lower fangs. There was a rogue-vamp blood-family in Bavaria back in the fifteen hundreds. They had upper hinged fangs and stationary lower fangs. They were curved and were used for tearing out the victim's throats. Naturaleza 2.0."

Naturaleza vamps treated all humans as prey, to be used, hunted, drunk dry, abused. They called humans cattle. Mithrans, like the vamps in New Orleans, weren't much better, but at least they gave lip service to the importance of humans. And then the date hit me. "Berkins was turned in 1512."

"Revenants are most easily raised by their sire or the sire of the bloodline, the big kahuna of the clan bloodline. So if the person who turned him, or said big kahuna, is currently in New Orleans, that person might be able to raise him as a revenant."

It took a single breath to clarify for me. "An EV is here?"

"Yeah. A European vamp. At least one. That's what Alex thinks."

"Why? Why show up and tip your hand about who you are?"

Eli opened the limo fridge, popped two Coke cans, icy and dripping with condensation, and held one out to me. I drank, not even tasting the cola. "Insufficient data."

"So who would it be? Who would the master be?"

"The Kid thinks it might be Louis Seven."

Yellowrock Securities had recently received info about the European Court of Mithrans. Louis VII was a powerful vamp in the inner cadre of the vamp-emperor. He had been a king himself in France when human, and had been called Louis le Jeune, or Louis the Young. Or the Younger, for short. Funny about the way it matched with the Youngers' last name. "Okay. Louis Seven. Was he on the roster as one of the EVs we might expect as part of the parley?"

"Yeah." The European vamps were planning to take over the U.S. hunting territories and cattle, which meant coming to visit Leo—a visit he couldn't refuse—and then killing Leo. The negotiations for how many vamps, which ones, how many of their humans, and how long their stay would be had been ongoing for months. I hadn't bothered to do much more than scan the bios of the players because they kept changing with every diplomatic snag. "The Kid sent me a history lesson on Louis the Young," Eli said. "You want it?"

"Not really. But I don't think I have a choice." I sounded grumpy because I didn't particularly care for history, but with the layered motivations of the long-lived Mithrans and Naturaleza, history was not only important, it was vital to staying alive. History had always been about people I loved being dead, or undead people trying to kill me or Leo, or both. I slouched back on the leather seat, prepared to be bored.

"Louis was a Capetian King of the Franks from 1137 until his supposed death at age sixty, in September 1180. But he was really turned by Eleanor of Aquitaine during their marriage. He swore to the Vampira Carta, but he's bloodthirsty and still thinks of himself as the French king."

"Yada yada yada. Old fangheads. Got it."

Eli leaned toward me, elbows on his knees, hands dropped and fingers folded loosely together holding his Coke. "This is where it gets interesting. The line of the Capetian Kings ruled France from 987 to 1316, thirteen generations in almost 330 years. Then the line ran out of male heirs and the direct line of the House of Capet came to an end in 1328, when there was no surviving male heir. When the last Capet died, the throne passed to the House of Valois." Eli went silent.

I sat up and stared at him. His posture was casual and relaxed, deceptively so. The lights through the heavily tinted windows created shadows that seemed to crawl across his face. "Valois," I said. "That's important. Somewhere in my notes Grégoire was intro'd as Blood Master of Clan Arceneau"—I dredged up the phrasing—"of the court of Charles the Wise, fifth of his line, in the Valois Dynasty, turned by Charles—the well beloved, the mad—the son of the king." Grégoire, or Blondie, as I called him when I was being obnoxious, was Leo's secundo heir. And Leo's BFF. And Leo's lover. "If a Capet or a Valois is in town, then Grégoire could be in danger?"

"And Leo. And some of his people. And if Alex's line of reasoning is correct, one or more may be here. In the city."

"Ahead of the official parley. Sooo. Maybe to cause trouble to divert our attention from something bigger. Or as part of a sneak attack, to be followed by a bigger sneak attack? Something they've been planning for years? Decades?" I put it together with what I already knew. "A king of France—" I interrupted myself as a stray thought intruded and went backward in history. "And Hugh Capet was turned by . . . ?"

"The bag of bones hanging in sub-five basement in vamp HQ."

"Well, crap." I rolled the half-empty cola can across my forehead, hoping the chill would cool off my brain. The Son of Darkness, or what was left of him, was hanging in the lowest sub-basement of the Mithran Council Chambers, and he was Leo's source of power, an addictive blood-meal, and nothing but trouble, even back when he was sane-ish and free. As a piece of undead flesh with no heart, he was a bargaining chip or an excuse for a vamp war.

Everything in the vamp sub-basements was trouble, from the paintings and mementoes stored there, to the SOD, to the redheaded bloodsucker prisoner named Adrianna. I'd killed her a few times already, and each time Leo had brought her back. She was a future problem, though, not part of this.

Deep inside, Beast thought at me, *Cold mountain stream. Good water. Not stinky water here. Want to go home.*

"I know," I muttered. "I know." I waved away Eli's questioning expression and drank down the Coke, hoping for a boost in my metabolism. Caffeine and sugar are two of the few stimulants or depressants that work on my kind. "So the vamps who are rising revenant are tied into the historical line that sired Grégoire."

"Yes."

"Is it too big a jump to be worried that any still-living vamps who were made by the Capetians might respond too? Like Grégoire?"

"Might have already done so," Eli said grimly. "We've been out of pocket." He reached for the gear bag and returned my cell. We'd been offline for a little over five minutes. That was about the max we could manage while working. We turned on the cells and I texted the Kid about dinner, with a phrase that meant *record our conversation.* It said simply, "Takeout from Marlene's." Alex would record everything said and we could go back over it later, picking out details.

"I have a feeling that Leo's appearance at the wharf tonight wasn't happenstance but to prove something to himself," Eli said. "Now we just have to get him to tell us what and either confirm or deny our speculation."

"I'll get right on that." I tucked the cell in my jacket pocket and finished off the Coke as the limo door opened and wet, fog-dense air billowed in. Rain was starting, which would decrease the fog but make driving just as dangerous. The chauffeur stood there with an umbrella over his boss. Leo slid across the seat: dry, elegant, relaxed, and satisfied. The devil in an eight-thousand-dollar Brioni suit.

Lights pulled up behind us, a second limo arriving. The six others—vamps and humans—raced through the rain to the car and tossed two body bags inside to the floor, and five of them got in after. They pulled away at speed. The sixth vamp came to the window where Eli sat and tapped. When the window went down he held out his open palm. "Key fob," he said. It was Tex, a vamp turned in the eighteen hundreds, tall, rangy, and with a distinct Texan accent.

"Why?" Eli asked.

Leo said, "I've arranged to have your vehicle taken to the Council Chambers where you may retrieve it, that we might speak in privacy."

It was an order, politely stated. Tex would take our SUV and do exactly as Leo had said, but during that time it would be searched for information about us and our activities and scoured for bugs, and new GPS devices would be implanted in case the one in the SUV's computer system was somehow disabled. All this because I refused to be bound to Leo, which would have allowed him access to my mind and guaranteed my loyalty. He had tried a forced binding once and it hadn't worked out so well for either of us. Binding a two-souled skinwalker is harder than it looks.

Expressionless, Eli handed over the fob. Tex gave me a minuscule apologetic shrug, trotted to our vehicle, and drove away, too fast for conditions. The window went up and Leo's limo followed more slowly, the tires silent on the asphalt, the movement of the vehicle almost undetectable.

"Update?" Eli asked.

Leo sighed, a totally unnecessary breath, and let his TV-bonhomie face fall into more normal, arrogant lines. "It has been a vexing evening." He reached for a bottle of champagne I had only noticed as part of the background, in a silver bucket. He went through the process of opening the top, as if the steps soothed him. When the cork burst out with a soft pop, he poured the bubbly stuff into three glasses and passed us each one. Out of politeness, I sipped. I'm not fond of alcohol, except a good malty beer, but maybe Leo would talk fast if I seemed to go along. The bubbly wasn't as good as Coke—not even as good as canned Coke— not that I'd ever say that. I've learned a few things in my time in NOLA, and keeping my mouth shut is one of them. Well, most of the time.

"You understand about bloodlines among Mithrans?" Leo asked. We nodded. "Some blood-family lines produce certain traits more strongly than other lines. The Damours line produced a greater and longer-lasting devoveo, leaving its scions permanently insane. The Shaddock line produces a trait for a shorter and simpler devoveo."

"Grégoire's sire's ancestor produced dog-teeth fangs," I said, cutting to the chase.

Leo's left eyebrow quirked up above his glass. He looked amused. "Indeed. Your Alex has been industrious."

"He isn't my Alex."

"You are Clan Yellowrock. Of course he is yours, along with Eli. And Edmund."

And there was the big issue. The big change in my life. The biggest change ever. I had a family now and it had grown more complicated when the vamp Edmund Hartley moved in with us. And became my primo. That was unprecedented. A nonvamp with a vamp main servant—a butler of sorts. A butler, bodyguard, secretary, personal healer, financial advisor, upholder of my honor, personal fighter, and hairstylist. In vamp eyes it gave me more power than most vampires ever had. I still didn't know who had come up with the idea, Ed or Leo. Not that it mattered. I'd been backed into the position. I hadn't seen it coming fast enough to avoid it. And I didn't know what it meant, how to stop it, or how to protect myself and the Youngers from its ramifications.

I put down my glass and met Leo's eyes, those amazing black-on-black eyes that sparkled with power and intelligence and amusement. He was teasing me, but this I couldn't let go. "I own no one. No one owns me. That includes you."

"Of course, *ma chérie.*" But his eyes said, *Yes you do. And I own you.*

"I'm. Not. Yours."

Leo breathed out a laugh, that silk velvet sound he used to charm and mesmerize. He inclined his head, a regal gesture that made him look kingly. "Your Alex will know only bits and pieces. The Capetian bloodline was descended from the first sire of the line, Hugh Capet, who gave rise to a Naturaleza line of blood drinkers with caninelike fangs, upper and lower. The unappealing trait bred out. The Valois line, from which Grégoire was sired, did not have the lower fangs. Nor did the bloodline that followed Valois, the House of Bourbon." Even more silky, Leo finished, "Nor did the house that followed Bourbon, the House of Orléans."

"Orléans?" I sat up. "Wait. The French kings were mostly vamps. And they ended with the House of Orléans? So . . . some of the EuroVamps we're expecting think they own New Orleans."

Leo nodded and sipped, unperturbed. "Events seem to suggest that we have a visiting Capet or Valois who is raising these revenants. He or she has put out a call and they are responding to that call. But our people have not been able to determine who they are or how they reached our shores. There have been no unaccounted chartered jets from Europe, no known Mithrans presenting papers for entry, nor are there sailing ships at the Port of New Orleans."

"Sailing ships?" I asked.

"My eyes among the European Mithrans had suggested that they would prefer sailing."

My eyes meant his spy, the woman referred to as Madam Spy, as if that were a title of importance. "When they can have a cruise ship?" I asked.

Leo pursed his lips at that, as if rethinking.

"Five-star chefs, power when there's no wind, lots of hunky humans, twenty-four-hour entertainment, swimming pools, gambling. And a speedy crossing. Maybe the vamps own their own line. How much faith do you have in your Madam Spy?"

"Perhaps too much," he murmured, and sipped his bubbly stuff. He pulled the cord from his hair, releasing it from the queue; the long black strands had curled in the damp air. "She has been unreliable at times."

"Cruise ships come and go all the time from the port," I said. "No one would notice a cruise ship. But a sailing ship full of vamps? That would have hit social media immediately."

"Hmmm." He sipped, thinking more. "Cruise ships. And

with the updated intermodal terminal, they could also come upriver aboard a cargo ship and debark at night with no one the wiser."

"There would be security. Electronic monitoring of the docks?" Eli said, his tone making his explanation a question, the way a minor soldier might suggest something obvious to a superior officer. Eli continued to impress and surprise me with his social skills. "There are easier ways to get in."

"If they are in my city, they are few," Leo said. "I would know if the entire grouping of European Mithrans had all come ashore ahead of the parley, as some sort of"—his hand made a little rolling motion—"preemptive attack."

Eli looked interested. "How would you know?"

"I am master of this city." At our blank looks, Leo said, "I am master of the land, of the Mithrans, and of the humans in it. A few Mithrans or Naturaleza might enter without my knowledge—Peregrinus' groups, for instance—slowly over time, but not in the number that the Europeans wish to bring."

"And how many is that currently?" I asked. Because the negotiations were stalled again, this time on that all-important final number.

"Their current demand is for lodging, food, and entertainment for some fifty Mithrans and their one hundred fifty to two hundred humans." He smiled and said wryly, "I would know."

I accepted a second Coke from Eli, exchanging it for my glass of champagne, which he appreciated far more than I did. "And they expect you to pay for their lodging?"

"They do," he said, his tone taking a decidedly subdued turn. "Their demands are based on progress."

"Don't sound like progress to me," I said. "It sounds like extortion or protection money or something."

"*Progress* is the term for a king or emperor touring his country," Leo said. "Land was always held in the name of the monarch, and when he or she wished to visit, it was the responsibility of the noble landowner to host the entire court. Such a progress could be considered a blessing or a punishment. A blessing if the monarch arrived and departed swiftly. A punishment should the monarch remain, draining finances and resources unto penury."

"And *your* city belongs to *them*?" Eli said, emphasizing the pronouns.

"It isn't my city, according to the United States government. When they bought the Louisiana territories, they bought the land here, but few of the Mithrans agreed with Napoleon's right to make the sale, as Napoleon was human and not of the regal line of Mithran rulers. They have long disputed the transaction." Leo relaxed in his seat, still sipping, his mood seeming to mellow. "Their most recent disputation was in the World Court. Acting as a displaced royal family, they accused the United States of theft of their territory and potential homeland. The International Court of Justice declined to hear the argument in 1962. They went silent then, until now, but I never assumed that they were satisfied."

"So let me see if I got this right," I said. "The EuroVamps are mad because Napoleon sold the Louisiana territory to the U.S. They sued and lost. They sent Peregrinus and his *ménage a trois*—or allowed them to come—to cause trouble and to see how easy it might be to take over. Maybe to test the waters and see how powerful you are. They also encouraged the Naturaleza vamps from Atlanta to try to take over. And now they've taken a new direction and plan to claim the land in person."

Leo set his crystal glass down and actually clapped. "Excellent, *mon chat*."

"Again. Not yours. Why didn't you ever tell me all this?"

"As you say, you are not mine. When the binding did not take as planned, everything became—I believe you call it—'need to know.'"

"But what if the Mithrans are here, in the States, but not in port. Maybe they came ashore in Mobile or Charleston or one of the Texas ports, and only a few came to NOLA. All the rest would need to get here is charter a bus, a jet, or a line of limos. They could get here overnight, easy peasy. So a few could be here, and any vamp who has bloodlines or bloodkin here would be forced to offer them shelter, right? Like Grégoire?"

Leo's expression underwent a series of complex changes.

Stating that Grégoire was a potential danger to Leo was like throwing a boulder into a pond when we had just been skipping stones until now. "Grégoire is safe in the Council Chambers," he said stiffly, all his feathers ruffled. Not that he had feathers. "But . . ." He took a slow breath, the fingers of one hand stroking the cuff at the other wrist, giving himself time to think. "I will move him to rooms adjoining mine. Just in case one of the Capetian line arrives at the Council Chambers unexpectedly."

I knew who Leo feared the most. Grégoire's Valois blood-sire. Le Bâtard was a bastard of royal blood, a pedophile like Berkins. Leo's lover and Le Bâtard had a nasty, evil, and complicated relationship. Yeah. Things were coming together. "Would Grégoire know if Le Bâtard arrived in New Orleans? Would he tell you if Le Bâtard didn't want him to? Could Le Bâtard use mind games to force Grégoire to help him get into vamp HQ?"

Leo shrugged, the gesture still elegant, though his face told of uncertainty in his own judgment and insecurity about his loved ones. "Grégoire and I drank from each other upon rising. I have asked Katie to join us for the duration. It would be far better if my home was ready for habitation."

"Yeah. I know." If I sounded sarcastic, it was because Leo's Certificate of Occupancy had been requested and denied twice, each time for some minor offense after Leo had tried to bribe his way into getting the CO early. That bribery attempt had resulted in one complication after another. Now the house sat empty and Leo was stuck in HQ. Which meant that he'd have to put two hundred people up in some hotel. Royal progress as punishment. He'd be bankrupt in no time keeping them satisfied.

"Would they go through the proper channels?" Eli asked. "Would they have passports or visas? Or are they likely to sneak in?"

"They're royalty," I volunteered, thinking it through. "Modern law means nothing to them. Homeland Security, U.S. Citizenship and Immigration Services, trying to control Mithrans who ruled the world before the Western Hemisphere was ever discovered by Europeans? They'd blow raspberries at the idea of being forced to follow modern laws."

"Raspberries?" Leo asked.

I blew a mouth fart. Leo laughed, looking delighted. "Excellent. Please tell me you will do that when the Europeans arrive."

"To their faces," I agreed.

"It is unlikely that they would feel obliged to follow laws of any kind," Leo said. "See how far my Jane has come. She thinks in terms of royalty now. My Enforcer," he amended before I could complain, lifting a palm in a gesture for peace.

Faker. "So if they sailed from France," I said, "aboard an unknown boat, and got off at an unknown port, on an unknown date, then they could be anywhere."

"But not in the city in any numbers," Leo said.

"Right. I've got some maritime people I can talk to," Eli said, "without going to the authorities. Yet."

"And when it reaches the point where we need the authorities?" I asked.

"Homeland Security, U.S. Citizenship and Immigration Services, and multiple branches of the U.S. military can be at the dock on the Mississippi River in no time, to stop them from coming ashore," Eli said, satisfaction edging his voice, as if he was looking forward to a battle: U.S. government lawyers, law enforcement officials in suits, and uniformed military with things that go *bang*, versus royal, self-important suckheads. Since Eli was more a boots-on-the-ground kinda warrior, I knew who he was rooting for in that contest. Guns blazing all the way.

"Excellent," Leo said, drawing conclusions even faster than Eli and I. "Should that occurrence appear to become likely, I'll see that the lovely Carolyne has prior notice."

"Carolyne?" I asked.

"The reporter from the news channel. I found her delightful."

I sighed. Leo's sex drive was over the moon, but then, all vamps had supercharged libidos. "I have one more question," I said. "The vamps who rose as revenants. How did they get from Europe to New Orleans originally, during their undead unlives?"

"They escaped the French court and came to the Americas, where they swore to Amaury Pellissier. My uncle."

"That same uncle who pinned the Son of Darkness to the basement wall? The Son of Darkness who turned Hugh Capet and the dynasty that included Louis le Jeune and Le Bâtard? In the French court?" I clarified.

"Indeed," Leo said, pouring himself more champagne. "It is a complicated situation. Tiresome in the extreme."

"Tiresome. Yeah. That's the word I'd have used too," I said, thinking of the dead sailors.

Leo totally missed the sarcasm. "With my people, there is always a threat of armed conflict, of battle in the streets," he said, unperturbed. "You will prepare for that eventuality. I shall address the political aspect. And we shall meet again to discuss potentialities."

The rain hit like a thousand fire hoses as we turned onto my street, and I muttered, "Just in time. It's like I have a rain djinn." New Orleans in early winter was an evil creature, usually warm, with highs in the sixties and low seventies. But when storm fronts came through, the temps and rain and wind could change instantly. Like this storm. And me without an umbrella.

The limo stopped in front of the house, and my partner and I dashed from the car to the front porch, where we huddled under the front gallery for another half second while the Kid opened the door for us. The air inside was warm and dry and wonderful. We had been unprotected for less than three seconds and were wet to the skin.

This storm was the worst I had ever experienced in New Orleans: colder, lashing, and it was almost angry feeling, though that was anthropomorphizing the weather patterns. I had enough problems without a sentient climate.

As the Kid closed the door on the squall, lightning shattered through the air. Thunder boomed close by. I had yet to get over being hit by lightning. I faked it pretty good, but that ozone smell in the air and the prickles of electricity that meant a big storm still got to me. "I'll be in a hot shower," I said, disappearing into my room.

CHAPTER 3

You Offer Me Your Blood? Freely?

I dropped my gear bag and gobag on the small rug at the foot of the bed and my soaked clothes on the bathroom floor. The shower in the attached bath—what my honey-bunch called an en suite—wasn't huge, but the hot water was plentiful and the water pressure was glorious. One great thing about New Orleans was the water. It was everywhere, surrounding the city, wrapping around it, trailing through it. There was no shortage that ever meant conserving what was a precious commodity in most parts of the world. Well, except after hurricanes, when water surged in from the Gulf of Mexico and the city's supply was contaminated. During and after Hurricanes Katrina and Rita, potable water had been in short supply and shower water had been nonexistent for weeks. Months in some parts of the surrounding area.

I laid my forehead against the shower wall, the tile cold under my forearms, and let the water beat down on my head and back. Looking down. Studying myself. I was too skinny again, legs more sticklike, belly too flat, no hips. Not much in the boob area. Muscles too defined to be truly healthy. Females needed more body fat than males to keep our estrogen cycle steady. Or so said Aggie One Feather when I last visited her. Aggie was the *Tsalagi*—Cherokee—elder I visited for advice, information, and spiritual healing. Aggie knew me well enough to notice things like weight loss and had become mother-hen bossy. I had lost a few pounds since the lightning event. I had developed new scars, traceries of lightning that weren't visible unless water was pouring down me, like now. Then I could see the old burns. No one else had been in a position to see them but me. I'd kept Bruiser out of my shower since I first saw them. Eventually, after I shifted shapes enough, my skinwalker magics would heal me. If everything went as usual. I wasn't sure how big an *if* that was, yet.

I flexed my hands and relaxed them. They worked great. No residual problems from the strike that had fused the flesh together, trapping foreign objects in the scorched tissue. No problems at all except the ones that were left in my brain. And I was dealing with that situation. Mostly.

Eli had recognized that I had a problem when he caught me flexing my hands over and over. He had quietly asked what other symptoms of delayed-onset PTSD I was experiencing. Post-traumatic stress disorder. We had been sitting at the dinner table eating steak and potatoes when he broached the subject, and all sorts of things had come tumbling out of my mouth. Things I hadn't even known I was feeling. Eli had made me talk about what had happened, the night I was struck by lightning, talk about every single detail. Over and over. He shoulda been a shrink. Maybe I'd buy him a couch for his birthday and see how long it took him to get the joke.

However, all jokes aside, it had helped to know that what I was experiencing not only had a name but was suffered by others. Including him. The condition had a lot of symptoms, a lot of variables. Learning that had been helpful. And he hadn't told Bruiser yet, though I knew he wouldn't keep my secret much longer. Secrets were dangerous to mental health. He had assured me of that, which was odd considering how many secrets the former Ranger was keeping, like the source event of his own PTSD.

I was expected at Aggie One Feather's soon to be taken to water again, in an ancient Cherokee ceremony of purifi-

cation and healing. That would help too. And I'd eventually
get around to telling my boyfriend about my condition.
Maybe. If it didn't go away fast enough.

What I hadn't told Eli was that he was going to water too.
Aggie had secured the services of an old Choctaw man to take
Eli to water, since women and men had differing ceremonies.
And since it meant being naked. No way was I comfortable
being around Eli naked. Just . . . wrong. So Eli's ceremony
would not be the Cherokee version, but Aggie thought the
Choctaw ceremony would do. Would help. We'd see.

I turned off the water, dried with an oversized bathsheet
that Eli had ordered from some high-end store, oiled my skin,
and toweled my hair but left it down rather than drying it.
I'm not a girly kinda girl, but I have great hair, or so said
Bruiser, black as night, straight as good bourbon. Unbraided,
it hung down below my butt, and it would dry faster if I left
it loose and long. I pulled on layers: a long-sleeved silky undershirt, long-sleeved cotton tee, fuzzy sweatpants, and wool
socks and joined the boys in the main room.

Eli had showered in his usual ninety seconds and was
already lying on the couch, taking up the space of three people. Alex was playing some international war game on his
computer, the werewolf Brute at his feet. Pea, or maybe it
was Bean, since I couldn't tell the grindylow littermates
apart, was curled on Alex's shoulders, her steel claws groom-
ing his hair. Which looked horribly dangerous. And Edmund
was coming in the side door, wearing a rain-wet, dark suit, a
glimpse of his gorgeous collector car, parked in the narrow
lane. The smell of storm and vamp blood mixed on the breeze
close behind. His knees buckled. He fell forward.

"Ed!" I shouted.

Beast shoved into my brain. I/we leaped across the room,
Beast-fast, catching my primo before he hit the floor. His
blood smeared my hands. He slipped through my grip until
Beast's nails snagged on his clothing. I eased him to the
wood floor, his head on my thigh. He was bleeding from
dozens of cuts. His dark suit was rain and blood soaked.
"Call Leo," Eli said to Alex. And he sliced his wrist, verti-
cally, to keep from harming the tendons that made hands
and fingers work. Placed it at Edmund's mouth.

Eli had his battle face on: no emotion. No reaction. Edmund looked dead. His fangs should have flipped down. He should have ripped into Eli's arm. He should have vamped out, insane with hunger. But he did nothing, which was infinitely worse. Eli pressed his bleeding wrist to Edmund's mouth, gravity draining the blood in over Ed's tongue. Some drizzled out his lips. Pooled in his cheek.

"Come on," Eli demanded. "Drink, you sorry, fanged piece-a'-shit."

Nothing happened. Except watery blood pooled slowly on my floor. "Jane," Eli said. "Call him."

"What?"

"You're his master. He's healed you, so he's tasted your blood and shared his own with you. Call him. Make him drink. Keep him alive."

I started to say I had no idea what he was talking about, but Eli snarled, "Do it."

I started to say I didn't know how, but Edmund looked like death-still dead, real dead, not undead. I closed my eyes and crossed my legs in a half-guru position. *Beast?* I called my carnivorous half. She didn't answer, so I took a breath and dropped slowly into the Gray Between. Silver mist shot through with blue-black motes of power filled my mind. *Beast? I know you're here. How do I call Edmund?*

Beast does not know.

Gimme an idea. He's . . . dying.

He is dead. He is dead for longer than Beast is alive.

Beast didn't lie well, if at all, except by obfuscation. A thought occurred to me. *How did you call kits when they got away?*

She made a little mewling, coughing sound, which wouldn't help at all.

Then I remembered the electric velvet feel of Sabina's magics on the air when she called the Mithran vampires of New Orleans for a *gather*. And the raw, slicing power of Leo calling his scions to him prior to a feeding frenzy. That magic was all vampire, rich and deep and potent as death itself.

I reached out into the Gray Between. Took the silver mist and motes of my skinwalker magic into my . . . not hands. Into my mind. I usually used the magic to shift into an animal for which I had enough DNA material. But when I called Beast, it was different. Easier. I . . . I just thought about her, called her into being. I opened my eyes and looked down at the vampire. He was surrounded by the Gray Between. In the mist of my magics, he looked dead, pale and bloody and unbreathing, heart not beating.

"Jane!" Eli snapped. "Now!"

I gathered up my magic and slapped Ed with it. A red streak appeared on his cheek. "Drink, you sicko blood-sucker fanghead."

Nothing happened. I hit him with everything Beast and I had. And again.

The vamp coughed. Swallowed. A strangled sound of relief escaped my mouth. Eli put his wrist back at the vamp's lips. Ed swallowed and swallowed. His fangs flipped down slowly on their little bone hinges. Edmund's hand lifted to grip Eli's arm, guiding it more fully to his mouth. His lips closed around the wound, wasting no more blood to dribble on the floor.

Eli hissed. "Son of a . . . gun." He grunted in pain as Ed bit deep.

I let the Gray Between of my skinwalker magic fall away.

And that was when I smelled the stench of silver mixed with vamp blood. Toxic. Deadly. I touched a slash on Ed's side and the smell puffed out like putrefaction. Edmund had been cut with silver blades. He was really and truly dying.

"Alex?" Eli asked. "When?"

Edmund's eyes opened, white sclera and brown irises. His gaze focused on me as his eyes bled slowly black and his pupils dilated. Blood flushed into the vessels and his clear sclera went scarlet. He was vamping out, deliberately, con-trolled, even while poisoned with silver, tortured with blood loss, and dying. He was still dying. Such a slow vamping-out took power, a lot of power, for any vamp, even one in the best of undead health. Especially for a vamp who had been poisoned with silver.

Alex said, "Leo's sending Tex, some female named Dacy Mooney, Brandon and Brian, and Wrassler to help." I started to say something about the names, but Alex continued, his tone full of dread, "It'll be at least half an hour."

His eyes on me, Edmund sucked. And sucked. Time

passed. It seemed forever. Eli went slightly pale. Started smiling. He sat on the floor. Boneless and limp. His head tilted to the side and he stretched out beside the vampire, who was still bleeding onto the wood flooring. Silver in Ed's wounds was keeping him from clotting, from healing.

"How long?" I asked Alex.

"Twenty-two minutes before they get here."

"He won't last that long." I knelt beside Eli and pulled a blade from a sheath at his spine. I slid up my sleeve and sliced my wrist, saying something my house mother would have washed out my mouth for. It *hurt*. I said it again as the sting expanded and blood welled into the open flesh. Edmund stopped sucking. His eyes were still on me.

"Take it," I said. "Don't make me call you a fanghead piece-a'-crap. 'Cause I will. Now let go of Eli's wrist and take mine before you kill my partner and I have to take your head."

Edmund's eyes went from mine to Eli's, and shock flashed across his face. His mouth released, fangs sliding free. "I have taken too much," he whispered.

"Yeah. But two vamps are on their way to help. One of them can feed you and the other can heal Eli. Now drink."

His eyes went back to the blood that was now coiling around my arm in a spiral. He looked sick, ashy, starved. He needed to drain a few humans to heal, and yet he was holding back from attacking me. "You offer me your blood? Freely?"

I knew what he was asking. Freely sharing blood was part of the binding ceremony between master and primo. Edmund had freely given me his blood several times when I needed healing. Half of the sharing. If I gave him my blood freely, that was a second part.

Edmund's eyes fell from my arm to Eli, cradled on the floor. His lips widened the same way Pavlov's dogs salivated. Unconsciously. Needing.

"Jane?" Alex asked, warning in his tone. He was standing over Edmund, a silver-plated vamp-killer pointed at the vamp's cervical spine.

"Yes," I snapped. "Freely."

Edmund's eyes whipped back to mine, and I had a moment to wonder if I had been played before he released my partner and snatched my wrist. His tongue cold as a body in a morgue refrigerator, he licked my arm free of the trailing blood and dipped into the wound. The pain was instantly eased, the anesthetic in vamp saliva so effective that he bit through the slash and started sucking and I didn't even notice.

The pull was oddly familiar. *Kits*, Beast thought at me. *Suckling. Like kits.*

I blinked, closed my eyes, and the world faded from view. I was in my soul home, the cavern where I communed with Beast, with my own spirit, and with my memories. It was the memory of the first place I ever shifted forms, before I ever stole Beast's soul in an accidental act of black magic, blood magic. Before my family died. When I was a child and happy. It was the place I went to when I needed healing or solace or when I needed to learn stuff.

Before me was a fire flickering with warm yellow flames, tossing shadows on the smooth stone walls. The smell of fire eating black walnut wood was slightly sour, dry on my tongue. Across the fire pit was Beast, lying in a curl, so her head was on her paws, thick tail around her side. Golden eyes were staring at me, lazy, happy eyes. At her teats were kits. Suckling. Five of them.

Like kits, she repeated the thought. *Suckling.*

As in the way of dreams, I was suddenly sitting beside her. I put out a finger and stroked the head of the one closest to my ankle. It was soft and warm and smelled of milk. I looked at my other arm in the real world.

Not exactly, I thought back, seeing nothing remotely kittenlike in the vamp hanging on my arm. But the sensation was pleasant, nothing like the experience of Leo and Katie when they attempted to bind me against my will. *I should have killed them for that*, I thought.

Did not want you/us to go back and kill them, Beast said.

That wrenched my attention from the kits, fast. *You stopped me?* Understanding rolled over me in a tsunami of comprehension. *Stopped me from . . . even thinking about killing them. Didn't you?*

Jane needs vampires to survive Europeans. Needs vampires to save littermates. To save Angie Baby and EJ and all witch kits, many more than five.

I could just send Yellowrock Clan into safety. Back to the mountains. Why did you stop me? Secrets. You're still keeping secrets from me. What do you know? I demanded.

Edmund sucked and sucked, his mouth moving on my wrist without pain, but with a sensation I couldn't name. Tingly. Cold.

Beast went silent for a long time, as the tingles raced up and down my arm and pulsed into my bloodstream with every beat of my heart. My heart rate was beginning to speed. Racing. My breath came fast. Edmund was taking too much blood. Even with all his control, he was draining me. *Beast!* I commanded.

She thought, *I/we will not die.* In the deeps of my mind the kits vanished. Beast rose to her feet. Her lids closed and opened, in the lazy way of cats. She turned and pawpawpaw'd into the dark.

"Dang it," I snapped aloud, and opened my eyes. And realized that Edmund's eyes were on mine. Without asking, I knew what he was thinking, feeling. He had experienced the entire conversation with me. Just like when Leo healed me that very first time. "Oh crap," I said.

But Edmund was still dying. Fast. The pool of blood around us was spreading. My sweatpants were soaked with it.

Edmund released my forearm and reached up toward my face. His fingertips were cold as death, pale and ashen. I reached for him with my skinwalker magics. Felt myself falling into his mind. Into a dream not my own.

The house was dark, lit only by a single oil lantern in the front room and a single candle in one of the back rooms. The four large rooms that comprised the downstairs were fraught with winter chill, the house buffeted by icy blasts, the timbers creaking. Frost in intricate patterns caught the lantern light, sparkling on the precious window glass. Snow piled against the house in deep drifts and fires burning on the hearths could do little but hold the worst at bay. There were no customers on this blizzard night, snow such as Charleston had never seen—perhaps eighteen inches by morning.

Yet even in the cold, Sara's face was too hot. She was feverish, thrashing in ill dreams. She had taken some disease from one of the gentlemen callers over the summer and had not been given time from her duties to be made well. Instead she had been worked and worked, man after man, used and left sicker each time than before. And oft as not giving the patron the same disease she had contracted. Disease not acquired from the air, or some melancholic of the liver, as many chirurgeons suggested, but from the numbers of men she was forced to service and the abuse she suffered in her chambers.

"Heal me," she whispered.

He flinched and found her eyes on his in the night. Once they had been a laughing bright blue, a strange tint in her dark-skinned face. Her coloring—half white, half black—had drawn her much attention from the townsmen. "I have given you my blood a dozen times. It is not enough," he whispered. "Here. Take watered wine. There is opium in the cup I have stolen from the master. It will ease your dreams and your pain."

She turned her mouth from the cup, her blue eyes holding tight to his. "Make me what you are. I know that you can."

"No," he whispered back. "I cannot." But he had thought of it. He wanted it. But where would he keep her while she wandered in her mind? How would he feed a scion for ten long years of devoveo? "I have no lair to keep you safe. I am but a slave, like you."

"No," she whispered, turning her cracked lips to press a kiss to his hand. "You will never be a slave such as I. You will never be used as I have been. You must turn me . . ."

The front door opened.

I was ripped out of the dream. Chest heaving.

Not dream. But memory. A memory of Edmund's past. This was bad. This was very bad.

The stink of vamps and the smell of Wrassler blew in. Help was here. But that also meant that there wasn't time to deal with the shared memory or to figure out what it might mean. "This stays between us. That I shared your memories," I whispered to Edmund. "Between us." The command pulled through my blood, electric, heated, charged with potency. And it bound him to my demand. His eyes widened, a human reaction of surprise and hunger.

Shock followed through my blood, shock and guilt. Guilt that I had power over him, that I could command him. That I had made him some sort of mental slave. This was what it meant to bind another. This was what Leo had tried to do to me. This was what I had tried to avoid my entire time in New Orleans. And now instead of me being bound, I had bound Edmund. My stomach went sour at the realization and at the knowledge that I couldn't deal with any of it right now. I needed time to untangle the mess I had made.

Edmund eased his fangs from my flesh. "Yes, my master," he murmured, his eyes holding mine, the light hickory-hazel brown irises gleaming. "Do not feel guilt. I am yours to command."

I scuttled across the floor. Vamps poured into the house through the front door. Within seconds of the vamps arriving, I bolted to the backyard, pulling up the Gray Between as I stripped. Not thinking. Not thinking about Edmund and what I had done. Rain slashed me with frozen claws, icy and miserable on bare skin.

It hurt to change fast—it *hurt*—but I didn't have time to shift a slower, less painful way, and time was urgent in the storm and rain. The scent of Edmund's blood and the blood of his wounded attackers would be gone in minutes, the trail lost in the downpour. And I didn't dare become dog to track waning scent patterns. When I became any form of tracker dog, I got lost in the scents and feared I'd never find myself again.

Beast tore out of me. I fell to the ground as Beast thrust herself through my skin, bending and breaking bones, muscles stretching and tearing.

Was heaving breaths, cat-gagging. Alex strapped Jane's waterproof gobag around my neck. Held plastic cup of vampire blood to nose.

Smell good. Smell strong. I/we lapped blood. Licked small cup clean. Was still hungry in belly but strongness raced through body.

Alex slapped Beast on butt.

Snarled at littermate Alex. Pulled paws under belly and stood. Needed food. Needed cow or deer. Needed to hunt and pounce and kill and eat. Growled. Shook pelt like dog. Was wet.

"I can't leave," Alex said. "Not with vamps in the house. Be careful."

Hacked at Alex. Padded to porch, to door where Edmund had come into den. Blood was everywhere. Edmund blood, rich and strong. Licked at blood. Some was good. Some was also silver. Looked up at Alex. Was man now. Held white-man gun in one hand, pointed at floor. Fingers on safe place called slide.

"I'll clean up the mess," Alex said.

Sniffed with *scree* of sound, lips back, sucking air over tongue and scent sacs at top of mouth. Smelled strange vampires, their blood mixed with blood of Edmund. Blood. Silver. Death.

Beast? Jane thought.

Am Beast.

Can you smell him? Oh yeah. There it is. I got it.

Jane nudged Beast brain. *You need to stop taking canine scent genes in when we shift to dog. It's getting crowded in here.*

Strange vampire blood smell. Strange vampire ambush-hunted Edmund. Two vampires. Strong vampires. And humans, more than five.

Okay. We'll talk about it later. For now, use those dog scent genes and track back on Edmund's trail.

Beast sniffed. *Beast wants good nose without being ugly dog. Do not want to be tracking dog, but do want good dog nose.* Jane started to think Jane thoughts. To argue. Put paw on Jane and made her silent. *Will not talk to Jane about nose.*

Muzzle to ground, like dog Beast did not want to be, followed blood trail through rain. Alongside of house. Past Bitsa, covered with cloth. Past Edmund car, fancy car that Alex loved, with top and seats made of dead cow. Car was cold. Edmund had been on paws—on foot. Edmund did not have paws. Stopped at metal gate at end of alleyway. Stuck nose and muzzle through bars and sniffed. Looked. No people in rain. People were smart. Rain was cold and Beast was hungry. Even with vampire blood in belly.

Gathered self tight, looked to top of fence with metal flower. Leaped, pushed off flower with front paws, then back paws, over metal gate, and landed on smooth not-stone path, what Jane called sidewalk or concrete.

Uptown, Jane thought. *Ed came from uptown. Bleeding all the way.*

I/we began to trot, avoiding round places of streetlights. Rain fell, slowing. Water gurgled through downspouts. Tinkled off roofs. Plinked onto cars. Splashed as Beast trotted, covering much ground. Jane thought Jane thoughts. Sulking. Good word for juvenile kit. Sulk.

Beast was insulting me so I ignored her. It continued to rain, though the water didn't penetrate Beast's double-layered pelt. We had worked in Beast form in the rain before—rain being the normal for New Orleans at any season—but not in such cold weather. Her breath blew twin plumes of vapor into the night. Her paws splashed through puddles and runnels of water. Rain made the city smell fresh, releasing ozone and ions on the air. The scent of blood and vamp faded and I thought we had lost it, but we found it around the next corner, a puddle of blood and rainwater that had no outlet except across the concrete. The scent faded again, to reappear further on. Beast trotted around corners, doubling back, searching, nose to ground, keeping to the shadows. Melting into the dark when a car came past. She was smarter than any mountain lion. Adaptable. Reactive. Going on two hundred years of life would give any animal excellent survival instincts.

Even with dog genes incorporated into her brain and nose, Beast wasn't the best tracker. I'd have better luck with a bloodhound nose, but I'd had problems lately changing back from canine to human. Without a handler and a leash, I could lose myself and stay dog forever; noses and the scent part of dog brains were that strong. Alex had known all that. He had understood what I was doing and why, possibly even before I raced outside.

The rain stopped. Started again. We passed restaurants almost empty of tourists. Bars full of drunk tourists. We passed churches next to Creole cottages, and we chased off a small pack of junkyard dogs with a single growl. Which made Beast chuff with laughter and victory. We passed cemeteries, the smell of old, *old* death and limestone and fresh white paint. We trotted beneath the I-10 interstate and were halfway to Highway 90 in what felt like a long way from home, though Beast wasn't tired, just wet and grouchy. Mountain lions aren't long-distance cats like jaguars or cheetahs, but in the cold, with the air decreasing the effect of heat buildup, we could travel a long way. A female *Puma concolor*'s hunting territory might cover a hundred fifty square miles.

Beast stopped. Looked both ways. Shoulders hunched. *What?* I thought at her, flooding back into her forebrain. I/we slunk close to a parked car and waited for two motorcycles to pass.

Like Bitsa, she thought, *but not like Bitsa. Does not have Harley growl like Bitsa.*

Okay, I thought. *I loved the bike too, though not so much in a downpour. But why are we stopping here?*

Beast trotted out from the protection of the car and down a narrow alley between two houses. The ground and walls stank of feral male cats, territory spray, strong musky stinks.

Stupid cats, think they are lions. But smell Edmund. He was here. With cats.

Where? Inside the house? I looked around, through Beast's eyes, seeing the world in silvers and greens and blacks and grays of Beast's night vision. I/we sniffed the air. Edmund's scent was everywhere and nowhere.

Smell of Edmund on top of house. Smell of vampires and blood-servants inside house.

He was spying on the house. They came out and found Edmund. They fought here? What is this place?

Smell of Edmund blood and silver. Smell of vampire blood and strange blood-servant blood. Smell of white-man guns and steel. Edmund fought.

They fought here, I thought. *Then Edmund got away. They chased him.*

Human died here. Vampires drank female inside.

That made sense. The vamps—what vamps?—had found a victim and charmed and mesmerized her. She had brought them back to her house. She was dead inside, the smell of death coming through the cracks in the walls. Beast pushed me down, out of the forefront of her brain, taking control again.

Beast is alpha. Beast has hunted. Nose to ground. Want cow.

You did what I asked, Jane thought. *Thank you.*

Jane is po-lite. Po-lite does not feed Beast. Sat down in dark place beneath plant with big leaves. *Feed Beast.*

I have nothing to feed you.

Smell dog. Big dog on chain. Could eat dog, Beast suggested hopefully. *Is on chain. Would not fight long. Could not get away.*

I bet dogs taste bad. How about this. We shift back to human, call a cab, grab a bucket of chicken, and go home, where it's nice and warm and dry. Then we can hunt alligator in the swamp on a full moon night.

Jane has been Beast two times this night. Chased vampire who killed revenant. Tracked Edmund. Am hungry. Want cow. Want to hunt cow in Edmund car on full moon night.

Yeah, I don't think that's gonna happen.

Want cow. Want to hunt cow in Edmund car.

That's between you and Edmund. Jane sent image of Beast talking to vampire, making funny puma sounds. Was not funny but Jane laughed.

Jane bound Edmund like dog on chain. Edmund will let Beast hunt in Edmund car if Jane makes him.

Jane went silent. Beast groomed paws. Paws were wet with rain and tasted of gasoline and exhaust and rats. Was bad for Beast but would heal when Beast shifted again.

Alligator on full moon hunt, Jane thought. Jane was mad. She pulled up Gray Between and reached into snake that was Jane. Jane-snake was not quite right but was good enough. Like Beast with dog nose was good enough. Was maybe better. Bones began to twist.

CHAPTER 4

Put Down Your Pin Sticker

I woke lying in the dark beneath the dripping leaves of a banana plant, my too-long black hair wrapped all around me, but at least that was better than some places Beast had left me. I tied my hair in a knotted tail, opened the water-proof gobag, and dressed in thin layers and flops. My stomach was cramping like I had swallowed a nest of water moccasins. Shivering, I pulled my unofficial cell—one Leo couldn't trace—and called Rinaldo.

"Who dis is?" he answered, instead of hello. I could hear kids screaming in the background, the TV on a sitcom. The cabbie was off duty with the nearly defunct Blue Bird Cab Company but he sounded mostly sober, and he offered to pick me up when I gave him an address two blocks away from the house where Ed had fought and bled. "Twenty minute," he said, and disconnected.

I jogged through the rain, holding a dripping hand over the flip phone, while calling in a DB to vamp HQ, with the words, "Dead body. Looks like vamp attack." I gave the address and disconnected. A good citizen would have called 911. I wasn't a good citizen. Leo's team would make sure the body was found and the death looked like an accident. One of his private labs would do a full forensic workup, an arrangement I had suggested to keep track of paranormal crimes that we didn't want reported to the police, for some reason. Leo would also do what he could for the victim's family, children, parents.

And then Leo would send me to find and kill the vamps who'd killed the girl in the small house. They were also the vamps who attacked Edmund. A life for a life. Yeah. He'd demand the vamps die.

The wait was short, but when Rinaldo arrived he wasn't driving a Blue Bird cab but a black four-door sedan. He saw me, shoved open the front passenger door, and shook his head when I squelched inside. I was soaked and trembling and gratefully wrapped myself in the oversized towel he tossed at me. I took the cup of hot coffee and sipped while he idled at the curb. I'm not a coffee drinker, but there was plenty of sugar and cream in the travel cup too. "This is good."

"Why some big-ass famous vampire killer and assistant to de devil out in de storm in you underwear?" Rinaldo asked in his Frenchy accent.

I wasn't wearing any underwear and my clothes were sticking to me like a second skin, my real skin showing through, though Rinaldo turned his head away, politely, which was nice. I no longer had huge vampire-hunter/vampire-employee secrets from Rinaldo. But he didn't know everything.

"I'll answer that if you tell me why you're not picking me up in a Blue Bird car."

Rinaldo made a snorting sound, very Frenchy, a sound I'd heard in cafés and restaurants among the locals. "Traditional cabbies, we losing money against Uber cabs. Closed down. I now self-employed Uber driver too. I make more money. I pick my calls. Dat part I like. But I hafta pay my own taxes, I do, and I hate me some math." He shrugged. "You turn."

Rinaldo stood about five feet seven and had been a little paunchy at one eighty, but he had lost weight, was dressed nicer than when he was a cabbie, wearing ironed khakis and a golf shirt. He had also stopped trying to cover up his bald spot with a comb-over. He looked good. "You smell better. You gave up smoking."

Ruefully Rinaldo said, "Ha-ha. You funny, you is. My little one, she crawl up in my lap and she say, 'Daddy, when you get sick like Mrs. Marillett, I gone get a oxygen tank for you. 'Cause I love you!'" Rinaldo shot me a look. "I ain't had me cigarette in two months. Hardest two months a' my life. But can taste food now again. Dat a good part. You answer my question now."

"I was chasing vamps. I ended up without my coat, no shoes, and wet to the skin."

"Dat ain't no answer. You want burgers or chicken?"

I pointed to a small Cajun eatery and bar on a corner. The painted sign said EBO'S NO. 2 FANCY. "See if they got boudin balls? Get me a few pounds?" Rinaldo slowed and parked as I fished out two twenties from my gobag.

"You ever gone tell me you secrets? I thought we become friends of a sort."

I studied Rinaldo's earnest face. He needed a shave. Renewed rain beat against the windows. A sudden gust of wind rocked the sturdy car. I was glad to be out of the rain. And I was out because of Rinaldo. He had been there for me when I needed him. I had never done anything for him except tip well. Yet he knew only what the general public did, nothing confirmed by my own words and my own trust. "You're right. We are friends. I'm not human. These are the clothes I wear when I'm tracking a vamp."

"Goo' enough. Dat a start." Rinaldo opened an umbrella and jogged through the storm to Ebo's, leaving the sedan and the heater on so I'd stay warm. It felt odd having a . . . a new friend. I hadn't had many—none if I was honest—in my life until earth witch Molly Everhart and I became pals, and I was grown by then. This felt . . . itchy.

Rinaldo jogged back through the rain, a huge paper bag under an arm. The car door closed on the storm once again and he handed the bag to me, offering with his other hand the second twenty and change. "Keep it," I said. I unfolded the bag and held it out to him. "Want one?"

Rinaldo, who had no idea how hard it was to give the first boudin ball away and not chow down on it myself, took a ball and a handful of coarse napkins. "Jist dey one. I watching my girlish figure, donchu know."

In companionable silence, Rinaldo and I ate and made the ride back to Yellowrock Securities while wiping grease off our faces and hands and licking our fingers. There was nothing like the food in this city. Not even back home in Asheville.

I sat on the sofa, wrapped in a blanket, surprised that it was only near midnight, that dawn hadn't found the world yet. I had agreed to be fed vamp blood by Dacy Mooney simply because I was more tired than I thought I would be, even after eating a steak and fries, and I needed to be in fighting form. With a master vamp nearby to feed me, I was taking the cheater's way out because the night wasn't over. I had too much to do. Too much to think about. So I drank the blood of the heir of Clan Shaddock while she told me why she was in town, visiting from Asheville. She was checking on Shaddock's scion, Amy Lynn Brown, which was no surprise. Amy was the miracle vamp whose blood brought new vamps from the devoveo—the madness that freshly turned vamps experience for ten years or so after rising—in record time. It was expected that the European vamps would want Amy for their very own slave, and no one was giving her up. Amy could easily be the cause of a World Vamp War.

I listened with half an ear, drank maybe a half cup of Dacy's revitalizing blood, and made little *ummm* noises in the appropriate conversational places. I watched as Dacy fed Eli again and carried my hunky partner up the stairs to his room, Alex sprinting along to make sure the blond Tennessean didn't try anything inappropriate with his blood-drunk brother. I watched as Tex and then Wrassler fed Edmund again, and the Onorio twins, Brandon and Brian, helped my primo—my primo, for good and real, now—into bed in his nook under the stairs where we kept our weapons.

Brandon—or maybe it was Brian; I didn't look for the mole that differentiated them—said, "He's living in a Harry Potter room. Long fall for a master of his own clan."

The other twin said, "No windows. There is no room with no windows but this one."

"Still. Long fall."

"Indeed." The conversation ended. There was no doubt that they had intended me to hear it. They had nothing to say to me as they closed up the shelving unit that secured the daytime sleeping place of my primo. I had nothing to say to them either, remembering Edmund's memory of the dying slave in the blizzard. Silently, I watched as they all left the house.

Moments later, Alex stood in the opening to the foyer, shoes on his feet, real pants—the kind that covered his legs to his ankles—and plaid shirt over his T-shirt. "Since my blood-drunk brother is healed and sleeping off the treatment, I plan to go out. Okay with you?"

I looked at Alex blankly. I could count on two fingers the times he had left the house to "go out" since he and Eli moved in. And then I remembered and quoted back to him. "'Game con in town. Small one,' but you got friends who'll be there. Go. Have fun."

"Right. Call me if you need me." He waggled his cell at me. Undoubtedly his other electronics were in the gobag slung over his shoulders. "You'll watch Eli?" he asked unnecessarily.

"Of course," I said, also unnecessarily, but polite.

And then I was alone but for the sleepers.

I sat now on the sofa, with an afghan wrapped around me, wishing there were a fireplace in the room, and wondering which walls originally had one. The house was built when fire, probably coal fire, had heated every room. There would have been fireplaces in each, but we had none and now that I thought about it, there were brick-built chimneys on the roof. Maybe I should invest in finding the original fireplace locations, tear into the walls, and have them rebuilt. They would make the place feel more warm and cozy in winter.

Or . . . Maybe I should run home. To the mountains. Not that I'd be any safer there.

I had bound my primo. I had glanced into his mind and he into mine. It was freaky and weird and I had a deep and abiding discomfort at the intimacy of the contact.

Almost as bad—Beast was still keeping secrets from me. Big ones.

She hadn't wanted me to kill Leo for trying to bind me. We had instead bound him and tied him to our soul home. And when his binding to us had severed, something had been left in its place. What had really happened in the meta-physical moment when Leo was set free? What had it all meant? Was Leo's being bound to us part of some bizarre plan Beast had hatched? But long-term plans went against Beast's nature in every way I could think. So why had she done whatever she had done? And what else was she keep-ing secret from me?

My cell rang. I looked down at the screen to see Molly's face and name. My BFF was calling at an odd time. Unless it wasn't her. I tapped the screen and said hello.

"Hey, Aunt Jane," a tiny voice said. It was Molly's daughter.

I curled tight on the couch and said, "Hey, Angie Baby. What are you doing up?"

"Me and EJ and Mommy and Daddy are going out of town. So I had to call you now. My angel said to tell you something."

My heart and my magic leaped in dread at the words. The angel Hayyel had started a lot of the troubles in my life. "Okay. Like in a dream?"

She yawned hugely and her voice was sleepy-sounding when she said, "Nope. He waked me up. He said to tell you it was raining and the storm was dan-ger-ous. You have to make some 'cisions. He said your magics was gonna be a problem but you can fix 'em. Or . . . I dunno, maybe he can fix 'em? And if you do the right things everything will be okay. Okay? I'm going back to bed, Aunt Jane. I'll see you when we get back from Daddy's camping trip. I love you."

"I love you too, Angie Baby." The call ended.

My heart was racing. My breathing was too fast. Angie had a dream. Right? Except that with Angie I never really knew. She was probably the most powerful witchling on the planet. And I knew for a fact that angels talked to her.

I pulled the afghan closer and tried to sleep, but my eyes kept popping open with every little ping or pop of the house settling. To relax myself, I put a nine-millimeter and a short-bladed vamp-killer on a small table, close to hand. It didn't help.

*   *   *

A little after two a.m. I heard keys at the front door, and it
opened again. Bruiser's clean citrusy aftershave and heated
Onorio scent blew in as the cold blew out. He closed the
door after him. I didn't look up. We didn't speak. Instead
I heard him enter the kitchen and the sound of water scud-
ding into the teakettle. The sound of the stove lighting with
a soft *whoosh*. The softer sounds of him preparing tea. The
warm scent of chai on the air. The sound of a paper bread
bag opening and the fresh smell of a bakery loaf filling the
house as he toasted slices. The delectable scent of salmon,
both smoked and raw. The sound and smell of cucumber
being sliced as cucumber sandwiches and salmon tartare
on toast points were prepared. At two a.m. Something soft
and heated opened inside me. With the exception of the
Youngers, no man had ever cooked for me. And Bruiser
was fixing me an elegant meal of cucumber sandwiches and
salmon tartare.

Cucumber sandwiches. Not thin-sliced beef. Not cinnamon and sugar. Cucumber. And watercress. And soft cream
cheese. Raw fish. My honeybunch was making me a soothing
treat.

He came to the couch bearing a tea tray and two humon-
gous mugs. One of them said, WHEN LIFE GIVES YOU LEM-
ONS, THROW THEM AWAY AND GET SOME BACON! It was a
new mug, and I felt my mouth pull into a smile at the sight.
Bruiser's mug said, I LOVE YOU MORE THAN BACON.
Both mugs were full of steaming chai and a big spoonful of
melting Cool Whip. My new primo would think we were
heathens. My smile fell away. My new primo. For reals. I
had bound another sentient creature. Slavery of the worst
sort. And Edmund knew a thing or two about slavery.

Bruiser set the tray beside me and placed a cloth napkin
in my lap. In the middle of the table he placed a plate of
cucumber sandwiches; a second plate of salmon on toast
points; a huge, heated, white chocolate macadamia nut sugar
cookie on a glass dessert plate; and a single white rose with
a long stem and no scent. He took my hand and wrapped it
around the mug. The ceramic was warm. My smile came

back. I held the mug with both hands and sipped, the taste speaking of good memories and the house mother I had loved best, Belinda. I should have the Kid track her down so I could tell her how much she meant to me. Maybe someday.

Bruiser pushed my legs over, kicked off his leather loafers, and curled up beside me. His Onorio warmth was better than any fireplace, and I tucked my toes under his leg. He pulled the afghan over us both. We sipped. Silent. Content. I even ate one of the veggie cheese sandwiches in between the salmon. The snack soothed me almost as much as the company.

When I was warm inside and the mug was mostly empty, Bruiser said, "Ed will survive. He'll need to be fed the blood of the Son of Darkness tonight, and by as many masters as will offer, but he should be well in"—Bruiser waggled his hand, his elegant fingers looking longer in the shadows—"two days? Three at the outside."

A heavy load I hadn't acknowledged fell off me and my shoulders relaxed for a moment. I licked the vanilla-flavored whipped topping off my upper lip and said, "That's good. Thank you for telling me. But. I bound Ed to me tonight."

Bruiser nodded, as if I had said something innocuous, like *It rained*, or *Good tea*. "You saved his life," he said. "Eat your cookie."

I picked up the cookie and took a bite. It was made with butter, lots and lots of butter. It tasted like heaven. I nibbled as the flavors washed through me, in a color like yellow flowers and sunlight. With the last bite of cookie, I gestured at his mug. "Do I love you more than bacon or do you love me more than bacon?"

"I love you more than bacon," he said, a smile in his voice.

"I love you more than bacon too," I said. "Unless I'm hungry. Or Beast."

"In either of which cases I will bring you bacon."

My lips pulled up again. "I like my bacon cooked. Beast likes hers raw."

"Duly noted."

I finished the cookie, licked my fingers, and picked up the flower. Sniffed it. "I like that you give me flowers that don't stink."

"I like that you give me interesting bottles of wine."

I nearly choked on my tea, making a noise suspiciously like a giggle. Days ago, I had stopped at a wine shop and ordered a mixed case of wine to be shipped to him in a fancy wood crate. He had received the twelve bottles of Boone's Farm. The flavors had ranged from Orange Hurricane to Strawberry Margarita to Blue Hawaiian to Fuzzy Navel, and the gift was in honor of what Bruiser thought was a dreadful confession. He had admitted to me that in the seventies he and a female vamp-to-remain-unnamed had gotten violently drunk on Strawberry Hill–flavored wine (and Strawberry Hill–flavored Bruiser) and had raced around the city on his motorbike, dancing at every bar they could find, before motoring up to the fountain in Jackson Square and vomiting in it. He had barely gotten the vamp housed before sunrise. I hadn't known he had a motorbike, or that he had ever been less than suave and sophisticated. I had been delighted with the tale, hence the prezzie.

I'd been even more delighted that we'd shared a bottle of sweet Fuzzy Navel wine with po'boys from Coop's Place, curled up together on his gallery. It had been a magical night, so much so that I'd shared a few tidbits from my own youth.

I'd talked about Bobby, the sweet little boy I'd befriended and taken under my wing in the children's home when the other kids picked on him. Had admitted that the phrase *taken under my wing* was synonymous for beating up several kids who abused him physically or verbally. Admitted that I had practically broken the record for time spent in detention. Bruiser said he found my stories and me "delightful." And then he had proceeded to kiss along my throat and up to my ear. I'd never been called delightful. I was pretty sure it gave me the quakes.

The next morning I had woken to find a pair of boxing gloves on the pillow beside me, ancient gloves that smelled of sweat and blood and time. They had been his from the same year he drank wine. Now I had them hanging off one of the short posts at the head of my bed, and I fell asleep at night smelling Bruiser even when he wasn't there.

And now he loved me more than bacon.

That was more lovey-dovey talk than we had said to each other ever. Preceded by BACON complementary mugs, that was, like, practically the magical three words. Almost, *I love you.* Or maybe even better, because the magical phrase was just a statement of fact without qualifiers. This was *more than bacon.*

I sipped my tea. He sipped his. He loved me more than bacon. I loved him more than bacon. He wasn't disappointed with me for binding Edmund. He didn't worry about me out in Beast form hunting killer vamps; he knew I had the skills to take care of myself. He made me tea and cookies and cute little sandwiches just because.

Life couldn't get much better than this.

Around 3:30 a.m. Bruiser took a call and kissed me on the cheek before he left my house. I checked on Eli, who was sleeping with a happy smile on his face. He didn't wake when I walked up the stairs. He didn't wake and shoot me when I leaned over him to check his breathing. The former Ranger was out cold, sleeping deeply, with good dreams, for the first time since we met. This seemed like a good thing. I should make him drink vamp blood more often.

Because I was the only protection tonight, which felt odd after so many months with the Youngers living here, I checked the house doors, made sure there was a round in the chamber of the weapon by my bed, and crawled between the sheets. The warm scent of Bruiser on his boxing gloves lulled me into dreams.

What felt like only minutes later, I woke to the echo of a deep, reverberating growl. I took a slow, still breath, parsing the scents. Someone was in the house. In my room. Two someones. I smelled werewolf and Anzu: Brute, the white were stuck in wolf form, and Girrard DiMercy, who looked human but was not. And magic. I pulled on Beast-speed. In a single move I rolled from the mattress, throwing off the sheets, picked up the nine-mil, and bent my knees into a shooting stance. The sheets were still in the air when I off-safetied and pointed the weapon at the location of the scents. The entire move took maybe half a second.

They stopped, frozen in place like a bizarre tableau in a wax museum. Gee was holding his sword to the werewolf's throat. Brute was snarling. My closet door was open. So was the side door, and a fine rain was blowing in, filling the house with icy, wet mist. Both doors had been closed when I fell asleep.

Beast's night vision turned everything into bright silvers and greens and whites. More than enough to see that Gee was wearing all black, with a black kerchief over the lower part of his face. And a brimmed hat. And a black lace shirt with cuffs that hung dripping. He was dressed like a cat burglar/sword master from some Renaissance romance novel. Dramatic, as always. But the sword, that was real. And he knew how to use it.

"It's loaded with standard ammo. Lead won't kill you, Gee," I said, my voice casual, "but it'll hurt."

Gee slowly turned his head to me and pulled down the kerchief to expose his face. Brute kept his predator's stare on the small, pretty man and growled again, a deep, low vibration that I could feel through the floor and the soles of my bare feet. The wolf wasn't sopping but wasn't totally dry either. He'd been here a while. The soaked man was the interloper. "So here's what I think happened," I continued, taking in the condition of the house beyond my door. "An hour or so ago, Brute came in through the wolf-door panel Eli installed, because Brute belongs here. Sometimes. Gee does not, but you came by anyway. And then you cast a sleepy-time spell of some sort over the house and walked in. Brute, who for some were-taint reason didn't succumb to the spell, caught you walking into my house and going through my closet."

"You have that which belongs to me." He was talking about a magical item I had confiscated from a big honking witch-versus-vampire fight in a little town west of New Orleans. It looked like a laurel-leafed crown, and it was a powerful amulet. That was about all I knew, but that was enough for me to keep it out of the hands of anyone who wanted it.

"Nope. It may belong to the Anzus as a group or to one or the other of you, but *le breloque* is mine until I discover its true and full provenance and powers. Put down your pin sticker and step away from the closet. I really don't want more blood on my floors tonight. I intend to collect on that boon you owe me from way back and don't want to fritter it away by accidentally killing you."

"This storm," he insisted. "It is fed by ancient magic. If you give *le breloque* to me I can end the storm. I can save your people."

It could be a pathetic attempt to bargain for what he wanted. Except that the only times anyone wanted *le breloque* was when there was a storm overhead. Interesting. Did its power increase with storms? Give the wearer control over them? Allow the wearer to gain power from the storms? It was all conjecture; without answers, birdman was getting nothing. "Still no."

Gee slashed the sword up, around, into the sheath in one single flourish. My finger, which had begun to compress the trigger with the movement, relaxed. Gee said, "I bring a message from Sabina, the outclan priestess of the Mithrans."

"I'm listening."

"You are not going to put away your weapon?"

"Nope. Talk."

"Sabina has had a vision of the bubo bubo. She says, 'Purify yourselves. Be ready. The time has come.'"

With the storm blowing in, it was chilly in the house, even with the warm, fuzzy nightclothes I had worn to bed. I shivered at the prophecy. Sabina had an in with the spiritual world that I didn't understand at all. She knew things. She knew I was a shape-shifter. She associated some ancient vamp prophecy with the bubo bubo, the Eurasian Eagle Owl, which I had once turned into so I could pry into secret vamp ceremonies. Yeah. This was from Sabina.

Ancient people purified themselves before battle, or before some great life change, and Sabina wanted me pure. Not good. Not good at all. I wondered how much of this had to do with the girl earlier tonight, the one the vamps drank down and drained and left dead.

"Message delivered," I said. "Get out of here. And next time you break into my house, I'll shoot first and ask questions later."

"As you said, it will not kill me. Rounds are lead."

"As I said, it'll hurt like a mama. Get out the way you came in. And shut the door behind you."

Gee vanished, almost vamp-fast, and the door closed as he left. I slid the safety on and set the weapon on the bedside table, angled for quick access. "Thank you," I said to the wolf.

Brute tilted his head to me and his tongue lolled out of his mouth, comical in the dark.

"Lemme guess. When you came in and found that the door to the gun safe was closed, you trotted your wet, dog-stinky-self upstairs to the Kid's bed and made a nice damp nest."

Brute grinned at me. It was a doggie grin, showing teeth.

"You ever do that to my bed and I'll kick you out. For good."

Brute looked at my bed. To a dog, the alpha's bed was the very best place, the only place, to sleep. I had let him onto my bed on a very few occasions when I was ill or hurt and his werewolf warmth had helped me to heal, but he didn't have permission to go there at will. I had caught him standing in my doorway more than once, staring at my bed, thinking about jumping up there and rolling his scent all over it, doggie-claiming the alpha bed. But this time Brute looked from the bed to the closed side door. And then to the closet, making a point that he had saved the day. Or the night.

"I mean it," I warned.

Brute snuffled and sat, looking from the closet to the back door, and then growling, repeating in clear dog-speak that he had saved me. That he deserved a reward. I almost offered him a doggie treat but I knew that this was more than just a desire for a crunchy bone. He tilted his head again and whined, looking at my bed and then at me. This was a werewolf negotiation.

"Fine," I said, though it wasn't. "I recognize your service tonight. Therefore I promise to look for a dog bed—" Brute growled again. I blew out a breath that caught the loose black hairs around my face and made them fan out in the dark. "A memory foam mattress I can put in the hallway upstairs for your use—whenever the Everhart/Truebloods are not here, until such time that Evan Trueblood agrees you can stay in the house with Angelina and EJ. Until such time, and when they are here, you will sleep in the weapons room." I thought over what I had said and figured I had covered most of the angles of a paranormal negotiation. "Agreed?"

Brute snuffled agreement and turned away, to trot back upstairs to his stolen nest. I went to the side door and cleaned up the rainwater. Then I placed a call to vamp HQ and got Del, the primo to Leo Pellissier, the Master of the City. It was the middle of the business day for a vamp household, and the primo sounded confident and in control. We chit-chatted for a bit and then I said, "Is the priestess in Council Chambers tonight?" Council Chambers is a more polite way of saying suckhead HQ.

"No. Why?" Del dragged out the words because any proper verbiage from me was always a warning.

"The Enforcer has a formal request to make, of the primo of the Master of the City of New Orleans. May I speak?"

"The primo of the Master of the City of New Orleans is attentive to the Enforcer," Del said, pure suspicion lacing her words. I was seldom so formal. I was seldom even faintly polite.

"The Enforcer would be honored to call upon, or to receive a phone call from, Sabina, the outclan priestess of the Mithrans."

"Oh." Del sounded nonplussed but continued with the proper, somewhat formulaic responses. "I will pass along the message. Is there a subject that should attend the request?"

"Yeah. Tell the priestess that I need to talk to her about Anzus—Anzii?" I queried midsentence, "and *le breloque*'s purpose—which may or may not have something to do with storms like the ones currently brewing over New Orleans. Please."

Del repeated it back to me, I said that was perfect, and she went silent, though I could hear her tapping on her tablet. "The primo will happily pass along the request exactly as worded."

"Thanks."

"You still owe me a spa day."

I always owed Del a spa day. "Find a spa with a steam

room, massages, and facials, and we can go Saturday and take Jodi."

"Wait. Who is this and what have you done with Jane Yellowrock?"

"Ha-ha. It's cold and miserable. A massage, a hot rock to curl up on, and some pampering sounds wonderful."

The hot-rock part had come from Beast. If Del thought it was odd, she didn't respond to it. "Deal. And I'll let you know what the priestess says."

We disconnected and I found myself staring at my back door. Gee DiMercy shouldn't have been able to get in. The door wasn't broken or splintered, and the lock hadn't looked scratched, so either Gee could pick a lock leaving no traces, which was possible, or he had used magic to get inside, which was also possible.

Gee was a bird, an Anzu, a creature once worshiped as a storm god. We had recently hunted together, both of us in Anzu form. I'd had a good long look at Anzu DNA when I shifted into the form, and that DNA was not from Earth, but it did look a lot like *arcenciel* DNA. Could there be a connection between all the weird stuff? Between Sabina's bubo bubo prophecy, the storm overhead, the dead female in the small house, the vamp attack on Edmund, *arcenciels* (rainbow dragons who could shape-shift into human form), and *le breloque* . . . Nah, I was reaching. Or hoping that I could tie it all together in one lovely package with a bloody red bow. I had learned that with vamps and other paranormal creatures, it was better to be safe than sorry, and nothing was ever easy. So I had lots of smaller problems and not one gigantic problem with a single resolution.

I checked on Eli, who was still smiling in his sleep, trotted back downstairs, and crashed again, sleeping until a rumble of thunder waked me.

CHAPTER 5

You Look Like Shiii—Crap

Torrential rain was blasting the side of the house, and the old structure groaned against the wind. Even brick wasn't proof against some storms. I checked the weather on my official cell and found that the storm off the coast had moved closer to shore and a second storm that was sliding south along the Mississippi River Valley hadn't slowed its descent. If one of the weather fronts didn't change course, we'd have a big one, a storm of the century according to some reports, though no one in New Orleans was panicking yet and no evacuations had been ordered. Since Katrina and Rita, the back-to-back hurricanes that had devastated the state, most Louisianans took evac orders to heart.

I patrolled the house, checking the windows and doors, putting sponges where rainwater was blowing through, and watching for dark rings on the upstairs ceiling that might mean water damage. I pressed my hand to the shelving unit that hid the weapons room and Ed's bed beneath the stairs and thought about checking on him. But he had made no demands to be let into the house, and if he wanted outside, he had access on his own through the trapdoor. Vamps were unpredictable at the best of times, and silver-wounded vamps were the worst. Most didn't live, and the ones who did were pretty nutso for a long time afterward. I worried that waking him might send him rogue and force me to have to kill him. Killing a friend wasn't something I wanted to do. Ever. Especially a vamp bound to me.

He needed time asleep to heal. *Chicken*, a small, mean part of me whispered.

The wind outside howled. The bushes against the house smacked like finger bones tearing at the walls to be let in. Lightning slammed into the earth nearby, so close I could feel the blast through the floor and a tingle of electricity ripped across my skin. For an instant the Gray Between of my magic stuttered around me, a silver mist shot through with darker motes of power. Deep inside me, Beast padded close, her golden-amber eyes watching. Then the Gray Between closed. Fear pebbled my skin. That had never happened before. I swallowed, fighting to keep my breathing steady, to control my desire to grab a blankie and hide in my closet.

This was the first major storm since I was stuck by lightning—an attack that turned out to be deliberate and not an accident of nature. I forced myself to walk to the kitchen, get a bottle of water, and drink it while standing at the kitchen window looking out at the street and the rain. Dawn and night battled each other in the clouds overhead. Rain fell so hard there wasn't time for it to run off, and water began to rise in the streets. Lightning struck again. The Gray Between danced through me and vanished.

"I don't like this," I muttered to the storm. Then added, "Ducky," and laughed, the sound strained. "Water off a duck's back. Betcha that ducks never get hit by lightning."

A transformer blew, an explosion that would have, should have woken Eli. I heard nothing from upstairs. The power along the street went off, leaving the house and the nearby parts of the French Quarter dark. A car pulled slowly down the street, water cresting before it like a bow wave. The wind was cold outside, and the gusts were strong enough to shove through the cracks and crevices of the house, bringing the wetness of mist and rain that collected into the sponges I had placed at doors and windows. I'd learned the sponge trick from Eli. As long as I cleaned up the sponges before the water penetrated the paint and wood, I could avoid water damage. We usually took care of storm prep together.

Lightning *struck, struck, struck*, three times close by. I fell to my knees as I entered the Gray Between and my time-altering magic leaped and stretched. Outside, the sound of the rain deepened, its descent slowed to nothing. I didn't know what was happening to me, but it couldn't be good. I looked down at myself to see that my skin was shining in a pale, weird pattern, like heat lightning flashing across my skin. Then the place where my magic originated snapped back and time returned to normal. I fell flat, my skin tingling and burning. I felt sick to my stomach and figured I was already bleeding internally from bubbling time. Using that part of my gift was life-threatening and not something I wanted to happen all by itself.

Brute padded down the stairs and moved close to me, snuffing. Then he shifted his body at an angle, blocking my way or . . . making himself a support. That. I put my hands on his back and pushed partway to my feet. His fur was warm and dry and—

Lightning struck again, a flashing, booming explosion of light and sound. Close. The Gray Between skittered through me, lightning fast. Brute leaped away, yelping. I fell again, landing on my backside. "Sorry," I whispered. "Something's wrong." He dipped his big head once and chuffed in agreement, his body a massive brightness in the dark. My own skin was glowing through my clothing in lightning patterns up and down my legs and arms. I lifted my shirt to see them on my belly too, though less bright there. I blinked against the light, and the glow faded to normal skin.

Though there was a pause in the lightning, Brute stayed far back as I made it to my feet, staggered to my room, and opened the closet. Because I don't believe in coincidence. The Mercy Blade, once a storm god, in my closet in the middle of a late season tropical storm still gathering strength outside. Shaking, I gripped the jamb on both sides and rose to my toes. On the top shelf was the witchy item that every-one wanted, a wreath made of metal, neither silver nor gold, but something in between that looked like a peculiar mixture of hues, maybe white and yellow gold mixed together. The upper part of the circlet was carved or shaped in ascending points in what Alex thought might be laurel leaves, with the base carved or incised with markings that could either be decorative or some unknown early language, triangles and circles and squares and lines in no particular order. There were no stones or other ornamentation.

Le breloque in French, *la corona* in Latin, the crown was plain by comparison to crowns I'd seen in movies and on the Internet. The wreath was similar to ones the ancient Romans and Greeks used to indicate royalty. But this one was magic. A pale haze of power was glowing in my skinwalker sight. I could smell the energies wafting from it like ozone from a power plant.

The wreath, like the other magical trinkets in the closet, was under a *hedge of thorns* ward created by Molly. She was part of the Everhart witch bloodline and was married to Evan Trueblood, one of the strongest male witches alive today. Before Molly and her hubs had left NOLA after the witch conclave, she had recharged all my little-to-never-used toys and the ward that protected them from anyone but me. They had once been in a safe-deposit box, but I had a feeling that Leo had access to them there, and I had brought them all home, securing them under magic.

Including the thing I called the Glob. It was a weapon. Or I was pretty sure it was. It had started out as a black-magic, blood-magic artifact called the blood diamond, a spelled gem empowered by the sacrifice of hundreds of witch children over hundreds of years. It had once been evil, but things had changed. The diamond had changed. Now it was a brilliant white diamond, the stone itself transformed through magical means, when it was placed in close contact with a sliver of the Blood Cross, with iron discs from the spikes that had pierced the feet of the three men killed on Golgotha, and with my blood. I had been struck by lightning while holding it. An angel and a demon had fought over it. They had maybe fought over me too. Not sure who was winning that one. Now it was the Glob, a diamond/silver/iron thingamajig doohickey. And I had no idea what it could do.

Lightning cracked nearby again, the light blinding, reflecting bright off the pale painted walls. My skin glowed in
the new odd patterns as the Gray Between opened. Outside
of time, the wreath sparked. A bright white flash, brighter
than the lightning, with the incised symbols darker, a purple
color, like amethyst. In the silver energies of the Gray Between, with time stopped and bubbled, the wreath writhed
like a brilliant snake, or like a vine caught in a thrashing
wind, pulling in power from the air as if eating it.

It was absorbing power from the lightning.

An internal shudder raced along my spine at the sight of
le breloque kindled by lightning. Sparking with power,
power that was unclaimed. *Unclaimed*. It was in my pos-
session, but its magic was still unclaimed. I knew, without
knowing how, that the unclaimed part was important. In
the moment outside of time, the lightning began to dim.
Time resumed with a crash of the downpour, leaving the
world storm-dark and the scent of ozone in the air.

Eli, Ed, and Gee had been with me when I acquired the
wreath, and I was pretty sure that Edmund knew what *le
breloque* was, but he had never admitted to it. We had first
seen it in the dark of night in a rainstorm. Like this one,
though not so electric. And now the wreath was acting up.
And so was my own magic. "Crap," I whispered to Brute,
who was standing beside my leg. "There're connected somehow." He didn't respond except to flop to the floor with a
thud.

I closed the closet door and settled to my bed, pulling
the covers over me, and Bruiser's boxing gloves close for
the comfort. I breathed in his scent, the scent he'd worn
before he was Onorio.

Lightning hit close by and the wreath sparked again, a
light in the night, growing brighter with each strike, easy
to see now, outlining the cracks around the closet door, far
brighter than the silvers of my own power. But at least this
time my own magic didn't alter time. I was sick to my stomach, nausea churning.

Lightning flickered again and boomed as it hit, closer
now, and all the magic sparked, but the closet didn't catch
fire and neither did the sheets, so I pulled them around me

in a cocoon, staying put and warm. And worried. I had been right about one of my postulations for the purpose of the crown-amulet. It sucked in power from storms.

Eventually the storm settled, quieted, as if it lost power with the dull gray skies. The wreath calmed too. It was too large to put in a bank vault. But I had a feeling that if the storm didn't abate for good, *le breloque* would continue to absorb power until it did . . . something. Exploded, maybe. I couldn't keep it here; I couldn't store it elsewhere. I wondered if Gee would kill me to get *le breloque* back, which would suck, as I would then die for possessing something I didn't want.

The world was dark and wet and dripping, a soppy, foggy morning, after a night that lasted far, far too long. The air was blustery and chill, the rainwater running in the streets incongruously colder, like the chill of melted sleet. Sabina hadn't called. Eli hadn't woken. Brute snored at the front door. And still I sat.

In front of the house, a car pulled up and stopped, engine running, lights brightening the windows. I heard a car door open and slam, the splash of running feet, followed by Alex coming in the door, moving fast, tripping over Brute, who didn't move. Alex reeked of garlic, pizza, and energy drinks, his eyes manic, his curly hair standing out in moisture-tight ringlets. His dark skin glistened with rain. He could be a heartbreaker if he ever decided to.

"How's my bro?" he asked, putting down his electronic gobag on the foyer floor and picking up the sponges there, squeezing them out in the ornamental bucket in the corner.

I thought, *So that's what the bucket's for.* It had appeared there a month ago and I hadn't known why. Hadn't asked. Hadn't cared. I wasn't much for decorating. But placing the bucket near the doorway to wring out the sponges that absorbed rainwater that seeped or blew in was perfect and made sense, in a totally nondecorating, totally practical way. "Still sleeping."

There must have been something in my tone because the usually oblivious teenager tried the lights, which were still off, before coming into the room. "You look like shiii—crap."

"I feel like crap."

Alex made a quick circuit of the kitchen and living area, wringing out sponges, redepositing them to catch the next band of sideways rain. When he was back in the foyer he asked, "Why's the wolf in the hallway?"

"I think he's worried about me." I managed a partial smile. "Or your sheets were too wet to be comfy."

"Holy crap!" Alex said, using my swear words and dropping the bucket with a clatter. "You let him on my bed?"

"You try stopping a three-hundred-plus-pound werewolf."

Alex stomped up the stairs and yelled, "You damn wolf. I hate you!" A moment later he shouted, "My sheets smell like dog. Arrrrr. There's brown stuff on it. Holy crap, it's shit. He scuffed his butt on my sheets. I'm gonna kill you, Brute!"

I snickered softly. Brute snorted. Alex thundered down the stairs, pale sheets flapping in the almost-morning light, to the laundry on the back of the house. The storage room/gear-cleaning room/laundry room/mudroom had once been a canning room for fruit and veggies. I didn't know what Alex was going to do back there without power. And when he cursed again, most imaginatively, I figured he had forgotten that small fact. I didn't say anything about the cussing or the smell that emanated from his clothing and pores. He had a teenager's temper and lack of control. I'd wait until he wasn't so riled.

Brute and I were still sharing a laugh when Alex rounded into the foyer again. "Why doesn't he ever get in your bed? Or Eli's? Why always mine?"

"Maybe he's our Goldilocks, and it has to be just right. Which makes you the baby bear."

"Not funny." He stood in the doorway and glowered down at the snorting wolf. "Not funny! And why's Eli still asleep? And why are you still sitting in bed?" he shouted.

I let the last of my amusement flow away and said, "I'm getting Brute a very expensive bed. I think he'll stay out of your bed now. Yes, Brute?"

The werewolf breathed out what might have been a promise. Or not.

"And Eli's still asleep because he's blood-drunk on vamp blood and because Gee DiMercy put a sleepy-time spell on the house. And I'm still sitting here because I hurt too bad to get up."

In an eye blink, the Kid morphed into Alex, or the Alex he had the potential of being when he finished growing up. He made another fast tour of the house, checking the windows and doors and tapping on walls, which was strange. When he came back, he was wearing Eli's shoulder harness and two of Eli's guns. For the last few weeks Alex had been to the gun range almost every single day. We had discovered that he had a gift for shooting. Scary good. With a lot of practice, he might be better than Eli, who was an expert military marksman with a variety of weapons.

"House is secure," he said. "I tapped on the shelf to Edmund's room and he cursed me, I think, in some foreign language. Sorry I lost my temper, sorry I cussed, sorry I went out last night, and I'll get a shower as soon as we're secure."

Tears burned my eyelids and my shoulders slumped. "If you had been here you would be asleep like your brother. Thank you. I think my magic needs Aggie. Will you call her and make sure we can come to water today? Sabina sent a message via Gee, telling us to purify ourselves. I have a feeling that we shouldn't wait."

Alex picked up my cell and punched in my code. Which I didn't know he knew. He pulled up Aggie's number and I heard it ring. "Who's us?" Alex asked oh-so-cautiously as it rang.

"Eli. Me. And you. That is, if you haven't eaten anything this morning. You have to be fasting."

He turned away slightly so I couldn't see his face. "Good morning, Aggie One Feather," Alex said, speaking like an adult. Totally adulting. More tears gathered in my eyes and a single one slid down my face. "*Egini Agayvlge i*," he added, using her Cherokee name. "This is Alex Younger calling on Jane Yellowrock's cell. The outclan priestess of the suck—vampires said we all needed to come to water. Something big's about to happen." He listened a while and then said, "Yes, ma'am. Yes, ma'am. Yes, ma'am." He put a hand over my phone and said, "She said we have to come before the storm gets worse again. She said she won't take men, but she knows an old Choctaw man who will take Eli and me. That the ceremony isn't as good as the Cherokee one, but that it will do."

Which was essentially what she had told me. "We'll have to wake up your brother," I warned. Eli had done serious active duty. When woken unexpectedly, he came up fighting.

"I can handle it. And I'll drive." Into the cell, Alex said, "Clan Yellowrock will be there in an hour." He listened and then said, "Yes, ma'am. I understand, ma'am. That's just what we call ourselves." He disconnected.

"Problems?" I asked.

"She says there are only a few Cherokee Clans, and Yellowrock Clan isn't one."

I knew what he was saying and it was something that I had figured out in the last months, since we missed the big October tribal meeting. But I wanted to see how Alex would handle it, so I let him talk.

"We can't call ourselves Yellowrock Clan when we go through the adoption process into the Cherokee tribe. We'll be adopted by Blue Holly Clan or Panther sub-Clan, and by the clan elders, not you, specifically. Nothing we can't handle later," he assured me. "Aggie said she would sponsor us, or whatever they call it, and not to worry. But before the official adoption process, we'll need to talk to the elders and ask how it'll be handled." He changed the subject. "I'll get my bro. Can you get dressed by yourself?"

"I'll figure out something."

Well. That was interesting. The Kid was growing up fast.

I watched as Eli and Alex were loaded into the rattletrap pickup. Aggie's "old Choctaw man" looked about seventy, wore his black and silver-streaked hair in a short, deer-hide-wrapped tail down his back, and was dressed in loose work jeans, work boots, a short-sleeved T-shirt, and a sweat-stained cowboy hat that a fifties Western TV star might have worn. There was a hole in the crown that could have been a bullet hole, and a feather that looked like a turkey-buzzard flight feather in the band. He looked old, but he moved like a well-oiled machine, easy and smooth. Once he got my family loaded into his truck, he turned and studied me. Staring, reading, not speaking. His face was grooved and lined and his eyes were a black so deep they made Leo's look pale. He touched one finger to the hat brim, got in his truck, and drove away.

I wasn't happy about the Youngers heading off with a stranger into a ceremony that had been known to expose all sorts of things about one's inner self. And Eli was on the edge of aggression after the night he'd been through. He needed calories, but he wasn't getting them until we had done what Sabina wanted. Get pure.

Feeling like I had baked in the sun for hours, I eased out of the car. I hadn't paid attention to myself since my flesh had glowed so brightly from the lightning, but my skin had remained red and burned looking. I was wearing clean sweats and a pullover hoodie and soft shoes. I wasn't wearing armor or carrying arms, not to the house of an Elder of The People.

My hair was again tied back in a knot and thumped silently against my back as I walked toward Aggie's house. The door opened before I got there and a brown nose appeared at knee height. The nose was attached to a brown-and-white face and long floppy black-and-brown ears. Aggie had a beagle puppy. She better not try to make me take it. Last time I was here, she had given me a cat. Fortunately I was able to foist it off on Molly. Aggie was standing behind the dog. She asked, "Are you here to go to water?"

That was pretty much the same question she had asked the last time I came for the purification ceremony.

"Yes." With Aggie, it was always safest to agree.

"Are you fasting?" Aggie asked, again repeating the same sequence of words, like a formula she had memorized.

"Yes. I'm starving."

"Go get in the car. Our things are already in there. I will get *Elisi*." She meant her mother, the one I called *Uni lisi*, which was a term of respect rather than one of endearment. *Grandmother of many children*, a title used for a tribal or clan elder, one who knew the old stories and had old magic and even older secrets of healing.

I climbed into the Toyota's backseat, knowing better than to call shotgun. I settled in, buckled in, laid my head back, closed my eyes, and was instantly in that strange almost-sleep where my body felt paralyzed but I was aware of everything: my own breathing, my own heartbeat, the sounds of water pattering onto the car, the permeated smells of the old women, the puppy, the mean old cat they had adopted, and a strong scent of coffee.

Aggie and her mother got into the car. I heard it turn over and felt the motion as it eased down the road. The wipers squeaked back and forth; rain tapped down softly. That precise sound of tires on wet roads filled the car, soothing, and then we traveled down a series of shell roads, which would be shining bright even in the gray light and rain. The sound of the tires changed as the shells on the roadway became sparser and the roads became progressively less maintained. I knew the moment we veered onto the two-track trail, the car bouncing into and out of potholes and over washboard ruts. I'd been here before.

As the four-by-four Toyota crawled down the ruts, Aggie again explained the ritual of going to water, unconcerned if I was listening or asleep.

In my near dream state, I heard every word, and as she spoke I drifted back into myself, feeling oddly and unexpectedly rested and free of pain. I sat up when she finished, and I stretched and decided that since she had used the same formula this time as last, I should too. "So, we go in the woods, throw up, talk to God, and go for a swim in the bayou that's full of snakes, nutrias, and alligators."

Aggie and her mother laughed, the sounds like water rippling over stones. "Thought you was asleep," *Uni lisi* said. "We walk you through the ritual prayers."

I hadn't done much praying lately, in or out of church, so maybe this would help me in more ways than I had thought. When I stopped, which wasn't often, and considered my own soul, which was never unless I had to, it was dusty and dry and scoured by winds. It was also dark as a cavern, and I suddenly worried that no soul should ever be so dark.

"Your vampire priestess, she call us today, before dawn." *Uni lisi* watched me absorb this in the little mirror in the sun visor. I nodded. "She old and powerful. She know you a war woman, so we take you to water as a man, like last time," *Uni lisi* said, returning to the general outlines of the last time we went to water. "After, you will be cleansed inside and out; your spirit will be open and restored. You will be ready for battle or pain or difficulty, and you will be without the shadows of the past that darken your soul."

"We know you worship the Christian god," Aggie said, again following the same ritual steps as before. "The old beliefs say the Great Creator made us. Some say the Creator still listens to us and some say he is gone, but all say he left three guardians to watch over us."

I nodded, my hair rubbing loud on the seat back. Cloud-to-cloud lightning brightened the sky, lambent and gentle-looking. Around us fog closed in. Rain splattered the old car.

"In Cherokee ritual, the numbers four and seven are important," *Uni lisi* said. "Four guardians of the four directions, seven when you add in the three guardians left by *Unelenehi*. *Unelenehi*, is the Great One. You call on this name when facing east. *Selu* was first woman, the corn mother. Her husband, first man, was *Kenati*. There is also the great female spirit which we call *Agisseequa*. But going to water is no hard and firm ritual calling on a specific god or a specific spirit. You call on who you want, who you want to lead you, who you want to clean you soul."

The small Toyota turned into the same pine trees I remembered from before. Aggie braked and turned off the car. *Uni lisi* continued the narration. "This not like baptism. This a way to recognize our *Tsalagiyi* roots and heritage, to call on the past to lead and direct us into the future. It your ritual, the way you pray, the god or spirits you believe in. We done said what we needed to say. Come on. Sun done rose. We late."

I bowed my head to them and murmured, "*Lisi*, elder of the People, and *Uni lisi*, grandmother of many children, thank you for taking me to water." They each nodded regally and left the car for the rain. I peeled myself out of the car and followed them into the woods, flip-flops squelching on the rain-soaked ground.

Aggie's hair had grown out and both women wore their hair braided, Uni lisi's down to her hips, the thin white tresses laced with the black of the midnight sky. Their bodies moved with grace and elegance and I felt awkward and noisy in my flops.

I had worn flip-flops last time too, though for different

reasons, and now the flops splattered rainwater up over me even as more rain fell through the pine needles. The trail snaked through the trees to the edge of the muddy bayou, though the water was much higher now, drowning the roots of the trees, and it moved faster than I remembered. I finally took off my flops and carried them.

We stopped and my stomach cramped with the memory of what was to come.

Aggie hung her black cloth bag from a branch above a stump and peeled off the lid from a coffeehouse travel mug. Steam curled out into the cold, winterlike air as she set it on the stump beside a small freezer bag containing a bit of native tobacco, harder and harder to find these days. She gave neither to me.

The smell in the cup was different from what I remembered. It still smelled like boiled tree limbs and lichen and pinesap, but now it also contained something more bitter. I remembered the odor and the effects of it from my last time in the sweathouse. Peyote.

Aggie opened a small thermos and poured some of the contents into the plastic thermos cup, giving it to her mother, who guzzled it down and moved into the trees. Aggie drank her own dose in a single gulp and made a horrible face. She poured a third cup and handed it to me. "Drink. Purge. Then come back and drink that one, the whole thing." She pointed at the second mug. "And follow the ritual."

"Why is this time different?" I asked as her face continued to twist in distaste.

"You take strong medicine now. Drink." Aggie closed her thermos, put everything back into the black bag, and turned quickly into the trees. Dual sounds of retching moved through the pines. The breeze sprang up, a whipping wind, and I clenched my teeth against their clatter. Big bad vampire hunter not able to take a little chill, when the older women seemed fine? No way.

She hadn't explained the next part of the ritual, and that was surprising, as carefully as she had kept to the original format. But she had left the travel cups and the small freezer bag on the stump below the branch where her carry bag had hung. I tossed back the first drink, this one exactly like the first time, and ran deeper into the woods, gorge rising with each step. I gagged. Gagged again. I stumbled and fell to my hands and knees as the emetic hit and my previously empty stomach cramped. Everything inside me came up, from my toes to the top of my head. I vomited until I tasted bile, remembering the bitter taste only then. It felt like I was turning inside out, retching hard. All the energy left my body, and I was limp and shaking. I had no idea how I was going to get to my feet again. And I had most of the ritual still to go.

Beast rolled beneath my skin, sick and angry. *Jane is stupid kit. Let human shaman give bad things to Jane again. Foolish stupid! Like bad meat. Kit mistake. Foolish. Sick!*

I agree, I thought as the herbal drink flushed through me with a roil of vicious cramps. I got to my feet and yanked off my clothing just as the last of the stuff hit bottom and my body rejected the potion, this time from the other end of my digestive tract. Just like last time, it took forever and I was even more sick and weak when it was over. I looked at my legs, arms, and belly and the moonlight-pale scars there. The scars that hadn't yet healed from the lightning strike. The scars that the lightning had illuminated like some kind of claiming. And there was that word again. *Claiming.*

In a pouring, drenching rain, I stumbled back to the stump and cleaned myself with the baby wipes in the bag, then put the waste in the garbage bag Aggie had left for me. Quivering with reaction and fatigue, I sat on my folded clothes, the smell of pine sharp and sneezy. I was hollow, tingling, drained. But like last time, the cramps subsided; any hunger I had misted away. The rain eased. Energy flooded back into me. But the cold air struck against my sweat-streaked body and I shivered even as heat flushed through me.

I lifted the second travel mug and drank down its contents. The taste was so bad that I nearly lost it and held the foul stuff down by an effort of will.

Stupid foolish stupid kit! Beast raged inside, her golden eyes glaring at me, her claws digging deep into my brain. Then suddenly she was gone. My mind was clear and lucid and empty of Beast.

CHAPTER 6

Peyote Made Everything Weird

I picked up the smaller plastic bag, opened it, and sniffed the dark brown tobacco, perhaps two teaspoons of curled leaves with a raw, rich scent. Less than last time. I stood and faced east, the sky a deep gray, clouds building. Thunder rumbled, a temblor beneath my feet. The world went brighter, lighter. Thunder grumbled again and this time it didn't stop, a long, drawn-out sound that lasted a minute or more. When it finally faded, I could see curls of magic around every tree and blade of grass, and purling across the water in the fog that was still rolling in. The magic of the land danced and sparked, amazing iridescent hues of blue and brown and green and yellow, like Mother Nature on drugs, except that I was the one on drugs. The peyote was working. And maybe something stronger.

Taking a pinch of the tobacco in the fingers of my right hand, I thought about what Sabina had said. *"Purify yourselves."* Purification was an ancient thing, spiritual and holy and dangerous, but necessary to face hard times, battle, or great danger. War.

I faced east, lifting my fingers through the blue twinkling mist. I didn't remember what I'd said last time, but it seemed important to keep the ritual similar, as if treading the same sacred ground. "I call on the Almighty, the eternal, the Elohim, the god in three." I dropped the bit of tobacco and it fell across me, bright red motes on my skin, and an echoing red from inside me.

The motes. The motes the Damours released when I killed them. My goddaughter told me the motes of magic were still inside. As was a dark shadow, poised next to my heart. This was what I needed to purify. This darkness, this remnant of blood magic, this shadow that lived inside me and beat with my own heart. It kept the Damours' magic alive even when I tried to kill it. I needed to be free of it.

Raindrops splatted onto my skin, hard and punishing for a few moments as I curled around the tobacco, keeping it dry. The raindrops left little droplet-shaped white spots before they trailed down me to the ground, and the spots on my flesh turned red. My breath was heated on the cold air, puffing bright, a sign of life, pink as a baby's toes.

I turned to my right, facing south. "I call upon my skin-walker father. I call on the skinwalkers who have gone before me, but without the taint and dishonor of *u'tlun'ta*. Those valiant ones who died in war, with the blood of their enemies in their fangs. Hear me."

I dropped a bit of the tobacco. It too fell against me, and this time it burned, hot as sparks from an ill-built fire, catching the wind, skirling in the magic of the mist. Rain thundered down, putting out the sparks where they burned, the rain purple and glorious. I laughed and my laughter joined with the rain and fell to dapple the ground. But my breath was brighter, a richer shade, like blood mixed with water.

A stick cracked behind me. My flesh tightened. Shoulders hunched. I was not alone. If I had ever actually been alone before. I didn't look. I didn't want to see.

I turned west, holding up a pinch of tobacco, wet in the rain. The drops pelted down, icy as sleet on my bare skin. My feet were black from the mud I stood in, and black mud splattered up my legs like dark tears. I remembered the term *Unelenehi*, who was the Great One. "I call upon the self-existent, eternal god Yehovah, who is the god who creates." When I spoke these words, my breath was red, scarlet as the Damours' magic, and shadowed black with their evil. Evil they had placed inside me and no matter how hard I tried, I couldn't get rid of it . . . or at least not alone.

I had been five at my first kill. I could still see the hilt of the knife in my small hand as the blade pierced the white man's flesh. I could hear his screams, though his mouth was bound. All this was stored deep in my soul. The dark spot grew, expanded. It beat like my own heart.

I realized that the Damours' dark magic had combined with the evil done to me by my grandmother when she taught me to kill. Together, they had become something else. Something much more powerful than I had understood. Something that conflicted with the sacred name of the Almighty.

The wind swirled around me and the tobacco was drenched from my fingers to wash down me, across my body. Where it touched, it trailed hot and scalding. Some small part of me knew that the ceremony shouldn't go like this. Something was wounded and broken in the ritual. Or in me. I had gotten off course. But if I stopped, the black mote of shadow would be forever with me. Endlessly a part of me. And the scarlet motes would eventually destroy me, eating me from the inside out. Like what they were doing inside me each time I bubbled time. They cut me. And I bled.

Ahhhh . . . I thought. The foreign magics cut me. My body then tried to vomit them out of me, tried to free me of the evil motes and the shadows.

My breath went hot and noisy in my lungs, like a roaring sea in a blizzard, a whiteout of clarity and understanding.

I turned right again, now facing north, shuddering so hard I thought I might drop the tobacco pinched in numb fingers. My heart beat erratically, shaking my chest. "I call upon El Shaddai, the all-sufficient one, the feminine of the godhead. El Shaddai, that aspect most often associated with the Holy Spirit, hear my call." I felt the presence behind me move closer. Colder than a glacier on the flesh of my spine. I hunched my shoulders against the pounding rain.

Beast growled low in my mind, the sound far away; the place where she usually hunched was vacant.

I slid my feet through the mud, rotating back to the east, and scraped the last bit of wet tobacco to the tips of my fingers. I closed my eyes, my body grayish with the cold. I let the pinch of tobacco fall into the rain. "I seek healing of and freedom from the dark shadow that grows within me. I seek the destruction of the purpose of another's power, that power manifested in scarlet motes that infest me. I seek wisdom to cure my weakness. Strength in battle. Purity of heart and mind and soul."

The air sizzled. The wet ends of my hair lifted. Terror zapped across me like electric sparks. Rain shattered down. Wind slammed into me like a fist. I nearly fell. Lightning struck. It ignored the trees and hit the center of the bayou only twenty feet away. The brilliance stole all vision from me. All but the vision of magic.

The darkness that lived inside me was close to the surface, the shadow beating with the rhythm of my heart, the scarlet motes zipping through me, painful as barbed wire. But as I watched, the Gray Between opened around me and silver motes of my own magic reached inside me and began . . . herding the scarlet motes. Like prey.

I dropped my arms and slumped forward, following the bright and silver colors of all the motes as they raced through me. My dark silver power moved the scarlet motes into some kind of weird geometric design. They moved from my left fingertips to my right toes, to my head, to my left toes, to my right fingertips, and back to my left fingertips. I held my arms out to the side like Vitruvian Man and . . . the motes formed a pentagram. *Holy crap.*

Before, they had been unfocused, unstructured power within me, the magic random. Until now. There now was a working, one organized like a witch working—geometric and steady. This ceremony and my skinwalker magics had stirred it all into some different path, some new purpose. I knew that it was possible for a working to take black magic, overcome it in some kind of great battle, and then use it. But it took testing and fire and suffering, and I had endured none of that. Yet the darkness within me was changed.

Memory surfaced, full of blood and terror, my fangs tearing the head off a blood-servant sent to kill me. Memory of being shot by El Diablo, one of Derek's men, in a bayou. Of shifting into Beast in the back of Leo's limo. Of nearly dying on the floor of sub-five basement in HQ, after fighting and defeating the Naturaleza vamp De Allyon. Of the first instant I bubbled time. Of achieving the half form of the fighting skinwalker. Maybe . . . Maybe I had been tested all along? Maybe my magic had been waiting until I was whatever I was now to fix me. To fix itself.

Rain again drenched me, black bayou mud splattering up to my knees with the force of the drops landing. My breath came fast. The mist rose around my feet and ankles, up my calves, a pearled shimmer of moisture and magic and peyote dreams, leaving me breathless but exhilarated. I traced the pentagram within me and discovered that my stomach was no longer hurting. My heart felt lighter. Cleaner. My breath blew shades of red, dispersing light from scarlet to fuchsia to palest pink. To crystal clear.

Around me, the world was bright, sharp, each raindrop distinct and glistening and full of magic light.

I gathered all the things we had brought and wove through the trees upstream in the general direction I had taken last time, the earth sucking at my bare feet, water swirling around my ankles, muddy and thick.

The trees opened out at a slow, easy curve of the bayou, a place that had once been a tight twist of water. Smoke blew across me, black and choking, kerosene to start a fire of wet wood. In the center of the tiny clearing, Aggie and her mother were sitting beneath a canvas tent top, one coated with polyvinyl chloride so that the water ran off. The tent was just a covering with no sides, held up by a metal framework. The wind caught the top and billowed it with a hollow, flapping sound.

Aggie and Uni lisi were sitting on flat stones, situated on top of what looked like garden cloth, the kind that let water through but not plants. Like me they were naked, except for small beaded bags hanging on thongs around each neck. Their clothes must have been in the bags beside them. I could see their magic, Aggie One Feather's a deep, dark lavender, near purple. It should have appeared soft, like a flower, but it was hard and stony, like amethyst. Uni lisi's was much darker, a purple so deep it looked nearly black, shot through with white light, and the white was crystalline and pointed, sharp, like clear quartz arrowheads. Dangerous. Deadly.

Peyote made everything weird.

The fire smoked and stank and Uni lisi called to me. "Sabina call us and so we got one them young men to set up tent and bring us kerosene and dry wood. Not too dry now but it be okay."

I realized that I had stopped. I pushed against the earth with the soles of my feet and floated over to them. My own magics floated behind me, silver and red and black and gray in a swirling pointed star. Violent shades of stone and blood. But my breath was clear as purest water in the midday sun.

I took the third sitting stone and settled to its flat surface. Aggie jutted her chin to the green pine boughs and I scattered them in a circle around us. Aggie had called it a protective circle. Witches called it a witch circle. No matter what it was called, circles have power and the pine boughs began to glow a pliable, deep green, the color of emeralds. Aggie put several of the green branches on the fire and wet pine smoke billowed up, black and green and choking, glowing with power. Smoke gathered in the low canopy above and writhed there. Small fingers of smoke and blackness trailed from the tent covering and out into the clearing.

Aggie said, "No evil can cross the circle or enter beneath the scented shelter of smoke. We are warded here, the three of us, against malevolent spirits."

Uni lisi stood and faced east. The last time I had seen her naked, her skin hung in folds from her arms and thighs, and her rounded belly looked like a deflated balloon. Now she looked decades younger, her power enfolding her, magic meant for battle, for the might of war. She raised her hands to the place on the horizon where the sun would have been had the clouds not eaten it. She pushed apart the clouds and a speck of blue showed through, blue sky and a lance of sunlight on the horizon. She said something in Cherokee, words I should have understood but no longer did.

I decided in that moment that when my job here was done, I would go to North Carolina and the college or university that taught Cherokee. I would learn, and perhaps I would remember.

"This is a good thing," Uni lisi said. I realized I had spoken aloud and clamped my mouth shut.

Aggie began to speak, a chantlike pulse to her words, the cadence formal, whispered into the mist that grew up around us. The world ducked and rolled with the smoke. Last time, I had placed my palms flat on the ground for balance. This time, I began to rock slightly with the words, back and forth, as her chant rose and fell. Rose and fell like a boat rocking on slow swells of the sea. Through my body the motes coursed, the star-working inside me doing whatever it wanted to, or whatever the Almighty had told it to. If I hadn't been drugged out of my mind, I'd have been afraid.

Sleet began to fall, beating sporadically on the canvas tent, bouncing on the wet ground, melting in seconds. I had chill bumps all over me, and yet I felt hot, feverish. The fire before me flamed and smoked and my eyes watered as magic stung them. Tears coursed down my cheeks, hot and burning, just like the last time I was here. Everything was the same this time. Except the storm, the cold, the vision of magic, and me. I was different. I was very different. My magic was changing, flowing in a pentagram. Salty, hot tears splashed on my chest. Beast, eyes glowing, moved through the darkness that was the I/we of our two souls. She stared at the pentagram of power for many lines of chanting, then padded into the front of my mind. I knew my eyes were glowing gold when Aggie One Feather faltered in the chant.

"Do not fear," Beast said, speaking through my mouth, her voice rough, her tone stilted. "Beast will not eat you."

"Are you a devil? A demon?" Uni lisi asked, shaking her head. "I saw no evil spirit inside of *Dalonige'i Digadoli*."

"*Dalonige'i Digadoli*. Yellow rock, yellow eyes," Beast said. "I am the other inside with her."

"Ahhh . . . Like a spirit animal," Uni lisi said happily. Her magics danced and shimmied around her with delight.

Arms high, Aggie started speaking again and her words now had magic. Green sounds and yellow sounds and the blue of the sky sounds, the peyote showing me the power of the past and the color of power. Her words, still unknown to me, floated around us, through the glowing smoke, and when her chant ended, she dropped her arms.

Rain tore from the skies, melting the fallen sleet, and I understood what the saying meant—the bottom fell out. It was beautiful, the way water cascaded down, greens and blues, a shining miracle of glory. I laughed, and my laughter was golden, dancing among the raindrops.

Lightning flashed.

The Gray Between sputtered and stumbled. The smoke stopped moving. The magic that was Aggie and her mother stopped moving. Everything around me stopped, except for me. Except for Beast, who watched through my eyes. Everything stopped. Except for our magic. The red motes still flashed through me, in the star shape, chased by my own silver motes, the geometries of energy and matter, $E = mc^2$. Altered by time. Einstein would have been awestruck.

Beast said, *Smell deer. Want to hunt. Want to hunt cow.*

"You can't hunt cow if there are only deer," I said, reasonable and calm and wise-sounding. I reached into my chest and took the shadow mote that beat along with my heart. I pulled it out and turned it from side to side. It was still connected to me by a long silver shadow-chain that trailed through my body and into my soul home. I knew this. I knew if I cut it I would die. I also knew it was an evil. My evil. I'd have to deal with it someday. For now, I held it to the east, to the rising sun. "I accept that I wanted to kill the white man who murdered my father. I accept that I felt joy when he screamed as I cut his flesh. I accept the knowledge that I took delight in his pain and experienced ecstasy in his blood. I accept my part and participation in the experience of his death. And I . . ." I stopped, thinking carefully about my words. "I forgive myself for my part in it. I forgive myself for existing always for death, and so seldom for life. I offer this shadow of death to . . . to Adonai. If you want it. I no longer do."

But the mote remained attached to me, to my soul, to my soul home. I pulled on it, feeling a resulting pain in my heart with each tug. I let the shadow go and it snapped back into place, thundering against my heart. It skipped a beat. Time cracked and shattered, like an egg hit by a silver knife. The world moved again.

Aggie opened the beaded bag hanging around her neck. From it, she pulled a tobacco leaf, whole and wrinkled and dark brown; she held it in her left hand, and onto it she sprinkled small fists full of other dried and crushed herbs from her larger bag, calling out their names in English for me. "Sage for cleansing, sweetgrass for life and joy, a single sprig of rosemary for potency." Aggie pulled a yellowed leaf and some roots from her bag. "Mullein, the last of the year's fresh. Yellowdock taproot. Wild ginger."

Uni lisi added a final herb, and just like last time, Aggie didn't speak its name. It was a sacred part of going to water, secret. Aggie rolled the herbs all together into a fat cigarlike cylinder, though it wasn't intended to be smoked. She tied it with hemp, creating a smudge stick. She took a burning twig from the fire and lighted the smudge stick, holding the flame until the herb tube was lit and smoking. Standing, she handed the smudge stick to Aggie, who took it, rolled to her knees, and bowed, facing east. I didn't remember the bow from last time.

In slow, circular motions, she smudged the air around her mother. The woman looked old again, a grandmother rather than a war woman, and she was silent, her magic still, her eyes closed. She was smiling peacefully as she slowly turned, lifting each foot and placing it back down, the dance of being smudged, of allowing sacred smoke to caress and spiral and coil around her legs and back and belly, up over her face, the smoke purifying each part of her. She lifted her braids and the smoke curled around them like the snake that lived in the heart of each being. She breathed the aromatic smoke and was purified within as well. Her magic glowed brighter and brighter, the purples giving way to clear, with a flash of periwinkle blue and the gold of mica.

Aggie held the smudge stick to me and turned her back. I came to my knees and bowed to the east—and the God who didn't want my sin—brushing the smoke up her body like the fingers of angels. She lifted her feet and held out her hands, as if to step upon the smoke or catch it and hold it. She unbraided her hair and I held the stick so the smoke passed through it, lock after lock. She turned, lifting a leg so the smoke could touch the back of her thigh and curl over her buttocks. When every part of her had been blessed, she opened her eyes and sat.

With a slow gesture, Aggie indicated her mother, and I gave the old woman the smudge stick. It was more than half gone and it smelled heavenly. I turned to the side as each of them had and closed my eyes. The smoke was warm, curling up from my ankles, fragrant and rich. I breathed it in and my heart rate sped; my body, which might have been chilled, warmed. I turned a half step, then another, lifting my arms, moving into the smoke. I lifted my hair, which was free of its usual braid and wet from the rain. I fluttered it through the smoke.

Around me the rain slowed, splattered, stopped. The fog had enclosed us, a glistening blanket of white, a magic that met the magic of the fire and the magic of the smudge stick. Together they coiled and twisted. Sleet again shushed down, a slow, irregular patter.

"*Dalonige'i Digadoli*," Aggie said. I quaked with the words, with hearing them spoken properly, in the whispered syllables of the language of The People, the Cherokee. "*Dalonige'i Digadoli*."

I turned and turned as Aggie's mother smudged my body and my soul, the herbal stick rising and falling, the aromatic smoke brushing me inside and out. Even billowing around the shadow in my soul. Ah . . . Cleansing the shadow as it cleansed me. Maybe there was no way for the shadow to be given away, cut away, or taken away. Maybe it was a part of me, for always.

The last time I had gone to water, my father's voice had called me to the ritual. Today there was nothing but the sleet that fell with that erratic shushing sound, and the sight and feel and . . . oh, the taste of magic on the air. Magic had a hint of sweetness and a hint of bitter, like dark chocolate. I liked it. The magic of the smoke wrapped around the shadow within me, as if tying itself in place.

The magic smoke loosened, as if I had been contained in a balloon, its sweet bitterness trapped, and the balloon was unknotted so the taste could escape. Not an image that actually made sense, except to the peyote dreams. But the pressure of it lessened except where it lay tightly wrapped against the shadow on my soul.

I opened my eyes. I was alone beneath the canvas tent, the green pine branches that had formed the protective

circle removed and placed in a pile. Uni lisi was standing
in the sleet, her back to me, her skin hanging and wrinkled,
so very unlike the drugged vision of the old woman and her
magic. She walked past the swirling, muddy bayou, the water so cloudy that a sixteen-foot-long alligator could be
inches below the surface and I'd not have seen it. Aggie
followed behind her and I followed them through the muck
beside the bayou and down into a small pond. It was outside
the current of moving water, and it was clear to the leaf-
coated bottom. It was also free of alligators. I stepped into
the pond after them. The water was warmer than the air,
its bottom thick with the slime of the rotting vegetation.

I could hear the murmurs of the other two as they prayed
and dipped beneath the water. I moved to the side and softly
said words I hadn't planned to say. "Creator God, I seek
clarity of mind, wisdom, strength in battle." I bent my knees
and sank beneath the water. My hair caught in the current
of my own movement and brushed my body. I stood, sleet
peppering my head. "Adonai, I seek understanding of the
scarlet motes that move throughout me, magic not of my
making, but somehow merged with my soul." I sank again
beneath the water. I came back up. "El Shaddai, I seek to
be enough, to do enough, to sacrifice enough, to save my
friends and my family, as you are enough to succor the
world." I dropped beneath the water. Something touched
me as I moved, long and linear and sharp on one end. A
stick, I hoped, not the claw of some creature testing my
flesh. But I didn't look and it floated to the bottom.

"Redeemer, I seek purity of heart, purity of mind, purity
of soul, and, if not freedom from the darkness that is tied to
my soul, then acceptance of it." I dropped again and rose
again. And this time when I opened my mouth, I started to
cry, throat tight, tears streaming down my face, so hot against
the *plink* of sleet. "To the spirit of my own uni lisi. I seek . . ."
My breath juddered in my chest, as new understanding
bloomed open inside me. "To forgive you. To forgive what
you made of me. To forgive that you taught me to kill. That
you pushed me into the storm as *we-sa* and abandoned me.
That at every part of my life, you neglected or abused my
soul, my spirit. My own lack of forgiveness until this time has

allowed the dark shadow to find a home in my heart and to have power over my spirit." I dunked myself. I stayed deep this time, letting the water carry away the pain that I never even knew was there. The pain of betrayal and abandonment. I felt something detach from my chest and slide away. The magic had wrapped the darkness. Waiting for me to understand. Waiting for me to release it.

I hadn't had to cut the darkness away. Or give it away. Or hope that God would wrench it from me. I just had to let it go. There was an empty place there now, a hole in my soul, waiting for me to fill it. I stood. When the black water drained away enough to speak, I said, "To *Elisi*." I sobbed, choking, and had to stop until I could breathe again, this time talking to my mother, so very long ago. "I forgive myself for not being strong enough or old enough or war woman enough to stop the men who hurt you."

I slid under the water and back up. "To the spirit of my father, *Edoda*. I forgive myself for the torture of your killer. For the vow I made in your blood. I was a child. But I knew what I did. I *knew*. And though I am *fiercely*"—I grated out the word—"glad of their deaths, I have carried the pain of the vengeance for all these years. And I am forgiven." I slid beneath the water once more and stood. Opened my eyes.

The magic synesthesia was gone, the fog just fog, the water just water, my breath just breath. I felt clean and free inside as I stood in the small black-water pond. I knew the water was not really as warm as I perceived it. I was hypothermic. But again, I didn't care.

I gripped the hand that appeared before my face and let Aggie One Feather pull me to the bank. She was stronger than she looked. But then her magic had shown me that about both of them, their strengths and their mighty power, and their terrible purpose.

We dressed under the tent, my flesh ashen with cold. The strange burned and scarred places were gone, as if I had never been hit by lightning. Shifting shape hadn't healed me. But facing my own dark demons had.

We dragged the tent down and set it under the trees far above the waterline. The rain put out the fire even as we worked to gather up all our belongings, but I still used the small shovel to toss mud over the smoking coals. Together we walked back to the car and got inside. Aggie turned the heater on high and we drove away.

We were nearly back to the small house that the two women shared when Aggie One Feather said, "You must take your family and make them your own. Claim them, according to your clan, according to the Cherokee Constitution and the old ways. This will give you strength within your own heart and at your own hearth."

I thought about the Youngers and Edmund. Bruiser. The Everhart/Truebloods. Shivers snatched me up and my teeth chattered, but I talked anyway, though the words sounded odd. "We pppplanned to go through the adoption ppppprocess this past October, but we couldn't ggggget to a ppp-powwow. Nnnnnext October for shshshsure."

"Do not delay beyond that," Uni lisi said.

"Yes, mamamama'am."

"One last thing," Aggie One Feather said as we turned down her street through the rain. "From the words you spoke in the water, it is clear that we must speak of your lineage. When we first met, you said that your father was of Panther Clan and your mother was Blue Holly Clan. But Panther Clan is a subdivision of Blue Holly, and the tribal elders would not have allowed them to marry. Your father was Panther Clan only after he married into Blue Holly Clan and, as a skinwalker, the clan grandmothers likely gave him the secondary Panther Clan designation. The old woman you call uni lisi was Panther Clan and she had yellow eyes like you and like him, but she would not have been his mother. The clan relation was too close. Do you understand?"

"My father's birth clan would have been something else," I said, feeling even lighter than after I walked from the bayou. "So that my grandmother with yellow eyes, the old woman that I recall in my few early memories." My throat tightened again. "She was related as a skinwalker, but may not have been my biological grandmother. Or may have been a grandmother from many generations up the line." I felt my mouth pull into a smile, tight and sere. Somewhere deep in my soul, I had hoped this.

Aggie turned off the Toyota and we sat in the driveway,

none of us eager to go back into the cold, not even to get inside to the warmth of the tiny house. I let my mind wander through the revelation. The old woman who made me kill two men as a five-year-old child, the old woman who forced me into my bobcat shape and threw me into the snow on the Trail of Tears, she wasn't my real grandmother.

Softly, Aggie said, "You have many memories, buried, suppressed. Memories of your mother. Of whom you never speak. Memories of your clan and tribe. Of the grandmothers who would have taught you to farm and how to gather foodstuffs, how to live off the land. How to make pottery or weave baskets. Even as a child of five, you would have begun learning such things, and you have no memories of this?"

I shook my head. "Nothing." And maybe that should have frightened me, that I didn't remember, but I had forgotten so much. This was only one more thing. The face of my mother. The vision of her hands working. The sound of her laughter. Was that all still buried inside me, in some place that could be found?

Aggie said, suddenly sounding stern and staring me down in the rearview mirror, "Last thing. We told your brother this. When you take the Youngers into your Cherokee family, they will not be Yellowrock Clan. That would be according to vampire tradition, not Cherokee tradition. So you will have to adopt them twice, once into Panther Clan as your grandmother chose for you, or into Blue Holly Clan. Then once into your own clan as the vampires do. Understood?"

I ducked my head, hiding my reaction from Aggie. "Yes. I understand."

The rattletrap truck bearing the old Choctaw man and the Youngers pulled down the street and idled at the drive. Alex and Eli got out of the truck and shut the doors. Without looking our way, they went through the rain to the porch and waited. They looked different too. Tired. Wan. Worn out. Aggie One Feather and her mother got out of the car and we all trooped inside, silent, frozen.

Inside, the old women once again fed us a king's feast.

CHAPTER 7

The Crown of the Orcs

It was nearly ten a.m. when we drove back into town, Eli at the wheel. He had spent the night feeding a dying vamp and being healed and the morning puking and voiding. He looked exactly like a human in those circumstances should. Wan, pale, slow moving, and weary. Eli never looked tired.

The rainstorm hit again as another band of showers wheeled across us. The air was warmer now, though not by much, and the rain was free of sleet. Lightning blasted again, multiple strikes, and my magic responded with a flicker of the Gray Between, which made me less than happy. I had hoped going to water would free me from that, but at least it wasn't as intense as before.

We were turning into the French Quarter when Alex, sitting in the backseat, said, "Got a problem on Bourbon Street. Mob forming. Cops have been called in. SWAT. The gang task force." He was scanning reports on his tablet and through his earbud. Eli tapped on the radio to a local channel that gave news, weather, and traffic updates every ten minutes.

Alex said, "They called in ambulances but ordered them

to take shelter on the uptown side of Canal Street. Shots fired."

Eli turned right and then left and began the slow process of fighting traffic to bypass the riot. Lightning struck again. And again. Each time, my newly altered magics reacted and fluttered inside me.

Alex said, "Dispatch says lightning hit the pavement at the corner of Bourbon Street and Bienville. Arnaud's is on fire." The Kid's voice sounded funny and I angled the sun visor's mirror so I could see him. He looked intent. Older. As if he had matured in the last twelve hours or so. "Two rioters are receiving medical attention from bystanders and cops until medic gets there," he said, "but the downpour is so bad that traffic came to a standstill and the ambulances aren't moving." He shook his head, tight ringlets bobbing. "The Royal Sonesta Hotel has been invaded by tourists escaping the rain, but the gang followed and brought the fight into the hotel. The lobby and restaurant are being trashed."

Eli took more side streets. The storm worsened, the wipers not much help against the deluge. The SUV created a bow wave, and I remembered the truck from this morning doing the same thing. Lightning hit-hit-hit, blasting the entire world in flashing lights. Making my body spark and the time-bubbling reaction quake on and off. It also sent shocks of something different through me and I thought maybe the lightning might be exciting my new pentagram magic. Things fluttered inside me.

"Annnd the power is out," Alex said.

Eli said nothing, his hands steady on the wheel as he took us far away from our house, trying to stay free of the snarled cars, circling slowly around to come in on the downtown side of our street. A half-hour drive across the French Quarter took over an hour and when we got home, there was no parking. Oddly enough parking on our little one-way street wasn't usually difficult to find but, with the storm, today was different. Cars had pulled off the roadway and taken all the available spaces: people sitting inside, fogging up the windows, checking e-mail and talking on the phone.

Eli found a space one block over, which meant that we

ducked and ran, getting soaked again by the time we got to the porch. We were met on the front stoop by Brute, growling, guarding the entrance, not letting us in.

With the storm getting stronger again, I had a feeling what the problem was. Lightning slammed down two blocks over, and my suspicions were confirmed. My bedroom windows, to the left of the door, flashed. *Le breloque* was still sparking and it was brighter than ever. It was still soaking up power.

Brute stood, blocking the door with his impressive body. "You have to let us in," I said. He snapped at the air inches from my hip, and I belted him right in the nose. Hard. Brute yelped and leaped into the rain. Eli keyed open the door, and we dripped all over the foyer getting gear in. Alex tossed us dry towels and began replacing the sponges. We had power, which was a blessing. Eli trotted up the stairs, cell phone in hand, probably calling Sylvia. Brute walked in, shook his heavy white coat all over the walls, climbed on the sofa, and licked his nose and jowls and other body parts. I headed for my room so I didn't have to watch.

I would never hit a dog, but werewolves were not dogs. They had human thought patterns and they were contagious, hence the blow to his nose and his pride. Werewolves were dangerous, and since Pea—the grindylow who acted as were-creature law enforcement, judge, jury, and executioner in New Orleans—clearly wasn't here at the moment, I had to protect my team.

In the closet, the wreath was no longer sparking. I reached up and deactivated my BFF's *hedge of thorns* witch-working that kept it safe and touched the metal. It was neither hot nor cool and it didn't zap me with some kind of spell, so I lifted it down. It looked the same. It looked fine.

I carried *le breloque* to the small table beside the unused reading chair in my bedroom and shoved the pile of clothing onto the floor. The wreath went on top of the table in what looked like room décor for a nerd or geek. The crown of the orcs or something. In an old gobag I found an even older MP3 player and plugged it in to charge. While it was charging, I set it to play some of Ricky-Bo's music, the anti-moon spells created (by my BFF's husband) to keep him from going insane when the full moon tried to force him into his black wereleopard form. Rick was an old boyfriend. And a werecat stuck in human form. Maybe the same music that kept his were-magics under control might keep the wreath magics from blowing up. Maybe not. Maybe I should have left it under the ward. Magic was dangerous when handled wrong, but until the lightning struck again I wouldn't know if I had been smart or stupid.

I started to turn away when the air sizzled, the lights flickered, and thunder boomed, all in a half second. My body shimmered. *Le breloque* sort of glowed but without the sparking light of before. "Go me," I said. I texted Molly and Evan—the creators of the spells I used—and sent them pics of the wreath and the MP3, with detailed description. They were, by now, on vacation down in a gorge somewhere in the Appalachian Mountains camping, so it would be a long time, maybe days, before they replied, but I had done my best.

I hung up my wet clothes to drip and took the hottest shower I could stand, soaped up, and scrubbed with a sponge that was meant for the kitchen sink but worked well for dermabrasion and restoring circulation. But the moment I was all soaped up, the lightning decided to hit again. *Of freaking course.* The Gray Between opened and time bubbled. My shower water stopped falling. I said a slow string of words I'd have had my mouth washed out for as a child in the Christian children's home.

This had happened before, and when it did, I saw visions of the future and its trail into the past in the drops. I had decided not that long ago that I had no business trying to save the future or fix the past, and I tried not to look at the possibilities that lay within each drop, no matter how tempting. Instead, I danced around in the small space, letting the droplets I touched enter the Gray Between with me, but there wasn't enough to rinse. I needed to keep a gallon bottle of water in here to rinse with. Hindsight and all that. For now, I was covered in drying soap. I opened the stall door, not an easy process, but I made it without breaking the glass, and peeked into the bedroom. *Le breloque* looked fine. Kinda glowy, and with sparks going off above it, but nothing that looked like it might catch fire. I got back in the shower to wait.

Shortly, the Gray Between flickered off and I was able to rinse away the soap that had tried to dry on my skin. If this was going to keep happening, I needed to plan better. I shut off the shower and dried, standing in the steam. Slathered on some scent-free moisturizer and sprayed some cleanser on the tile walls. The house was cleaned once a week by someone from Katie's Ladies, but that wasn't often enough to prevent black mold from growing in damp corners. New Orleans weather meant a whole 'nother way of living compared to living in the Appalachian Mountains.

Within minutes I was dressed in jeans, a T-shirt, and a sweatshirt, warm slippers on my feet. But I made a decision not to go armed. Metal blades and metal firearms seemed like a stupid idea in the middle of a lightning strike, though the weather cell had moved off. Mother Nature probably had a belly laugh at me in the shower, dancing around like a monkey in a barrel. I towel-dried my hair and put it into a tail. The weather was too wet to braid it and I wasn't interested in using the hair dryer in this storm. The house had old electrical wiring and I worried about being electrocuted. I worried about lots of things that had never bothered me before.

Back in the bedroom I pulled the covers over me on the bed, checked e-mail, and watched the wreath for a while. Just in case. It seemed fine now that the lightning was gone. Once I was satisfied about safety, I followed the smells into the kitchen. Bacon. Eggs. Grits with butter. Hot tea and coffee. Eli, who had showered with his usual Speedy Gonzalez efficiency, was busy with the fry pan and the protein, and Alex was making pancakes. That was still a surprise. Alex being a real and contributing part of the household team was stunning. The Kid was growing up.

I took a seat at the table and sipped the chai that was already poured into a huge red soup-sized mug that said No Such Thing As Too Much Tea in a whirly font. Inside, at the bottom of the mug were the words, in a tiny block font, *you've just been poisoned*. We had started buying funny mugs not long ago and now had a nice—or rude, depending on the mug—selection. I had bought this one myself because it was funny. And if Leo ever took tea here, this was *so* going to be his mug.

I contemplated the scene and realized that something felt different. Beyond the stove's exhaust fan and the banging of the occasional pot or pan, it was weirdly silent in the house. No tinny TV in the background, no quiet video game going on the speakers, no music on the Kid's headphones. I hadn't been aware of the low-level noise of two other people living with me, one a teenager who lived twenty-four-seven with earbuds and music playing. The noise level had built up slowly, and now it was gone. Alex had no electronics on. At all. I sat back and sipped and watched them.

They were dipping food onto plates, working together as if they were two sides of one whole, when I said, "You wanna talk about it?"

Eli turned off the fan, which only increased the silence. They loaded up the table with food, sat, and looked at me. Alex said, "I had to puke. And shi—"

I heard a thump under the table, Eli kicking his brother. I stuffed a slice of bacon into my mouth and chewed, lips closed. Trying to hide my laughter.

"And void my bowels. That's how Mr. America here phrased it." He thumbed at Eli. "I had to smoke some tobacco that made me cough my lungs out, drink this gross drink that tasted like pond water, puke, and *void my bowels*, and then sit in the freezing rain, *naked*," Alex's voice rose, "and listen to this saggy old dude—and lemme tell you he was saggy in folds you could hide this in." He held up a serving spoon and I still managed to keep my laughter off my face. "And listen to him sing, which he could not do, at all, in a language I did not understand. And then I had to get into the muddy water and dunk myself. *Seven freaking times*."

"Uh-huh," I said, finishing off the bacon and digging into the eggs, which had been cooked with onion and little bits of pepper and cheese. It was heavenly.

"I swear that I could feel an alligator swimming around my legs."

"He squeaked," Eli said. "Like a four-year-old girl."

"Did not."

"Did."

I lifted my mug and said through a mouthful of food, "So you enjoyed it?"

"Totally," Eli said. "Ready to do it again. Anytime."

"You people are crazy. My family is insane. Bonkers."

"But family," I said. Just to clarify.

"Family," he agreed. "But you all should be chained in an insane asylum. I'm getting pizza for supper tonight. Period. No *if*s, *and*s, or *but*s about it."

"We can do pizza," Eli agreed.

Alex glared at him as if expecting Eli to change his mind or say, "Psych," but he didn't. I got up and poured them more coffee and me more tea. Family breakfast—the way it was supposed to be. If it weren't so cutesy, I'd get matching mugs that said that.

I said, "What do you think about restoring the house?" Eli looked interested. He was handy with hammer and nails and power tools and other home remodeling equipment. He had replaced the windows along the side of the house with extra-tall, narrow French doors and working shutters. I looked out into the living room. "I was thinking you could find and replace the fireplaces with gas ones."

"No. Wood," Alex said. "That way, when the zombie apocalypse comes we can have wood fire for heating and cooking."

"When the apocalypse comes," Eli corrected, "we'll grab gobags and head for the hills. Some little holler Janie tells us about."

"Until then, we need a bigger house," Alex said.

"No," Eli and I said simultaneously. Eli added, "We just need a better use of space. I've ordered a Pendleton King Revolving Gun Safe. That'll give Ed more room in the gun room."

I remembered something I'd seen when Eli and I were sparring not so long ago, and I had ended up, breath knocked out, hurt, on my back, staring up at the ceiling. "There's a small attic door in the corner of the upstairs hallway." Both boys looked at me. "I've never been up there or even looked up there."

"If there's space, I'm calling dibs," Alex said. "Man cave. Game room."

"If there's space," Eli said, "and windows that can be lightproofed, it should be for the fanghead. I'll check it out over the weekend."

"Spoilsport. Your turn to wash dishes, bro," Alex said, shaking his head. "I'm gonna be busy monitoring HQ's security measures. You need me, poke me. I'll have music on."

"I'll put in a load of laundry," I said. Both men raised eyebrows at me. "What? I can do laundry." I hoped. I made a trip through the house, gathering wet clothes. In the laundry room, which did not originally contain a washer and dryer, I studied the units, trying to remember which was which. I vaguely remembered the one that opened on top was the washer. Directions were printed on the inside of the top. "Easy peasy," I said, loading the clothes according to the instructions and adding liquid detergent. I hit the start button and was rewarded with the sound of water jetting into the tub.

"Hey!" Alex shouted. "Get in here!" I darted back into the living space.

Eli was gripping a nine-millimeter in each hand. I found that I was holding a coat hanger. Because of the lightning, I had left the bedroom unarmed, which now felt all wrong, and I put the coat hanger down before they noticed that I had planned on defending myself and them with a thin strip of metal.

"What's up?" I asked.

"There's a second riot near the corner of Jackson Avenue and South Robertson Street. It started with a lightning strike." Alex popped open an energy drink and downed it. Lightning slammed down all around the house, the glare blinding, the noise like thunder. Thunder on steroids and meth. Sleet made sizzling and popping sounds against the windows. Sleet. In New Orleans. Eli holstered his weapons in a double rig of his own devising, both weapons at his waist, but well hidden beneath his tee.

"The storm's getting worse again," Alex said, concentrating on the tablets on his desk, tapping and swiping. "The forecast is all over the place. The temps have dropped by ten degrees in the last four hours."

Eli said, "It's early for an ice storm but not impossibly early. With the storm on the Gulf moving north and the Arctic edge moving south along the Mississippi, bad storms should be expected."

"But one front is supposed to give way to the other. These are heading right for each other and now the National Weather Service thinks they'll meet right here. Like a storm apocalypse."

Lightning hammered the earth again. Lights went out. *Le breloque* glowed in the darkness from my bedroom door. I shimmered into the Gray Between and back out, my silver magics passing through me in a Vitruvian Man pattern, a witch pattern, a pentagram. I didn't like this. At all. But at least time didn't bubble.

"Don't believe in coincidence," Eli said.

"Nope," Alex said.

"So it's witch shi—crap, or vamp crap, or Gee DiMercy, the storm god, crap." Alex shoved his moisture-kinked hair up high, where it stayed in place.

"How about we gear up and check out HQ?" Eli asked me. "The ballroom upgrades should be nearly done by now."

I nodded and went to my room to change. Again. Outside, the storm blasted the earth.

We played rock-paper-scissors and Eli lost. He donned a military poncho when he went to bring the SUV around. In appreciation, I made a double espresso for him and a chai for me while I waited, and poured them into insulated travel mugs. Win-win as far as I was concerned.

On the way to the Mithran Council Chambers, better known at Yellowrock Securities as Fanghead HQ, among other less-than-respectful names, he gave me a litany of the security upgrades and I listened with half an ear. The European vampires were coming sometime, whenever they finished yanking Leo's chain and got around to the actual visit, and Leo was planning to hold the initial reception in the ballroom.

We were turning the corner to the drive when the power to the streetlights—which had come on because of the darkness of the storm—blinked off and on and off as the power fluttered. The entire city went dark. Eli's cell rang, the call coming over the car's electronic system. "Derek," Eli said, seeing the name on the car's synced coms system. "Go ahead."

"There's a security problem at HQ from lightning strikes. I've got men checking it out."

"Copy. We're on the way to inspect the back entrance and the ballroom," Eli said. "We'll be on coms if needed."

"Copy."

The connection ended and I decided I needed to confess the problems with my magic. "So, there's this little problem," I started.

Eli didn't say anything. He didn't react at all. At the words *little problem*, he had entered the Jedi voodoo stillness he achieved when he was shooting. "The storm?" I continued. "The one that's making *le breloque* spark? It's making my skinwalker magics spark too. I'm doing the whole time-travel thing almost every time the lightning strikes. I thought it would be better after going to water, but it did it again in the shower."

"Go visit Sabina if she's in. Or the crazier one, Bethany. Both of them know what you are. Both have witch magic of one kind or another. They may have thoughts about what's happening. But stay away from the electronics and the windows."

At the last part, I wanted to go *Duh*. I wasn't in the mood to visit either of the priestesses, even if they were old enough to be awake in the daylight. One was spooky crazy. The other one was just nutso. I avoided interpersonal interactions with them like I would a plague victim. But it was all good advice. I said so. Eli gave me his battle nod, more of a twitch than anything else. We pulled around back to check out the spike strips in the entrance drive and the laser eyes and the cameras, but as we braked, the lightning got worse, the cold got colder, and the rain got harder, throwing up a thick white mist to mix with the odd fog. It was disconcerting and my magics did the time-stutter again. So I left Eli to the inspection and ducked inside between lightning strikes.

Once in HQ, I wandered the halls, seeing only humans because even though it was storm-dark out, it was still technically daylight, and the noon hours were the middle of the sleep cycle for vamps. Lightning came in groups—bunches? clumps? gaggles?—and my magic continued to splutter and sputter, sometimes bubbling time, sometimes not. I discovered it was wise to simply stop in place each time it bubbled and wait it out; otherwise I'd appear to vanish to the humans around me. I didn't want stories of ghost-Jane to start circulating. The stops made me acutely aware of HQ. The carpet or wood flooring or tiles under my feet. The lighting. The security cameras placed prominently in corners. The real cameras better hidden in picture frames and light fixtures. The colors, textures, decorative and architectural elements that seemed to flow from one area to another. Leo had money, and his personal and business space screamed class. Not something I knew a lot about. His people screamed it too, in the way they walked and moved, their posture self-confident, the quality of their clothing and uniforms. Leo had spared no expense making his people feel comfortable. He never had. They looked cared for and they smelled safe and happy. I'd been in vamp households and clan homes before, and few were as contented-smelling as this one. That implied that they really liked it here. How much of their contentment was because they were blood-bound? Addicted to vamp blood. High on blood. They had asked to become bound. Signed contracts for that. Entered into the blood-meal relationship with eyes wide open, knowing that once addicted, they could never leave, not and maintain the youth and vigor that vamp blood gave them. But that was the case in every vamp home. What about this one made it smell happier?

As I maneuvered through the hallways, I found my hand on my throat, at the place where Leo had bitten me. When he had tried to force me into a blood-bound relationship. Had he expected that once I was bound to him I'd want to stay that way? And why had he claimed me? I had to believe that it was to keep me from being claimed by the EVs. I was a valuable resource he didn't want to lose until after the EVs were defeated. And . . . when binding me didn't work, he gave me a primo. Sneaky bastard. I needed to talk to Leo about a lot of things. Someday. When the world wasn't trying to fall apart.

Mixed in with contentment, the hallways were also full of the other scents that permeated a vamp's household, that mixture of dry herbs and wilting funeral flowers, sex and excellent coffee, gunpowder, blood, and sweat. The smell made Beast—a predator herself—sit up and take notice. *Good vampire smell. Smell George. Smell Leo. Mates . . .*

Yeah. No. Down girl. Not plural. Not the fanghead. Only Bruiser.

Beast hacked with laughter.

Not knowing what else to do (and feeling a sense of disaster in the worsening storm), I stopped humans to talk about the weather. I wasn't the chatty type, but their surprise at my noticing them seemed odd. I always noticed—the way they moved, the way they smelled—I just didn't engage in useless conversation. Even now. This convo about the weather was important because the weather was not acting like itself. Not that the humans had noticed. No one had any ideas about the weird storms, and most locals pointed to the fact that New Orleans always had weird weather. "What's new?" was the most common reaction. As the minutes passed, I reached the lower levels, where the effect of the lightning was less. It seemed that being underground even a bit abated my magic's reaction to it and the stuttering of time eased.

I ended up in the workout gym, where I discovered Gee teaching swordplay with two wooden sticks to an advanced student. The woman was Ro Moore, a self-proclaimed Alabama backwoods hillbilly, boxer, wrestler, and MMA cage fighter. Ro had no fear and didn't believe that there were limits of any kind on her abilities. She was putting on a show for the gathered security types in the Spanish Circle form of sword fighting, also known as La Destreza. She'd be peppered with bruises tomorrow, because if Gee was holding back, it didn't show. The clack of wood staves was so fast I had to pull on Beast-vision to follow. With each hit, Gee was whapping her hard, but the slender, muscular woman wasn't backing up. She even managed three touches on Gee, which humans never did. I didn't know which vamp she was drinking from, but whoever it was had given her remarkable strength and speed. Sword work seemed to be something Ro was born to do, her prominent shoulders, narrow waist, and long arms giving her a long reach, longer than Gee's. But Gee was inhumanly fast. He backed her up a step. Then two.

Ro ducked beneath Gee's staves, dropped to one knee, and swept her other leg out to impact Gee's knee in a move I had learned in the dojo. Gee's leg buckled and he nearly fell. Instead, he swept around and caught both of Ro's practice sticks in his, did some kind of swivel motion, and ripped them from her hands. There was a collective intake of breath among the watchers and an instant of silence as the sticks flew. They smashed into the wall across the room in a clatter.

But by then Ro was dead. Not dead as in lifeless, but as in flat on her back, Gee's staves at her throat, crossed for a scissors move that would have sliced her head off had the staves been blades and the fight been real. One of his feet was on her abdomen; the other pinned her right hand. She was immobilized. And Gee was ticked off.

"Who taught you this move, human?" Gee demanded.

"An old man named Clementine. A cage fighter who thought I showed promise."

Gee backed away, crossed his staves in front of him, and bowed. "You have done well. Next time follow it up with a strike to the jaw and one to the heart. Go ice your knee. Drink from your mistress this evening. You will need healing, as will I."

Ro rolled to her feet and backed away, far enough for Gee to miss if he was planning a sneak attack. She crossed her hands as if she still held staves and gave him a deeper bow, but without taking her eyes from him. Smart woman.

Gee was about to call the next student when I pulled my magics close to try to keep them steady and said, "A moment of the Mercy Blade's time for the Enforcer?"

It was a formal request. I was getting good at using the ceremonial speech of vamps, which worked better than,

"Hey you, Bird Brain. Got a minute?" My invitation was all proper and curly, like calligraphy of the mouth.

Gee scooped up Ro's staves in addition to his own and headed my way. He was dressed in skintight black, his dark hair tied in a short queue, and he sauntered across the floor as the gathered humans dispersed into small groups. Gee was fine, despite the blow to his knee. Whatever Ro had kicked, it hadn't been his real knee, but some other bird body part hidden by glamour. A lot of people now knew he was bird-shaped in his natural form, but he didn't show that off unnecessarily.

Oddly, Troll, Katie's primo, helped Ro out the back door, which claimed Ro for Katherine Fonteneau, aka Katherine Louisa Dupris, Katherine Pearl Duplantis, Katherine Vuillemont. Katie was Leo's heir, owned the oldest continuously operating whorehouse in New Orleans, and never showed any interest in her blood-servants or scions learning swordplay.

I was watching the pair so tightly that I missed the toss and caught the staves only inches from my face. Barely blocked the Mercy Blade's strikes, three clacks of wood against wood. Parry and block were often considered cheating in the vamp version of La Destreza, though the archaic rules were confusing. I blocked three more strikes and caught my balance. Attacked, circling my staves, still heated from Ro's hands, circling, thrusting, moving forward, drawing on Beast's speed in addition to my own skinwalker speed.

Fun, Beast growled deep inside. *Play with mouse.*

Lightning struck, a *crash-smash-bang* of thunder that shook the building. HQ, struck by lightning. The Gray Between ripped open and the world went still and silent. Gee's face was frozen in a look of intensity. His lips were slightly parted so he could breathe steadily, his feet were planted securely on the wood gym floor, and his black hair was a solid glisten where the light hit it. His glamours were an interlocking, underlying patchwork of power-reds from scarlet to crimson to cerise. Lots of blanketing shades of lavender and grape and periwinkle and amethyst. And all glowing with magic to Beast-vision. I stepped back from Gee's staves to keep from drawing him into the time bubble with me.

In the room beyond I could see the blood-servants and

-slaves, watching us with a sense of expectation and excitement. All but Ro, whose eyes were narrowed and cataloging the scene that Gee and I made. I walked toward her and took in Troll's expression and the protective hand on her arm. Interestinger and interestinger.

Back at Gee, I realized that I wasn't cramping. My stomach wasn't constricting; I wasn't throwing up blood; I wasn't nauseated. I looked at myself in the Gray Between. My body was a shadow of matter. My souls were golden wisps of light, swirled around one another, intermixed. Beast moved up into the forefront of my brain and panted, watching what I was watching, understanding what I was understanding. Maybe better than I did. My magic was in a pentagram, a star geometry, stable motes of power moving like the new normal in the slice of time around me. But the scarlet motes always seemed to be moving just ahead of my skinwalker magic. Leading instead of being herded? That was a scary thought. The one perfect thing about my magic was the empty place against my heart where the shadow of murder had been. Now there was a feathery light there, bright and sweeping. Light. That was unexpected.

Either the storm was doing something to my magic, or being taken to water had done something to my magic, or the new Vitruvian Man motes had done something to my magic, or some combo of the three. The star shape, or pentagram, had proven to provide the best geometric and mathematical stability for magical workings, and was best when five magic users came together to work energy to a purpose, what laymen called a spell. I had five of the little red motes zipping through me and around me, in a working that appeared to be part of me. Either it had fixed the problem with my skinwalker magic or it was about to try to kill me.

Beast. Talk to me. What's happening here?

Angel Hayyel happens. Purpose of light. Like purpose of Beast is to hunt.

That isn't overly helpful. Got anything more?

The angel Hayyel had appeared in my presence once, and his hand had changed me and everyone in the room with me. No surprise that the celestial being was an ongoing problem. *Beast?*

Beast didn't answer. I knew she had talked to the angel who had appeared in my life for all of maybe four seconds. And I knew that the angel's time with Beast was longer than his time with me. And whatever he had done had created this ability to bubble time. It had given others certain skills and certain gifts and certain punishments. I wasn't sure what bubbling and bending time was—a gift or a penalty. Maybe both.

I'd gotten too close. Around me, time stuttered and Gee's staves moved several inches in a swing that would have impacted the side of my head had I not ducked. Instinctively, Beast pulled on the bubble of time and it stabilized. Now that . . . that was interesting. And I had seen how she did it.

I gripped my staves and went behind Gee. Without touching him, I set the hard wooden shafts in two delicate places—assuming his bird had parts like humans did—leaned in, and the Gray Between dropped. Sound slapped my eardrums like two palms clapping on the side of my head. I yanked the staves up and back, snapping one stave between Gee's legs and one against his throat, yanking him back against me and applying pressure all at once.

Gee made an *eep* and froze in place. His breath made a whistling noise. A blood-servant hooted approvingly. Others applauded slowly, as if still trying to figure out what they had seen. Or hadn't.

"Enforcer," Gee greeted me, motionless and formal.

"Bird Man," I greeted him back, softly. "How's it shaking?"

"I have nothing that shakes. I am healthy. And you, Enforcer? Are you well?"

"I'm good. Okay, how about this. You drop your staves, I let the pressure off your nuts—you do have nuts?"

"Yes," he breathed. "At the moment in a most uncomfortable position."

"Continuing: I let you go, we bow to each other, and we chat off the record." I hoped this took us from formality and fighting and into conversation.

"You wish to gossip?"

"Sure. Why not?"

"Agreed."

Gee dropped his staves. I stepped back and crossed my

hands at the waist, the staves sweeping out behind me. We bowed in that formal manner and I set my sticks on the floor.

"Would the Enforcer care for tea?"

"I would."

Gee snapped his fingers and Brenda Rezk inclined her head. It looked like the security person from Atlanta was learning how to be a servant, which was part of every good blood-servant's job. She was a prideful but resolute woman, determined to move up in Leo's ranks and doing a fine job of it, though serving tea didn't look like her cup of the beverage. The fact that she was working directly with Gee, however, suggested that she might be up for the number one or two security spot when the new Master of the City took over in Georgia.

I placed my staves into Brenda's hands and followed Gee from the gym into the cleaner-smelling hallway. Less sweat and blood and fighting pheromones and more soap, shampoo, food, coffee, and tea scents. Gee led the way to the small room that was used as a consultation room and gestured me to one of the sofas. I had few happy memories of this room simply because bad stuff had happened here. But I took a seat and tea was delivered by a gray-liveried servant wearing white gloves, overseen by Brenda. Tea and little sandwiches and a small plate of fruit. Beast sneered. I ignored her.

When the servants left, Brenda closed the door behind her, guarding the hallway and our privacy. I said, "I think I whupped your butt in there, dude."

Gee poured tea and pushed the sugar and cream to me. I wasn't the patient type except when hunting, but I managed to not look up. I added sugar and cream, tasted, added a bit more of each, wasting his time as he was wasting mine, and settled back with a satisfied sigh. The tea was good.

"You twisted time," he said mildly.

"I did." It had been caught on tape a few times. It wasn't like it was a secret.

"Only *arcenciels* can twist time."

"And Brute," I said.

"The werewolf?"

"Werewolf touched by an angel. And me. Also touched by an angel."

He thought about that as we sipped and ate sandwiches. They were nearly as good as Bruiser's cucumber sandwiches. They'd have been better with beef and bacon, but no one had asked me.

"I see," he said, after an extended time.

"Angels and *arcenciels* and Anzus were on Earth and interacting with humans at about the same time, and of them all, only *arcenciels* could be trapped and their magic used. Only *arcenciels* could become magical slaves." They could be trapped in quartz crystal and their time-altering gifts melded to the will of the owner of the crystal. I'd seen it. I wondered if *arcenciels* were the mythical source of the djinn trapped in bottles for their magic, though the rainbow dragons were trapped in crystals, not lamps. "Did you know a winged dude named Hayyel?"

Gee's mouth turned down in distaste. "I am not permitted to speak of messengers, celestial warriors, creatures of light, or time."

There didn't seem to be much to say to that, and Gee looked like he was thinking hard. I waited him out and sipped some more. It was really good tea. Only the best for the suckheads and their employees. I poured myself a second cup and warmed Gee's cup.

"I may not offer to speak of many things, but in return for that information I will gift you answers," he said at long last.

Meaning that if I asked questions, he might be able to respond. "Goody. Two for starters: Why is Troll helping Ro Moore? What do you know about the storm overhead?"

"Tom, the primo of the heir of the Master of the City, Katherine, is helping Ro Moore, the heir's new Enforcer. It was decided that all our top three Mithrans should have Enforcers. This will increase their importance to the European Mithrans. You will have an Enforcer as well."

I laughed. "An Enforcer will have an Enforcer? You already stuck me with a vamp primo and a werewolf."

"The head of Clan Yellowrock will have an Enforcer," he clarified. "It has been decided," he added, making it clear it was out of my hands. "It has been suggested that Eli Younger will become your Enforcer."

Time didn't bubble again, but my heart did skip a beat.

An Enforcer took first challenge to all blood duels. Eli was great with firearms and hand-to-hand and things that go bang. Not so much with long swords. And then I knew exactly what to do, as clearly as if God himself had stuck the idea into my head. "Nope. You know that boon you owe me? The one from way back? I'm claiming it. I want you as my Enforcer."

Gee DiMercy splashed tea over the cup edge onto his hand. His face contorted into some kind of horror. I just grinned. "Welcome aboard Clan Yellowrock. Get with Eli for your place to sleep at the house. Maybe Ed will share his nook under the stairs. It'll be tight but I think you can manage it. Ed's good with hair. Maybe he'll groom your feathers for you." I set down my cup, stood, and opened the door. "And I think that concludes my business here today." I closed the door and smiled up into my honeybunch's face. "Hi ya, Bruiser. Thought I smelled you in the hall."

Bruiser returned my smile, his brown eyes warm, his Bruiser/Onorio scent like citrus and . . . Onorio. That was a scent all his own. Beast started a purr that I barely kept inside.

He said, "If you're finished baiting the locals, would you accept an invitation to join me for a trip on a boat?" He held out a hand and I placed mine into his heated one as we walked to the elevator.

"In a storm? Sure. Why not?" The elevator doors closed and we ascended to the ballroom level in back, talking as we moved.

"You heard?" I asked.

"I heard. Onorios have very good ears. Leo will be displeased at your presumption," he said with a secretive and delighted twist to his lips. He lifted our clasped hands and kissed the back of mine in that old-world charm that made my heart melt into a puddle of goo. Bruiser was pleased at what I had done.

I wasn't sure when it had become important to please another person, but it had happened around the time that Yellowrock Clan had first been mentioned. Clans, in the Cherokee tradition, had rules and regs about interpersonal relationships; pleasing and supporting each other was a big, if unspoken, part of that. I didn't remember much about my own Cherokee tradition, but I remembered that. Just as important, at some point over the last few months Bruiser had stopped being Leo's footstool and started being Onorio. That meant he'd started putting me before his former master. This change had nourished the small bud of happy now growing inside me. Happy was scary. I had never done happy. "Leo can kiss my pretty, golden-skinned bottom."

"No. He cannot."

The happy bloom got bigger. So did the scary. I wasn't sure I had really been happy since my father died. Happiness and death were mixed up inside my head from that juxtaposition, as if being happy meant waiting for death to happen. Together we exited the building to stand under the porte cochere. "Wait. Did you say I'd be joining you for a trip on a boat? A *boat*? Unless you got an ark out there, I'm not interested in going on a boat in this weather." Bruiser opened the passenger door of one of Leo's limos, armored and heavy and very familiar. Especially the floor of this one. I looked at the floor and he read my mind.

"Sadly not today. But soon. I promise."

I slid in and removed the top from a bottled Coke I took from the tiny refrigerator. I had never had a bottled Coke—real glass and everything—until recently, and now the flavor of canned or plastic-bottled Coke—aluminum or plastic and a touch of *bleagh*—had begun to pall on me. I figured that the glass bottles were intended for Leo and the cans for the hoi polloi like me, but that only made them taste better. Bruiser slid in beside me. He wasn't dressed in his usual dress pants and dress shirt, sleeves rolled up, but in jeans, a T-shirt that traced his abs like a lover's hand, and a navy wool pea jacket, unbuttoned. With butt-stomper boots. There were two rain ponchos resting over the seat across from us. And rain boots. And life vests. The limo pulled away.

"You were serious. We're going out on the water in this gale."

"We are. There is something you should see."

"Ducky. Not. My magic is reacting to the storm. To the lightning specifically."

"I saw." His eyes rested on me, his lids low, his lips quirked up on one side with delight. "On the monitor, along with the entire security team, and Eli, gathered in the main security office. When you vanished, reappeared, and pinned the Mercy Blade, they broke into spontaneous applause."

"Yeah?" Okay. I could live with applause.

"Yes. You took him. He dropped his weapons. And you didn't vomit blood or grow claws. It was impressive. And something that might get leaked to our enemies. There were a lot of people in the room and not all of them are fully trustworthy."

"That could be a good thing or a very bad thing. But we're going to a *boat*?"

"A very nice boat with a snug cabin and a teakettle."

Bruiser had never taken me on a very nice boat with a cabin and a teakettle. "It's about the storm, isn't it?"

His face went grave. "It is."

"And about my magic changing?"

"Possibly that too."

CHAPTER 8

A Felon with Employment Offers from the ÐOÐ

The limo trailed through the streets to the docks at Bayou Bienvenue Marina off Highway 47—Paris Road to the locals. The marina led to several bodies of water, including the Mississippi River Gulf Outlet Canal, Lake Pontchartrain, and Lake Borgne.

Bruiser and I raced onto a very nice boat and into the snug cabin with its teakettle. I wasn't up on my nautical terms. But the boat was wide and the hull didn't go down into the water much, which seemed smart in the half-swamp, half-navigable waters around New Orleans. It did move around beneath me, though, and Beast turned tail and disappeared. I guessed she didn't like the blustering wind that buffeted the boat or the unsure footing. My stomach didn't like them either.

There were thumps and jars above us as the sailor types—a captain and a first mate?—got us ready to shove off. Bruiser poured me ginger tea and watched me sip it, sitting cautiously on a bench attached to the wall and floor, my poncho dripping and my borrowed rain boots puddling storm water.

I put a smile on my already-green face, downed the tea, and got ready to pretend enjoyment.

The mate shoved us off into the storm. The water, even in the protected areas, was worse than choppy. It was heaving and cresting and the wind was gusting. I stood and braced my feet, gripping a railing at my shoulder level. I swallowed down my gorge and said, "So where are we going on this little three-hour tour?"

Bruiser laughed. "*Gilligan's Island*. How could a youngster like you know about *Gilligan's Island*?"

"Reruns."

"I could stand being shipwrecked on a tropical isle with you." Which made my toes curl in my boots, or would have if they weren't clawing through my boot soles to get a grip on the shifting floor. "But for now," Bruiser continued, "we're taking the outlet that leads to Lake Borgne, out just beyond the Lake Borgne Surge Barrier." He patted the upholstered mattress-seat-huge-cushion beside him. I thought I might toss my cookies and spoil the moment, so I attempted a smile, rebraced my feet, gripped the shelving rail, and held on. Fortunately it wasn't a terribly long trip and the lightning had eased. Again. Which was really odd.

When the boat slowed and I could let go with one hand, I sent a text to Alex asking him to track the spates of storm activity. It seemed too regular to be natural. Almost like clockwork. Not that it went away entirely, or enough for me to let go and stand on my own two feet. "What I want you to see can be seen only in the storm," he said, extending his hand.

I gave him a look. A mean look. But the compassionate one I got in return suggested that I'd sent him a seasick look instead. I took his hand and let him help me onto the deck.

He stood behind me and wrapped one arm around me, holding me close. With his other hand, he pointed out in the rain and wind, and across a mucky sandbar. At first I didn't see it, but then I realized that my eyes were slipping past something, almost as if it were pushing my attention away. "*Obfuscation* spell," I said.

I felt his jaw move beside my temple, close enough for me to hear softly spoken words. Bruiser was taller than me, so the sensation was both familiar and unusual. "The spell was never intended to work with rain. Unlike light, which can be reflected or refracted, the rain hits the boat and trails down it, giving us an outline."

"You discovered this how?"

"Coast Guard investigated a fisherman's report of a ghost ship and asked the local Mithrans to check it out."

There was something in his tone that suggested he knew my next thoughts even before I voiced them. I pressed my head against his and said, "A water witch with strong air witch tendencies must be aboard. The storm systems colliding feels wrong. Not natural." He waited until I said the more likely possibility. "But since the witch conclave ended and the witches and Leo are in each other's pockets, this is either an unknown witch group attacking New Orleans, or a powerful water-witch-turned-vamp." I wrapped my arms around his, holding us together. My nausea slipped away, replaced by an adrenaline spike that I knew he could smell. "There are no witch-vamps among Leo's own who could do this. Therefore, there is most likely some unknown European vamp-witch sitting in a spelled boat, just off our shores."

He nodded. "I hope you don't mind, but I asked Alex Younger to research the histories and see if he can discover who might be causing the storm. He's binging on energy drinks already."

"Yeah," I said softly, watching the rain conflict with the *obfuscation* spell. "Can you tell how big the boat is?"

"We can't risk getting close enough to get a firm reading, but smaller than Her Royal Majesty's *Queen Mary Two*, larger than a tramp steamer. If the winds abate, we'll send a drone over it. But it's big enough."

Big enough to ruin our safety and our lives. Got it.

Bruiser said something to the captain and guided me back inside, where he poured another cup of ginger tea. He left me sipping while he returned to the deck and chatted sea-type stuff with the captain. Manly stuff about Mississippi River men.

Mississippi River men were legendary. They knew the river, every turn, every sandbar, every wreck buried in mud.

Nothing moved up or down the powerful waterway with its shifting bottom without them. The entire nation's trade depended on them. I could feel the pull of Onorio magics, new to me, potent and surging as the tides, as Bruiser encouraged the maritime types to like him, to trust him, to talk to him like a friend. When he had won their trust, he asked how the Mithrans who protected the city—that's what he said, *protected the city*—might discover who among the elite group of river men had been contacted to bring the ship's passengers ashore, or the ship to a berth. They started bandying names back and forth. All palsey-walsey.

I sat on the cushioned bench for the trip back and texted. Eli got a full description of the boat with a suggestion that he contact those people he had mentioned, the ones in Homeland Security, U.S. Citizenship and Immigration Services, and the multiple branches of the U.S. military. If a ghost ship was coming ashore, we'd need all the help we could get. I queried the Kid for updates. There was nothing new except a small fistfight turned gun battle outside of Arceneau Clan Home. There was a magical storm and multiple riots at the same time. Riots in a storm. People didn't riot in storms.

Grégoire, Leo's boy toy and second in line to the Mastership title, was safe in HQ, but I had never believed in coincidence. Arceneau Clan Home would be my next stop.

Leo's limo maneuvered the streets through the storm and the traffic that looked like a dozen kittens had attacked a ball of yarn, Bruiser and me tapping and swiping our electronic devices. The intimacy of the twenty-first century. Not. But we felt an expectation of Big Bad Uglies heading our way, and good coms made us safer.

Brandon and Brian were standing under the small porch roof at Arceneau Clan Home, decked out in the Enforcer version of riot gear. A moving van was out front and burly blood-servants and -slaves were loading up the house's contents. "Grégoire's moving?" I asked.

Bruiser's lips twitched with satisfaction. "No. Leo decided a week ago that the accommodations at any of the five-star hotels in the city were"—his voice took on a French accent similar to Leo's for the next few words—"'simply not up to Mithran standards.' In his position as host, he decided to garrison half of the Europeans here and the rest of our visitors in the Council Chambers. Scrappy drafted the letter on parchment with all proper calligraphy, Leo signed it, and it went on its way, airmail. Leo found the entire ploy entirely too amusing."

I didn't comment on his use of the nickname Scrappy. Leo's secretary's real name was Lee, but I had been calling her Scrappy because of her red hair and fiery temperament. It had caught on. Maybe even with Scrappy. "But the purpose was to divide and conquer?"

"Exactly. The soldiers will be billeted here."

"I like." Pulling our ponchos over us, we stepped into the downpour. Water ran in the streets and had been running long enough that the filth had been deposited into the city's drainage system, leaving the surface of the earth nice and clean. The city even smelled fresh, an uncommon occurrence. Walking in the rain, I stomped once in a puddle. And stopped. I hadn't intended to do that, not consciously, but the splashing water was kinda nice. I stomped again, the water spraying up over my boots. Bruiser was watching me, a look of . . . something . . . on his face. He held out his hand, I took it, and together we wove through the workers who were carrying out priceless antiques covered with plastic. We were met in the entrance of the Clan Home by the Robere twins.

"Howdy, boys," I said. "So tell me about the security upgrades. Alex has all the deets but I've left it to him. Oh. And the hidden cameras Leo authorized and had Derek install without my oversight? I totally get it now, with the plan to park some of EVs here."

"You knew about those?" Brandon said.

"Of course I knew. Derek and Pauline Easter are good, but they're amateurs. The Kid is a felon with employment offers from the DOD. He's better than good."

The twins exchanged looks, one of those multilayered communication things twins can do. "We see," they said together. I just narrowed my eyes at them and walked into the three-story house. It was larger and deeper than it looked from the outside, forty-six feet across the front, and twice that deep on its small lot. The central hallway led past a wide staircase in the foyer, the floors and stairs carpeted with Oriental rugs in shades of blue and gray and black. The dining room was off the foyer, with a hand-carved cherry-wood table and chairs and loads of china showing through glass doors of the built-in cabinetry. Across the hallway from it was a parlor filled with antique upholstered furniture, statues, and objets d'art. Gilt-framed paintings hung on the right wall in the wide hall, and a mural graced the left.

The scent of coffee and tea lingered on the air from a butler's pantry that separated the dining room from the expanded kitchen added on in back. There was also an old-fashioned music room behind the parlor and a library behind that. Staff quarters were on the left at the back of the house, for the servants, including security. Arceneau Clan Home was überfancy and überexpensive, tasteful in ways I had yet to become comfortable with. The cameras were set into the light fixtures, complicated things with sensors and on-off switches. When the place was swept for electronics, Alex or someone at HQ could deactivate them and then reactivate them once the EuroVamps felt secure. The cameras were everywhere. And even with my experience, I couldn't spot them.

"Tell me about the gunfire," I said when I was done with my inspection.

Brandon said, "In the middle of the lightning storm from one of Dante's circles of hell, a car pulled up and six unknowns, male, jumped out and attacked the movers. Fists. Then blades. Before we could intervene, it escalated into gunfire. We got the movers under cover, but a neighbor had already called NOPD. Since it involved gunfire and was in an upscale part of the city, law enforcement showed up quickly. At which point it appeared that the gunmen would turn on the officers."

"We stopped them," Brian said. "I assume Alex will have acquired the security footage."

Which I couldn't wait to see. "Okay. Keep us informed," I said.

I wandered through the ground floor of the house, and on the way out, I passed the mural on the wall, the one I

had seen before, that attracted my attention on so many
levels. I stopped to study it. Closely. More intently than ever.
I realized that one of the vamps in the mural had dog fangs.
Which Bruiser had to know. "Onorios," I said, using my
Enforcer tone. "This blood-family with dog fangs. Details."

Bruiser stepped up on my left, one twin on my right, the
other behind me. Onorio scents and heat enveloped me.
"Bouvier," the twin from behind said. His tone suggested
that I should know and remember this already. Things were
ticking in the back of my brain but not fast enough.

"Remind me," I said.

Brandon, to my side, pointed. "Rousseau and his favorites,
Elena and Isabel." Rousseau was the formal way to refer to
a clan head, though Rousseau Clan had been disbanded
during the vamp war not long after I got here. His fingers
moved. "Desmarais with his Joseph, Louis, and Alene." The
first names indicated a blood-servant or much lesser scion;
the vamps were obvious by the fangy display.

Brian leaned over me, his body touching my spine. "Lau-
rent with her favorites, Elizabeth and Freeman." Freeman
was black and gorgeous and I had little doubt why he was
both free and a favorite. "Renee with his master, St. Martin." He went quiet. St. Martin was associated with the Damours blood-family, the family of witch-vampires I had
helped to kill. They had been powerful and evil and dangerous. And their red motes of power were still trapped
inside me.

"Bouvier with Ka Nvista."

The vamp master and Bouvier clan head at the time had
dog fangs, which I hadn't noted before. His blood-servant
was Cherokee, her name meaning dogwood. She had yellow
eyes like mine and she was likely a skinwalker, though no
one who was alive both then and now had ever remarked
on any similarity in our scents. She was beautiful, with long,
braided black hair and lost eyes. Her master would have
savaged her beautiful throat with the double fangs. "Bouvier and the Damours. Did they hang together back in the
day?"

"Yes," Brian said. "They did. As did other masters and
scions from time to time. The Damours were a sensual and

sybaritic family. They attracted many of the restless young, the dissolute elder, and the bored." He didn't sound particularly approving, which relieved me in ways I didn't take time to look at too closely.

I pulled my cell and texted the Kid to go through the old records databases to look for all witch/vamps who used to hang with the Damours and see how common the dog-fanged vamps were among the group. But Alex had beat me to it, texting back, *I started that research the moment the first dog-fanged revenant appeared.*

Why? I typed back.

Because everything else bad in this fuc—messed-up city traces back to the Damours, so why not this too?"

He typed that so I could see his near-cussing. But he was right, and maybe he was more clearheaded than I was right now. Vamps were long-lived and had different views of future plans, potential goals, and multiple methodologies. They could harbor vengeance in their hearts for centuries before they enacted it against an enemy. It was called the long view.

Do any of Leo's current scions have dog fangs? I typed back.

Checking. A moment later he typed back, *No.*

I pocketed the cell beneath my now mostly dry poncho and said to the three Onorios, "Thanks. I have things to think about." They all stepped back, in synchrony, which felt weird, and created a passage out the front door. Just before I reached the door, I turned, retrieved the cell, and stepped back to take a couple of dozen photos, using several different filters, just in case I needed to reference it later. I sent them to Alex's and my own e-mail addy and text number. Then I pocketed the cell again and left the house. Bruiser waited for me at the limo, holding the door open against the fine, misty rain, but when I slid in, he didn't follow.

"Shemmy will take you home," he said. "I need to be here at dusk with the twins and that's only two hours away. You haven't eaten sufficiently. I smell your hunger. Stop for something to eat. Cochon's maybe."

"Shemmy?"

"His father was Jimmy and his mother was Sheba. Not

the queen." His lips curled up slightly at beating me to the question.

"Shemmy it is. Does Shemmy have any special gifts, training, or abilities?"

"Of course. Your second insisted."

My second was Eli. "Good to know. Later, then."

"Later, love." He closed the door, leaving me in a state of bemusement. He was British, so calling me love was like Eli calling me Babe. Inconsequential. But it felt like more, as if he was getting closer and closer to the three little words. No one had ever said them to me. No one. Unless I counted the claiming by my werecat ex. But not love. Not ever. I wondered how I'd feel when it happened. If it happened.

"Howdy, Shemmy."

"Miz Yellowrock," Shemmy said, politely.

"No need to be fancy." I swiveled my body around and put my booted feet on the seat. I leaned back my head and blew out a breath that spoke of exhaustion. "Jane is fine."

"Jane it is. I hear you give nicknames. What's mine?" I looked up at Shemmy, who fit the general physical parameters of Derek Lee's security team—the shaved head, big, muscled, physique of the former military. "You can't beat Shemmy. It's perfect."

Shemmy pulled away from the curb just as my cell beeped with a call from Alex, and he didn't wait for me to say hello. "A revenant broke the iron bars over the front doors of a church—a freaking church—on Jackson Ave, walked inside, and killed two people. In daylight. Plus there's a riot still taking place nearby. It started during the last lightning. Sending you and your driver the address and directions. The storm is bad there, so be careful."

"Of course it is," I said, hearing the wry note in my voice. "On my way. Don't call your brother. He's busy at HQ. I'll handle it." And Eli was exhausted, not that I'd say that one.

Alex treated me to a silence fraught with import, the kind that meant he was thinking fast and on several levels. "Sure," he said, in a tone that meant he disagreed with my assessment. I was drawing a lot of interpretive conclusions. Odd for me. "The revenant is still there," he said, "and the cops have the building surrounded." He clicked off.

"I'm just trying to be nice," I said to the blank screen.

I turned the cell off, knelt on the floorboard of the limo, and slid my fingers around the edges of the flooring. The bottom of every limo had a store of weapons, caches that Eli had discovered as part of the latest security upgrades. We had known about the weapons in the sidewalls and nooks and crannies, but that was for handguns. This one had blades and shotguns and silver ammo. I chose a double-barreled shotgun and loaded it with silver-pellet birdshot. I'd rather have my own Benelli and silver fléchette rounds, but there was a problem with collateral damage—humans I might injure or kill by accident. For that reason I took two .380s and set them into old-fashioned leather holsters. I pulled the unfamiliar rig on over my clothing and hooked an adjustable gorget around my throat. There were two motorcycle jackets in the bottom, and I took the smaller one, even though it smelled like Leo. The scent would indicate to another vamp that I belonged to the MOC, which I hated, but the second jacket was too large.

I heard a discreet *click* and Shemmy spoke over the limo's intercom. "Ms. Yellowrock, Mr. Pellissier wishes you to know that the media is present at the church."

"Is it the woman from WGNO?"

"Carolyne Bonner is indeed at the scene, Ms. Yellowrock."

"And how is the local ABC station getting to scenes with revenants faster than anyone else?"

"It is my understanding that she has been permitted to cultivate a source high in New Orleans' Mithran politics."

Which meant that Leo was letting her into the center of things in case he needed to feed someone news with a slant. This was interesting, but not newsworthy. As I used a speed-loader to load silver/lead ammo into extra .380 magazines, I snorted in soft laughter at the word *newsworthy*. Even I knew my internal play on words wasn't really funny. Nerves maybe. It had been a long time since I went up against a revenant alone. They were superfast, were hungry as zombies, and never stopped. They were as hard to kill as bayou roaches.

I closed the deck cover and sat on the bench seat, looking out into the rain. Overhead, lightning flashed cloud-to-cloud, sparking the sky, as if angels were playing laser tag with real laser weapons. Thunder rumbled. The limo plowed through the streets and puddles the size of small lakes. I had lived in NOLA for two years, give or take, and I had gotten used to storms, wind, and rain, rain, more rain. But this was something else. This was making me itchy, getting up under my skin. Inside me, Beast was prowling, the tip of her thick tail twitching slightly.

Ahead, a mob of kids was playing in the rain. Drenched to the skin, jeans held up in one hand at the waistband to keep the water-heavy denim in place, they stomped and gestured and raced. An instant later, I realized they weren't kids and they weren't playing. This was the riot.

"How many?" I asked Shemmy.

"I can see . . . fifteen clearly, Ms. Yellowrock. Another twenty or so are half hidden. The fog and rain are so dense that even though I see forms at the street corners, racing back and forth, I can't tell how many. I can guesstimate we're looking at more than fifty. NOPD is five minutes out."

"Which means more like twenty." I called Alex and asked, "Do we have an update on the revenant's location?"

"Yeah, but we have worse worries. Grégoire says his sire is in New Orleans. Derek says he's freaking out in HQ. Trying to get outside in the daylight."

He was being *called*, demanded to join his sire. It was a psychic link that the script and fantasy novel writers got right. That calling meant that Le Bâtard was in New Orleans, on the city's soil. My insides made a little quiver and shake. "Sit Wrassler on him. And give him a job. Get Grégoire to list all the hotels, restaurants, gin joints, and haunts Le Bâtard might frequent. Get him to list all the people he might want to see, steal, or kill. Get another list of all Le Bâtard's scions and grand-scions. Keep Blondie busy."

"Good idea. When did you get all touchy-feely, Janie?" Before I could answer, he said, "The church janitor, name of Babeaux, is holed up in a closet with a layperson. They have cell phones and sent footage out to the press of the revenant. Loading that up to your cell now. Babeaux says he can hear the revenant in the sanctuary, tearing the place up."

"Ms. Yellowrock," Shemmy interrupted. "We'll have to go directly through the riot to reach the chur—"

Lightning struck the earth about two feet from the limo. The blast was so bright it seared my eyeballs. The sound so loud it deafened me. It fried the cell's electronics, burning my hand and adding the stink of burned plastic and ozone to the air I gasped in. The light and thunderclap went on and on as the Gray Between opened up around me. I dropped the ruined phone and it hung in midair.

I clutched the Gray Between energies to me and shoved the limo door open on the far side of the vehicle. Dashed through the stationary drops, getting soaked, refusing to see the future possibilities in each. I sped through the riot, taking away a gun from a furious-faced teen, tripping his adversary, knocking a bullet from its trajectory toward the ground. I didn't stop all the violence, but since time was no longer an issue, I made a circuit of the riot area and helped where I could.

By the time I finished, the lightning bolt had nearly completed its descent and I was having trouble controlling the Gray Between. I was growing claws, and golden hair was sprouting through my skin. Beast was trying to push her way through. Sometimes it didn't hurt, but this time it hurt. Bad.

I need hands to pull a trigger and hold a stake and a vamp-killer, I warned her.

Beast is not doing this, she said back.

I sprinted toward the church and the revenant. *What then?*

Storm. Light from clouds. Magic.

Something else is pulling my skinwalker magics to the surface? Just like it's bubbling time.

Yes.

Well, that sucks.

Something moved in my peripheral vision and I looked around, seeing nothing at ground level. I glanced up into the storm. Above me, in the Gray Between, an *arcenciel* hovered, her wings out and her tail caught in the moment of lashing. It didn't look like Soul, rather, the other one I knew

of, the juvenile *arenciel* named Opal. The light dragon was
horned and frilled, her long hair copper and brown, her body
scaled with red light and a hint of sapphire. She was half
human-faced, half dragon. Her teeth were eight inches long,
sharp and pearled. The scales of her snake body glistened
like the opals for which she was named. Her wings were
pearled bronze, marked by small feathered flourishes here
and there.

The Gray Between usually allowed rainbow dragons to
see me working outside of time, and since they could bubble
time, they could trace my whereabouts through it. This one,
though, was not using the ability to bubble time, but was
still in normal human time. Dancing in lightning. Magic.
Magic was affecting them too. The storm was magic, and
more so than I had guessed. It was a good thing humans
couldn't see magic, or the locals would be firing handguns
and automatic rifles up at them, hoping to bring down a
trophy-dragon.

The church was white adobe-like stuff on the outside,
rain-damaged palms and small trees along the outer walls.
Broken concrete and shell-based asphalt paving the parking
lot. I dashed into the darkness. The entrance walls were
white plaster, recently painted.

The Gray Between flickered, my joints popped and expanded, and my hips narrowed. Pelt grew down across my
face and over my limbs. I darted into the sanctuary, though
Catholics probably called it something else. The altar area
was a huge arch. Plaster dead saints stood on stands, and
plaster angels held up candelabra. Stained-glass windows
were pictures of Bible stories. The ceiling had been repaired,
and scaffolding was still in place. The smell of paint and age
hung on the air, mixed with fresh blood and old death. I
passed by a life-sized crucifix. Two church pews hung in the
air as if levitated, caught in the moment of no-time. They
had been thrown by the revenant.

She stood, arms raised in fury, about halfway down the
center aisle, feet braced to either side of a body. It—he—was
dressed in black and might have been wearing a clerical
collar, though the blood that drenched his shirt hid that.

His bald head was sitting atop the gold cross behind the altar. He looked vaguely surprised.

The revenant was wearing a dress of rags and one shoe without the heel, the other foot bare. She was scorched, and smoke curled up from her, spiraled and coiled. She was half on fire, burned, psychotic, and a lot rotted. She stank like last week's roadkill. She had been called from the grave, she had been out in the daytime, and she was the dead undead, so she had good reason for the poor fashion sense and the stench. It had probably been decades since she bathed.

I pulled the unfamiliar silver-plated vamp-killer and tested its balance by swiping it through the air, loosening up. It was hilt-heavy and was too lightweight for what I wanted. But it was what I had from the cache in the limo. I pulled it into a backswing. Rushed her.

The lightning dimmed. Thunder reached its highest pitch. The pews dropped several inches, starting to fall as time unbubbled. I leaped. Vamp-killer high. Screaming.

Time took a jump, paused, and caught up with me.

The revenant saw me, heard me, turned her head to me as I left the ground. Opened her mouth to reveal the dog fangs. She leaped at me. Inside my swing. The pews fell with twin crashes and splintered wood flew. Wood shards stabbed me. The vamp and I met about three feet off the ground. Slammed together in midair.

Her head twisted, a snakelike, inhuman move. Fast as a shark. She bit down. Catching my right shoulder in her fangs.

We landed hard, her on top, shaking me like a dog. My hand went numb. It dropped the vamp-killer. The weapon and a longer reach were a detriment now, anyway. This was close-in work.

Left-handed, I pulled a shorter silvered blade from my belt. Gripped it tight in my knobby hand. Stabbed up under her ribs, at her heart.

Which in a revenant didn't work. My training and experience were working against me. Muscle memory a hindrance.

She grabbed my head in clawed hands. Rammed it against

a pew. I had a moment of blackness, shredded away by the pain. She shook me again, teeth in my shoulder, hands on my head. She was ripping my arm off. My blood sprayed across the room and up, to spatter on the newly painted ceiling far overhead. I adjusted my grip and stabbed under her left ear. Cut toward me. Severed her carotid and jugular, her trachea and esophagus. Nothing changed. Except my blood pooling, spreading under me. The sound and vibration of her growling into my shoulder stopped.

I stabbed again, working the blade back and forth, severing tendons. They were old and tough and it wasn't easy. I was screaming in pain, in battle fury. Her head lolled forward. But her jaws didn't unclench off my shoulder. I sawed. Panted. Mewled in agony. She shook me, my whole body sliding on the wood floor, through my blood. Things tore inside my shoulder joint. Blood shot into my right eye. Into her face. Her eyes opened and she stared at me. She started drinking; the sucking sounds were just *eww*. Even if it hadn't been my blood she was drinking.

I yanked the knife out, movements clumsy, and placed the tip of the blade into the jaw joint. *Temporomandibular joint.* Yeah. Odd the things I think and remember when I'm probably dying.

I shoved it in and cut backward. Her bite decreased, but she was healing. Focusing on me. Aware of me. Gaining sanity. I had to end this now. Or die. I turned the blade. Stabbing back into the vertebrae. They were brittle and they cracked. Her bite softened more. Using my legs, I rolled her over. Pushed at her and her fangs pulled through my flesh with a slow, sickening sound. Her eyes dulled.

Silver caught my eye. Swinging down. Fast.

Her head separated from her body. She collapsed beneath me.

Eli stood above us, looking down. There was a light in his eyes I hadn't seen before. "Babe. Shift. So I can kill you at my leisure."

"Kill me?" I whispered.

"For taking her on without me."

I laughed, or tried to. Pain zinged through me. Lightning

boomed. Beast ripped the Gray Between open and I shifted. The last thing I saw before the change took me was human-shaped fingers. I was changing back from fighting half-form to human, which was a good thing, as it was still daylight-ish. If I'd changed to mountain lion, I'd have been stuck in that form until nightfall, an irritating glitch in my skinwalker energies.

CHAPTER 9

Sword of the Enforcer

"You want to tell me why you took her on alone?" Eli's voice was low, almost a whisper. The way he sounded when he was seriously ticked off.

I licked my fingers, cleaning the burger juices off them, thinking. He had sent Shemmy to get me a dozen burgers and fries and a couple of two-liter Cokes. He had waited until I ate every single bite to ask me anything at all.

I almost said, *I came alone because you were nearly drained of blood last night and were weak*. But I figured he might just shoot me. I almost said, *You were busy*. Ditto on the shooting. I settled on, "I was stupid?"

"Very."

"Thank you for the clean clothes? And the food?"

Eli grunted. He was sitting on an undamaged pew beneath the crucifix, bent forward, forearms resting on his thighs. His hands no longer held a weapon but dangled between his knees. He skin was very dark in the church's shadows, his hair buzzed close, brown scalp showing through, gray eyes looking charcoal. Eli was a seriously pretty man. And was seriously ticked.

I was on the floor at his feet, eating like the calorie-starved person I was after so many shifts and half-shifts in quick succession. Oh. And nearly dying. Nearly dying is hungry business. Plus my hair was a mess and I didn't have lipstick with me. Not that I'd ever say that to Eli. No freaking way.

Though I might look a mess, the magics coursing through me, the ones that now formed a star, and were so different from my usual skinwalker magics, felt steady and smooth and relentless. So that was good, right? Except, Eli. Ticked. Dangerously ticked.

"Babe. Don't do it again. Even disabled I'm better than nothing."

He said it as if he'd been disabled and had still held his own. The scar on his collarbone shone white above his black tee, which was rain soaked, though no longer dripping. He had acquired more scars since coming to work for me, pale streaks on his neck and across his chest, but I seldom noticed them, not in competition with the white, puckered scar on his collarbone.

His dress pants were soaked. His skin was covered with chill bumps, gleaming in the church lights. The jacket he'd worn to HQ was gone. When he breathed, steam blew from his mouth. It was unexpectedly icy in the old church.

"I won't. Pinkie swear?" I held up my little finger, crooked.

There was an instant of silence, then Eli laughed. An actual out-loud chuckle. "Babe." He shook his head in resignation.

"I know." I dropped my hand.

Behind him, NOPD detectives and crime scene techs were working up the scene, which was hard to do with the bodies being in several places, scattered all over the church. With the perpetrator crumbling to ash. And with her being dead three times now. The paperwork was gonna be a disaster, I thought. Fortunately not my problem. The crumbling to ash was the weirdest part. I'd never seen such a thing, but then I'd never seen a thrice-dead vamp out in daylight and then dead on holy ground. I was expanding my horizons and not in a good way.

"We need to talk and you need to know something before we go back outside," he said.

"That sounds ominous. Not as ominous as a revenant chewing on my shoulder, but bad enough."

"Alex asked a question. One I hadn't thought through."

I nodded for him to continue and wadded up the garbage.

"Why are all these vamps buried with their heads? It's common knowledge that vamps killed with silvershot, blades, or stakes can rise as revenants."

I thought back to the only buried vamps I'd seen, in a mausoleum in the vamp cemetery. The vaults had been raided and the bodies tossed around. I honestly couldn't say if they'd had their heads or not. "I don't know. That sounds like a very important question for Leo."

"Another one, then. Why were these suckheads buried in human graveyards instead of the vamp cemetery?"

"Huh. More questions for the MOC. That it?"

"No. Bruiser is outside, dealing with the media and with law enforcement for the riot and for the crime scene here."

"And that's important because . . . ?"

"Law enforcement includes PsyLED."

It took a moment for the words to sink in. Another moment for my brain to catch up to my suddenly speeding heart. He didn't mean Soul. He'd just have used the name of the Senior Agent. Eli meant someone else. I stood up from the floor, slowly, carefully. Just as slowly, I weaponed up in the gear Eli had set aside when I shifted. Nine-mil. Vamp-killers. I wished I had the Sword of the Enforcer. It had a scabbard and looked important. So did the blade Bruiser had given me. That one would work too. I needed more weapons.

"Jane?"

I pulled my hair back and up into a tail, then tied it in a knot and twisted it around. "Phone," I said, holding out my hand.

Eli placed his in my palm. I dialed HQ, the direct line to Scrappy, Leo's newish assistant. "This is Lee, Mr. Pellissier's assistant. How are things progressing, Eli?"

"This is Jane. If I'm arrested, I recommend Eli Younger for my replacement as part-time Enforcer. Derek will need help, at least until this EuroVamp crap is handled."

"Arrested?" she squeaked.

I hung up. Handed Eli his cell. "Keep outta this," I said to him. "It's personal."

"Got that. Still gotchur six."

There was nothing I could do about that. Free will and all. I spun on the toe of my boot and stalked into the rain. It wasn't pouring as hard, more a steady patter instead of the previous downpour and alternating sleet. The lightning had resolved into a faint and distant rumble. The strange wet mist was back, though, thicker than ever, and I strode through it, my off-the-shelf combat boots splashing. I wasn't in Enforcer gear—no spectacular leathers, no specially de-signed boots, and there was no way I was putting on the gorget until it had been steamed clean of my own blood and the damaged links repaired. But I was dressed in black, a long, lean form, my gold nugget necklace my only jewelry, weapons, and a scowl the devil himself would have admired. From the way people backed away, I knew my eyes were glowing gold, Beast close to the surface. It was her snarl on my face.

I stalked to the flashing lights, blue and red emergency vehicles resolving out of the fog, cops and techs and detec-tives stepping back. I caught his scent on the wind, slight but undeniably his. Wereleopard. Black wereleopard. Ricky-Bo LaFleur. The SAC, senior special agent in charge of the Knoxville, Asheville, and Chattanooga PsyLED office, and several other states if assigned by his superiors. My ex. We had things to say to each other.

Well, maybe it was clearer to say I had things to say to him. Not all that long ago, Rick had promised to kill my honeybunch and take me back, as if Bruiser were his personal threat and I was a toy to be fought over. Not. And Not.

I caught Bruiser's scent, but not the smell of his blood. He was still okay. Something tight and twisted unclenched inside of me. But he was standing with Rick, his form tall and controlled, looking like a male model, a passive metro-sexual. Utterly deceptive. I had seen my sweetcheeks fight. He was deadly. He'd fight if attacked, but would he be fast enough? Were-creatures were faster than human eyes could follow. The fear returned.

I strode from the fog, long steps, straight between them.

Stopped, nose to nose with Rick. Unlike the cops behind me, he didn't pull away. "Talk. Now," I said. "Bruiser, we'll be a minute."

"Of course, love."

I heard him turn and move away, about ten feet. Onorios have very acute hearing. He was giving me the pretense of privacy but still covering my back. Eli, disobeying orders, took up a position at Rick's back. The corner of Rick's eye twitched. He was a predator. He knew when he was being stalked and cornered. He looked different, older, worn. His black eyes still flashed and his hair still fell over his forehead in a small black curl. In the weather, it had formed into small ringlets at his collar. He was swoonworthy. He had also broken my heart, embarrassed me in front of the entire vamp city, and taken off with another woman, a curvy, sex-on-a-stick, gorgeous wereleopard. A creature like him. I had grieved. But I was done with that months ago.

I smiled at the memory, showing too many teeth, and snorted a breath at him. Big cat to big cat. The first steps of a challenge. "Ricky-Bo," I whispered. "The last time we talked personal crap, you said we can't be together, but that eventually you'd find a way out of this 'were problem.' Then you said, and I quote, 'If you're sleeping with him,' meaning Bruiser, 'I'll kill him and take you.'" I dropped my voice, so low even a wereleopard had to tilt his head to hear. "Understand this, you foul piece of scum. You and I are done. I'm with George Dumas," I said, using his real name to make sure there could be no confusion. "You touch my Bruiser and I'll take your head so fast you'll still be blinking as you fall in two. Anything happens to my Bruiser by an outside force or person, and I'll take your head. My Bruiser disappears, and I'll take your head. He stubs his toe and I'll make you pay. Are we clear?"

"Threatening a federal law enforcement officer?"

"Damn skippy."

Rick's face relaxed. Rain dripped from his hair and trickled over his forehead. "I'm sorry I hurt you, Jane. I'm sorry I shamed you. I'm sorry I was such a lousy human being that every single person who matters to me in New Orleans wants to punish or kill me. Including my mom." A smile touched his lips. "She likes you. Still asks after you."

I didn't respond to that one. Rick's parents were amazing. So were his sisters. I had liked them. A lot.

"I was magicked," he said. "Not an excuse. There is no excuse. But you should know. I was spelled a long time ago, a blood spell, through my tattoos, but the working was left unfinished. When the incomplete spell was mixed with two types of were-taint, that messed me up. Bad.

"It took time but I'm free of it now. You and George are safe from me." His smile widened. "But the day you two break up and go your separate ways, I'll be back. Promise. And this time I'll be the one doing the courting."

Rick had told me only part of the real tattoo problem, but I elected not to comment on that now. "Sometimes things die, Ricky-Bo. And they stay dead."

His smile fell away. "Sometimes," he agreed. "Talk business now? And tell your second to put away his blades."

"You know Eli's my second?"

"I know a lot of things."

And I had to wonder how and why. "No. I'm done with you. Eli. Bruiser. Limo." I turned and walked away from Rick, through the rain to the limo and Shemmy and something more to eat. I was starving, and there was a fine tremor running though me. Nerves and not something to do with the new magics pulsing in the shape of a star around me and through me.

In the limo, Bruiser found towels and passed them to us. He handed me a box of energy bars and candy bars and I tore open a Snickers and munched down. Heaven. He had an odd look on his face as I ate. Sorta . . . *bemused* might be the right word. "What?" I asked.

"My Bruiser?" he asked.

I flushed scarlet and wanted to fall through the floor into the weapons container below our feet. "Ummm. He threatened to kill you."

"So you laid claim to me?" His tone was full of peculiar emotions, feelings I couldn't name. Didn't understand. Except that he wasn't teasing me. His eyes were warm, like melted milk chocolate with flecks of hot caramel, but gleamed like brown obsidian, a high sheen.

"Seemed the most"—I hunted for a word—"most expedient way to keep you alive." I resisted squirming in my seat like a four-year-old.

Bruiser's lips softened and parted, his bold, sculpted nose casting a shadow across his face. "Thank you. No woman has ever wanted to protect me."

I frowned and almost said, *No man ever wanted to protect me either*, except that was a lie. Eli protected me. Leo protected me when it suited his course of action and future goals. Alex and the Robere twins. The Mercy Blade a time or two. I met Bruiser's eyes and the smell of Onorio in heat flooded the room.

Beast peeked out, making my eyes glow. *Mate*, she thought.

"Get a room," Eli grunted.

"I intend to. As soon as possible," Bruiser said, his eyes still on me. And my blush, which had cooled, burned even hotter.

Beast might as well have been rolling in catnip, she was so happy.

Eli wasn't the eye-rolling type, but if he had been, now would have been the time. He dragged our attention to business. "Without prior authorization of the governor, Rick is the official who has to authorize Jane's use of force—unless there is a direct threat to the populace, in which case she can act unilaterally."

"Rick?" I said, sitting up in my seat. "Not Soul?"

"Soul isn't here."

"She will be," I said, remembering Opal in stasis in the lightning. That seemed important, but nothing came to mind. "Soon."

"PsyLED has law enforcement control here, even over the feds," Eli said. "This is Rick's show. So keep that in mind."

Bruiser laughed. It wasn't a nice laugh. But Beast liked it even better than the Onorio heat.

"Moving on," Eli said. "Alex uncovered some evidence—other than Grégoire's panicked assertion and the rising of the revenants of their line—that Le Bâtard and Louis Seven are both in town. It's possible that they're in the Roosevelt Hotel in the French Quarter. The tip came from Grégoire's boys just before they disappeared."

Bruiser's eyes sharpened and his entire body came alert, all without moving a muscle. "Disappeared?"

"Brandon and Brian aren't with Grégoire and won't answer calls," Eli said.

"That is very strange. And unexpected," Bruiser said.

"We got pics of this Louis and Bâtard?" I asked.

Bruiser passed me his cell phone. On it was a photograph of a small painted portrait. I studied the likeness of the two men pictured there. One was pretty, with curling brown hair, the other wore a van-dyke beard that accentuated a cruel mouth and hard eyes. "Louis," Bruiser said, gesturing to the pretty one.

I grunted and passed his cell back. Heard the muted click and Shemmy said, "Excuse me, sirs, ma'am. But we have a report of a revenant rising in St. Louis Cemetery Number One. There's already video of skeletal fingers pushing through a mausoleum wall. I'm assuming you want to go there?" Shemmy sounded eager, as if he found all this entertaining as heck. Let him get chewed on by a dog-fanged vamp and see how entertaining it was. I stretched my shoulder, peeved. I liked that word. *Peeved.* It was more refined than saying *pissed.*

"With all speed," Bruiser said, swiping his cell. "It's nearly dusk and we'll have undead Mithrans responding to Le Bâtard's call as well as revenants. This will get messy."

"We need better gear," Eli said.

"Correction, Shemmy," Bruiser said. "To St. Louis One by way of Jane's home, please."

The limo made a quick right turn, throwing me against Bruiser. I stayed there for a moment longer than necessary before sitting up straight. I didn't know about other limos, but Leo's limos didn't have seat belts. When I sat up, I started braiding my hair into a tight-fighting queue.

"That will get *us* gear," Eli said. "What about you?"

"I relayed a message from the Enforcer"—he glanced

down at me—"to have a cyclist meet us at Yellowrock Securities with my gear."

I was responsible for the MOC having motorcycles, all white, all exactly alike. Crotch rockets, fast, responsive, and popular among the blood-servants, especially the younger males, some of whom had been reprimanded for racing in the streets at two a.m. last week. Now they had permission to drive too fast.

"Sure. Whatever. And why are you going at all?" I asked.

Bruiser slouched in his seat, one elbow braced on a seat arm, fingers latched across his middle, legs out and crossed at the ankle. He looked good. More than good. And the way his eyes fastened to me, heated and intense, I'd say he knew it. I had seldom used the word *sexy* in my thoughts about anyone, but oh my God—the man was hot. Freaking. Hot. Sexy didn't even begin to cover it. Or uncover it. A dozen visions of Bruiser naked on my bed or his or in the shower raced through my mind.

"Again—" Eli started.

"We know," I interrupted. "Get a room. You wouldn't be so difficult if you weren't fighting with Sylvia."

"Again. I am not going on a cruise."

I grabbed the strap at the door to keep from being slung across the limo as Shemmy made a fast turn and braked in front of my house. The driver said, "I'll stay right here unless traffic makes me move, in which case I'll circle the block and come back."

"Back up and block the street, emergency blinkers on. I'll text when we're nearly ready," Bruiser said, opening the door. "If there's traffic, they can wait."

"I love my job," Shemmy said.

We got out and ran for the front door, just as a crotch rocket motorcycle roared the wrong way up the street.

Inside, I shut my door and pulled out one of the newest sets of fighting gear sent by Leo. This wasn't as pretty or as expensive as the three sets of fancy leathers he'd sent last time. The pretty ones were for formal occasions, and the one damaged at the witch conclave had been sent off for repair. The new leathers were not showy, but utilitarian; they had a dull finish that didn't catch the light, and they didn't squeak when I wore them. The fancy ones did. Eli was working on fixing that so I didn't embarrass myself at the next official shindig, but for now, I was in matte black.

I drew on Beast-speed, stripped fast, and yanked on the long silk underwear that gave a layer of protection between my skin and the anti-spell silk lining of the leathers. I slid into the pants and zipped the jacket. My leathers, and the straps and buckles that held my fighting gear snug, had been adjusted to me, the fit tight but breathable. They were spelled with anti-spell workings by the witch coven in Seattle, the coven that spelled the government's military armor. My gear had plastic armor inserts at groin, elbows, and knees—the favorite vamp dinner sites—and fine sterling silver mesh between the layers to keep vamps from biting down. I put on my own gorget and leather wristbands.

I weaponed up, threading on the harness designed to carry maximum firepower and blades. If the revenants had started coming out before dusk, I had no idea what might happen after the sun set.

Fun, Beast thought at me.

"Not," I said to her. I added mags loaded with silver ammo in the utility pockets. I zipped them closed and folded over the Velcro pocket tabs to keep them in place.

As I seated the Benelli in its new Kydex holster, my door opened and Bruiser entered, shutting the door behind him. Without looking at me, he dropped a satchel on my bed, dumped out his old Enforcer gear, and stripped. It wasn't pole-dancer erotic, just economical and efficient. Jacket, shirt, shoes, socks, pants, undershirt, folded and placed carefully on the bed. He left his boxer briefs on. The lights and shadows touched his body like living marble, like David under the hands of Michelangelo. *Good lord.*

Chest hair tapered to his waistband. Pecs to die for. A six-pack that needed no makeup or special lighting. Or even posing. Just there.

He bent over the bed and spread out the leathers and weapons. A small birthmark peeked out, high on his inner thigh, shaped like a jagged scar or a bolt of lightning—which was coincidence for sure—so pale it didn't show in most light, and I hadn't noticed until recently. I could see it perfectly just now. I'd bitten that mark the other day. Playfully. Very playfully. Heat zinged through me at the memory.

If I still had my cell I'd have taken a dozen shots as he moved. I might have moaned a little. His lips widened. He knew I was watching. His scent warmed, changing from the citrusy scent of his cologne to the heat of Onorio in a heartbeat, more like caramel and heated brown sugar, with a hint of something spicy. He looked up at me, his eyes nearly closed, as if he too was thinking about that last time we were able to take off a day and play.

Mate, Beast purred.

"Oh yeah. Definitely," I said aloud.

Bruiser slid into the leather pants, his looser on his frame than mine on me, his pockets bulging with gear. He didn't zip up, his leathers open hanging on his hips, his black boxer briefs perfectly exposed and uh, bulging with gear of a completely different sort. He stood, his jacket held by one finger, his chest bare, and slanted a look at me. "You're not making this any easier."

"Huh? Oh."

"We could just stay here and let the security team handle the twice-risen undead."

"We could. Probably should," I agreed, still staring. His muscles had been sculpted by fighting and a judicious lifting of weights. His body was beautiful, not something I had realized the first time I met him. I'd just thought he was a blood-meal and sex partner to Leo who also was Leo's knee-capping muscle.

Thanks to vamp blood he was scar-free, except for two very pale bullet scars on his chest. I was pretty sure he should have died from them, but drinking vamp blood has its perks.

"If you keep looking at me like that I'll never get my leathers on."

I flashed him a cheeky grin, walked to the door, and opened it a crack. Blocked the view both ways with my body. Over my shoulder I said, "Pretty sure you need a cold shower to get the pants zipped now." I slipped out, hearing his chuckle. "Showoff," I said through the door.

"Ready?" Eli asked.

He was decked out in leathers too, despite the fact that

when we first met he had declared he'd never wear them. Once he'd seen how well mine protected me from injury, he had changed his mind. I had picked up my stakes on the way out and stuck silver ones in my fighting queue.

Outside a car flashed its lights. The limo, idling. A horn blew from down the street. Then two more. Then longer and more strident.

My door opened and Bruiser walked out, his boots silent on the wood flooring. He crossed the space to me, encircled my waist with one arm, and yanked me to him. He kissed me. Hard. Demanding. Plundering. He bent me back. A tango dance move that put all the important parts in very, very close proximity. Heat blossomed through me like bombs going off. And I had no doubt that if we didn't have an emergency, we'd be in my bed right now.

I gripped his shoulders and kissed him back. And again my throat made that sound, that almost-moan that I couldn't keep silent.

Bruiser broke away but held me bent over, all my weight on his one arm. "I know," he said to the others, his eyes spearing me. "Get a room." He whirled me upright and opened the door. Strode out into the dark and the rain. Eli cursed and followed.

I followed too, but quite happily. Now I knew what other women meant when they said a kiss left them floating. I was sure my boot soles were landing about six inches off the ground. I slid inside the limo, the door closed, and Shemmy sped off, me holding on to the emergency strap.

We reached St. Louis Cemetery Number One just as darkest night fell and the heavens opened up again. We got out at the corner of St. Louis and Basin Streets and raced to the nearest entrance. The deluge was stunning, the water beating down on us heavy and pounding. It already stood an inch on the sidewalks, falling too fast to run off.

Metal screeched and clanged—old iron being wrenched and torn. A gate flew at us and we all ducked. The revenant walked out of the entrance, holding something. A human leg, which he lifted and started eating. Lightning flashed and boomed, close by, thunder rolling. But my energies

stayed put, stable. Beast shoved her way to the forefront of
my brain, her vision turning the world silver and gray and
sharp green.

Bruiser pulled his sword and took off the revenant's head
in one clean sweep. He was good. He had been Leo's Enforcer once and he had over a hundred years to master *La
Destreza*. The revenant fell and Bruiser kicked the parts in
different directions, striding into the unlit cemetery. I didn't
know if it was always unlighted or if the storm had put the
electricity out in a different part of the city. But watching
him move through the rain in wet-streaked leathers was an
erotic exercise all on its own. *Holy crap*.

St. Louis Cemetery was the oldest in New Orleans, containing the first bodies laid to rest in the 1700s, all
aboveground. Statues adorned many of the mausoleums.
Angels and crosses were everywhere. Stone children. The
savior with arms outstretched, Jesus on the cross, the statue
defaced, his legs broken off. Iron gates keeping back the
riffraff from the tombs of the wealthy, vault doors bricked
and cemented over. Carrara marble. Plaster. One tomb
painted blue. Xs in red paint on others.

Red flowers spun into the air, lifted by a sudden wind,
and then were knocked to the ground. It was gusting and
frigid, forcing the rain beneath my collar to stream down
my spine. Palm trees lashed the night, branches flying.

The voodoo priestess Marie Laveau was reputed to be
buried in the cemetery, but really, who would know if she
had even died. I had never asked if she had been turned,
taken another name, and lived as a vamp today. It was possible.

Over the smell of the rain, I caught the scent of fresh
human blood and bowels released. Vomit and urine. The
sharp tang of fear and despair. And the older stink of revenant. I pulled my vamp-killers, turning my head at each
small space between mausoleums, waiting for attack.

Bruiser turned down an . . . aisle? Walkway? Eli and I
followed. And we found them. Beer bottles were everywhere. A lantern that could survive the deluge cast soft
light. Illuminating three revenants, feasting on humans. At

least two victims, by the number of heads, but there were five legs, so that was wasn't anything to go on.

They looked up at our appearance, dropped dinner, and dove at us. These had feasted well and they were fast, nearly as fast as a normal fanghead. I whipped the vamp-killers in a scissors move and took out the one near me, cutting her in two. Bruiser took out the man with a clean beheading. The first two crumpled, dead again.

Eli hesitated as a child dove at him. Fangs flashing. Eyes empty and wild. A child vamp. She couldn't have been more than twelve. He hesitated. Bruiser stepped in and took her head.

The act was necessary. Completely essential. Yet the ease with which Bruiser moved shocked me. There was no hesitation. Just a fluidity of motion that was like death on the wing.

Eli's mouth opened as the child's head flew and spun into a puddle. He got a strange look on his face, as if he'd seen a ghost. Or was reliving something from his past. Yes. That. He stood, there, frozen, weapons down. Vulnerable. I knew, through personal experience, that being taken to water this morning had brought him closer to his past, his memories, his own private hells, the ones he'd lived through courtesy of Uncle Sam. And they had risen up and attacked him all at once.

Bruiser gripped his own bloodied blades in one large fist and grabbed Eli's jacket. Rain slicked his face as he shouted over the downpour, "Not a child. She looked like a child, but she wasn't. Her name was Joan Bennett and she stood only four feet nine. She was staked and beheaded in nineteen forty-three for killing two humans." He shook Eli. "Not. A. Child."

Eli focused on Bruiser. Took Bruiser's hand in his and pushed it away. But he wasn't back yet. He was somewhere else, someone else. Emotions locked down. Feeling nothing. Remembering everything. It was the first time I'd seen evidence of the PTSD symptoms that probably helped end his career in the Rangers. I didn't know what to do to help.

"She had her head back," I said to Bruiser over the downpour.

"All of them do, and all were beheaded at their deaths," Bruiser said, his tone grim. "We have to—"

A gust of icy wind blew the lantern over with a clatter. Battered us. Sudden dark enveloped us and I pulled hard on Beast's night vision. Inside me she growled low. I stumbled against the wind, a howling banshee, and regained my footing. The rain, which had come in waves all day, again pounded down so hard it threw up a white mist as the droplets shattered on impact.

Over it were strange scraping sounds, like flesh against stone. Revenants poured out of the cracks and crannies and rushed down the walkways. Blind eyes zeroed in on us. Seven revs. Bruiser stepped close, placing Eli between us, his back to me. I turned and faced away too, my partner in a safe place until he got his head together. Revs weren't built for wind. Three slipped and I dispatched two of them. Bruiser took a third one.

They were on us. I stabbed and cut, but they were too close. I tried to pull on the Gray Between, but I couldn't find it, the place I reached for inside myself empty. And for the first time today, there was no lightning. No way to take them down from outside of time. I stabbed and cut, stabbed and cut. It wasn't enough.

One latched on to my elbow, getting a mouthful of armor and silver. She wasn't deterred. Her mouth smoked. The stink of burning vamp rose against the beating rain. I dropped my longer blades and drew the short ones. Stabbing, aiming at heads, cutting across eyes. The female on my elbow pulled me down. I landed on one knee, feeling something wrench. This was going to end badly unless Eli got himself together. Beast screamed in rage, the sound tearing my throat.

I smelled Edmund.

CHAPTER 10

Their Heads Should Loll Over and Bounce as They Walk

Long blades flashed. Edmund took down three vamps, moving so fast and lithe it was like watching water slide down a rock face. Bruiser matched his stance to Edmund's and suddenly the revs were all down. We were standing in ankle-deep water and vamp entrails and remarkably little blood.

Edmund turned to me. "You will never leave me out of a fight, mistress. Do you understand?"

"You were hurt. You nearly died, you idiot."

"I am well."

"Yeah." I raised my voice over an icy gust of wind that whistled through the mausoleums. "Who attacked you?"

Ed's face twisted in something that might have been self-anger. Or indigestion. The words seemed to drag out of him when he said, "I do not know. I did not know the scent of their blood. I did not see their faces."

Lightning struck, hitting close by. The light was shocking, brightening the entire St. Louis Cemetery Number One. The water around us carried the electric charge, zinging up our bodies. Finally, if a little late to help in the fight, I bubbled out of time. The female vamp's head was still attached to my arm, and so I used the blade of the knife and worked it between her jaws. She had been a freshly turned vamp before she died the second time, and her four small fangs hadn't penetrated the leathers, the silver, or the plastered interior armor. The jaws finally released and the head fell away from my shoulder and the bubble of time. Then it just hung there.

Beast sent me a memory of a dog she had seen once. The reddish dog had a half-rotted rabbit in its locked jaws, foam and spittle all over the rabbit. The dog was moving in faltering circles. Rabid and dying. Beast had hated the smell and had moved far away and out of the dog's territory. I sniffed. That smell wasn't present here, so that was one good thing.

I worked my elbow joint as I made sure all the vamps were separated from their heads. Eli was still staring around, his eyes not seeing, his face slack, but he was uninjured. Satisfied, I knelt down to study a vamp and head, lit by the lightning, caught in stasis. The cut that separated the head from its shoulders was clean, but above it, closer to the jawline, was a fine line, reddish and jagged. I realized that I was seeing a line of very, very fine stitches, the tiny circled and knotted ones made by a plastic surgeon. The head had been removed to bring about a second death, then reattached postmortem. For burial? That made sense. A vamp mortician had made her pretty for a coffin viewing. I hadn't been to a vamp funeral. Maybe I should have. Because now I knew that some vamps buried with the head reattached could get up and move again.

I moved through the nonfalling rain, from head to head, checking, and all had the dog fangs and the stitching. I figured all the previous revenants had it too, but the thread was so fine I hadn't noticed. So either there was something different about the dog-fanged vamps themselves that allowed them to rise for a second undeath, or there was something unique about the reattachment that allowed the head and neck to regrow together in the coffin. I needed to talk to someone who knew about vamp funerals.

I stood and checked out Eli, who was in the act of blinking against the rain. I thought that might be a good thing. The experience had thrown him into a stasis of his own, one probably from the Middle East, not a place associated with rain. The weather might bring him out of it.

Edmund was looking where I had been standing, and he was royally ticked off. Bruiser had a different look about him. It was protective. Which was just so sweet. I looked up into the storm and the lightning.

Three *arcenciels* were right there, in full dragon form with dragon heads, not the human-shaped heads they were capable of presenting. Wings out, hovering above me, a couple hundred feet high, hanging in the air. Soul and Opal were beautiful and feral in their rainbow dragon forms— pure magic that humans had not been able to see. Soul was staring where I had stood, and I was pretty sure she was saying something to me. I returned to my original spot and waited until the Gray Between let me go.

It juddered and shuddered and snapped back into time. Darkness and the storm dropped over me, blinding, the torrent sounding like a jet engine. Soul dropped down to within inches of my face, glowing with rainbow lights. "Someone rides the dragon," she hissed, her lips moving over her blade-like pearled teeth. "Close. That one seeks to cage us. Our sister must be set free."

Beast was close to the surface and narrowed my eyes on Soul, adoringly. *Littermate*, she thought at me. *Littermate and not littermate.*

Which made no sense. Beast was working through something.

I might have blinked, because Soul was gone. After the nonminutes in the bright light of the lightning I had lost my night vision. "Jane?" Edmund queried, spinning in the rain to find me.

Eli rammed into Edmund and the two fell, rolling in the puddled rain, wrestling. Edmund taking a flurry of blows. Grunts and cursing. Far too much violence for whatever had happened between them to spark this. I wondered if the magic in the storm was causing their aggression, and the riots in the city too. I drew on Beast-strength and waded in. Grabbed an arm of each and spun them around, throwing them both flat into the puddles.

"Stop it right now!" I yelled. Both men froze, bodies on

the ground, eyes moving to me, to each other, and away. "Get up and act like you have some sense. The storm is making people—men in particular—violent and aggressive. Maybe it's calling the revs and having the same effect on them. Whatever it is, we have to stop it, not fight each other. You idiots!"

I looked up and caught a glimpse of *arcenciels* dancing in the storm. I slashed rain out of my face. I was wet to the skin, the silk underwear clinging to me.

"We should leave and call the police," Bruiser said. "This is an active crime scene. And it's possible that PsyLED will have some idea about why the revenants are rising."

"Sure. Whatever." I was still ticked off at Ricky-Bo. Including him or his agency in anything I did was galling. Not so long ago, PsyLED hadn't existed and vamp physiology was unstudied and unknown to the medical and forensic communities. Now, thanks to a certain fight in Natchez, where my team took down over two dozen vamps, the feds had vamp bodies to study. They probably had lots of knowledge by now. Thanks to me. Thanks to Rick.

I found and put away my weapons, still wet and gooey, because I had no choice, and led the way out of the cemetery. The entrance of the cemetery was blocked by cop cars. Standing in the rain, beneath an umbrella that was being buffeted by the decreasing wind, was Rick LaFleur. I walked past as if I hadn't seen him. Bruiser stopped to talk. *Men.* The rest of us got in the limo and Shemmy lowered the privacy wall to toss us towels.

"Ms. Yellowrock," Shemmy said, excitement high in his voice, "Derek and a small team have gone to the Roosevelt to search for an unknown vamp."

"Mith—" I stopped. Why should I care how the fangheads wanted to be called. "Go on. They're heading to search the Roosevelt," which was a five-star hotel in the French Quarter.

"Their party includes vamps to create access via mesmerizing. That's it. Except that Mr. Pellissier sent a new cell for you. Same number, everything up until three hours prior to you losing yours has been restored." He tossed a new matteblack cell at me, and I caught it out of the air. Like the old one, it had an armored case and was a cell that Leo could track. I flipped it open and scrolled around. Apparently someone had downloaded and backed up all the content from my previous cell every few hours and then downloaded it onto this one already. How kind. Not. Sneaky li'l bastard going through my private info. Rage thrummed through me.

Beast pressed a paw on my mind and extended her claws, pressing down. Clearing my mind. I had always known that Leo had total access to my official cell, the very reason I carried a throwaway, a burner phone, for private convos. So why my anger? The storm was affecting me too. "Just ducky," I muttered.

"What, mistress?" Edmund asked.

"Stop calling me that."

"Yes, mistress." I could have sworn he was smirking, but there was nothing of that on his face.

I sighed and followed Edmund's lead, drying myself off with the big fluffy towels. Fangheads have the best stuff. Top quality all the way. The stink of wet leather and gun oil and New Orleans wet was potent in the car. I also smelled fresh tea and followed my nose to a paper cup of coffee-house chai latte in a cup holder. I thought I loved Shemmy. I took it and drank. Heaven in a cup.

Eli, however, just sat, his face scrunched into lines, his hands gripping his weapons, too tight, skin white. I pressed the towel over my head, squeezing the water from my queued hair. From behind the towel I asked Ed, "So you're my primo?"

"Yes, m— Yes."

"So if you know something, and I need to know it, you'll tell me." Edmund didn't reply and I dropped the towel to settle a mean little smile on him. "Yes or no, primo?"

"If I can answer, I shall," he said carefully. Which meant that he might know stuff he had sworn to keep secret.

Vamps always had secrets. But this should be common vamp knowledge. "Are vamps always beheaded after they die a second time?"

"If their master is not able to revive them, yes. No Mithran wants to return as a revenant."

"And then their heads are reattached for the grave."

"Yes. For the services." I saw enlightenment dawn in his

eyes. "But their spines and tendons are not reattached. It's cosmetic only."

"So properly interred vamps shouldn't be able to rise from the grave, heads in place. Their heads should loll over and bounce as they walk."

"No. They should not be able to rise at all." Edmund looked troubled. He oughta.

"But the dog-fanged vamps are rising, walking, seeing, eating, and drinking. Making either the vamps themselves different or the method in which they were prepared for the grave different. Who are the vamp morticians?"

"Mateo and Laurie Caruso," Edmund said, "of Caruso Family Funeral Services. For the last two hundred years and more." He sounded unhappy about it. I had to wonder why.

"Vamps?"

"Yes."

I thought about his tone and the unhappy look on his face. "Mateo and Laurie Caruso. Do they have dog fangs?"

"Yes." He looked utterly saddened at speaking the word. The kind of sad that spoke of a personal history, one filled with heartbreak.

"You and Laurie. You used to have a thing, didn't you."

"If by 'have a thing,' you mean did we have a romantic relationship once upon a time, yes. We were . . . close."

Bruiser got in the limo and began to wipe off on the fluffy towels. The storm had lessened again, and beyond the patting sounds of Bruiser's towel, I heard nothing. "Shemmy," I said, "take us to Caruso Family Funeral Services."

Bruiser stopped patting and looked at me, then at Ed. Comprehension dawned in his eyes. "Oh. Bouvier clan."

Just in case he wasn't on our page, I said, "Dog fangs. All the risen revs had them. Heads, mouths, eyes, ears, legs, arms, everything works and nothing should work at all."

"Yes." The limo pulled away as Bruiser retrieved a small cell from a pocket of the limo and punched in a number. When Scrappy answered, he said, "Tell the Master of the City that his faithful Enforcer and his faithful Onorio are en route to Caruso Family Funeral Services." He listened a moment, said, "Thank you," and disconnected.

"Faithful?" I asked.

"There is only one funeral home in the city for Mithrans. If we have to kill the Carusos, I wanted to remind Leo that we do so while still being loyal to him."

"Why?"

"Mithran funerals and burials are very circumscribed, sacred, and private affairs," Bruiser said. "Almost holy. Without the Caruso family, there will be no one to provide the correct interment procedures for the city's undead. Things will become difficult."

"Uh-huh. Okay. I'll keep them alive if possible. But if they're raising the revenants or helping the people who are, then they go down. Unless I can use them."

"Understood," Bruiser said. Then he did a strange thing. He turned off his cell before gesturing that we all do likewise. We all did and then held the cells tightly beneath an armpit to muffle any remaining mic. "One thing you should know," he said. "Leo's eyes among the Europeans has not always been reliable."

Leo's eyes refereed to Leo's Madam Spy. That she had not always been reliable suggested that she was either easily confused or a turncoat, a double agent, spying for Leo and giving intel to both sides. That sucked. And that was possibly deadly. I nodded and we all turned on our cells. I quickly texted Alex to find and turn off the security system at the funeral home. This was Enforcer business, not cop business. And if the morticians were EV spies, planted here a couple of centuries ago, then we needed to keep the Eurotrash from discovering that we were onto them.

Eli shook himself. Blinked. Looked around the limo until his gaze settled on Bruiser. "You killed a little girl?"

Bruiser repeated his previous statements, nearly word for word, his tone careful, his eyes on Eli's hands, close to his weapons. "Her name was Joan Bennett. She stood four feet nine, and she looked like a child. She was staked and beheaded in nineteen forty-three for killing two of her human servants. Not a child. But you were seeing a child."

Eli frowned, his eyes staring into a past only he could see. "A little girl blew herself up. Killed three of my men. Nearly killed me. She was maybe ten." His eyes filled with tears and he blinked against them. "I saw her coming. There was nothing to suggest that she was a danger, but . . . I knew it. Somehow. And I didn't take her down. I just watched her walk up to us and . . . If I'd just shot her, my men would have lived." Eli's expression didn't change. His hands clenched and then released. Rain dripped off his fingertips. "I couldn't do it. I knew what she was going to do and I couldn't . . . couldn't do it. I just stood there." A single tear gathered and fell, trickling down his rain-slicked face. And still his expression was stone.

We all sat as he cried, silent, terrible tears. I wanted to take Eli's hand, give him a hug, but I didn't know how. The limo took corners carefully, Shemmy as involved in the pain as we all were. Outside, muted thunder rumbled. My magics stayed silent, contained.

Edmund slid across the seat to him and took up a towel. Silent as well, he dried off Eli, starting with Eli's head, which he pressed like a benediction. Eli's neck, shoulders, and arms. He dried Eli's torso and slid to the floor to dry Eli's legs and behind his knees. Down to his feet. From the floor, without looking up at Eli, Edmund said softly, "There is no going back. There is no revival of our humans. There is no erasure of our horrors. No healing except of time and she is a vengeful mistress, leaving scars that are forever. But there also is no proof of foreknowledge, only of twenty-twenty hindsight. You guessed. You did not know. Knowing is only for God." Edmund lifted and dried Eli's hands. He said, "Your hands are clean. Not stained with blood. You need not carry the blood of your men. Only their memories."

Eli took a breath that quaked in a sob.

Edmund returned to the seat, next to my partner, his nearness a comfort if Eli wanted it. After that we rode in silence.

We pulled through Faubourg Marigny, a mostly residential area of the city, and Shemmy pointed out our destination as we rode by, a street-side recon. "You want the double-gallery house with the star jasmine blooming out front."

It was the wrong season and too cold for jasmine to be blooming. The temps at freezing should have killed the flowers, even if the plant itself survived. A sense of unease slid across me. There were few two-story buildings in the nearby blocks, and the brick building housing Caruso Family Funeral Services stood out as different, even though it didn't have a sign advertising its services. Like most vamp businesses, it didn't publicize.

I said softly to Edmund, "Vamp funerals and the vamp mortician or morticians who reattached the heads of the dog-fanged vamps. I want to know everything."

"Clan Bouvier began a climb to power as lesser Mithrans who provided services to and for other, more powerful Mithrans. They cared for scions in lairs, they cared for sick human servants who contracted diseases not eased by their master's blood, they helped to care for and educate children of the body."

Vamps sometimes were able to have children of their own bodies, though that was uncommon and I had no idea why. But such children were rare and cosseted and adored. I had killed the creature masquerading as Immanuel, Leo's "child of his body." Losing the person he had thought was his son had driven Leo nearly to madness. It was a miracle he hadn't killed me.

And then it hit me. "Did they care for Immanuel when he was a child?"

Edmund hissed, putting the death of Leo's supposed son together with the Europeans. "Yesssss . . ."

The long view. A plan in place for decades. Perhaps for centuries. And then I come along and kill the pretender and set everything awry, force a new plan into motion. "Go on," I said. Beyond the armored windows, thunder rumbled. The tires sprayed water in the streets up under the floor of the limo as we circled the block, and I could feel the vibration through my boots.

"Bouvier took as blood-servants human doctors and nurses and the mortician family, and they turned those who were most loyal. They chose bankers as scions. They made friends among the powerful humans in the city, the politicians, the movers and shakers as they were called. Bouvier did favors. They recruited among these powerful humans for the useful and capable and not simply the beautiful. They also served Mithrans faithfully. Which meant they learned secrets from the Mithrans they attended and from the humans they turned. They grew covertly powerful. And because I believe that I know what information you seek, I will add, the Bouvier clan were allied with the Damours. The clan and blood family shared blood. Fostered scions. They were close."

I put together what I knew and was beginning to guess. "And Bouvier's attachment to Bethany Salazar y Medina, the outclan priestess? Was she part of their little clique?"

Edmund shifted a puzzled gaze to me. "From time to time, I do believe that she associated with them, though to say she was allied would be incorrect. Outclan priestesses do not align with either clan or blood-family. Why do you ask?"

"Bouvier appears in a mural on the wall in Grégoire's house. He had someone I believe was a Cherokee skinwalker on his arm, a skinwalker like me, named Ka Nvista." But she had smelled like flowers. That was what I'd been told. My own scent smelled of predator and aggression to strange vamps. They hated my scent until a stronger vamp accepted me, and then they settled. No one who had met and smelled the scent of Ka Nvista and then smelled my scent had ever put us together as similar creatures. "I don't know, but there's something there. Some connection. Bethany had my blood in a healing just after I arrived in the city. I believe that she knew what I was."

"We've circled the block, Ms. Yellowrock," Shemmy said, again pulling past the brick building. "Everything looks okay. I'm parked three houses down. It looks as if the power is out along part of the street."

I pulled my blades and cleaned them on the damp towels. The sterling gleamed in the darkness. "You all coming?" I asked the group, keeping my voice casual. They all said yes, even Eli. I shot a glance at Edmund, who gave a minuscule nod. He would watch over Eli. My vamp primo would watch over my human second and business partner. My life was so weird I scarcely recognized it.

I opened the limo door and got out, into the storm. As I bent forward, rain blasted down my jacket neck, icy and miserable. I now officially hated rain. But I marched through six inches of running water to the two-story house.

I had learned a lot about New Orleans architecture listening to the boys talk, and a double-gallery house meant that the front façade was composed of stacked front porches with a flat roof over the second-story porch, columns, and a low-pitched roof over the rest. Two windows, sometimes three, like here, and entry doors were traditionally on the right.

I stepped to the sidewalk and through the small gate, across the porch. I banged once on the door and would have banged more but it opened with a creepy movie squeal of unoiled hinges. Moving fast, I slid into the darker shadows to the left of the door. Bruiser took right, along the wall, and crossed the room. He had a sidearm in a two-hand grip at his thigh, visible as a darker image than Beast's vision of Bruiser himself, who was lit up in greens and bright silvers, leaving wet splats across the wood floors, beading on the rich Persian carpet. Edmund entered and moved straight across the room, vamp-fast, with a little pop of sound, to the far wall. He carried blades and I'd seen him fight. He was a way better swordsman than me, so I put mine back and readied a .380. I'd rather have a larger caliber, but I might shoot a human by accident. Smaller rounds meant decreased killing capacity.

I moved, stance balanced, deeper into the small front room. Eli took my place. The only truly human among us, and without low-light goggles, he stood just inside the door, guarding our exit. Caruso Family Funeral Services was unlit, and it smelled odd. Vamp lairs and residences usually smelled of a strange mixture of blood and sex and herbs, but this one smelled of other scents. Dead lilies. Dead something else.

Dead mice. Dead baby birds in hot summer, rotting in nests, when there has been no rain, Beast thought at me.

I didn't ask how she knew that. We moved on, through the business, into the hallway, past offices, empty according to the scents. Bruiser cleared the first room; I cleared the second. The third room took up most of the breadth of the house, a large viewing room, currently empty except for side chairs along the walls. The next room was a carbon copy of the former. The smells grew stronger, coming from the back room, and Edmund was standing to the side of its door.

"Locked," he said softly, too softly to be heard by human

ears. "Steel bolted at top and bottom. Steel casing. There will be no taking it down, short of explosives."

Coms had been left behind. I moved through the dark, back to Eli. "We have a secure door," I murmured to him. "Steel core in steel frame. Those bolt locks that go into the framing."

"I'll handle it," he murmured back.

I turned and he stopped me with a raised hand. "I'm sorry," he said.

"For what?" I was honestly curious and maybe he heard that in my voice, because his scent changed, flooding with pheromones of relief.

"Babe." He shook his head. It was man talk for so much more than just *Babe.*

"Dude. Yada yada. We good?"

He chuckled. "We're good." He holstered his weapon and started digging in his pockets as he followed me down the hallway. "Did Alex get the system shut down?

"I texted him and I don't hear sirens, so I'm guessing so."

Eli knelt at the door and pulled a mini flash, one so bright it hurt and I had to look away. "I don't have goggles. Back away to preserve your vision," he said to us. To me he added, "Text Alex. Tell him what's going on."

I backed to the far end of the hallway where I could cover the entrances and the offices. No one was there, but we had once seen a small room with a witch circle drawn on the floor that allowed mutated vamps to transport in, just like in *Star Trek,* but without the crazy lights or sound, or Spock or Scotty at the controls. That was in Natchez too, and though this situation was nothing like the one there, something, probably the magic output here, kept reminding me of it.

I texted Alex again and got a text in reply: *Security off. Pulled latest building plans. Retrofitted with electronic hurricane and vamp shutters. Walls insulated and soundproofed in 2009 with gel-foam liquid.*

I typed back, *K.*

Got a note in reply. *Get the dog-stinking-werewolf out of the house!!!!!!* which made me snort out a laugh. Brute had a coat like the offspring of a Brillo pad and a long-haired sheep. When he got wet, he stank, and New Orleans weather meant he stank pretty often. That would get better if I'd bathe him. And Alex would complain less when I got him a mattress of his own. I made myself a note to stop by Walmart and see about a mattress. And a plastic covering like they used in nurseries and nursing homes to protect it from wet and smell. And a bleachable mattress covering. I never wanted a pet and here I had a full-time werewolf and a part-time grindylow. Again with the weird life.

Eli was still busy, and I had my cell out, so I checked my business e-mail. I hadn't done that in a while and I had offers for two jobs back near Asheville. With an unexpected ache, the mountains in winter called to me. I had a sudden vision of a snow-covered chasm as viewed from some tall, bare-branched tree. The smell of the air was clean and sharp and frozen. Below me, a deer picked his way through the snow. Beast's vision. Beast's memory.

I closed the Kevlar cover and stuck the cell in my driest pocket. Maybe I needed to invest in a special dry-pocket something or other. I needed to do more research. There were advantages to being Leo's Enforcer, and the pretty, pretty toys and gear were part of that.

"Fire in the hole," Eli said, racing into the office near me, pulling me in after him. I got a glimpse as the others ducked into rooms too.

The *whump* was more muffled than I expected, shrapnel flying down the hallway, ricocheting off the walls. The freed door whammed against the wall. Soft light, like candlelight, brightened the hallway. The cloud of plastic explosive and detonator blew through the air, an acerbic scent that curled under my tongue and filled my mouth with bitterness. Behind it came the smell of the locked room. Dead things. Dead vamp blood, old and new.

Eli was just behind Edmund into the room. I moved slower. Holstered my weapons. According to the poster-board-sized note propped on one of two white enamel embalming tables, the Caruso family was long gone. It said, *The Caruso family has returned to Europe. Please inform the Master of the City that we are no longer his to rule. Laurie Caruso.*

"They knew we were on the way," Bruiser said.

"There's dust on the floor and evenly on the poster," Eli said, bending over the paper. "They've been gone a while."

I looked up at the dim lights. Some kind of battery back-ups. And a great idea. We needed that in our house. "Ten bucks says they left when the ghost ship entered U.S. territory, whenever that was," I said.

"Ghost ship?" Edmund asked coldly but politely, his tone telling me that I wasn't keeping him in the loop.

"You were asleep," I said, resting my forearms on my weapons. I walked through the room, my wet clothing depositing drops here and there. I explained about the spelled ship in Lake Borgne as Eli checked for booby traps in cabinet doors and the body refrigerators along one wall. I found a bright yellow door marked with a red diamond-shaped fire hazard sticker. Eli cleared it and I went in.

The room was really a closet, metal walls, metal shelves, a sprinkler overhead, battery backup lighting. On the shelves inside the metal room were metal cans of chemicals: formaldehyde HCHO of various indexes—whatever that meant—formalin, something called pro-line primer, pre-injection and drainage fluid, things I felt were pretty normal for human embalming and should be pretty much the same for vamps. There were boxes of lye and an arsenic container. Arsenic hadn't been used in human burial since the early twentieth century. I spotted a small refrigerator-freezer at the back, the kind advertised for dorms and small break rooms. There had been a larger refrigerator in the main room. I had to wonder why there was a tiny one in the fire closet. I squatted and studied the fridge.

"Babe?"

"Take a look at this. Think it's booby-trapped?"

I moved back and Eli lay on the slightly dusty floor, his little mini flash checking out the rubber seals and the back. "Good place for a bomb," Eli said as he worked. "Flammable chemicals everywhere. Contained space is good for creating a high aerosol concentration of said chemicals." He rolled to his feet, back to the calm and fit Ranger I remembered. "I can't see anything, but that's not to say there isn't a device on the inside, triggered upon opening. I suggest we leave it alone. If Leo wants it open he can get NOPD's bomb squad in here."

"Works for me," I said, backing away and closing the door behind us.

In the main room, Edmund was studying the contents of a cabinet. It was full of supplies in small boxes. Musingly, he said, "The heads of the revenants were reattached with a pale pink silk. The traditional line for Mithran head re-attachment is braided silk, a white or pale gray line." He took a pink box from the shelf and removed a spool of silk. "This is what the Carusos must have used on the revenants. It's pink and it feels"—he made a face as if something tasted bad—"odd to the touch."

I took the spool of pink thread from Edmund's hand and studied it. Outside, lightning bracketed the windows with brilliant light. The thread sparked. Hot, potent magic pulsed into my fingertips and I dropped the spool. "Holy crap on a cracker." I shook my fingers and stuck them in my mouth. "I'm burned," I said around the fingers. "Blistered."

"Whatever is calling the revenants awake is tied to the thread they were preserved with," Edmund said. "Interesting."

Eli had checked out the big fridge-freezer and tied a long cord around the handles. He said, "Everyone out so we can open this." We all moved out of the room for the opening, and with us all standing behind the now-broken door frame, Eli yanked on the cords. Without explosion or fanfare, the doors opened and bright appliance light spilled into the room along with refrigerated air. Overhead, the lights came back on, and I squinted at the glare. "Clear," Eli said, coiling the cord and sticking it back in his pocket.

There were more fluids inside, and I pulled the cold bottles out, silently reading labels, putting them back. Only one bottle was unlabeled, a brown glass bottle in the door. It was sealed with a cork, which I eased out, like I'd seen Leo do a champagne cork. Decorking seemed to be a guy job, among humans, vamps, and Onorios, like taking out the trash, or hammering nails in boards. Not that I couldn't do trash and nails. I totally could. But they felt it was a man's job. Cleaning their own toilets, that they were less receptive to. I eased the cork back and forth until it slipped free. The stink of vamp blood filled the room.

Edmund whirled to me. His shoulders hunched, fangs slowly *schnicked* down on their little hinges. "Edmund?" I asked. His eyes bled scarlet and his pupils dilated. He was vamping out. This was not good. I had a feeling it was bad form to kill your primo on the first full day of business. I pushed the cork back into the bottle. Took a vamp-killer by the grip. "I will end you," I said.

"And I'll fill you full of silver, bro," Eli said. He had two handguns aimed at Edmund's back. I stepped to my right and out of his angle of shot. "You already got silvered up this week. Twice could finish you."

Bruiser said, softly, "Jane, call him."

"Do what?"

"You shared blood. Call him. Someone else is trying to influence him, someone he once trusted and with whom he shared blood. Only a stronger master can ease him from this path."

"Not sure how to do that."

"He's fighting the call. Give him something else to think about."

"Beast wants to hunt cows from inside your fancy car," I said instantly. "With the top down and Eli driving around a muddy field. You don't calm down, I'm taking her hunting." I leaned closer and grinned, showing teeth. "She'll claw up your leather upholstery. Maybe scent-mark your carpet."

Inside me Beast perked up. *Hunt cow? In Edmund car with no head?* Which I figured was her way saying with the top down.

"Yes," I replied to her aloud. "With the top down and a mountain lion in the passenger seat. She'll pull a dead cow into the car and feast on it. Entrails everywhere. It'll be a bloodbath."

Edmund swallowed. His lids closed and stayed that way for three seconds. Opened. "You wouldn't."

"Oh, yes I would. She wants your car. *Bad*. And she wants to drag a full-grown cow into the seat and sit there, looking out over a pasture while she eats it."

Beast will hunt cow! In Edmund car!

Ed's eyes started bleeding back to human-ish. His fangs folded back on their little hinges with a snap. "My car is a Thunderbird Maserati 150 GT. It is a 1957 prototype for which I paid over three million dollars. One does not hunt in a Maserati GT. One does not—"

"If I have to kill you, the car is mine," I interrupted.

"I—" He stopped. Focused on me. "What happened?"

"I opened this." I held out the brown bottle. "And you decided to hunt *me*. Then there's the storm. I'm guessing some combo of the two?"

Edmund accepted the sealed bottle and brought it close to his nose. He took a tiny sniff. With a pop of displaced air he was gone. I caught the bottle before it hit the floor. "We'll take this to Leo," I said to Bruiser.

"Indeed."

I frowned. *Indeed* was a Leo word. Formal and . . . Leo-ishy. This place and this bottle were having an effect on my people.

I tucked the bottle under my arm and said, "Let's go to HQ."

Fortunately, Edmund was sitting in the limo when we got there, staring out the far window at the storm. I gave the bottle to Shemmy and had him raise the privacy panel. "To keep the smell away from our fanghead."

I got the feeling that Shemmy was disappointed, that he liked being part of the action, but he complied, opening the communication channel instead.

"Don't pout, Eddie," I said, crawling in to sit beside the vamp.

His head turned to me in one of those inhuman gestures they can do. "I am not pouting," he said distinctly. "Pouting is for children. And my name. Is. Not. Eddie."

"Good to know. HQ, James," I instructed.

"My name isn't James," Shemmy said, helpfully.

"Picky, picky, picky," I said.

CHAPTER 11

Đid You Know You're Being Tailed by PsyLEĐ?

On the way to HQ, we got notice from Scrappy, Leo's secretary, that a small cruise ship was trying to dock and that all sorts of local, state, and federal officials were on site. Leo wanted us to check it out. Of course he did, in a rainstorm that was getting, if possible, worse. This night, like the previous one, was never-ending, and I'd had only a half hour nap, at best.

By the time we made the necessary blocks and avoided one-way streets and congestion caused by the storm, the ship was motoring back down the Mississippi for international waters. I got a quick look at the boat, hoping I could tell if it was the invisible ship in Lake Borgne, but I couldn't tell diddly. I watched the byplay of the multiagency law enforcement and government people standing and gesturing in the rain.

Bruiser said softly, "On site is one state senator, two ICE agents—immigration officials—two suits from the Secret Service, four marked cars. Two FBI agents, there." He pointed to the man and woman with oversized umbrellas. "Two detectives from NOPD out in the middle of the night, when there are currently no dead bodies and no weapons of mass destruction. All of this is anomalous."

"Why don't you go to talk to them?" I said. "I'm the MOC's female Enforcer. You can be one of the guys."

"Or you could just kill them and save us some time," Edmund snipped.

I swiveled in my seat. "Or you could swim to the cruise ship, climb on board, find out who's there, what they want, and save us even more time," I said.

Edmund made a sort of blowing noise and looked away again. I had a feeling the smell of the blood bottle was still getting to him.

"What was in the bottle?" I asked him. "Whose blood?"

"It was . . ." He shook his head. "I do not know. But it reminded me of the aroma of mixed blood, when the Mithrans gathered and Katie was put to the earth, to heal." He was watching me as if he wanted me to say something, admit something. No way was I admitting that I'd been there in bubo bubo form. Not happening. An uncertain silence built.

Bruiser looked back and forth between us. Having nothing to add to the conversation, he opened the door and said, in one of the typically British turns of phrase that occasionally slipped out of his mouth, "I'll try not to delay you unduly." He left the limo, walking to the gathered officers, his body limned by the headlights. He was beautiful, and his butt, in the wet leathers, was simply amazing.

"Stop," I said to Eli before he could tell me to get a room. My partner chuckled evilly.

Moments later, Bruiser walked back, his body again caught in the lights, rain falling lightly onto him. He got in and said, "No one will talk to us, officially. But I know one of the officers. He'll talk to Leo. HQ, Shemmy."

"A cop in Leo's pocket?" I asked as Shemmy slid the limo into gear.

Bruiser said, "The officer's father was with NOPD back in the day. He warned Leo about a small group of officers working directly under the mayor of the time. They were planning to get something on Leo, make it look as if he had killed a child, stir public sentiment. Leo was able to head off the trouble, and the officers left NOPD and went to work in other fields. Leo offered the man a boon in return for his information. And he then fed that man his own blood for two years as he fought and beat cancer, an aggressive stage four colon cancer. In Leo's pocket. Yes."

Which made me feel all slimy for suggesting it was something else. I didn't like Leo, but in his own way, he did some good.

My cell pinged and it was Alex. "You're on speaker," I said.

"I have all the security video of the ship attempting to dock," Alex said. "And by the way. Did you know you're being tailed by PsyLED?"

"I knew," Shemmy said. "We picked him up on way to the docks. But he was holding back, so I waited to tell you."

"Rick," I said, a growl to the name. "Next time tell me."

"Yes, ma'am," Shemmy said. "Sorry ma'am. He's parked just down the block in the alley. Shall I pull up next to him?"

That made me grin. "Sure. Block him in. Let's consider it an invitation to a private tête-à-tête."

The limo made a three-point turn as if we were on the way out, at the last moment maneuvering closer to the mouth of the ally, blocking it, and throwing the narrow space into deepest shadow. Rick got out and walked to the limo, though *prowled* was more in keeping with his grace and balance and catlike movements. He leaned in my open window, studying us all with eyes that saw more than a human's would.

"Were there vamps on board?" I asked.

His Frenchy-black eyes flicked to me and back to Bruiser. "I'm sure that if Mithrans were aboard, they would have notified the Master of the City according to proper protocol," Rick said, his voice bland with the lie.

"Riiiiight," I said.

"Who called you about this incident?" Rick asked. "Nothing went out over the usual channels or the airwaves." None of us answered. "Move along, nothing to see here." He stood and went back to his car.

Alex said over the cell, "These are not the droids you're looking for."

Eli's lips twitched, his eyes going from me to Bruiser and

back. "Did you really threaten to kill the PsyLED special agent?"

"She did." Bruiser's face softened. "HQ, Shemmy. Alex, let's see the security footage of the ship trying to dock and its passengers trying to disembark."

"Sending it to the limo computer system," Alex said. "Flip up your screen."

Bruiser raised the extra-wide video screen covering the privacy panel. The scene had been captured by several cameras, from different angles, and we watched as a dozen men in military camo and automatic rifles surrounded the space where the gangway—gangplank?—would have touched U.S. soil. On board, a small clump of black-clad humans seemed to be trying to dock the ship. There was no audio, but we got the general idea. A lot of posturing. A lot of shouting through a megaphone. A lot of head shaking. Eventually the ship pulled away. Nothing happened. So who was aboard besides the crew in black? Who were the passengers and why were they denied permission to dock? If it was vamps, they would never do something so public for no reason. And if there were old and powerful vamps on board—the EVs come calling before the agreements were reached—they would have had the ability to get the humans to do anything they wanted, at least long enough to get several vamps ashore and drink from them. Unless one of the cops was a witch. A well-prepared witch might have shielded the law enforcement types from being rolled. If there were vamps on board. There were too many unknowns.

Eli said, "I don't get it." I studied the agents and cops on the screens. "Let's get stills of the plainclothes people and see if we can match them up with known local witches. Send the stills to Jodi and Lachish Dutillet." Jodi ran the woo-woo department of NOPD. Lachish was the leader of the NOLA coven. If one of them didn't know the witch, then he or she was very well hidden.

"Can we get video from farther downstream and from across the river?" I asked.

"You think this might have been a ruse? Yeah, okay. If it was the European vamps, they knew they wouldn't be allowed ashore," Eli said.

I lifted my thumb, twisting the palm open, in a *What else could it be?* gesture.

"It'll take a while," Alex said, "but yeah, I can pull from private security video."

Shemmy said, "HQ is down one block. Just so you know, the PsyLED agent tailed us here."

"Of course he did," I muttered. But Rick didn't try to follow us through the back gate. He rolled away through the rain into the darkness. Over the coms system I heard Alex say, "The cruise ship that was trying to dock? It just vanished. The Coast Guard vessel following it downriver said it was there one second and gone the next. They're tracking it by its wake now, but it's nearly impossible in the dark."

"Copy," Eli said.

It was still predawn as we pulled in behind Derek and his top men. Some were team Tequila, from the first time I met him, and some were team Vodka. There was not enough left of either team to make one single full unit. There had been battles. Too many battles. Too many injuries and deaths.

We deserted the limo under the porte cochere, Bruiser and Edmund parting and moving in different directions. Eli hung with me and gave Derek one of those manly nods that accepted the other's presence without being too happy about it. Everybody around here had a history. "Any luck?" I asked Derek as we went inside out of the wet and cold.

"Le Bâtard and Louis—the Deadly Duo—haven't been to the Roosevelt, or the Hotel Monteleone, or Dauphine Orleans, or the Omni."

Deadly Duo. I liked that. I liked even better that Derek had started assigning nicknames the way I did. Not that I'd ever say so. Instead, I said, "You covered a lot of territory."

"We broke up into small groups. Less conspicuous. Each group took a vamp to let us get where we needed." He grimaced, his full lips scowling, as he said the last part. Derek hated working with vamps. Hated that they could roll most humans so easily. But he used the tools at his disposal, always had.

He continued, "One team did get a tip where an unknown vamp might be. It seems there's a five-star vamp inn we didn't know about."

"Not the Acton House?" The Acton House was where famous vamp visitors of the twentieth century had stayed, including the Son of Darkness, one of the most powerful vamps in the world, on the good part of his visit. Since then, the SOD had been hanging on the wall of Leo's basement. Worst vacation spot ever.

"The St. Emilion House," Derek said, leading the way into the lower, back entrance and up in the elevator. "According to our source, it's discreet, gated, and has ten staff per bloodsucker. We did a drive-by. Place also has more cameras than Fort Knox. I doubt that it has anyone staying there right now because it's for sale. I called Scrappy on the way back and she asked Leo about it. It's one of the properties that went on the market after the last vamp mini-war."

The elevator doors opened and Eli placed the blood bottle in my hands. As the doors closed on us, he drew his weapons. Derek and I both raised our brows at him. "Edmund was a little aggrieved when he smelled the contents." Eli nodded at the bottle. "If Leo loses it, I can shoot him, standard ammo. It'll at least slow him down and let us get a door between us."

Derek let a grin pull at his mouth. Like Eli, he was former military and if he showed amusement it was for a reason. "Legs, I think I'll tag along to see how this goes down." He led the way from the elevator to Leo's office and knocked on the door. When Scrappy answered it, Derek said, his face emotionless, "The Enforcers and Yellowrock's second."

Scrappy was looking relaxed and more rested than the last few times I had seen her. She stood aside and left as we entered, the smell of pepper and papyrus and the fainter scent of ink on the air. And blood. Scrappy looked mighty happy as she left. I wondered if Leo's redheaded assistant had been lunch.

We moved silently across the piled carpets in the hallway, and the perfume of other vamps infused the air. The faint trace of tea in Katie's scent and Grégoire's pale green odor of freshwater streams and summer gardens, this time overlaid with a dissipating reek of fear. And then blanketed with the scent of recent and sweaty sex. Lots of sex.

The furniture had been moved out, a few essential pieces

shoved back, to line the walls: the desk, its chair, the armoire, which had been pushed to the side, and a smaller-than-normal tea tray were still present. A second built-in fireplace had been exposed on the wall where the armoire had been and it was burning merrily. A round, king-sized bed had been placed in the center of Leo's office, a silk fitted sheet hiding the mattress itself. It was covered with velvet throws; chenille throws; a puffy, fluffy, silky comforter; a dozen or so pillows; and three vamps in various stages of undress. I stopped hard at the end of the hallway. There were things I so did not want or need to see. I already wanted to stab out my eyeballs.

Leo (pretty sure he was buck naked) lay closest to us, on his side, his bare feet dangling over the edge of the mattress, a thin, shiny sheet tossed over his hips, his head on his arm. Long black hair dangled over the side, curling on the ends. Katie was in the middle and definitely naked, the small fleur-de-lis brand on her upper arm darker than I remembered, the scar brown and uniform. She had been branded before she was turned, possibly as a crime of the French state of the time. Delicate and erotic, she was posed languidly on the mattress, facing Leo, the covers underneath her. Grégoire, farthest from the doorway, was at her back, one arm holding her close to him, spooning, his face buried in her nape, her ash-blond hair tangled in his lighter locks. At least he was under the covers. Mostly. The important bits.

"Boss," I said calmly.

"Do you know why the revenants are rising?" he asked, opening his eyes, cutting to the chase.

"Yup."

Leo brushed the hair out of this eyes and sat up. His hair was longer than I remembered, a good six inches longer. It lay on his shoulders and across his chest in a tousled disarray. Sex on a stick. "Proceed," he said.

I filled him in on the discoveries of the day, including the pink silk line we found at the funeral parlor. "We also found a bottle of something that made Edmund freak out. It's possible that it's used in the embalming process. Maybe it—"

Leo thrust out his hand in a *give it to me* gesture, imperative.

I looked at Eli, who moved into the room where he could cover all the vamps. He centered one weapon on Leo, the other on Grégoire. "You get Katie," he instructed Derek. Leo vamped out. So did Katie. Grégoire didn't move except to twitch the arm that hung off the edge of the mattress.

"Blade," I said to Eli, assuming that the boy wonder already had one in hand.

"Got it."

"Explain yourselves," Leo said around his fangs, in the soft velvety tones of the mesmerizing fanghead.

Derek sighed and drew a weapon. "Standard ammo, boss. You try to kill us, go into a feeding frenzy, we'll shoot you, let you heal. Come back at a better time."

"It's what a good Enforcer does," I said. Leo scowled at me, but I stepped close and extended the bottle to him. The Master of the City of New Orleans, way underdressed for a business meeting, wrapped his pale fingers around the neck of the bottle and pulled it from me. Without removing it, he sniffed the cork. Stopped, his eyes narrowing, his head tilting to the side as if to access an old memory. But he didn't go nutso or try to eat me. Instead, his fangs retracted, his eyes bleeding back to human. He was beautiful and, for a moment, uncertain, perhaps even terrified, though he hid it instantly. He extended the bottle to me. I took it and stepped back.

Leo took a breath deeper than he needed for speaking, as if to settle himself, and said, "This contains the blood of Louis the Seventh. And Le Bâtard. And a dozen others I recall from long ago." He lifted his brows. "And the blood of Titus Flavius Vespasianus."

As Leo spoke, Grégoire peered out with one beautiful blue eye. The scent of fear pulsed into the room. "I told you that Le Bâtard is here."

Leo said, "We have no eyewitness proof of his presence in the city. Be still, my love." But things were moving in the back of Leo's eyes, like pieces on a chessboard, rearranged and reorganized and reconsidered. Leo was still in the game. Musingly, he said, "If the age of the rising revenants and the scent of this blood are indicators, some plan of our enemies has seemingly been in place for two hundred years. The Caruso Family were originally Clan Bouvier, but if they have been the willing spies of the Europeans, they may have set a strategy in motion that we only see with the rising of the revenants."

Grégoire's face slowly eased away from Katie's shoulder, his eyes bright with tears. "I told you. I am doomed."

Leo leaned back, exposing waaaay too much of himself, and stroked Grégoire's pale white shoulder. Katie pulled a golden comforter over Blondie. "You are safe, my darling," she said. "Remember that you are safe here. We three are enough to defeat them all."

"No one is doomed," Leo said softly, a faint smile on his face, his eyes turning to me in speculation. "We are quite safe. All is according to plan."

I frowned, not liking that I seemed to be part of his plan. "You know why the revenants are rising," I guessed.

Leo rolled back to us, set his eyes on me, and readjusted his silk covering. Thank God. "Revenants rise from the second death when they are not put properly in the ground. There are myths that they might be raised by choice and the will of their masters, for use in battle, where there is a need for confusion, fear, and where large numbers of inconsequential bodies might be lost without harm to the plan of battle." He stopped, watching us all.

He wasn't going to tell us outright. Either he was playing with us the way a predator played with his dinner, or he wanted to see if we could figure it out on our own. I hated guessing games. "Okay. You brought your core people into HQ. You think Le Bâtard and Louis Seven are in town. You think the boat that tried to dock is tied into some arcane plan by the Europeans. You think it's possible that the Europeans are . . ." I stopped, realization dawning. I met his eyes. "You think they're sitting offshore, ready to come ashore the moment agreement is reached on the parley, not giving you time to get plans laid. You think they're raising revenants to make it harder for you to keep order in your city, and to turn the local officials against you."

"You are becoming sagacious and perspicacious, my catty Enforcer. Titus Flavius Vespasianus was a powerful general, who became the Roman emperor Titus," Leo said, crossing his ankles, bending his elbow, and propping his head on a hand. The scant covering slipped again, just enough, and I willed my eyes to not look down. "As a human, he and his second-in-command, Tiberius Julius Alexander, besieged and conquered the city of Jerusalem, which had been occupied by its Jewish and Mithran defenders. The siege ended with the sacking of the city and the destruction of its famous Second Temple. He returned home and gained the throne, ruling Rome for two years before he was turned by his vampire concubine, a woman he captured from the fall of Jerusalem. He is the undisputed ruler of the European Mithrans."

I remembered the story of Sabina, the other outclan priestess. She had been turned early in the time of the first vamps. "Sabina?"

"No. Not Sabina," Katie said. She pulled a chenille throw from beneath her and wrapped it around herself fully.

Thank God. One covered, two to go.

She slid out of the bed, stood, and went to the armoire, from which she removed two bottles of wine, both red, and three glasses. "Another turned him. Long true-dead."

I couldn't tell if she was telling the truth, but she had no reason to lie.

"Though Titus Flavius Vespasianus signed the Vampira Carta," Leo said, speaking of the legal papers that passed for law among vampires, "he did so against his will. He is still the ruler of the vampires, all vampires, Mithran and Naturaleza. Humans are cattle to him. No one has successfully stood against him, though my uncle Amaury successfully kept these shores from his influence."

"Titus Flavius is strong," Katie said, applying a cork-screw to the first bottle. "Not as powerful as the Sons of Darkness, but his blood is potent. Some say it is by way of blood magic."

"The kind of stuff the Damours used?" I asked.

"Titus Flavius visited the island of Saint-Domingue during the time the Damours were landowners and slave owners there, free to pursue the most vile forms of magics," Leo said. He rolled off the bed, not taking the covers.

I averted my eyes fast, but not fast enough. I got the full frontal nudity and I could smell Derek's concealed amusement, laughing at my nude-body-squeamishness. This was one reason I'd never make it as a full-time Enforcer. *Eww.* I found myself staring at a painting of Katie, one I hadn't seen before. In it she was naked—Katie was always presented in a state of undress—lying in a bed with a man wearing a crown and nothing else. It was night through the windows of the painting, a quarter moon hanging in the evening sky. A woman stood at the window, her dark-skinned face shadowed, only her eyes bright, vaguely familiar. She was watching the couple. I couldn't place her but her eyes drew me. I might have met her. But the context didn't come to me. I played a timeline game, going back to the moment I met my first vamp—Katie—and moving through until now. I knew those eyes, but who she was, I didn't know, not with her forehead, lower face, and hair hidden.

The timeline game was better than watching Leo, Katie, and Grégoire, who still occupied the bed, his nether regions and his delicate boyish face covered, thank God. Grégoire looked fifteen, and he had been horribly abused by his creator, Le Bâtard. Katie crawled back into the bed and gathered Grégoire in her arms, his back to her now, covering her from chest to midthigh, her arms around him, holding a glass to his lips. He took the glass and sipped, and Katie's arms dropped into his lap. To his . . . Oh. My. God. I needed blinders. Or a fork to stab out my mind's eye. Stab, stab, stab. I stared at the fire, hoping the flames would blind me to the rest of the room.

Standing naked, Leo took a glass of the red wine as well, the bowl cupped in his palm, and rolled the liquid up around the rim and back. "Good legs," he said, holding the glass to the light, one arm high. Showing off. Naked. Dang it. And my nickname was Legs. Which he knew. Leo sniffed the wine in tiny sharp bursts. "A nice blend of Merlot with a sterner, later-ripening Cabernet Sauvignon. Full in body, lush velvety tannins, and intense plum and blackberry fla-

vors. The Europeans will hate it. See that Lee orders a dozen
cases." He was smiling when he said it. "Overnight delivery.
And the other red?"

Katie passed him a second glass. "It is sweet."

Leo tasted and made a face. "Indeed it is. Too sweet for
me to simulate enjoyment. That one may be struck from
the list." He handed it back and looked at me. "My Jane."

I heaved a sigh. In the painting, the king had his hands
all over Katie. Maybe it wasn't so good to be staring there.
"Yes."

"You seem dismayed at my lack of attire. This is your
doing. We are practicing our parts in the grand play that
will shock and amuse the Europeans."

I opened my mouth and nothing came out.

"You once suggested that we play Petruchio to Katherine's shrew." He gave Katie a small bow. "My apologies,
mon coeur."

She shrugged a perfect shoulder. "I was a shrew to him.
I was a shrew to all of them. It was the title I deserved. But
only you conquered my heart, Leo."

"Are we done here?" I asked.

"When Titus Flavius Vespasianus arrives, you will play
your part, my Jane. Until then you are dismissed."

I grabbed the blood bottle, turned tail, and ran. Well,
actually turned on a toe and walked out of the room and
back to the limo. But with very long strides. Eli kept up with
me and I could tell he was laughing. When the door closed
on us I said, "Speak and die."

He laughed aloud. The sound was so rare, and so unexpected, that I didn't kill him.

We took a long detour on the way home, past the Acton
House, which was currently empty and for sale. I remembered the death of the most recent proprietor, a tiny woman
with pink hair, someone I hadn't thought to protect and
who had died thanks to my lack of foresight. Guilt, my old
friend, raised her ugly head and sank claws into me. Moments later, we pulled up in front of a larger house with a
small, discreet FOR SALE sign out front.

"St. Emilion House," Shemmy said.

"It would be a good investment," Eli said, his tone too even to be casual.

"Uh-huh," I said. "Why? We have a house. And you said we could rearrange the space to make it work."

"We can. This one would make a great investment for the Europeans' visit."

I swiveled in my seat and stared at him. "This house, in this part of town, would go for about—"

"Fourteen thousand a month."

Up front Shemmy started coughing, probably to cover up laughter.

"Are you out of your mind? We don't have that kind of money."

"Just keep it in mind."

"You win the lottery and you can buy the house. I like it where we are. I won the house fair and square."

"Go ring the bell. Say hi."

My partner had a plan. Maybe nothing more than poking an anthill to see what climbed out, but it felt more like throwing rocks at a hornets' nest. I handed him the blood bottle, opened the door, and got out, leaving the car door open to the rain. "All the men are nuts," I said to the storm. "And naked. And Katie is nuts. And I must be nuts too, to be out here in the rain." I walked up to the gate, which was wrought iron, the top railing a good ten feet high, with spear points rising above that. I stared at the camera and rang the buzzer. The camera mounted on the left of the gate made a soft whirring sound and turned to me. I gave it my most forbidding face, though how forbidding I was, in the rain-drenched everything, I didn't know. I said. "I'm Jane Yellowrock. I don't know who owns this house but be aware. I know about it." I spun and got back in the limo, closing the door. "Happy?"

Eli laughed, that odd and wonderful sound. I wondered how often Sylvia heard it but decided it was better not to ask. "More so than you know. Alex thinks Louis Seven owns it from back in the seventeen hundreds."

Exhaustion wrapped her arms around me. I slumped in the seat. "You coulda told me. Home, James," I said.

"Not my name," Shemmy said easily, spinning the tires and taking us back toward the house.

Moments later, I opened my eyes. "On second thought, take me to Bruiser's apartment."

"Getting that room?" Eli asked.

"Shut up."

I crawled into bed with Bruiser. The smell of him filled my nostrils, the heat of him bathed my flesh, and he gathered me into his arms and pulled me close. In the cold of the storm, and with the dearth of insulation in his old apartment, his warmth was like a furnace and I melted against him with a small groan of pleasure. He slid one hand up along my hip, feathered it across my stomach, and cupped my breast. His mouth descended to mine and my moan softened. "Yes," I whispered. "This." Things proceeded to become a great deal hotter.

After a shower, a nap, another bout of fun and games, and another nap, Bruiser woke me at sunset with an early dinner of eggs with green and red chilies and ricotta cheese and shrimp and grits. Comfort food, high in protein, served in front of the burnt-persimmon living room couch, both of us wearing a pair of Bruiser's flannel PJs against the cold, and a cushy comforter tucked over us. New Orleans houses and heaters weren't built with cold in mind, and drafts were everywhere. Bruiser had a one-day beard, a scruffy look that made him look sharper, harder, and maybe a little mean. I liked it, and kept scrubbing my knuckles over the scratchy pelt. Beard. Whatever. His skin was hot beneath my knuckles. It felt good in the icy weather.

Our plates were nearly clean when the knock came at the door and Bruiser let Eli in.

The guys fist-bumped, which looked all wrong on Bruiser, but when he saw me watching over the back of the couch, he just smiled. "Breakfast?" he asked my business partner.

"I'm good. We got problems. Exactly one minute after dusk, a riot broke out near Tulane, one at the St. Vincent de Paul Society cemeteries on Piety Street, and a third one at Rosemary Place. College kids get riled and cut the fool from time to time, but there's nothing at Rosemary to incite a mob. It's a residential street." He dropped a heavy gear bag on my lap. It landed with a thump and a rattle. It mighta bruised me some too.

Bruiser said, "However, Carrollton Cemetery is near Tulane. Metairie Cemetery and Cypress Grove Cemeteries are near Rosemary. And the St. Vincent *is* a cemetery."

"Yeah," Eli said. "Cute jammies."

"Thanks," I said as Bruiser pulled up a map of the city on his tablet.

Eli sat on the edge of a white leather bar chair and said, "It forms a triangle, which might be witch magic."

"What it does is send us all over," I said. "Spread resources. Create discord."

Bruiser said, "Let's get to HQ first. We need to check some things." My partner had brought dry leathers. Admittedly they were my dress black set, and they squeaked when I moved sometimes, but at least they weren't drippy and slimy. I changed and tossed my wet leathers at Eli. "These need your special touch."

Bruiser removed a basket of rags from a long cabinet, each neatly folded. Folded rags? I had a feeling my honeybunch was a tad OCD. Eli stuffed the sleeves and the legs of the leathers with balled-up terry strips. It was better than I had done. I'd left them dripping in the shower. When this gig with vamps was over, we needed to invest in water-wicking, water-resistant poly-cotton-nylon suits. They were lighter weight and cost a lot less than the leathers Leo bought me. The military was coming up with mix-and-match uniforms and gear for all weather conditions, and the civilian providers weren't far behind. I was sure we could get the Seattle coven to provide anti-spell gear. For a price.

I stomped into my boots and followed the guys out. Shemmy was again behind the wheel and since he was part of the team for this gig, I took the time to look him over. Mixed race with brown eyes, bald head, ready laugh, and a physique that screamed bodybuilder. His back strained his pale gray suit, his neck was big enough to need its own horse, shoulders Atlas would have admired, and a waist tight enough to make a pole dancer envious. "Atlanta?" I asked, wanting to know where he had come from.

"Got it in one."

I nodded and took a seat next to Bruiser as the limo moved away from the curb at speed. I heard a faint *ding* and Shemmy raised the privacy panel to take a call. Above us, lightning lit the clouds like fireflies in a bottle, making the storm clouds look like puffy cotton balls and Christmas tree lights, innocent and nonthreatening, but I kept expecting them to trigger my magics. They didn't. It was almost as if the lightning were playing. Or maybe just warming up for the main event.

I tilted my head as a stray thought speared into my brain and took root. "What's happening to the SOD in this storm?"

Bruiser focused on me intently. "He's in sub-five basement. He's too far down to be, do, or feel anything. As far as I know his brain is still trying to regrow."

"Huh. Yeah. When I first saw him, he was clawing into the copper wiring. It was doing something to him, giving him a jolt of power. What if the storm is jolting him. Hitting his magic."

"Accelerating his regeneration," Bruiser said, evaluating my theory. "I'll take a look."

The limo swerved and accelerated. Bruiser hit a switch. "Shemmy?"

"The Council Chambers is under attack by revenants and members of the Bloods and the Crips. The gangs are working together, more or less, which Derek says is nearly unheard of. He's called in reinforcements."

"A ruse?" I asked. "Another one? Or the purpose of the riots, resources already divided, and so they strike at their central target." The two gangs were Derek's old enemies, and they had been fighting over his neighborhood way back when.

"Two enemy gangs working together?" Eli said. "What? Under some kind of truce? Or did some vamps pay them? Or drink them down and roll them?"

The limo swerved and slid on the water in the streets, hydroplaning, headlights bouncing across the buildings and reflecting from vehicles nearby. We sideswiped a car parked on the side of the street, fishtailed, and hit a second one on the other side. The impacts sent us grabbing for the emergency straps overhead. Mildly, Bruiser said again, "Shemmy?"

"I'll come back and call the police, leave a report and my card. Cops won't come, not for something small like this, but at least there'll be a record at dispatch."

Two blocks later, Shemmy roared up under the porte cochere and we boiled out of the limo to see people running away, into the dark. HQ's security team was pulling two wounded in through the back entrance. The attack seemed to be over. The thought was half formed when I saw a human shape dressed in black pants and red jacket roll across the top of the brick fence and drop to the ground. Then two more. So the attack was coming in waves. Slight forms, short and skinny, underfed. Teenagers. Maybe hopped up on meth. Or spelled by the storm to more extreme and violent tendencies. And there was zero chance that the cops would show up here.

As Eli and I watched, Derek, Wrassler, and a full security team dashed from the entrance and through the porte cochere, carrying truncheons and leather saps—handheld weapons made of leather with sand or lead pellets inside to knock someone silly. HQ's people were wearing vests under winter coats. Better than armor and guns. The attackers might be ready to rumble, but they were still kids.

The security team waded in and hit and smacked, going for kneecaps, elbows, and fists instead of faces and the sides of heads. Minimizing long-term injury, preventing death. They were trying to stop the kids without gunfire because they were kids.

Shemmy lowered the passenger window and shouted, "Security woman monitoring the cameras just saw someone go in a side gate? But we don't have a side gate." He pressed fingers to his earbud. "She says it's a revenant and six gang members."

"Side gate," I whispered. "Oh crap." To Bruiser I shouted, "Get to Leo's office! Incoming!" I pulled on Beast-speed and raced out the gate and around the block. The rain was pattering, but the fog was growing denser. There were cars and media vans arriving up and down the street, as if they had been alerted. I tilted my head away from any cameras that might be able to focus through the heavy mist and darkness.

It was hard to spot the small gate in the brick fence. It was overgrown with vines. A dark hole resolved out of the whiteout and I stepped inside. The rain stopped instantly. The silence was intense after the constant sound of drumming downpour. It was darker than the inside of hell.

The gate had been propped open with a long block of wood, allowing for egress. Ahead, flashlights revealed a revenant racing through the blackness, chasing a dozen older teenagers wearing gang colors just like the ones at the porte cochere. The rev was tracking them by scent, running blind. The group dashed ahead, waited until the revenant almost caught up, and dashed ahead again. They were leading it inside. I was reminded of Leo's comment about revenants being bodies a commander was willing to lose.

Beside me, a few feet inside the door, stood Rick. His hands were empty. Dangling. His face was hard with horror. He knew this gate because he had been carried out through it by werewolves when he was kidnapped. After which he had been tortured and raped by a werewolf bitch and her pack. But he seemed frozen, standing, doing nothing. PTSD. Eli, now Rick. The horror of memories that had broken them. The magical storm was affecting everyone.

I walked up to him and seized his face in one hand. Pulled him close, until he had no choice but to look in my eyes. "You can beat this. You beat it the first time. You can beat it every time."

He gurgled a laugh, sounding like a death rattle. "Beating I can do. But am I going to have to relive it every damn time?"

"Probably. But you'll survive that too. Beat that too. And you can have a good life."

"Without you."

"Without me." I let his face go and walked into the dark. But not before I saw movement in the gate. Carolyne Bonner and a cameraman, filming me holding Rick's face in what had to look like a lovers' tryst. "Well, crap." I adjusted my weapons and took off after the rev and the kids.

CHAPTER 12

A Six-Foot Snowfall in Hades

Eli had followed and he fell in beside and slightly behind me. The passageway was narrow and stank of mold and kids, their sweat laced with violence and adrenaline. There was a faint reek of rot from the rev. They took the winding passageways through the place but bypassed the entrance leading up to Leo's office. Instead, we came out in the ballroom. In front of us, the group had raced across the wide space and ducked into a small set of hidden stairs leading down to all the basements. I stopped Eli, a hand on his arm. In Beast-vision, the room was silvers and greens. Empty. But something was wrong.

I sniffed. Again. We were definitely alone in the ballroom, in the dark, and the stink of the rev was strong, but there was something different beneath the other stinks, something that hadn't been there during the last inspection. I had smelled this scent recently. "Plastic explosives," I whispered. "If you wanted to destroy the ballroom where the EVs and Leo will meet to obstruct or delay the parley, where would you plant them?"

"The columns," he said, just as soft. "Bring down the roof and take out the windows. It could be repaired, but likely not in time for the EuroVamp visit. Plus it's quick. Strap explosives to the columns and bug out. Detonation from offsite."

"I smell magic too," I said.

"No reason magic can't be added to bombs. Military postulated magical weapons decades ago."

"So who planted them? Outside vamps or ones from inside? Never mind, I know the answer to that. Sleepers." We had enemies here at HQ. Always had.

If I'd been human I would have missed the sound of a sword being drawn. I whirled. Pulled a weapon. Racked back the slide. Aimed at the head behind. Before I could fire, he was gone. Popped away. A breeze touched my cheek. Movement from above as he leaped over us. "Behind us," I shouted to Eli. And fired at the second vamp.

Vamps are fast but not faster than a bullet. I nicked her in the rear as she popped away. Stupid. Humans were present. I put the gun away and drew a vamp-killer. More gunfire sounded. Kids and twenty-somethings poured in through the porte cochere entrance. And boiled in from the stairwell entrance. Part of the first wave had made it inside. Bruiser and Derek followed the group from the back. Gunfire sounded, echoing against my eardrums. There were too many combatants. More raced in from the passageway to the hidden gate entrance.

Outside, lightning crashed down. Hitting in the backyard of HQ. Into the small chef's garden. The world went bright and brilliant and full of glare.

The Gray Between ripped out of me. The world slowed, hesitated, stopped. Standing outside of time, my hands grew pelt, claws, but I willed my knuckles to stay human sized. They ignored me. I could operate a gun if needed, but not well. My face ached. Fangs pushed through my gums and I tasted blood. It freaking hurt. My shoulders expanded, my waist shrank. But my feet were human in the boots. The transformation stopped there. I was still me-ish. But time was stopped.

Beside me Eli faced a vamp, one I didn't know, redheaded, glowing pale skin, blue eyes. The one that had somersaulted over us and landed in front. Dang ninja vamp.

Eli was bleeding from a nick on the outside of his forearm. The vamp had a sword and it was descending on my partner, wicked sharp. Three rounds hung in the air between them. I calculated the speed of the bullets and the speed of the falling sword, one powered by a master vamp. The rounds would hit the vamp midface, but using my own blade, the sword would continue to fall, slicing though Eli's arm. I pushed the sword about three inches outside its current arc. It resisted, the vamp's muscles engaged, but I put my back into it and the sword moved.

As long as I didn't touch their flesh, they stayed in their own time. Or that was the way it had worked in the past. Things seemed to change a lot with magic, even mine. And one thing I didn't want was for the enemy to know everything I could do with time. So while it wasn't a perfect solution, this worked.

Eli safe, I stepped into the ballroom. In the bright light of the lightning, I counted two unknown vamps and seven gangbangers. Weird. It had felt like more. Chasing the kids up from the stairway were Bruiser, Derek, and some of Derek's security guys. Wrassler was firing down the stairs, his weapon aimed high. Cover fire. Derek and one of the new guys were firing at the gang kids, who were also shooting up the place.

I guessed that Gee and others were in Leo's office protecting Leo, Katie, and Grégoire.

I had time to study the two unknown vamps, the redhead, and the one I had shot in the tush. They were skilled and old, far older than they looked on first glance. They were vamped out and had old, old, *old* eyes. Both vamps were using two long swords in the La Destreza style. From their body positions I'd guess they were masters at the fighting form.

The shot one was pale skinned, covered in ancient blue tattoos in spirals and circles and wavy lines. I had seen someone like her once and made a mental note to find Koun and chat him up. In the shadows of the lightning strike, I saw something unexpected. Two vamps I recognized. One was named Callan, the other Fernand Marchand. Both had been enemies to Leo and had reason to hate me.

Callan had been a vampire kept in a cage at Katie's and I'd nicknamed him Corpse, verbally abusing him, allowing the vamps to torture him. Well, maybe torture was too strong a word, but they hadn't been playing tiddlywinks with him. He had served a vamp named de Allyon but claimed it was only because his master kept him alive. He had boxer's shoulders, the thighs of a cyclist, long, slender fingers, and an angel's face, but he'd been turned for his looks, not his brains. Or so I'd thought. When De Allyon had been defeated, Callan had asked to join Leo's power base and been welcomed in. He'd been healed by Sabina and fed by Christie, one of Katie's working girls. Now it appeared that his loyalty was lacking. Part of the attack on Leo's power base. And maybe the brainless part had been a ploy.

Fernand Marchand was a longtime troublemaker, had been a suspect in more than one security leak. Dark haired and jaded, he was the brother to Amitee Marchand . . .

My heart slowed and my fingers suddenly ached. The Marchands had come from France for Amitee to marry the vamp masquerading as Leo's son Immanuel, the liver-eater I had killed when I first came to New Orleans. Everything, every freaking thing, went back to Immanuel.

Immanuel and his friends had wanted to kill Leo and take over the city. Immanuel, Amitee, and Fernand had been traitors. Yet Leo had kept the brother and sister around even after his heir was killed. Why? Was it part of the homily that said we should keep our enemies closer? Callan and Fernand were standing together, Fernand's hand on Callan's shoulder. It would have been all cozy, lovey-dovey if Callan hadn't been pointing a gun right where I had been standing. I thought about hurting them both but put it off for now. There were other things I needed to see, and they might lead me to other enemies.

Too many enemies, too many plots. Only one thing was certain. This situation had nothing to do with the United States Navy or an attack on the military. That had been a feint or an unhappy accident. This was a direct hit on Leo and the fangheads on U.S. soil.

Spotting a kid in a red jacket and black pants dripping on the marble floor, I moved in. He was holding a nine-millimeter sideways in one hand. It was a street gang firing stance, one where aiming was more a general-direction thing, not target practice. I leaned in and sniffed, getting a good whiff of his weapon, his clothing, his armpits, and his breath. He was whacked out on drugs, cheap liquor, and vamp blood. I moved closer to him. Breathed in through my mouth, air moving over my tongue with a soft *scree* of sound. Vamp blood. And sex. A lot of both and recently. He'd been fed and rolled and seduced and sent on a quest. All by a vamp I didn't recognize. The kid was maybe fourteen.

Kits . . . Beast hissed. *Not sucklings. Not yearlings. But young. To be kept at mother cat's side, taught to hunt. Taught to survive. Not ready to be mated.*

Anger rumbled through me. I moved through the fracas into the area where the elevator opened.

Security was rushing from the parted doors, faces in that cold, hard combat mode that former active-military types always wore in emergencies. They wore SWAT-type flak jackets and they carried small subguns. Not good. They were about to kill humans, kids, gangbangers, for sure, but gangbangers who might have been rolled by vamps. I had to stop this.

Time juddered, sound beating against my ears. The lightning sizzled. Thunder hammered the air. Gunshots. Screams. Shadows and motion, and then it all stopped. I didn't have long. I ran to the first man racing off the elevator and grabbed him, yanking him out of his time and into mine. Into my arms. Up off the floor, using his momentum against him, spinning him. Letting go, I leaped back, leaving him hanging in midair. He'd fall and most of the others would land on top of him. A pileup. Time stuttered. Shuddered. Almost out of no-time.

I raced through the melee, knocking bullets to the floor, ruining aims by slapping against weapons, knocking guns out of loose grips. The vamp I had shot was nearly to the outer door. I leaped into the air and kicked her knee. I heard the bone break, slowly, snaps dragging through her flesh and into the air.

I touched her and she fell, screaming, into no-time. And time snapped back. I caught her, shoved a silvered blade under her chin, and carried her back inside. "Tell the gang-bangers to back off, or I'll toss your head into the battle." I sliced into her flesh. "Now!"

"*Detener*," she said.

Bullets chiseled into the walls, floors, people. Shrapnel flew. Screams and the smell of blood filled the air. I shoved the blade an inch into her flesh, into a blue tattoo, getting a nose full of silver-scorched skin and blood as I took a breath. "Louder," I growled.

"*Pararse! Detener!* Stop! Withdraw!"

Gangbangers whirled and vanished, darting into the rain. The ones who were cornered put weapons on the floor. Ten seconds after time went back to normal, the battle was over.

We lost the redheaded male vamp. Callan and Fernand vanished as they popped away at vamp-speed. The security types were mostly untangled in front of the elevator. And I was about a quarter of the way to Beast-form. Fortunately it was still dark and the storm still raged. I threw the injured vamp at Wrassler and growled, "Get her to Leo. Have him read her. I want to know everything she does, pronto."

"I know nothing that could be of use to you," she said, sounding Frenchy, not even bothering to struggle in Wrassler's arms.

"Whatever." To Wrassler I added, "Clear the area and get the bomb squad in here. There are bombs set up in the ballroom."

His eyes whipped around the room, taking in the changes to the architecture. "Copy, Legs." He yanked the vamp off her feet and moved away.

I shouted, "Eli. With me." By the smell, one revenant was still on premises and had made it down the stairs to the basements.

Before I could lead the way down, lights and sirens pulled up under the porte cochere. Rick LaFleur led the way in with members of local and state law enforcement, the men and women wearing navy rain gear with the letters NOGTF on the front. NOGTF was the New Orleans Gang Task

Force, a multiagency task force with the FBI. I spotted cops as they took off into the night after the running kids. Rick caught my eye and I gave him a single, hard nod. He returned it. He was dealing. Good. I raced down the basement stairs, Eli on my heels.

Down and down and down, through another passageway, and down and down, following the scent of the rev. But the twice-dead thing stopped before he hit the deepest basement and the thing that hung on the walls there. The revenant wasn't in sub-five with the Son of Darkness. He had veered off course into sub-four. I knew in my bones what the rev was after. Adrianna. The vamp Leo had kept alive despite all the times I had killed her.

Leo had kept Fernand and Amitee, and even Callan near him. He had a plan on how to use them all. I hoped he'd find success with all that. I figured it was about as likely as a six-foot snowfall in Hades.

I raced down the hallway, following the faint stink of rot. The Gray Between hovered around me as I ran; my fangs disappeared and my pelt shimmered into flesh. I returned to fully human without having to stop and change. Something was happening to my magics, but I didn't have time to analyze it. We spun around the corner and found ourselves staring down the barrel of a gun from floor level.

In front of the sealed doorway to Adrianna's prison, lying in a pool of her own blood, was Ro Moore, one of Leo's new security people out of Atlanta and Katie's new Enforcer. With her shirt, she had fashioned makeshift bandages that covered her left arm and shoulder, the sports bra beneath drenched in blood. A nine-millimeter was in her right hand holding a steady aim on us. When she saw us, she laid the gun on her middle, and her body quivered in what smelled like relief and pain.

Eli dashed to her, murmuring, "How many rounds? Where are you hit?"

"Two in my left shoulder, nine-mil. I think one punctured a lung." Ro coughed and blood came up with the expelled breath.

We now had WiFi in the basements and I called up to Bruiser, saying, "Wounded in sub-four. We need medic—"

Edmund popped into place at my side, startling me.

"—A-SAP," I said, closing the cell's Kevlar cover.

Ed knelt at Ro's side and peeled back her bandage. "You are the human female who fights in cages."

"Yeah," she gasped as he probed the wounds. She wiped her mouth with the back of her wrist. "I can usually take care of myself. But there were three of them. With guns." She chuckled and more blood splattered. "They don't allow guns in the pit."

"Wise decision there." Edmund ripped the strap of the sports bra from her, without jostling her body. "Are you averse to close physical contact with me? You are badly injured. I will need to—"

She coughed again and blood went everywhere. I could hear the fluid gurgling in her lungs. Edmund had been many things in his long life; one was a physician. He pulled a blade and sliced two of his fingers deeply enough that the blood wouldn't clot over too quickly.

"I am most sorry," he said. And he thrust his fingers into the wounds. She coughed and gagged and writhed, smearing the blood beneath her like some kind of artwork for a horror flick. Ed put his free hand on Ro's head and said, "Be still. All is well." His voice fell low, slow, the tone they use when they draw on their power to mesmerize. "All is well. Do you know how much the Master of the City approves of you?" he said in the same easy tone. "He sets you on guard duty, in the bowels of the building, an indication of how much he trusts you with his secrets and his body." Ed looked up at us and mouthed, *Medic!*

I had seen Ed heal with his blood and his magic. He had brought me back from the brink of death. But I wasn't human. Ro was dying. Fear sliced along my nerves and I raced back up the steps. Snagged two paramedics as they came in the outer door. "Downstairs. Elevator." I didn't mean to shove them and their gear and the stretcher into the elevator, but somehow that was what I did. They landed with a jumble and clatter of metal and hard plastic. I stabbed the button, trying to remember how to get to the sealed door once we got off the elevator and how many walls I'd have to punch out to get the stretcher through.

It took too long. Too long, too long, too long for the elevator to descend. I punched the button again. Maybe a dozen times. The elevator finally dropped gently down.

"Ma'am? What do we have?"

I turned to the paramedic and managed to take a breath. I saw my reflection in his eyes. My own wide and terrified. Face too pale for my usual golden-hued skin. I realized I had panicked. I never panicked. I— *Oh. The storm.* It was affecting me in lots of ways, more than I realized. I gathered my brain around me and forced my shoulders down, forced in a breath. I said, "Female, aged twenty-two to thirty-five. Two GSWs, left shoulder. Left lung penetration. Coughing blood. Possible hemothorax. A doctor is with her, but he has no equipment." I looked at my hands. There was a splatter of blood on them from when Ro coughed. I had panicked. That was strange.

The elevator stopped. The doors eventually opened. I grabbed up the medical kit, which probably weighed a good forty pounds, and sprinted down the hallway. Then stopped and waited for the paramedics to get the stretcher sorted out. It took forever. And I understood then that I really liked Ro. She had moxie, was resourceful and practical. And tough as nails.

I had never bothered to make a friend of her and that bothered me.

We rounded the hallway and the paramedics went to work, taking direction from Edmund, who gave them everything about her from pulse and respirations to the fact that her lung had partially collapsed and most certainly she had a hemothorax. More detailed and better medical information than I had known.

I watched as the medical types got IV lines going, started plasma expanders, put pads under her knees to restore some blood pressure to keep her from going more shocky. She was paler than most vamps. Blood-drenched. I couldn't stand here any longer. I needed to be doing something. I pulled a vamp-killer and the nine-mil, which I had safetied and holstered, all with a round in the chamber. Stupid. Unless I needed it in a hurry. Then maybe not. I felt as if I were waking up from a hazy dream. "Who's in the room?" I asked Eli.

"Ro says a revenant and a human wearing red and black."

"Okay. Let's do this."

Eli opened the door and took left; I took right. On the floor beside the cage against the far wall was a dead human who might have been wearing black and red. There was so much blood I couldn't tell for sure. I didn't have to check for a pulse. His throat was gone. A revenant wearing gray rags had his back to us, and he didn't turn, too busy trying to get the cage gate open. The mesh was tightly braided and woven stainless steel, coated with silver, and it cut and burned through vamp skin like a blade through butter. The latch was the highest-quality steel and spelled. And the dead human hadn't thought to bring lock cutters.

The door closed with a sharp sound and the rev whirled to us. There was life and light in his eyes. And blood and tissue and dog fangs at his mouth. But he telegraphed his move and I was already in a hard backswing. He dove for us. I took him down with the vamp-killer. His head bounced off the ceiling and landed on an empty cage. His body dropped. I knelt at it and studied the neck. The pink thread was pulsing with magic. I lowered my face and sniffed. There was the faintest trace of mixed vamp blood on him, the same mixture that was in the blood bottle. Which I had misplaced. Maybe in the limo. So much had happened in the last few hours, I was uncertain. Oh. Right. I'd last been holding it in the limo and had seen Eli take it. It was safe, wherever he had stored it.

I looked into the only occupied cage, into the face of the beautiful fanghead who had tried to kill me the first time she saw me. Her red hair was long and curly and as wild as she was, and she was dressed in jeans and a loose-woven, pale aqua sweater. Beneath the sweater, on her upper arm, gold gleamed. She was wearing a snake bracelet, one that danced with magic in a dozen shades of red, charcoal, and black. I had taken her jewelry away from her. It was all infused with magic and she was not allowed magic. Yet she wore magic tonight.

Outside, lightning struck close again. I felt it in my bones, an electric zapping that hurt. But it didn't do anything to my magic because it never found me. Instead, the magic in the lightning, or perhaps only a tiny bit of it, as Adrianna didn't burn to death on impact, found the bracelet. The gold lit up. The lights overhead flickered off and on several times. Adrianna gripped the mesh and leaned into it. Lightning swirled into the mesh, sparking and glinting, before vanishing. There was no stink of her flesh burning, no smoke. Adrianna opened her eyes, stared at me, and laughed.

The cages. They were brand-new. The mesh was a different design. The metal bright and clean and untouched by time and prolonged contact with vamp flesh and blood and air and water. Shiny. Either they weren't really coated with silver, or Adrianna had gained a silver immunity, which would be very, very bad.

I pulled my cell and sent a text to Alex. *Get someone in here to make sure the sub-four scion and prisoner cages aren't wired into a power system, regular electric, security system, or somehow getting to the SOD. Make sure they are silver. Adrianna not burning to touch.*

He sent back, *K.*

"I remember those," Adrianna said. "I want one."

I looked into Adrianna's eyes. Pretty sane. Ish. *Holy crap.* Maybe the way to cure vamp insanity is a silver stake through the brain. "Eli, we need that bracelet."

Adrianna slapped a hand over her upper arm, hiding the gleam of gold. "Mine."

"Nope," I said. "Mine."

Edmund entered the room and looked around like a dapper decorator unimpressed with the décor. Until he spotted the rev head on the cage top. He showed teeth in predatory pleasure and said, "This is why I love working for you, my mistress. Never a dull millisecond."

"I smell blood," Adrianna said. She held her palm against the mesh, not burning. Not burning at all. "Give."

"No," I said. To Edmund, I added, "We need to get her bracelet off. Someone gave her more magical stuff."

"Good," Edmund said. "The hidden security camera should show us who and when."

"You installed a hidden surveillance camera?"

"Technically your second installed it, but it was my idea."

Eli snorted, and I got the feeling that Edmund's contribution was more in the vamp's head than in reality. "It isn't tied into the system. I'll pull the drive now and insert another. We can take it to Alex for review." Eli went to a spot next to the door and peeled back a length of tape that was the same color as the wall. Behind the tape, Eli had cut into the wallboard and planted a small camera. He removed a tiny drive, inserted another, and closed the tape over it. Unless someone was looking for a small hole next to the door, it was invisible. "It's in real time, so it will take a while."

I walked to Adriana, who had been watching us avidly. "Give me blood," she demanded.

"No," I said. "I won't. Edmund, will you liaise with Sabina and Bethany and get that bracelet off her?" My primo went still, that undead thing they do when they display all the life of a wax mannequin. I grinned at the wall, not looking at him directly, my Beast playing. "What? You thought being my primo was going to be all bloody fun and games? There's politics too."

Eli said to me, "He could bring in enough minor vamps to take it off her and deliver it to the house. Up to you."

Regally, I nodded my head at Edmund. "I am not averse to either method. Make it so, Number One."

Edmund went from still as wax to staring at me. "You are . . . teasing me?"

"Pretty much," I said. "I still need that bracelet, but it's up to you how I get it." I stepped to Adrianna's cage and rattled the gate. It was secure.

There was a faint pop of sound. Blood stench billowed into the room. I whirled to see a blood-splattered Leo in the open doorway. Blood ran in rivulets over his crimson clothing. Adrianna moaned.

"Leo?"

"*Où étais-tu?*" he whispered, the words strangled.

"What—"

"They have taken him!" he screamed. "They took my Grégoire. You were not here. You were supposed to be here." Leo dropped to his knees. Tried to catch himself with a hand on the jamb but slipped in his blood. He had lost two fingers on his right hand. He face-planted and lay still. His shirt was cut to ribbons, as was the flesh beneath. There was a knife sticking from between his shoulder blades. Behind me, Adrianna laughed, the sound low and mocking.

Things moved fast. Katie, Leo's heir, with the most powerful blood in the city, Dacy Mooney, the visiting heir of the Shaddock blood clan from Asheville, and others gathered to feed their master. Someone sent for Sabina to help feed him. Bethany, the other priestess, raced down the hallway to feed Leo, opening the flesh of her fingertips and smearing it over the MOC, sticking the same fingers into wounds I hadn't noticed. When he was at least stable, the vamps carried the MOC to his rooms. I followed behind, useless, and I finally got to see where Leo spent his private time.

The room was unlike the one Grégoire slept in, with its tapestries and fancy antiques and carpets. Leo's room had wooden floors, pale blue walls, and a four-poster bed with intricate carvings. There were three armoires, all closed; a single chair, a small table, and a bookshelf full of old books and scrolls and wax tablets, of the sort he had owned before his former home burned to the ground. Some things had been saved from the flames, perhaps these.

I pulled the chair into the corner and sat, silent, watching, a nine-mil in one hand. Just in case.

Katie entered after me, bringing Leo's dismembered fingers for reattachment. A hand reached out and snatched away the dagger in Leo's back. Edmund brought gray silk thread and a medical bag for sewing. Someone else took a liquor bottle off Leo's shelf and cleaned the fingers, dousing them in copious amounts of ethanol. Edmund grabbed the bottle and shoved it away, saying, "One does not use a thirty-year-old Macallan for dismembered Mithran limbs. One uses vodka."

I heard the words coming out of my mouth before I could help it. "Doesn't that cause cell damage?"

On his bed, Leo laughed, as if at my naïveté, and clasped Edmund's hand with his own. "I wish a taste of that elixir before you put it away. It's obscene to open that bottle and not taste." Someone found two cut crystal glasses and poured some of the Macallan in each, added a splash of water, and the two men clinked glasses. Sipped. Edmund sighed, the sound so longing that I had to figure he'd had nothing so nice since he lost his own clan. Lesser vamps probably didn't get the good stuff.

"Sire," Edmund said in thanks.

Around him other, even lesser vamps opened ancient surgery supplies from Edmund's medical bag and doused them with vodka. There was nothing in sterile packets, and the part of me that remembered my emergency medical classes cringed. But then, vamp physiology was not human in any way. So what did I know?

"Do you remember the last time I replaced a body part?" Edmund went on. "You offered a much less fine drink."

"We were on a battlefield," Leo said, his voice regaining something akin to the mellifluous tones it usually carried. "Scotch doesn't travel well, not in saddlebags in summer."

"Rotgut," Edmund said. "Swill."

"'Twas all we had, *mon amie*," Leo said, his laughter containing a faint wheeze of pain and grief over Grégoiré's kidnapping. Leo looked at me. "Save him." I nodded.

"Let's flip you over, sire, so the priestesses can heal your back. Removing that blade was unwise, whoever did it. Blades should be removed from bodies—even Mithran bodies—in the presence of a skilled surgeon or a master with particularly potent blood. Even a master can bleed out if the placement was especially skilled."

"What if the blade was silvered?" a voice asked from the corner of the room.

Edmund looked up at that. Sipped, while surveying the onlookers. Perhaps he was remembering his own brush with silvered death only a day or so past. "In that case, yank it out and bleed yourself inside the wound. Feed the Mithran. And pray."

If anyone thought the order to pray was odd, no one said so. In fact, a tiny vamp at the edge of the bed dropped to her knees and started praying to a handful of beads. It wasn't a prayer like I remembered from the Christian children's home where I grew up, and it was full of stuff about Mary. I figured it was Catholic and I had been wrong about her praying to the beads themselves. Another person dropped and started praying too, also with beads, this one talking to Allah.

Vamps. Praying. This was crazy. Except that their sire and master was injured, and his death would set into motion perilous changes. If Leo fell, with his city in chaos, and the EVs arrived, all of Leo's people were in danger of a second and true-death. I secured my weapon and escaped to the elevator and down, to find another madhouse where the NOPD bomb squad was defusing and removing bombs in the ballroom. The cops escorted me back into the elevator and instructed me to go up a level and out the front door.

Unfortunately, a crime scene investigation was taking place there. Two dead and drained gang members—kids— lay on the floor and the security system just happened to have gone out during this battle, so there was no internal surveillance of the fight or the deaths. The cops seemed to find that suspiciously convenient and wanted to talk to everyone present. Including me. And while Eli, who was sitting in a folding chair in the security room, had proof of our whereabouts on his thumb drive, taken from Adrianna's prison, he didn't volunteer that just yet. He wanted to upload the video first before turning over the drive to the cops, so we were stuck. Sitting. Waiting.

Alex, who had followed everything on video, called and talked to his brother about the fights he was reviewing on the security feed. Skinwalker hearing allowed me to hear it all. Alex had video of the ballroom brawl, or most of it, and he had the battle in Leo's office. "Le Bâtard and four other vamps came in through the secret side-gate entrance," he said.

Dread swarmed through me like hornets. I hadn't secured the gate after I entered. Nor had Eli. We had been keeping our exit open, but in hindsight that had been stupid. Very stupid.

"Grégoire fought, but Le Bâtard threw some kind of spell at him and Grégoire fell. That was when the sword-fighting vamps rushed Leo, five to one, and cut him to pieces. When Leo fell, they took Grégoire and retreated."

"Ask him if he can follow their vehicle," I said.

"Working on it now, Jane," Alex said.

"Have I told you recently that you do a great job?" I asked the Kid.

"Words are nice, but I'd rather have a car."

Eli snorted and ended the call.

We sat in the security office near the front door, unmoving, silent. I was thinking through the last hours, tying the events from now into events from months and months past. Tried to make sense of it all. Le Bâtard wanted Grégoire. Everything else was a feint? No, that left out the revenants and the ship at the dock and the invisible ship in the lake and the attempt to free Adrianna, and the bombs in the ballroom. Vamps never had just one goal for anything they did, thinking far ahead on the chessboards of their games. They always had multiple goals. Le Bâtard would take what he could from each attack. Yeah. That.

Dawn was approaching when a minor vamp walked up to me and handed me a box. It was plain, white, no tape, no bow, so it wasn't a present. "From your primo, Edmund Hartley. With his compliments. He said to tell you that disturbing the priestesses was not necessary. His exact words were, 'Brawn and bullets beat magic.'"

I let a corner of my mouth curl up, wondering if he had shot Adrianna to get the bracelet off her. Not asking, but still curious. I opened the box and inside was a gold snake, the one from Adriana's arm. And she had put up a fight getting it removed, if the blood on it was an indication. I sniffed the blood. The crazy woman's, all right. I rubbed my fingers over the gold, which was slick and shiny and slightly warm to the touch.

"Legs?"

I looked up. "Oh. Hey, Wrassler. 'Sup."

"I've been standing here for a good thirty seconds, talking to you."

Eli was watching me with narrowed eyes. Not concerned, exactly, but piercingly interested.

I raised the snake to Wrassler and asked, "Does this feel wrong to you?"

Wrassler was a seriously big man, like World Wrestling Entertainment big, and though he'd lost a leg and full use of one arm, he still fit the size ratio. Even more since he muscled up after the injury. He was big and bald and my friend. He took the snake and handed it back, fast. "It's spelled. Something dark."

I held the snake, drawing on Beast vision. Something dark, like a fog of moisture, wrapped around my fingers. I hadn't noticed that about the bracelet until now. The dark shadow was in the shape of a snake. The snake in the center of all things was what skinwalkers used to shape-shift. What if it was magic that worked contrary to my own? What if someone had given it to Adrianna knowing that I'd take it? I was full of conspiracy theories lately, but vamps lived for that stuff. I had no desire for anything dark magic in my life. I frowned at the snake. "You got a big hammer?"

"There's a maul in the tool shed out back. You want me to beat it out of shape, Enforcer?" He used the last word to remind me that because I was one of Leo's Enforcers, what I wanted had significance and weight, but I had to formulate a request into a specific order.

"Yes. Beat it out of shape. Then take it somewhere and have it melted down. Then give it to the witch coven and have them *Break* it. Charge the spell-cost to Leo." *Break* was a magical working to stop and destroy another magical working. I put the snake back in the box and instantly felt better. The box, though plain, was an anti-magic box. Cool. And yeah. The magic in the snake was of an attack variety, going after my own, maybe striking anyone's magic. "Once it's *broken*, bring it back to me."

"For the Enforcer." It sounded formulaic.

I figured that was agreement, and I gave him the box. "Thanks, Wrassler. How's the dating life?"

The big guy took the chair beside me. It creaked under his weight. "I never thanked you for setting me up with Jodi."

"I didn't set you up."

Wrassler scuffed a palm and sausagelike fingers over his bald pate. "Potayto, potahto. I'm crazy about that girl."

"I'm glad." And I was. Jodi was a cop, a successful woman in a man's world, but she had been lonely. So had Wrassler. They had thrown mournful, meaningful, lovesick glances at each other for months. They were perfect together.

"I'm gonna propose."

My happy romance-is-everything thought pattern crashed and burned. Jodi would have a conflict of interest if she married a blood-servant of the Master of the City. She would not be allowed to maintain her command of the woo-woo department of NOPD. She would be demoted, pushed aside until she was totally ostracized and powerless. And she would never leave the force. And Wrassler would never leave Leo. Jodi was totally human. Wrassler was a blood-servant and would live for a couple hundred years. This looked like a disaster waiting to happen. I hadn't thought this through. "Uhhh."

"I got the ring." Wrassler was holding out a small, black velvet jewelry box. He opened it with a thumb. Inside was a yellow gold ring with three diamonds the size of pencil erasers. I knew next to nothing about diamonds, and even I knew they were flawless. Nothing else flashed like that. Wrassler stood, pocketing the velvet box. "Just so you know." He walked away, the snake box in his other hand.

Lightning struck down. The Gray Between opened around me. Time skidded, twisted, started, and stopped. In the non-moments that took place, I caught a glimpse of the security system at my side. The lights, which should have been green or blinking green, all went red.

The lightning was shorting out the system. I turned in my chair and saw the snake box in Wrassler's hand. It was shining red, a line of red light, rippling like lightning coming from the front doors, crackling, hitting the snake, and then shooting through the floor. And down.

Toward the Son of Darkness.

CHAPTER 13

Landing with a Thump on the Polar Bear Rug

I spun up and into a sprint. Almost reached the main elevator before I realized it would never open for me, not in no-time, even if the cops and crime scene techs hadn't commandeered it. I whirled and raced for the stairs. Shoving the door open took effort and muscles strained to the limit. I dodged people on the stairs, more people than usual, thanks to the main elevator and half of HQ being off limits.

I took stairs, then hallways, then more stairs. It had taken weeks to map all the no-longer-secret passageways and stairways in the joint, and I was sure we had missed some. The architect had both a funny sense of humor and a good idea about hidey spots and ambush locations. I wound down and down. Past sub-four, where fanghead prisoners, like Adrianna, were kept, and into the lowest sub-basement, sub-five.

It was cold and dank and wet down here. The walls were spelled to keep out the water that would have otherwise dripped in and filled the place, thanks to the high water table in New Orleans. It was so wet right now that the whole place would be a swimming pool in minutes if the working failed. There was a faint hint of mold. A stronger tang of blood. And the reek of unwashed vamp. The Son of Darkness hung on the wall, still wearing the blood- and filth-encrusted clothing he'd worn when I had taken him down. The serial killer was still pulp and goo but was mostly human-shaped now, his long bones nearly back in place, his facial structure beginning to look normal. But his body was surrounded by a nimbus of red, a glow just like the one on the snake box. "Bingo," I said.

Time spat and shook through me and returned to normal. I watched carefully and the magics vanished. If I hadn't been using Beast-sight and my own skinwalker abilities, I'd never have seen it at all.

"Joses, son of Judas Iscariot," I said, pronouncing it *Yo-sace, son of Ioudas Issachar,* as he had himself two thousand years ago, when he and his brother took the crosses of Golgotha and tried to bring their father, Judas, the betrayer, back to life. "Joseph Santana."

He didn't move. He didn't breathe. His heart—not that he had one anymore, since I'd ripped it out of his chest—didn't beat. I had no idea how he was healing except that his body might truly be immortal. Even without a heart, which I had given to the witches. I needed to call Jodi and see if the heart was still fresh and healthy. If the heart hadn't begun decomp, that meant that I could take the SOD's head and the pieces would still live. Which would be freaky.

I thought about the smell of the blood in the blood bottle. And the pink thread on the dog-fanged revenants. Someone had used immortal blood on the head and neck of the dead vamps when they were reassembled for funerals. And they healed. Sort of. Enough to come out of the graves when called. That was why so many were buried in human grave-yards and not in the vamp cemetery on the far side of the Mississippi River with the other vamps.

If a sleeper agent had gotten some of that blood to the SOD at any point in the last months, that might be why the Son of Darkness was healing. Callan. Fernand. Amitee. Any of them might have gotten down here. I leaned and sniffed. Caught the stench of the mixed blood from the blood bottle. It still smelled fresh, which never happened with vamp blood until now. I traced the scent with my nose. It had been sprinkled all over the SOD.

This. This was why they had attacked HQ. To get down to sub-five and put blood on the heartless bag of bones.

I turned and walked back up the stairways and walkways and tunnels and passageways and back to the front entrance. Time flipped back and forth between stopped and normal as I walked through it all until I found Wrassler and Derek in conversation and told them what I had discovered. "Get a hose and wash him off," I said. "It's probably too late but it's marginally better than nothing. And find and secure Callan and the Marchands. They're in this up to their fangs." When neither moved, I said, "Orders of the Enforcer," which let them off the hook if there were negative repercussions from my decisions.

"I'll hose off Joseph Santana," Wrassler said, speaking of the Son of Darkness. "You handle the detainees." Derek nodded and turned on a heel without speaking. Wrassler raised his eyebrows and looked at me. "Why does he hate you?"

I shrugged. "My winning personality?"

Wrassler moved off, chuckling and muttering, "Winning personality. Yeah. Sure."

In the foyer, the cops were still questioning vamps, trying to get in the last interviews before dawn hit and the younger vamps became comatose and the older ones simply walked away. It would be hours before they talked to me, and I was done waiting. NOPD knew where I lived. They could come visit me there. I waved to Eli and walked out the front door.

There was a vamp central SUV parked in the big parking area with the key fob under the mat. I started the vehicle, flipped on the wipers, and drove home. I let my mind rove and wander as I drove, not trying to think anything in particular, not trying to make connections or deduce anything at all. Just letting myself meander internally. I had a bad feeling about a lot of things I had seen tonight and they seemed to lead nowhere. Which meant that they had to have a connection.

I pulled in an empty spot in front of the house and stopped. The lightning hit again, far off this time, and I saw the green

sparking glow in my bedroom. The initial traces of understanding washed through me as all the little pieces began to
line up for inspection.

The first time I had seen the magical thing called *le breloque* had been in a storm. A magical storm. A storm god, an
Anzu, wanted it. There were magical detonators on normal
bombs. Red magics on the snake and on the SOD. Mixed
blood on the VIP—very important prisoner. All the Europeans knew we had him, and maybe they didn't know he was
heartless. *Heartless.* Funny me. Except it wasn't amusing at
all. After seeing revenants rise, I had to concede that the
blood might heal the bag of bones. Maybe totally.

Whatever was going on was tied to the SOD, *le breloque*,
the magical storm, the *arcenciels* trapped in the magical
storm, and the European vamps. Leo said he knew they
hadn't come ashore en masse. But they were tied in with
everything that was going on, and Leo had to know that.
Sooo. Leo knew what was going on and he was letting it
happen. Or . . . He had thought he knew. And then Grégoire
was taken. Yeah. That.

I turned off the vehicle, got out, and looked up, seeing
only cloud-to-cloud lightning. I pulled on Beast's night vision, however, and I saw a great deal more. *Arcenciels* dancing in the lightning, not dropping into no-time. Three of
them. As if they were trapped in real time.

I walked inside. Wrung out and replaced the sponges by
the door. And opened my bedroom door. On my small table
was *le breloque*, glowing green, throwing green sparks. Red
motes raced through the green. The top part of the corona
was composed of laurel leaves. The bottom was a gold ring
with the odd symbols on it. Tonight I had seen a similar gold
circlet on the head of a king, his hands all over Katie Fonteneau, Leo's heir.

Looking down, I saw the red motes and the silver-gray
motes of my skinwalker energies inside me. Magic. Magic
that had been waiting to find its proper shape and form.
Waiting to awaken. *The long game.* I opened the small footstool and stood on the top rung so I could see the box of
magical stuff. It was sparking too, the same colors as the
corona that had once been a crown on a king's head. Care-

fully, I took the box off the shelf and placed it on the foot of the bed. I opened the box. Inside were magical trinkets, including a particular gem. The Glob had been part of the blood-magic spell that I had interrupted the night the red motes had entered me. Now the device was attuned to me, somehow, something I had known since it had been transformed inside my own lightning-scorched flesh. Lightning had changed it. Changed me.

Right now, it was being charged by the magical storm outside. I didn't touch it. Not this time.

Alex knocked softly on the door. I grunted and he stepped inside. "Two hours ago, two humans were allowed ashore from a cruise ship that may or may not have had vampires as other passengers. Their reason for being allowed on U.S. soil was stated as being 'to deal with government and public officials and appropriate paperwork.'"

I closed the box and put it back on the shelf. Slid my hand away from the *hedge of thorns* that protected it. Alex said, "Brandon and Brian were at the dock as Leo's lawyer and interpreters when they heard that Grégoire had been taken. They left the docks midnegotiation. An international incident seems to be brewing between what might have been European blood-servants, representatives of the Master of the City, and the U.S. government. The mayor's spokesperson is making a political commotion and squawking to the media about the MOC walking out of negotiations."

"Did Leo call the Roberes off?"

"No. That was unilateral."

"So, not Leo's decision."

"True. It's still a problem."

"But not an Enforcer job at this point in time."

"No. But Grégoire and Brian and Brandon all are missing."

I remembered the painting in Leo's office, Katie in bed with a man, a woman peering in through the window as the last piece fell into place. I knew who all three players from that painting were. "Katie was having sex with the king, the emperor Titus Flavius Vespasianus himself," I muttered.

"What?"

I shook my head, as if to shake up the things rattling

around inside it. "I'll be right back." I went through the side door, across the porch, and back into the rain as I dropped to the ground. By now I had been so wet for so long that I didn't even notice it except for the cold. That was pretty miserable, and I shivered. I passed my boulders and stopped at the fountain. It was a huge marble tulip full of rainwater to the petaled rim, with a miniature naked woman sitting atop, the sculpture finely detailed. It no longer splashed, because I had turned off the water, but the statue was of Katie, naked, complete with fangs. She rose from the middle of the fountain bowl, a small, carved stone perfection, a masterwork.

This house had been Katie's before she lent it to me and then gave it to me as payment for a service. I used her teapots to make tea. Sat on her furniture. I never liked her, but I had never worried that she was a threat. Bedbug crazy, yes. Dangerous, no. I turned from the fountain, raced up the shattered boulders in the former rock garden, and leaped for the brick fence, less than twelve feet from the top of the rock pile. I got a toehold on a small irregularity and shoved up. Now that I didn't have to hide what I was, I vaulted over and landed on the far side, splashing down.

I trotted to Katie's back door and banged.

Troll, Katie's primo blood-servant, opened the door, almost as if he had been expecting me. He looked pale in the predawn light, as if he had been fed on too often and too deeply. He was wearing a T-shirt under a hoodie and thick jogging pants against the growing cold. He was huge, all muscle and toughness, and the winter clothes were tight on his torso, loose on his lower legs and arms, layered for the weather. "Little Janie," he said.

"Troll. The Enforcer of the Master of the City of New Orleans and the greater Southeast USA needs to see the paintings of Katie."

His face didn't change but his scent did. A faint, barely-there alteration. It gained the taint of despair. I thought he might refuse me, but the title of Enforcer obligated him to back away. Only Katie herself could refuse me.

It was nearly dawn, in the middle of an unusual and epic storm. Katie's Ladies was empty of clients, the girls in their rooms doing whatever working girls who catered to vamps did in their off hours. I walked through the house. Troll followed me, and together we stopped at each painting of Katie, studying them all, one by one.

The house was elegant if slightly overdone, decorated in hundreds of shades of gold from palest yellow to darkest golden brown. There were paintings and statues and objects d'art everywhere, a lot of them of Katie. I ended up where I had intended, in the parlor, gold silk fabrics and the bigger-than-life artwork of a nude Katie hanging on the wall. I had first seen the painting when two vamps were tortured in this room, in silver cages. One was Callan. The vamp from the ballroom.

That horrible night, I had kept my eyes on the portrait of Katie to keep from having to watch the cruelty. That made me a coward in my own eyes, but my cowardice was something to think about another time. Or maybe never.

Now I studied the oversized portrait in detail, deliberately.

Katie was naked as a jaybird, standing on a mussed tapestry of some kind, in a field, with a brook nearby and lots of trees. The painting was done in daylight, with shadows falling as they would have in sunshine, which meant it was painted before Katie was turned. In the distant background was a building. Not a castle, more like a fancy palace. Behind Katie was a pedestal, and on the pedestal were two crowns, one resting at an angle over the other. But the brushstrokes and the colors of the pedestal were different from the cracked and shiny patina of the rest of the portrait.

I reached out and touched them, comparing the textures of the paints. The pedestal and crowns had been added later. I felt Troll moving closer, and the hairs on the back of my neck stood up. I said, "I don't remember this painting when I upgraded the house's security system, soon after I got to New Orleans."

Troll didn't reply.

"It was added after Katie redecorated, wasn't it?"

He remained silent, immobile. I didn't turn, but I felt and smelled Troll's tension and something like pain. More softly I asked, "It was sent here, wasn't it? It was a message. That the Europeans were coming and that Katie was to remember old loyalties." My fingers stroked again over the pedestal and its crowns. Crowns that, at some point, had been joined together and were currently glowing with each lightning strike in my bedroom.

I turned to Troll, studying him. He looked tired, worn, beaten. Avoiding my eyes, he slowly sat on the gold couch, fingers dangling between his knees, his sleeves hanging to his middle knuckles. He shook his head, the soft lights tacking across his bald dome. "I kept hoping that Leo would come here, would drink from me. Would know what my mistress was doing. He didn't. He remained far away."

As if Leo had known . . . "When did the painting arrive?"

"Just after you came to New Orleans. Prior to the first visit by the weres and the successful parley."

Were-creatures had come out of the closet recently, and the Party of African Weres and the International Association of Weres had visited Leo and reached a political accord, in what had probably been direct defiance of the Europeans.

"You know I have to stop her."

"And you know I can't let you harm her." In a move that would have impressed a vamp, Troll snapped his hands. Two small handguns dropped into his palms.

I was already moving. Kicked up my leg. Stepping into the motion, adding momentum and spin. He was a big guy, but a well-placed kick to the wrists beat weight lifting any day. I followed it up, stepping closer and swinging a fist into his jaw. The impact sent his jaw swinging, broken. My other fist landed slightly higher, a direct hit to his temple. He went down. Landing with a thump on the polar bear rug several feet away. Out cold.

On a human, the force and location of the hits would likely have resulted in a need for surgery on his jaw and possibly permanent brain damage. Movies that show the injured getting up and continuing the fight are just stupid. Most no-holds-barred fights end in less than a minute.

I took away the guns, sliding them out of the metal harness that had snapped the weapons into his palms. Secreted them in the couch cushions. While he was out, I sent a text to Eli and then did a back-side pat-down on Troll. Ignoring the broken jaw, I flipped him over and did a front-side pat-down, which was when I discovered the blades in his underwear. If he had been conscious I might never have found the blades. As it was, I turned my head to the side and worked in my peripheral vision when I removed them. They were warm and slightly sweat-damp. He might have tried to kill me, but I liked Troll and I never wanted to get this personal with the big guy. And he was Rick's uncle back a few generations. I might need Rick. No point in making him mad for getting fresh with a family member.

I needed somewhere to put Troll. I made a quick call on Katie's landline phone, as I had forgotten my own cell back at the house. I grabbed an arm and rolled the big guy to a sitting position and then up into a fireman's carry, keeping one of his broken wrists in mine. His scent changed as I re-positioned him. I staggered under the weight. "Holy crap, dude. What do you weigh? Four hundred pounds?"

"Three fifty," he said, his words muffled by the broken jaw. "Wimp."

"I broke your jaw and both wrists," I said as I carried him out the front door into the rain. Grunting. Breathing too hard. "Don't *wimp* me."

"I been drinking Katie's blood for over a hundred years. You think I couldn't evade if I'd wanted to?"

"So you *wanted* to be taken down?"

"I wanted to be taken to Leo and read," Troll said, "with no one the wiser."

I walked out the door and stood in a soft rain in the dawn light and thought about his too-soft words. Then I started hiking down the street, his weight making my joints ache. After a block, I said, "You can't say no to Katie, who is working with the EVs as a spy in Leo's camp. But you think the EVs are going to backstab her once they're finished with her. So you want Leo to know, and then take her down easy and lock her away. Give her a chance to become loyal to him again."

"Katie's always been loyal to Leo," he said. More sadly he added, "She loves him to the moon and back. But Le Bâtard has her younger sister prisoner. A vamp scion named Alesha Fonteneau."

"And the bastard is threatening Katie with killing the sister?"

"Yeah. Alesha is . . . was Leo's foremost spy in the European vamp camp, the one Leo calls Madam Spy. Le Bâtard found out. He hurt her. Bad. Sent photos to Katie. She lost it. Now stop asking me questions. I hurt. Get Leo to read me."

"Okay. Thank you, Troll."

He rumbled a laugh, the sound more pain than mirth. I walked on. Around me traffic increased, but no one even slowed down to look at me. In New Orleans I was either too dangerous to notice or just another street artist on the way to the corner I paid the city to use. Either way, not their business. A few minutes later, Troll said, "For reasons I don't fully understand, I trust you, Jane Yellowrock. Don't make me regret all this."

"I'm a sweetheart," I said, doing a little bounce and re-adjust. He grunted when his gut landed on my shoulder. "What's not to trust?"

When he could speak again he said, "You're a stone-cold killer, Janie. But you got morals. If this city survives, it'll be because you turned the tide."

"Your jaw healed already, didn't it?"

"Close to eighty percent, yes."

"Pretend to be unconscious when Derek takes you to HQ."

"Will do."

A heavily armored SUV pulled to the curb and the hatch opened. I dumped Troll into the back and pressed the button to close the hatch. I leaned in the passenger window to see Derek at the wheel. He looked like hell, wrinkled and rumpled, smelling of vamp blood, sweat, and gunpowder, a coms earbud in his ear. "Take him to Leo. He tried to kill me. He needs to be bled and read, and not by Katie."

"You think she's in with everything that's happening now?"

"She's in love with Leo. If she's a traitor to him, then Leo's enemies have to have some kind of leverage, forcing her."

I spun away, through the rain. "Legs!" Derek shouted.

I did another one-eighty, back to the window. "Alex is on the coms channel. He said you forgot your cell and he has a message for you." Derek put a finger to his ear. "Got it," he said to Alex. "There was a bank robbery overnight and the robbers raided over a hundred safe-deposit boxes. He says you had boxes in the vault."

Boxes that had previously been filled with my magical trinkets. Including *le breloque* and the Glob. But I had already removed the magical items and stored them in the closet at the house. Where Alex was, alone. The blood that wasn't frozen in my veins plummeted to my feet.

Littermate! Beast growled.

"Alex," I whispered. Louder I said, "Call Gee. Tell him to get to my house. To fly like a bird! Call Alex and tell him to get into the safe room! Now!" I whirled and raced through the rain and the water running in the streets and down the sidewalks.

"Jane? What? What? Alex?" he said. "Alex!" The SUV's engine roared and tires splashed as Derek pulled the SUV around and headed back to my house. Troll was still in back.

I raced through the rain and water, feeling the pull on my waterlogged boots, splashing through water that reached my shins in places. Glanced up once. No *arenciels*. Where were they right now? I tried to pull on the Gray Between, but it stayed stubbornly locked down. Fear did that sometimes. And of course, now that I needed to stop time, I couldn't access it. No lightning to help me along, and Beast wasn't responding. Without the time to center myself and meditate, my magic was not perfect. With the storm, it was downright undependable.

Taking the most direct route, I dove inside Katie's Ladies, raced through it, leaving the doors open, the walls rattling, and out into the rain in the backyard, toward my home. I pulled on Beast's strength. Gathered myself. Leaped.

In the instant of pushing off, Beast burst through me. Pelt sprouted on my hands and arms beneath my soaked jacket. My body wrenched, hips changing shape, feet trying to grow wider in the now-ill-fitting boots. Waist shrank, shoulders expanded, rounded, stretched. My upper teeth erupted with fangs, the bones rearranging. I grunted in agony, the sound part-growl. Hunger clenched my insides. Too many half-shifts, not enough food to fuel them.

At the crest of the brick fence, I shoved off with a re-shaped palm and landed in a crouch in the backyard. The iron gate to the side of the house was broken and hanging open, the metal twisted back and over. The side door of the house was in splinters. Again.

Beast-fast, I pulled one of the mostly useless .380s and racked a round into the chamber. My knuckles were too large to handle a gun, and I held it slightly to the side, three fingers pointing away, as I slid my pinkie over the trigger. It was an unconventional firing grip and my fingers were likely to get smashed when it fired, but it was all that still fit.

With my left hand I yanked a vamp-killer free. It all took three steps as I raced across the yard and into the house.

Alex was nowhere to be seen, but there was a bloody shotgun pattern on the wall, the holes made by .30-.06 buckshot, with a head-shaped section missing. Below the pattern, on the floor, was a revenant, trying to get back up. Hard to do with no face, no eyes. I took his head with a single swing of the vamp-killer. The head slid across the room and spun on its ear, beneath the kitchen table, where it banged around on the table and chair legs like a macabre game of pinball.

Tearing into my bedroom, I took another head. Blood erupted into the air and over my hands. This one had fed more recently and . . . I realized I'd just killed a vamp and not a rev. I dropped the blade and grabbed for the head, whirling in midair. Missed, its hair flying.

Her hands went limp. The body fell. She dropped *le breloque*. It bounced and rolled across the floor. Her head bounced too, landing upright, facing me. Female, blue-eyed and needle-fanged. Blowback on her face from where Alex had shot the rev. She was a stranger, like the others, old and long dead.

Fear I hadn't perceived released my heart.

I picked up *le breloque*, hooking the magical instrument over my arm, blood splattering. I also took the Glob and shoved it into a pocket, getting blood on it as well. That couldn't be good. The Glob warmed me all over in an instant, as if it knew what I needed and sent it to me, part of its lightning magic. I picked up the vamp's head by the hair. I'd carried them this way before, hair being the most expedient handhold.

As I moved through the apartment, I realized that sword

practice with the vamps in La Destreza had given me a lot more skill with my blades. Not so long ago, taking a head was a multistrike proposition, sometimes ending with a little sawing or hacking—though the extra strength of my half-form helped.

Wind whooshed through the house, wet and cold and miserable. I stood in my bedroom, holding a king's magical crown and a vamp's head. Her hair was tangled around my fingers like a twisted wet brown tail. A cell phone began to buzz, some reggae bell tone, probably Derek calling my partner. I'd moved fast.

"Jane?"

I turned to see Gee, standing in the doorway, two long swords out to his sides. "I haven't cleared the house," I said, my voice too low, too rough.

His eyes fell to the wreath on my arm but he didn't speak of it, instead asking the question that warmed more than my body. "Where is Alex?"

I knew the answer by the scents in the house, scents I hadn't parsed until now. "In the weapons room. He'll be holding a shotgun. If you open the door, try not to let him kill you. It would hurt him a lot."

"Your concern for my welfare is touching." Gee stepped closer, his eyes taking in my face, with the huge upper and lower cat fangs and my oddly shaped body. "Brandon and Brian are missing," he said, and I remembered the incident at the docks when the Robere twins had left the scene precipitously. The outcry from the mayor's office.

"You think they found Grégoire's attackers and are—" I almost said *dead too*. But none of them were dead. They couldn't be. I changed it to, "in custody of Le Bâtard and Louis le Jeune?"

"I don't know. Find them before it's too late." He held out a fist, closed around something rounded. I didn't really trust the big bird, but I held out my huge, big-knuckled paw. In it he dropped a small black stone, one with white inclusions in it. "It's called an Apache tear. If you need me, you can crush it. I will come."

I tucked the stone in my jacket pocket, far away from the Glob. The pocket was full of water. I had to get some water-wicking fighting armor. "I'll get some guards from HQ to watch my house, but will you keep an eye out too?" I looked outside and added, "Keep it and my partners safe?"

"If you will keep *le breloque* safe."

"I'll do my best. But people are more important than magical implements. I'll use it to save lives if necessary."

Gee hesitated. Slowly he said, "We have a bargain, little goddess."

Together, we went to the shelving that covered the weapons room and I tapped three times, waited, and tapped once. Tomorrow we'd have to change the knock code. Gee and I stood back as the shelves opened and Alex peeked out, his curls in high kink, his face ashen, a shotgun in a two-hand grip. His eyes swept the room, taking in the rev and its head. The head in my hand. He started laughing. It was mildly hysterical but at least it was laughter. "Kit," Beast said, using my mouth.

Alex dropped the shotgun. Gee swiped it from the air before it hit the floor and discharged. Alex fell into my arms, pale and shaking, making the wreath clank against my weapons.

I said, "It's okay. It's okay." I patted his shoulder awkwardly. "Gee is here to take care of you. He'll see that the rev is taken away and Leo's cleanup crew will take care of the rest. And I'll get you some of Derek's Tequila team."

"Sure. Fine." I heard him lick his lips, a dry, panicked sound. His heart was racing against my chest. "I gotta say. I may move into Ed's room. It's the safest place in the house."

I grinned. "Take that up with Edmund."

"Yeah. Right." He stepped away. "Thanks for coming."

I heard a vehicle door open as I touched his curls, stalked to the front door, and opened it. Nearly took a foot in my face where it was about to kick in the door. I caught the foot in midair—all those catlike reflexes—and held it high. Derek was balancing on his other foot, extended for the kick, able to stop momentum. It wasn't something he'd been able to do back when he was just human. I wondered if he knew that. I grinned a feral cat-grin, all fangs, and said, "Awww. You were coming to save me."

I dropped his boot and Derek shook his whole body.

Battle energies flushed through his skin, unused and rancid to my expanded scent capabilities, his body full of vamp power and strength. His eyes rested on the head in my hands. "Alex?"

I let the snark flow out of me. "He's okay. Thank you for coming."

"Yeah. Well. I like the Kid."

Meaning that if it had been me in trouble he wouldn't have bothered. Check.

I shut the door in his face, went to the kitchen, and set the vamp head in the kitchen sink. Put the rev head beside it. Opened the fridge. Took out a Coke can and popped it with a single claw in the ring. I drained it, letting the sugar and the caffeine hit my system like a sweet, high-kicking brick. "Oh. Praise baby Jesus and dance on the head of a pin." Before Alex could ask, I said, "One of my house mothers used to say that when she had her first sip of coffee in the mornings." Alex had stopped laughing and now looked troubled. I lowered my head to him and asked, "What?"

"Am I gonna be in trouble with Leo?" He swept his arm to the blast damage on the wallboard, the blood splatter, the heads, and the bodies, one in my bedroom with a bloody mess and one in the living room with much less blood but a stink of decomp.

I chuckled and opened a Snickers bar. I tossed the entire bar in my oversized mouth and chewed, talking as I did. "Not a lick. You did good."

"I may have nightmares. I may be having one now," he confessed. "And Jane? You look really weird in that form. Especially with chocolate in your teeth."

"Uh-huh." I told him about the blood on the Son of Darkness and my theories about the attack on HQ and finished with, "What else you got on the Big Bad Uglies?"

I heard a *ding* and Alex pulled a small tablet from his pocket, scanning and swiping the screen. Excitement began to overwrite the stink of fear in his pores. "Oh yeah," he mumbled. "That's good intel. Especially with this." He waggled the screen in front of my face. "The old vamps don't seem to understand modern tech. It's like following footprints in the snow." He gestured me to his table-desk in the living room, which, semimiraculously, was still upright. He opened a laptop-tablet and transferred the info from his small tablet to the larger one. "I tracked the ones who took Grégoire on traffic cams and the private security cams I had already acquired." Acquired. That was a hacker term for *hacked*. "I know where Grégoire is," he finished.

My adrenaline pumped hard. "And?"

"You sound like a cat trying to talk."

I grinned around my fangs and popped in another Snickers. He had a point.

"He's currently in the Garden District. Specifically at Arceneau Clan Home. The security system just went down, which means that Grégoire gave up the codes. Better hurry. I already called Bruiser to pick you up." Lights lit up outside, a car pulling into the slot next to the SUV I sorta stole. I pocketed the .380 and grabbed a heavy gobag with better gear and clothes and a nice fluffy towel. The bag was waterproof, thank God. I stomped into the blasting rain.

I opened the SUV door, threw my bag into the floor, and climbed in, wet leathers and leather seat meeting with a grinding squeak. "Hey, gorgeous," Bruiser said. And though I looked like the love child of a wet cat and the creature from *Swamp Thing*, I knew he was serious. He thought I was pretty no matter what I looked like. That alone melted my heart. Bruiser pulled away from the curb and I stared out the window, not wanting him to see what his words did to me.

It was still an hour before dawn when we parked down from Arceneau Clan Home. The house was standing open, the door wide and the house seemingly dark inside. Bruiser and I both pulled weapons. I chose the Benelli M4 and silver fléchette ammo, which had been in the huge gear bag. The combat shotgun could fire seven three-inch shells before I had to reload. It also could also accommodate my bigger hands and knuckles. Bruiser chose two long swords and two .45s with silver-lead ammo. He was going with the big guns.

Silently, we moved through the rain and the dark up to the front door. I stopped him with a raised hand and stepped in first, sniffing for explosives. Instead I smelled Brandon and Brian and Grégoire, but their scents were fading. Grégoire's captors had brought him here to get something, and it had to be something that would affect the EV's takeover of New Orleans. But Grégoire was gone. The twins had arrived only moments too late, if my nose was telling me things as it should. Overriding all of them, I smelled unknown vamps. Strangers. Were the Deadly Duo here? Did we have them cornered?

I held up three fingers and mouthed to my honeybunch, *Brandon, Brian, Grégoire, gone.* I pointed out the door, then held up two fingers. *Two unsub-vamps. Some humans. Maybe four.* I pointed to the kitchen at the back of the house. Bruiser nodded. Started inside. Stopped when a door opened and closed, unseen, the sound hollow.

A muffled scream sounded in the instant the door was open. A wind whooshed through. I caught a whiff of burning human flesh and terror and bowels and urine. Bruiser took an uneasy breath. Glanced at me in warning and question. I gave him a quick nod to show I smelled it too. But no one moved this way when the door closed. We slid into shadow.

Using standard paramilitary urban-operations, conceal-and-clear techniques, we slid from shadow to shadow and room to room, clearing each, moving faster than human, but still silent and far too slow. The sound of muffled screaming grew strong, but despite my instincts, I didn't rush back, not until I knew we would be safe. No point in giving them more people to hurt, whoever they were.

The place was deserted. No people, no furniture. No furnishings at all. Walls were cut, broken, shot up. Blood was everywhere. I didn't know whose.

Grégoire had gotten his people out. Grégoire's primo, Dominique, and Shaun Mac Lochlainn, her anamchara, were in Atlanta, with Del, Leo's primo and his lawyer, Del flying back and forth as needed to deal with Leo's legal needs in New Orleans and cleaning up the legal and physical mess that existed in Atlanta since Leo had defeated the Blood Master of Georgia. Grégoire's scions and blood-servants had been with him at HQ. He might have been a quivering ball of terror at the thought of Le Bâtard being in New Orleans, but he had still been thinking. Until he was taken.

We moved quickly to the back of the house and met at the kitchen door. A woman's voice carried through the door, smooth, velvet tones, accented, perhaps Greek. But definitely European. "Where are the Onorios Brian and Brandon Robere?" she asked. A muffled scream followed. Grunting. Then again, soft and pleasant, the woman asked, "Where are the Onorios Brian and Brandon Robere?" There was no mention of Grégoire. They had him already. The victim, clearly being tortured, screamed again. Through the door we heard, "I shall remove the choke gag from you and you will answer me, every question, this time. And then I will kill you quickly. If I sense prevarication, I will replace the choke and proceed as I have until now. Nod if you understand. Good boy."

Bruiser looked at me and his face was both intent and weirdly happy. He leaned in and whispered, "Six against two. No place I'd rather be. No one I'd rather be with. Not in all of my long years."

My heart did a little somersault and pirouette. Bruiser kicked in the door.

CHAPTER 14

If It's Ass You Want . . .

Time sped up with battlefield awareness. I took in the upscale kitchen in an instant. The kitchen stovetop burners were on, gas flames a bright, too-hot blue. Knives glowed red in the flames. Two foreign vamps and six unknown blood-servants. Another blood-servant was stretched out over the island, face up, arms and legs cinched back. Naked. Exposed. Torso and thighs burned where he'd been tortured.

Before I could blink, the vamps whirled and drew swords. Bruiser fired twice, fast, two-tapping the vamp closest to the tortured human. The other vamp popped toward Bruiser. The blood-servants swept toward me like a wave of death, blades in every hand. I braced the Benelli against my shoulder, aimed at the first human, midcenter, fired, the shot pattern tight and deadly. She fell. All sound blasted away by the shot. We had miscounted at four humans.

The others spread out, moving so fast I could barely follow, humans hyped up on vamp blood. I fired again, missing, wasting my expensive ammo on humans.

Stupid thought.

I aimed, fired. Fired. Hit a second human, too low for a

mortal wound, but she was down. Four shells gone, three left. Two humans down.

Three humans ducked behind the furniture, one on the far side of the island.

A fourth leaped atop the island. Even as her weight landed on one foot, she fired down at the man tied there. Three shots midchest. Pushed up, transferred her weight again, and fell onto me. I dropped back and down, the weapon pointed up. I had clear and complete focus on the woman's face as she fell. Onto me. Onto my shotgun.

Miscalculation. Shock at the sight of my face. Fear. In midair, she tried to roll away. I squeezed the trigger. Upper chest, center. Took out her sternum and everything beneath it, including heart. I rolled away and she landed on the spot where I'd lain.

Three down. Three bad guys to go. Two shots left before I had to reload. At the speed the humans were moving, I'd never get that done.

The human behind the island was crouching around the side; I took aim at where the head should appear. Someone outside my field of vision tossed a pile of kitchen cloths onto the flaming stove and slammed a bottle of something on top. It shattered. The scent of good brandy filled the air. The cloths ignited in a *whomp* of sound and bright light. Flames leaped high Beast retreated from the forefront of my brain, shouting into my thoughts, *Fire!*

I centered the sights on the very edge of the island. The human behind it stuck out his head just as the woman who had thrown the brandy rushed me. I squeezed the trigger. The top of his head burst all over the cabinets behind. It was still splattering when I rolled flat to my back, weapon pointed down along my body. Tucked my toes down hard. Fired.

Last shot. The weapon bucked slightly in my arms.

The female blood-servant dropped. I was out of ammo with one human left. Where was he? Where were the vamps?

The last human raced through the kitchen doorway and into the predawn, a blur of darkness. I rolled over again, now holding a nine-millimeter that had been in the gobag. Smoke roiled slowly across the ceiling. Flames danced up the wall and dashed across the ceiling, separating the smoke and sending it rolling faster. The room was hot. My wet clothing started to steam.

Fire dashed across the room. Ignited a tablecloth. The kitchen was empty.

Except for Bruiser and a vamp.

They were sitting together on the floor, the vamp's legs splayed like a child's in a sandbox. Bruiser sat on her lap, his arms around her, her head pressed to his neck. She was drinking.

I scuttled close to separate her from her undead life. But Bruiser's arms tightened, pulling her closer. Something dark and deadly crawled through me. Bruiser, loving a vamp. I centered the weapon on her head. Bruiser held up a single finger, telling me . . . Telling me to wait? Wait! While another woman sucked on him? My heart did a twisting dive.

Beast dove to the forefront of my brain and growled. *Mate. My mate. Kill other.*

"Bruiser?"

Bruiser's finger rose again. I realized the vamp wasn't drinking. She was sitting with her fangs at Bruiser's throat but not inside his flesh.

I saw it then. The magics. Dark red rose, the color of watered blood, clear and sparkling, as if it contained bubbles. Magic like champagne. Flowing from the female vamp and into him. Into Bruiser. *Into Bruiser. Into* . . . He was draining the vamp.

Onorio magics, unknown magics. No one had any idea what Onorios did. What they could do. Only that they were rare. And powerful. And that Leo had three. Or he'd had three until today.

Slowly, I lowered the weapon. Safetied and put it away.

Flames roared as my hearing came back online. Heat like an oven blasted across the room. In the distance, sirens wailed.

Hunched over. Gathered and holstered my weapons. Crab-walked to the human who had been tortured and checked his pulse. He was long gone. I knew him, but didn't remember his name. Jim? John? One of Grégoire's people. He should have been in HQ, safe. I had no idea what had made him stay here or come back here. It had been a deadly blunder, whatever the reason.

Something darkened the doorway. I found a nine-mil in my hand again. Pointed at Gee DiMercy. "Get out," he said. "The entire place is—" He spotted Bruiser on the floor. His eyes grew wide and a look of intense satisfaction settled there for an instant, like a bird touching down and pushing back off. The expression, whatever it had meant, disappeared.

"Why aren't you with Alex?" I demanded.

"Edmund is with him, as are a quartet of Derek Lee's liquor security. Arceneau Clan Home is burning," he said to Bruiser. "The fire department has arrived."

Bruiser nodded and reached around to the vamp's face. He closed her eyes and stood. Her magics were a taut, twisted layer pressed tightly to her skin. She was still alive. Undead. Whatever. Bruiser lifted and carried her from the room. I followed. Gee went around front. Or flew over the house. Whichever.

Out front, Bruiser laid the vamp's body into the backseat of the SUV. She was mostly unconscious, her eyes rolled back, her fangs out. She looked drunk. Gee walked up as the fire truck pulled into the driveway. Firemen in heavy gear piled out and began to disgorge hoses and axes and ladders. A rotund man was shouting orders. Rain fell in slow spatters, not much help against the fire.

Lightning struck close by. The Gray Between flickered on and off. Finally. Time did its little dance. I stood still, hating that the storm was in control and not me. I leaned against the SUV. Gee swiveled to me and focused on the space around me, where the Gray Between glimmered. He could see it. I said, "You told me that the storm wasn't natural. That it's magic. What kind of magic? Anzu magic?"

"Not a power I can control alone, but if you give me *le breloque* I can try to—"

"No. I remember you and the vamps and the witches fighting over that thing. Not happening. The storm. Is it witch magic?"

"Yes," Gee said, sounding miserable, looking up into the night clouds.

I glanced back at the house. Flames were consuming the back, a raging inferno leaping for the windows. The wind, reacting to the heat, picked up. The blaze thrust, voracious, to the front door and the pure air that poured through it, feeding the fire. The kitchen and its bodies were a ruin. If I hadn't used silver ammo no one would have known who had shot the humans. I'd be in an interrogation room as soon as the silver fléchette damage was discovered by the medical examiner. I wasn't the only one who used the rounds but I was the best known.

Gee said, "Adan Bouvier, in the mural that is no more, was . . . is . . . a water witch with strong air capabilities as well."

It was info I hadn't asked for. When someone powerful gives me information for free, they usually wanted me to do their dirty work. I should have socked him and walked away. Should have. "I'm listening," I said instead.

Gee looked up into the clouds. "If he is still among the undead, he is capable of creating such a storm."

I remembered the black motes of power in the clouds, when the *arcenciels* were flying there, cavorting in real time. "Was Bouvier a friend of the Damours?"

"Yes."

"What happened to Adan?" I asked. Adan was the fanghead who had owned Ka Nvista, a Cherokee slave with yellow eyes like me.

"There was an 'incident,'" Gee said, "and though Leo told others he was dead, there are those of us who know the truth. He went back to France."

"You think he's the water witch causing this storm, either on shore with the others, or still aboard the invisible cruise ship." I wanted Adan to be alive. I wanted it so much that my hands ached with the need. I wanted him alive so I could question him about Ka Nvista. About how she died. And more, about how she lived. And if there were more of us.

That hope, that need, I shoved deep inside, not sure when it had gotten loose.

"No," Gee said, his dark eyes exploring the downtown skyline, then the uptown skyline, back toward the French Quarter and the river, then toward Lake Pontchartrain (downstream, upstream, river side, and lake side, in the parlance of the locals), as if scenting something only he could sense. He said, "I believe that he is on land. Here in the city. Any witch worth her salt can cast an *obfuscation* working over the ship and vanish in the storm. But creating a storm such as this, that takes a gift not seen on these shores in centuries. And not one practiced aboard ship, but with a witch circle, one drawn on the Earth."

Bruiser's cell chirped. He tapped the screen and said, "Alex?"

"I'm safe. Tell Jane her cell is off again." His voice was manic, the way it sounded when he was overindulging on energy drinks. Eli and I had talked to him about the dangers of overdosing on them, but he was a geek teenager, ten feet tall and Kryptonite-proof.

I fished around and found my cell. It was in pieces; the only thing still intact was the Kevlar cover. I didn't remember picking it up at the house. I didn't remember breaking it, but it must have happened in the firefight inside Arceneau Clan Home.

"Did she bust another one?" Alex asked Bruiser.

I muttered something less than ladylike under my breath and tossed it to the SUV floor.

"Yes," Bruiser said. "She did."

"Ha! I owe myself five bucks." He continued, "I got three things: Vamps coming ashore in a rubber dinghy while the attention was focused on shore during the original altercation with the Feds and ICE. Brandon's and Brian's current whereabouts. And Grégoire's attackers/kidnappers on camera after they left HQ."

I stood straight. "Yeah? Grégoire first."

"Timeline: The EV vamps carried Grégoire out through the side entrance of HQ and gave him to two humans. He was bound and bleeding and unconscious. The humans carried him down the street and put him in a car. I got a partial plate. Found the car on the way to Clan Arceneau. Not long after, I got a visual on the Roberes at the dock and leaving at a dead run. They got in one of Leo's SUVs, but they deactivated the GPS on it and I lost them on the traffic cams. I reacquired the humans and Grégoire. They ditched the car on the Lafitte Greenway Trail and left on foot, where I lost them on St. Louis Street. Best guess is they got into one of the cars going past, but not sure which one. I'm backtracking through the footage to see where the Roberes ended up, but it's taking time to acquire the private surveillance footage."

Which meant he was hacking right and left. I should tell him to stop, but lives depended on his illegal abilities. I kept my mouth shut.

The Kid continued, "Sending you coordinates of the abandoned car. I'll call back when I have more." The connection ended and Alex's face disappeared from the screen.

I reloaded as Bruiser drove, glancing several times to check on the vamp in the backseat. She was vamp-sleeping, the breathless, dead look of the undead uncorpse. I said, "You drained her power, didn't you?" He didn't answer, just turned his wipers on higher as the rain became harder. "That's the Onorio secret power, or one of them. To be able to steal the magic of the undead. And that's why the vamps want Brandon and Brian. Because they're Onorios. Now, because one of the humans got away, they know about you being Onorio." Again he said nothing. "You're glowing. Full of power, like a Naturaleza vamp looks, after it's drained a human."

He glanced at me quickly and away, saying, "Do I repulse you?"

I pointed at my fangs. "Do I repulse you? Did I repulse you when I killed five humans back there?"

Bruiser smiled, his lips quirking up, eyes crinkling. "There is nothing you can do and nothing you might look like that would repulse me, Jane Yellowrock."

I snapped the nine-mil into its holster and looked at my hands. I wasn't sure if I could blush in this form or if it would show if I did. "Ditto," I said. "Not repulsed. Just glad you weren't necking with the vamp back there while I saved your ass."

"Not necking. And if it's ass you want . . ."

I looked out the window, hiding my pleasure. An arch in my voice, I said, "I'm willing to accept thanks taken out in trade."

Bruiser chuckled in the manly way they do when they're thinking about sex. He drove with one hand and took mine with the other. We drove the rest of the way to the greenway holding hands, not looking at each other, me with a silly little smile on my fangy mouth.

The car Grégoire had been taken away in was a black, four-door Lincoln, and it had been pulled off St. Louis Street and onto the greenway grass before it was abandoned. Bruiser slammed the SUV into park and we rushed to the vehicle through the rain. I grabbed Bruiser's arm as he reached to open the door. "Possible explosives," I said. "The bomb squad is going to make overtime today."

"I'll call it in," Bruiser said, and called NOPD. While he talked to dispatch and was put through to three other departments, telling the same tale each time, I walked around the Lincoln and sniffed things out. I caught the bloody spoor of Grégoire; he had been carried away. I started the muddy slog on the Lafitte Greenway, which wasn't as pretty as that might have sounded, being a treeless stretch of grass and not much else. However, their trail ended at tire tracks in the mud. They had switched cars. My shoulders slumped, though I followed the tire tracks for a dozen blocks, the vehicle heading lakeside, until the mud no longer left a trail. I had lost Blondie.

Back at the SUV, the bomb squad hadn't yet made an appearance, and the storm had gotten much worse, like an out-of-season hurricane, but with sleet and frozen rain. Even in half-Beast form I was shivering and miserable. Bruiser held my door for me, as if I were wearing a ballroom dress and not the soaked leathers. I was so getting some nonleather armor.

We had to find the witch who was bringing in the storm—hopefully Adan Bouvier. And locate Grégoire. And the vamps and humans who took him. And we had to stop all of them and then stop the boat offshore. At some point, I had read a text update from Alex that the Coast Guard was patrolling the waters watching for vamps and humans who might want to make it ashore, but in the rain and wind, humans would surely miss a lot. Clearly there were more than just two European vamps in town. Maybe the entire

EuroVamp contingent was coming ashore in twos and threes, ready to do that whole preemptive strike on Leo. My heart rate increased as a spurt of adrenaline shot through my bloodstream. Alex had said something about vamps coming ashore in a rubber dinghy while the attention was focused on shore. Too much was going on and I was confused and hungry and tired.

Using the SUV's onboard computer, I got Internet access, texted Alex, and got a fast answer. At the same time we were watching ICE and the feds and baiting Rick, a motorized dinghy carrying six passengers had come ashore, at least two of them vamps. Alex was working to identify them all now, and when he sent me some stills, I was able to assure him that two of the vamps were out of commission, one dead at the burned-out Arceneau Clan Home and one in the back of the SUV. The humans were DBs too. Considering the storm and the distance from their insertion point, I could likely account for all the hours between landfall and torture/arson.

Alex also sent me pics of the vamps and humans who had gone after Grégoire. My heart clenched and the blood froze in my veins, even though there was no surprise in his identity. One of the vamps was Le Bâtard. Grégoire's sire.

Bruiser's cell chirped again. He answered and listened. When he ended the call he said, "Let's go. We're needed at the Council Chambers, and the Mithran in the back will cook if left out in the sun too long."

I looked up at the sky and said, "Sun?"

Bruiser didn't even laugh. Seeing me shiver, he turned the heater to high and also ran the air-conditioner, trying to get some of the moisture out of the vehicle. In our short absence, it had grown colder and wetter and the windows were fogged. I hated New Orleans winters. And summers. The weather here nine or ten months out of the year. Hated it.

My honeybunch whipped the wheel and gunned the motor.

"You gonna tell me about the call?" I asked when Bruiser sped through a yellow light, turning over to red. Bruiser seldom ran lights, probably habits left over from the days when vamps and their servants ran under the radar and did everything possible to avoid the attention of law enforcement. Not today.

"You asked about the new cages in the scion prison. One was not coated in silver. Adrianna is missing."

"You are freaking kidding me." Though with my fangs it came out, *U r fek'g kiddick ee.*

"Sadly not. She was set free during the storm. There were security problems from two lightning strikes into the grounds themselves. It's dawn now, so she's gone to lair, but we need to—"

"Alex," I whispered, dragging at my burner cell, punching in the number. Alex was at the house, still terrified. Drunk on energy drinks. "Take me home! Take me home right now! She knows I took her bracelet." My voice shuddered in my throat and froze up entirely. Bruiser's foot hit the floorboard and the heavy vehicle plowed through the standing water. Alex's number rang. And rang. I texted him. And e-mailed him. Stared at the cell willing it to respond, but the blasted thing did nothing. Edmund was with him. But it was after dawn. Derek's security team was with him, but Adrianna was a powerful vamp, older than Ed. She might still be active in the daylight, as dim as the storm had left it. Adrianna was a bedbug-crazy vamp.

Bruiser tossed me a towel and I wiped off the windows and the windshield. Condensation gathered right back. The SUV became mired in early-morning traffic, many vehicles detouring around flooded parts of town. I called Alex again. Direct to voice mail. I called Edmund and Gee and left messages. I called Leo and left another one. And Derek. And Eli, the call I had least wanted to make, all going to voice mail. But not one of them called back to say they were on the way. I had to consider the reality that humans were expendable to vamps, even a valuable human like Alex and Derek's team. And maybe because of the storm, Eli and Derek were out of cell coverage.

I could shift. Run back through the cold to the house. Get inside through Brute's wolfie door. Shift back. Fight Adrianna bare-assed naked. I would die but it would buy

Alex time. I dropped down in the seat and reached for the
Gray Between. And reached. And nothing. It was closed
to me.

A scream rose in my chest. Frustration and fear. Erupted
into the SUV. My right fist came down. Crushed the dash-
board. It cracked from the impact site to the floor. The glove
box banged open, hitting my knee. My fist was buried in
plastic, wedged in place. I yanked it out, tearing skin, too
mad to feel the pain that had to be there. "I hate fangheads,"
I growled. Wisely, Bruiser said nothing.

Behind the clouds, dawn was a gray smudge in the east,
brightening the world just enough to make driving in the
rain even worse. The vamp in the back cooked slightly as
day dawned, the stink of burned undead tinging the air.
Bruiser tore through the streets, his bow wave throwing
street water up on every car nearby. Horns blew and we
heard cursing in our wake. Neither of us cared.

Bruiser yanked the vehicle hard left and slammed his
foot back to the floor as we entered my street. The vehicle
was still moving as I ripped open the SUV door and leaped,
using the vehicle's momentum and Beast-strength. Up over
the door and the hood, into the air, faster than the vehicle
was traveling, and into the street. Pulled two vamp-killers.
I drew on Beast-speed and tore for the house. Two bodies
were on the small front porch. Derek's men, nearly dead.
The door was cracked open. The stink of gunfire and vamp
filtered out. The stink of Adrianna. She was here.

I rammed the door with my shoulder. In an instant I saw
Alex on the floor in a puddle of blood. Shotgun beside him,
broken open. Shells scattered in his blood. I was too late.
This time I was too late. Rage shoved through me like lava,
incinerating everything in its path. Two of the security team
were on the floor in my bedroom, at Adrianna's feet.

Her hair was piled up on her head. She was wearing gold
jewelry on both upper arms. An indigo dress, wet to the
skin. The closet was open. The front door was still moving.
It banged into the wall behind it.

Adrianna spun to me. Already vamped out.

In a single leap, I covered the distance to her, swords out
to my sides.

She raised her hands. Magics the color of blood coiled around her. *Like snakes*, I thought.

I was still in the air when I brought the silvered blades down. And cut off her arms. The cuts so hard, so perfectly placed, I scarcely felt the jar as they passed through flesh and bones, just below the elbows.

She screamed. The ululation a piercing wail. The peal of a vamp in mortal danger. Dying. Her magics faltered. I landed behind her. On my bed. Whirled. With a single, perfectly placed swing, I took her head.

Blood gouged high, hitting the ceiling. She collapsed. I caught her head by the luxurious red hair. Blood scattered crimson across the room. Bruiser paused in the doorway, taking in Adrianna. Me. Holding her head by the hair, the head dropping slowly and spinning as her French twist came undone. The elegant hairstyle had never been intended to be worn this way.

Bruiser left the doorway and knelt by Alex. "Breathing," he said. "Barely." I nearly fell, the relief was so intense.

"Move, Onorio," Edmund said, appearing with a soft pop of air and more of the stink of burned vamp-skin. "And close the door if you can remove the knob from the wall in which it is embedded. My mistress does not know her own strength, and I do not choose to walk into the sun this day." Edmund. Snarky. Stinking of sunburn from a run.

Bruiser stood to the side and Edmund dropped to one knee. I cleaned the vamp-killers on my linens, sheathed them, and stumbled off the bed, the head still dangling. I'd caught her head. I went to work on the knob. Which was really stuck.

"The door!" Edmund roared.

I took a two-hand grip, Adrianna's head banging on the painted wood, blood splattering, and heaved the knob free. Closed the door. Bruiser rushed outside and brought in the female vamp he had drained. She was smoking hot. Like, literally. Bruiser carried her to the kitchen and dumped her onto the table.

"Where were you?" I whispered to Ed.

"At the Mithran Council Chambers dealing with problems there." Edmund sliced his wrist and the fingers of the other hand with a small steel blade. He placed the wrist at Alex's mouth, dripping in enough that Alex coughed weakly before swallowing. At the same time he stuck his fingers into Alex's neck. Deep into his neck. Where Adrianna had cut him. I looked back at her body. She was wearing a golden knife at her waist, the blade aged, made of many-times-folded steel. Damascene steel, they had once called it. I had such a blade of my own, though mine was curved and delicate, while hers was straight and covered with blood. Alex's blood.

"You're dripping," Edmund said distinctly, "blood and rainwater. Go away. Put that head somewhere. Check the injured humans. Clean up the mess. Make yourself useful." His tone was commanding, the cutting edge of a master vampire to his minion. In a more conciliatory tone, he added, "Mistress."

"Uh-huh." I didn't need the kind of smarmy obsequiousness that many masters demanded. I didn't even want it. But the tone reminded me that Edmund had lost his clan and his mastership over it to one less than deserving. He had given up power on purpose and I didn't know why. And he had attached himself to me, sworn loyalty to me and to my friends when he could have avoided it. He still had secrets, and secrets could be dangerous to me and to mine. Perhaps he was mine under false pretenses. But he had run through the French Quarter at vamp speed after dawn to help Alex. The only other vamp I knew who was capable of that was Leo. I shook my head, my black hair pulling at my wet leathers. We'd have to have a little talk about all this. Alex groaned; his lips, which had looked slightly blue, were pinker.

I looked at the head. I'd caught this one. Laughter burbled up inside me, inappropriate and hysterical. I swallowed it down.

I walked to the side porch and opened the empty cooler, dropped Adrianna's head into it. It landed in the corner, faceup, fangs down on their little hinges. From the kitchen I brought a five-pound bag of ice and banged it on the porch floor until the cubes were loose. I dumped the cubes over Adrianna's head, watery blood gathering in the bottom. I latched the chest and dragged it inside and to the laundry room, where I could keep an eye on it. The house hadn't been cleaned by Leo's custodial team, which meant there was old blood on the floor and bodies and heads lying where they had landed. I should put the heads together, like a collection of bookends or salt and pepper shakers or something. Instead, I put them all in the cooler and checked the humans. They were all alive and mostly coming around. Group concussion. Adrianna had been an old, powerful, fast-as-blue-blazes vamp to knock them all out before even one could draw and fire.

Bruiser was still in the kitchen with the captured vamp. She was no longer smoking and I figured he had allowed her to drink from his wrist to heal her. For the moment, she was holding his wrist and hand, gazing adoringly into his eyes, speaking with a sweet, feminine voice. She was a knockout: big boobs, tiny waist. Blond. I ground my fangs. I hated her.

I stomped back to my room and dragged Adrianna's body and the other vamp's body into the shower so they could drain. Cleanup crew should have been by. It seemed the Enforcer wasn't at the top of the night's to-do list. Stepping across puddles of goopy blood, I toured my house. Clearly Adrianna had fed well and deeply in the short time since she had escaped HQ, because the fresher blood was everywhere, tracked all over the dried, tacky blood. I was so not mopping this all up. I located another unofficial cell and called Scrappy.

"Lee Williams Watts," she answered. "Mr. Pellissier's personal assistant. How may I help you?"

"Jane Yellowrock," I identified myself. "Alex called for a cleanup crew ages ago. They. Are. Not. Here. Send a cleanup team and some bloodsucker healers to my home, now. I want them here in thirty minutes even if they have to fly. Got it? There's blood everywhere, a wounded security team, a re-dead rev in the living room, and two dead vamp bodies in the downstairs bathroom."

"Just the two?" she asked, sounding perky.

I looked at the cell. Considering my history, I guessed it was a legit question. I put the cell back to my ear. "Just the two. And the revenant. But there's a lot of blood. And I need two sets of leathers cleaned. They're soaked. And I need a new mattress. It's bloody too."

"I'll check the files for the brand and model and have a new mattress delivered by nightfall." I heard soft tapping as she worked. "A cleanup team with an armor expert has been dispatched with an ETA of forty minutes to an hour, due to the weather. I'll enter this number in as your new official cell phone and upload it with all pertinent data." She paused. "And I'll order you several more. According to my inventory, you've gone through a lot of them lately."

I sighed. I hated perky people. And fangheads. And blood. To my more-sensitive-than-human nose, it was already starting to stink, that sickly sweet reek of decay. "I'll also need a new security team on my house, and Leo's medical team to heal the ones that were on duty when the house was attacked. Tell Derek to send two vamps in a sealed car and a new team of"—I started to say four but changed it—"six. ASAP."

"Done. Anything else?"

She might be annoyingly perky but she was efficient. "Nothing. Thanks," I added grudgingly. I closed the cell just in time to hear Edmund retch. Wet leathers squeaking, I went back to the entry. He had his fangs buried in Alex's throat, but it didn't look as if he was enjoying it much. He was pale and shaking and he kept making gagging sounds. "Ed?"

He withdrew his fangs from Alex's neck and his fingers from the wound there. "I refuse to heal this child again. Not so long as he continues to drink poison."

"Poison?"

"The foul energy drink. That beverage comes directly from hell." He retched his way to the kitchen and propped his elbows on the counter, hanging his head over the sink.

"Vamps can puke?"

I spun to Alex, still lying in his own blood. "Hey, Kid. You're alive?"

"Halfway." He gripped his throat with one hand, tracing the scar on one side with his finger and the site of the punctures, now closed, with his thumb. "I didn't see a bright light. No angels. Didn't see fire and brimstone either, so that was good. But the last thing I remember was Adrianna attacking. I think she tried to cut off my head. Like I was a vamp or something."

Relief scoured through me like coiled steel and white light. "Yeah." I held down a hand and he took it, allowing me to draw him upright. "Question. If you had been too far gone to be healed, would you want to be turned?" I put an arm around his waist and gripped the top of his bloody pants to hold him standing. He was shaking and paler than any ghost was reputed to be.

"Until today, I'd have said no. I'd be too long out of the field. Woulda lost my edge. But now? I'm leaning toward signing the papers." He fingered his throat. "Hurts." He looked around him on the floor, at the amount of blood. "All that mine?"

My own throat nearly closed up on my reply. The blood was everywhere. It looked like gallons. "Yeah."

"Eli's gonna go apeshit."

I didn't fuss about the language because my new cell rang. It was Eli. I filled him in. My partner went dead silent and when I was finished, he disconnected. Without a word. To Bruiser, I said, "I'm changing and going to fanghead central. You coming?"

Expression blank, he looked up from the adoring blonde and said, "I'll stay here." It could be his natural reticence. Or more storm and magic. "Will report as soon I have everything."

There was something about the emptiness of his expression that reminded me of the lying, sneaky, former boyfriend, Rick LaFleur, but I knew that Bruiser wouldn't cheat on me, so the lack of emotion was something else. "You want to talk about it?" I asked.

He looked at the curvy vampette on my kitchen table and then back to me. "I now have a bond scion," he said unhappily.

"Another superpower?"

"Yes." He said, "And I have no place for her to sleep."

Edmund said, "I'll care for her. She can sleep with me."

"I'll change then and go with you," Bruiser said, his voice still empty. "Nicolle. Go with Edmund. He is the primo of

Jane Yellowrock. You will do as he says and obey him in all things so long as they do not conflict with your service and vows to me."

"Yes, my master." She released his arm and slid her feet to the floor, standing, all vampy and slinky, like a rain-damp sex goddess. To Edmund she asked, "May we share blood?"

"I was counting on it. This way, Nicolle," Edmund said, leading the way to the weapons room hidden behind the bookshelf. They disappeared into the dark cavern and the shelf clicked shut.

My sweetcheeks and I eased around the puddles and splatters of blood, stripped, toweled off, and changed clothes in the laundry, the only clean room in the downstairs. There was nothing romantic in the process, but I couldn't help but see Bruiser in my peripheral vision. Long and muscled, yet lean and hard. Every inch of him. His face was haggard, however. "You want to talk about it?"

He paused in the act of pulling a long-sleeved T-shirt over his head, his skin pale in the darkness of the storm-shadows. His brown eyes were troubled. "I didn't mean to bind her. I have no place to keep a blood-bound scion. And no desire to keep her. I only want you."

For a moment my heart warmed, and then I figured out why he was so upset and all my happy-happy-joy-joy leaked away. "She's going to want to sleep with you."

"Yes. Constantly."

Part of me wanted to laugh. Another part wanted to go drag her out of the weapons room and into the daylight and watch her burn. Beast murmured into my mind, *Mine. My mate.* Her claws extruded and she milked my brain. It hurt but the pain helped me to think. To Bruiser, I said, "Can you give her away?" *She's a thinking sentient being, not a slave*, I thought. But if she was bound, that was exactly what Bruiser had created. No wonder he was upset. I had bound Edmund. I hated that. What were we two becoming?

"I don't know," he said. "I need to talk to Brandon and Brian. I'm still . . . new? . . . to the powers of an Onorio." He pulled the tee into place and slid jeans up his legs and buttoned them. Tight and fitted to his butt. Bruiser had the best butt. And the best nose, Romanesque and proud.

I finished dressing in jeans and rubberized boots and layered tees. And all my weapons. It was daylight, which made us—mostly—safe from vamps, but not humans, though they were far easier to dispatch than vamps.

Kill, I thought, suddenly, stopping in the act of pulling my weapons harness over my shoulders. Not dispatched. Humans weren't errands. Or targets. They were people, and if they fought for one side or the other it was because they were bound, not free-willed. And I had killed five tonight. There was a time when I'd never have killed a human. New Orleans had changed me. Being around vamps had changed me. Having things, possessions, friends, family had changed me. I now had people in my life worth killing over. Bruiser had changed too, in a positive way, no longer a brainwashed vamp tool, blood-meal, and plaything.

I pulled on an old leather jacket and said, "I'm here if you need me. For anything."

Bruiser stopped, one hand just about to settle a nine-millimeter into its holster, his eyes finding me in the shadows of early morning. A faint smile touched his lips, lighting his eyes. "You have my heart."

It wasn't exactly the three little words, but it was dang close. I wasn't sure how to respond, but settled on, "You have me. Pretty much all of me since my heart is stuck inside." *Oh crap. Did that last part come out of my mouth? Yes. Of course it did.*

He snapped the weapon in place and reached me in one stride, an arm around my back, pulling me close, his body a furnace, his arm like heated steel. He hesitated, his lips hovering above mine, so close. His eyes held me closer, moving back and forth between my own, and his smile spread. His kiss was gentle, as if he had never kissed me before, as if he were unsure, uncertain if I would pull away. Something altered inside me. A thing, something I had no name for, filled me, soft and sweet as jasmine on the night wind.

I slid my arms over his shoulders and pulled myself into him. The kiss deepened and I sighed into his mouth. When he pulled away, we were both breathing harder, and Bruiser was still smiling, a strange light in his eyes. He said, "If your bed weren't bloody I would have peeled your clothes away and taken you right now."

"If the floor wasn't bloody I'd have taken you on the floor."

Bruiser spluttered with laughter and the moment was broken, though the sweetness remained as he dropped his head and laughed into my shoulder. His hold around me eased. "And that, my darling War Woman, is why you have my heart."

We were almost back to HQ when I got a call. It was Lee. "Getchur butt to the Council Chambers. An emissary from the Europeans is on the way. There's two on our shores and they're headed here, ETA about twelve."

CHAPTER 15

A Case of the Cheerfuls

We made it to the back entrance of suckhead command only two minutes before the EV emissaries arrived. Full daylight in the storm was dim and dreary, but it was daylight still, which meant human blood-servants as emissaries, not vamps. They would be someone's primo blood-servants, which meant vampy protocols had to be followed, though the lack of notice also meant some protocols could be ignored. The difficult part was deciding which protocols might be ignored without accidentally resulting in insult. Deliberate insult was a whole 'nother matter. Vamps were weird.

Leo's human delegation was gathered in the entry, watching on the security cameras as two human males drove up, parked, and stepped from their two-seater antique vehicle. It was the same two who were trying to come ashore when the Robere twins disappeared to hunt Grégoire. They were clothed in black, with purple shirts and ties, with black umbrellas shielding them from the rain.

Wrassler murmured, "Royal livery. But more important, where in the world did they get a Daimler in New Orleans? George?"

"A 1935 Straight Edge," Bruiser replied. "And I have no idea."

I looked at the car on the screens and back and forth between the two males. I had no trouble believing that Bruiser was a luxury car nut, but Wrassler was a surprise. He struck me as more of a sports car kinda guy, or maybe a muscle car from the sixties, basketball and beer, baseball and hot dogs.

Outside, the two humans walked through the storm, up the stairs, and into the airlock with its laminated "bullet-proof" polycarbonate glass. They passed through the entrance's X-ray device, which was part of the security upgrades I had instituted since I came to work for the MOC. The glass had been replaced several times in the months I had been here. "Bulletproof glass" didn't always offer the protection one might think. The emissaries stopped and, on the X-rays, I got a good look at the weapons they carried—plenty—and at the men themselves. Beside me, Bruiser talked with Raisin, the oldest human living at HQ, on the in-house coms system.

Bruiser muttered two names to her, with a vaguely Spanish accent. "Macario and Gualterio. I'd have expected minions, not the big guns."

They were both short by today's standards, at five-six and five-eight. Both had dark hair and deeply olive skin. Both were dressed in black wool suits that dropped to gorgeous shoes—Italian leather buffed to a shine. They were also armed to the teeth with blades and sidearms, though no one would know that by looking at them. Their clothing was so perfectly tailored that not a bulge showed. Once I had a good look, I stepped into the shadows so they couldn't see me in the bright foyer lights.

"They're both over two hundred years old," Raisin said over the speaker, her voice scratchy. "The message is, we are here and our masters are more powerful than yours. They have kept us young for centuries. They always were pretty boys, with excellent manners and lovely penmanship."

"Excellent fighters," Del said. Del was arguably the most influential human in New Orleans, and last I knew she was in Atlanta. Leo must have called her back to deal with the current problems. Today, even in the cold air, she wore a sleeveless dress in an odd shade of black, one with a red tint that became redder when the light hit it just right. Like blood-soaked cloth. She wore a sword at her side. Del was one of Leo's people that these blood-servants would have to kill if they wanted a chance at Leo and his fiefdom. The others were the Enforcers: Derek and me. *Ducky*.

Dacy Mooney, her mother and the heir to the Asheville clan, stood just behind her. I hadn't seen Dacy since she healed Edmund of silver poisoning. "I've watched video of them taking apart other swordsmen," Dacy said to her daughter. "You're better."

"Open the doors," Del instructed Derek, her voice quiet. Derek, an earbud in his ear and a mouthpiece hanging below his chin, relayed the message.

When the two visitors stepped inside and the doors to the airlock had closed behind them, the one on the right said, "Macario and Gualterio Cardona, primo and secundo servants of the blood to Louis le Jeune, Capetian King of the Franks, turned by Eleanor of Aquitaine during their marriage . . ."

I tuned out the titles and bloodline mumbo-jumbo and then grinned, lips wide over my fangs, thinking of what they would do when they got a good look at me in half-form. Wondering what they might do if I told them their speechifying was boring claptrap. Between fear and insult, they'd skewer me before I could enjoy the show. Inside me, Beast snorted. *Less than five humans against more than five humans. Jane/ Beast, Bruiser-mate, and blood-drinkers of Leo. Good hunters, more than five. We win.*

Probably, I acknowledged, taking in the Cardonas' scents: blood and sweet peppers and rich cream. Watching the way they moved and shifted or stood completely still, as when Del began to respond. "Adelaide Mooney, primo blood-servant to Leo Pellissier . . ." I zoned out on her words and watched the men, letting some of Beast shine through, knowing that my eyes were taking on a golden glow. It attracted the attention of the unwelcome visitors, and my grin widened as they focused on me in the shadows with laserlike intensity. Taking in my casual clothing and my apparent lack of weapons. Like theirs, mine were mostly out of sight. But my eyes, my fangs, and my pelt scared them. Beast purred inside, enjoying the change in their scents. Beast and I chuffed in amusement, showing more fang.

They flinched the tiniest bit but it wasn't because of me. I zoned back into Del's intro, replaying it in my memory, looking for what had spooked them even more than I had.

She had been talking about Leo's territory in terms of states, which I knew, but had added, ". . . over four hundred thousand square miles of territory under his personal domain, with more swearing fealty to him." Ah. The emissaries of the EVs had forgotten that the U.S. took up a lot of map space, nearly three times as much as the original fifteen countries of the European Union. Which meant that Leo, under his personal control, had way more hunting territory than any single EV monarch had and maybe more than Titus the emperor had. Go Del. It was a lawyer's zinger and I wanted to applaud. Didn't. But wanted to.

Del finished with, "No parley time has been decided upon by our negotiators. No parley location has been decided upon. No parley numbers have been decided upon. Yet you are here. Is this a declaration of war?"

Macario and Gualterio both reacted to that too, showing surprise, even if it was only by their scent patterns. One of them said, "We are here to finalize the negotiations, not create an incident. We wish peace between us and between our masters."

Liar, liar, pants on fire, I thought as their scents again changed. They were here to cause trouble at the very least. To start the war they denied at the very worst.

"What further accommodations do your masters require, beyond that already agreed upon or in negotiation?" Del asked.

"Information only," the one on the left said.

Del inclined her head, waiting.

Leftie said, "Our master wishes to know how many Onorios Leo Pellissier has in New Orleans. How many Enforcers? And how many outclan priestesses?"

"And if we disclose this information, will we be provided

with the same information from among the full delegation of European Mithrans, now in U.S. waters, aboard the ship hidden beneath an *obfuscation* working? The ship from which you disembarked only hours past?"

The speaker hesitated a fraction of second before saying, "Of course."

Liar, liar, pants on fire.

Del smiled. It wasn't a pretty smile, all warmth and welcome. It was a *gotcha* smile. Smoothly, she continued as if she hadn't paused. "As well as from the Mithrans and Naturaleza hiding in Pellissier lands and drinking of Pellissier cattle? That is assuming that your masters still maintain control of all their Mithrans."

I tensed and a faint tremor of shock trailed through me. Del had just gambled, and that was unexpected. She had just informed them that we knew the boat was offshore and under a witch-working. But she was also claiming to know with a certainty that the entire European delegation was aboard. Which I was certain that we did not know. To make it worse, she had told them that we knew there were EVs already ashore, and claimed that the two groups could have split into factions, that the EVs in NOLA might be unaligned or working to separate ends. Which they could be. Or not. It was a dangerous and brilliant tactic. If the emissaries claimed the Deadly Duo were part of their group, they then laid claim to their successes, mistakes, and failures. If the emissaries denied the Deadly Duo and their cohorts, then that left the EVs in Leo's hands and judgment. Last, she hinted that the vamps had been captured, which was total bluff. But the emissaries had no way to discern the truth of her claims in real time.

Del tilted her head, smiling, waiting. Showing teeth.

Following an uncomfortable length of time, Leftie said, "We speak for the Emperor Titus Flavius Vespasianus. No others."

Del's expression didn't change. The emissaries had just delivered any vamp on shore into Leo's hands. She said, "Ah. So be it."

The two blood-servants bowed, turned, and walked away, back into the airlock. Or tried to. The glass didn't open. Not right away. They stood there, backs to the small crowd. As stage exits went, this one was embarrassing. The doors slowly opened and they stepped through. The doors closed. And then Derek's man made them wait. And wait. And wait for the outer doors to open. Backs to the room. Standing. Silent. They didn't betray by so much as a twitch that they were unhappy with the waiting, but I bet myself that the airlock stank of irritation and maybe even a little fear.

And then they were gone, the luxury car rolling smoothly out the drive.

As soon as we were certain that the iron gate had closed behind them, Del turned to me. Instead of saying hi, she said, "Sabina is missing. I sent a contingent to the cemetery across the river, but there was no sign of her anywhere. No one has seen her, not since the attack here when Grégoire went missing."

"Someone sent for her to feed Leo when he was injured," I said. "When did she go back to the cemetery?"

"She couldn't be found," Del repeated. "She isn't here. She isn't at the cemetery."

Derek tapped his earpiece and said, "Alex just found video of a body being removed from HQ following the attack, two hours after Grégoire was taken. This one was removed by unknown humans during the time when we were healing Leo and securing the premises."

"Not so secure then," someone from the back of the crowd muttered.

Derek made a growl worthy of Beast.

"Sabina was kidnapped. That's why Macario and Gualterio asked the questions about Leo's people," I said, figuring it out.

"They know we've lost her and Grégoire and Brandon and Brian. They were baiting us. Del baited them back. Nice con, by the way," Derek said to Del. "But what did they gain by coming here?"

Del was still grinning. She had been having fun, lawyer-style, with the kind of verbal repartee she had enjoyed before she became Leo's primo and took over "protocol and political rubrics and other fusty duties," Del's words for boring crap.

"Since they didn't kill anyone, as a gambit, their coming here was pathetic," Bruiser said, "and I'm not certain to what end."

I looked sidelong at Derek. "Did your men get the tracking device on the emissaries' car?"

He gave me a single thumb-up. "Three of them. Just in case. One of which is currently off but can be turned on remotely. We also uncovered the owner of the Daimler Straight Edge, a human named Josh Martin. His only connection to Mithrans was through his last name. His several-times-great-grandpapa was the founder of Clan Martin."

My mouth formed a silent O as that settled into my mind, and I drew all sorts of pieces together. Clan Martin was now defunct; Adrianna had once been part of that blood clan. And Adrianna was now defunct too. Which I hadn't announced yet. For some reason I was keeping my mouth shut about the fact that I had her head in a cooler in my house. Gee would eventually tell, I was sure, but for now it could stay my own happy, bloody little secret.

I wondered briefly about Leo's long game. Vamps played chess with time, and Leo was usually a dozen moves in front of the other players. But these guys had been playing for centuries longer than he had been undead. I thought back, as far back as when I first appeared on the scene. "Leo let Gee come back to NOLA. Leo made palsey-walsey with weres, with the witches, and with *arcenciels*. And with me. What do Louis and Le Bâtard have?"

"No witches except those they turned. No humans with magical powers or magical items," Bruiser said. "No weres, to our knowledge. And if they have taken Sabina, they are likely having a difficult time holding her." He sounded pleased at that prospect.

And no one had said so, but the two also had a storm witch working for them. Or a faction of the European witches did.

But how did we all fit together in Leo's big plan? Did his plan include losing so many of his key people to the gang and revenant attack? Where did the European vamps have our missing people?

Suddenly Bruiser laughed. "Well done," he said to Del.

"They now believe Leo to be two steps ahead of them. They believe that we have people have watching Le Bâtard and Louis Seven. They'll abandon their allies, just in case. Even if there were no difficulties between the two groups, or a possible spilt, you created one."

Del looked as satisfied as Beast felt when she took down a boar.

"That's my girl," Dacy said. The heir of Clan Shaddock had been silent until now, but she looked tickled at her daughter's ploy. "And now, I've had too much sunlight. I'm for bed." She turned and left the foyer, her boots clapping and the fringe on her jacket swinging.

A blood-servant brought carafes of coffee and hot tea and set up a small serving table in the foyer. I accepted a cup and sipped the excellent tea, my mind shifting through threads of history and current events, through evidence, ideas, fang-head relationships, and conclusions. It was daunting.

Bruiser pointed to the stairs, the gesture telling me he had Onorio things to do, and disappeared into the bowels of HQ to chat with Leo, who was old enough to be awake and watching the confab on the coms system but was still likely healing from the attack, the stabbing, the silver poisoning, and the loss of fingers. Eli and I took our usual SUV back to the house, my partner silent as he drove through the rain. The storm had let up again as an arm of the slowly swirling weather system passed us and New Orleans' massive drainage system cleared the city of flood water.

Traffic was at a crawl when Eli casually said, "Nice weather we're having."

It wasn't funny but I started laughing, too long and too unsteadily. "Yeah. We need the rain."

Eli smiled, the twitch of lips that meant he had relaxed. "Alex texted me that he found some more humans and vamps who came ashore. They came in from Lake Borgne through Bayou Bienvenue Central Wetlands in an air boat. Private surveillance cameras got some pretty clear shots for night cams." He thumbed on his cell and handed it to me. He turned the wipers on high, trying to keep up with the increasing volume of rain. I checked the time and realized the rain was right on time. The magical storm had a specific and unrelenting pattern.

I studied the vamps sneaking into the country without going through customs. In the best still shot, they looked very unhappy, maybe even a little seasick, which gave me a case of the cheerfuls. One female was wearing a tall wig, which she held in place with both hands. She was dressed in an old-fashioned ball gown with a hoop skirt and lots of ruffles. She was soaked through and looked weighted down by the wet fabric and soaked wig, which had tilted alarmingly to the left. If the airboat sank or she was tossed overboard, she'd sink like a stone. "Do vamps swim?" I asked.

"Never asked. But this batch made it to shore fine," Eli said

"Sad, that. I'd like to see them tip over and Marie Antoinette sink like a stone. We got a name?"

"Not Marie Antoinette but close. According to Alex it's one of Marie Antoinette's ladies-in-waiting, Marie Claudine Sylvie de Thiard de Bissy, Duchesse de Fitz-James." Eli stumbled over the French, but it didn't matter. I got the gist. "She died in 1812."

"Right now she looks like it. She never got over the royal fashion styles of her time," I said. "Who's the vamp dude?"

"Charles the Second of Spain. He died the first time in 1700, childless. He'd probably been a vamp for years."

"Hmmm. He likes modern clothes and fancy suits. And the little female?"

"Her name is Alesha Fonteneau. She's so pale, I'd say she hasn't been allowed to feed. Prisoner, most likely."

"Oh," I murmured, liquid shock flooding through me. I knew that name. "The underfed vamp is Katie's sister. She's in trouble, a hostage."

"Do we need to go back to HQ?" Eli asked.

"I think . . . not." I quickly gave him a rundown on the paintings and Troll's broken jaw, and sending him to be healed and read by Leo. It was evident we needed a long and detailed debriefing. Things were happening fast and we were not keeping up. Someone was gonna get hurt if I wasn't careful. "By now, the MOC knows that Katie hid things from him and might be a spy in his court, willingly or not. That's all MOC business, not Enforcer business," I said. "So why did these vamps, in particular, come ashore?"

"Don't know." Eli turned into our street. "But whatever it is it won't make us happy.

"Babe?" he added. "We got company."

I looked up from the cell and spotted two witches on our front porch. Lachish Dutillet and Bliss. I hadn't seen either since the Witch Conclave and they looked good—or as well as soaking-wet women could. They were confronting two armed men on the stoop, two of Derek's six-man security sextet. Unit. Whatever. The former military types had weapons drawn and the witches were retreating slowly, while drawing up power, one from the storm and one from the earth. This day would never freaking end.

Eli pulled to a stop and I jumped out just as he lowered his window and let out a piercing whistle. I'd never heard him do that before, and I flinched. Fortunately he was looking away from me. The four near-combatants started too. Also fortunately, no one fired a weapon. No one died.

"Idiots!" I yelled as I slogged through the rain and the standing water. "Stand down!"

"We thought they had you captive," Lachish called.

I stomped my wet boots up to the porch. "I wish someone had me locked in my house, nice and dry and sleeping. Let's take this inside. Boys, report to Derek. And get a list of people he thinks is okay to knock on my door." I stopped. "Who fixed my door? It was busted in."

"That would be me, ma'am," one of the guards said.

I recognized him but didn't remember his name, and he wasn't wearing a name tag. "Wayne Mac something?"

He smiled with real pleasure at being recognized. "Wayne McCalla, ma'am. Fixing the door was my pleasure."

"Nice work," Eli said as he moved the door back and forth. It didn't even squeak. The witches stepped in and Eli closed the door behind us.

Inside, the DBs and puddles had been cleaned up, the house smelling like citrus instead of death. I hadn't even thought about that when I opened the door. I held in a grin at the imagined expressions on the witches' faces.

Alex had placed towels and bathroom rugs all over the

foyer, along with a metal rack that was usually in the laundry, used by Eli to hang his clothes when he ironed. In a basket were towels, blankets, socks, and robes. Smart boy. I'd have to give him pizza. I pulled off everything I could while maintaining some form of decency and wrapped up in my robe. The two witches stood and watched me. As I dressed I asked, "What can the Enforcer of the Master of the City do for the witches of New Orleans?"

"We've never seen such a storm," Lachish said.

"Cold," Bliss added.

"Uh-huh. I smell tea. Want some?"

"No," Lachish said. "I tried your cell phone. I e-mailed. Your cell's out of order or no longer in use and you haven't answered e-mail."

I chuckled, chucked my shoes and wet socks, and pulled on dry, warm, wool socks. "Little busy. And I've lost two cells this week already."

"New record?" Lachish asked.

I laughed harder and stood upright. Lachish looked like normal, gray-haired and a little stout, a woman who dressed to look more matronly than she had to. She had a dry sense of humor and depths I hadn't taken the time to explore or learn.

Bliss looked good, if good meant beautiful—Sleeping Beauty, with white skin, black hair, and witch energy that softened her even more. She looked like a victim and maybe she had been one once, but she was nowhere near prey, now that she had begun to learn how to use her magic. The little witch seemed to glow.

I knew that the local witches were in danger because of the EuroVamps. Would the fangheads try to turn them? Kill them outright? Kidnap them? I realized that I had been staring too long and asked, "You okay? The local witches okay?"

"You mean since the European vampires started coming ashore in small groups and casting storm magic?" Lachish asked, annoyed. "You didn't think to call us? Ask us for help?"

"Ummm." *Not really.* And that was stupid.

"For a very bright woman you do tend to overlook your assets," Lachish said. "Too much the loner for too long."

I couldn't argue with that. "Come in to the kitchen? Have some tea?" I repeated.

"Thank you, no. We're here with witch gossip."

I had learned that gossip in the Deep South was a *thing*. A very important *thing*. A newspaper society-column-innuendo *thing*. So witches here with gossip-mill info shouldn't be surprising, but that they'd offer it without the social niceties was. Normally, gossip was shared over tea and coffee, maybe some coffeecake or beignets. The fact that they were bypassing propriety meant the info was important and they were in a hurry.

I guessed. "You're here to tell me that a vamp-witch on board a ship in Lake Borgne is bringing in the storm."

She looked mildly impressed and then spoiled it with her next word. "No. The storm and the riots are being generated and controlled by an unknown witch on land, not on ship. We've managed to locate her general vicinity, near the Lafitte Greenway Trail."

That was where the car used to transport Grégoire had been left. I had assumed that the kidnappers had taken him far away when they changed vehicles, but what if they had just driven around the block a few times? What if they were keeping him hidden right under our noses? "Do you have any idea who it is?"

"Not one."

"What if it's a male witch?"

Lachish took a towel from the basket and handed one to Bliss, perhaps deciding that if she was going to stand inside she might as well not drip. "Your question and your expression suggest that you know more than we supposed," she said with asperity. As if blaming me for her inconvenience in coming here, in the rain, and getting wet.

"I don't know much, except a witch-vamp named Adan Bouvier was once strong enough to cast storms. He left for France a long time ago. He might be back."

"Another male witch," Lachish murmured. "And he's a vampire?"

I almost asked who the other males were, but now was not the time. "Yes. He's old. Like centuries. Like from before the vamps killed off all the European witches, back when the EuroVamps were turning them instead."

Eli was standing wrapped in a robe and looked like candy on a stick, if the look in Bliss' eyes was any indication. He asked, "Is there any way to tell if the witch is storm-making by choice?" When Lachish looked at him blankly he said, "He could be a prisoner."

Lachish shrugged and rubbed her head with the towel. When she came out from under it, her hair was a wiry cloud, but she looked more cheery. She said, "I'm not sure. I'll ask my coven. Either way, the storm's not abating and it's creating a storm surge. The pump system was improved and updated after Katrina, but it's not up to a prolonged surge. We think the witch is somewhere near here." She pulled a sealed plastic bag from her pocket and handed it to me. Inside was a scrap of a map of New Orleans with a red circle around one area. Alex took it out of my hand before I could get a good look and started tapping on a tablet, doing his electronic wizard thingy. I hadn't even noticed him standing in the doorway.

I'd had a glimpse of the location, however, in the second or so I'd held the map. Enough to guess that it must also be where our missing vamps and Onorios were. Lachish had tracked the magics to St. Louis Street, just off the greenway near where we found the car that took Grégoire. The greenway was three miles long, but this was the third tiny clue that pointed us to this section of the city. We'd been so close. Alex turned his tablet to us, showing a satellite map of the circled area. It was mostly houses except for one larger building that was a warehouse with a false front, a new metal roof, and a lightning rod mounted on the highest point. A lightning rod. In a magical storm with lots of lightning. If lightning struck it, what would the power be used for? To ground a witch-working? To power a working?

"It's a trap," I said.

"Of course it's a trap," Eli said, a grin on his face that looked a little like a death's head, all ferocious teeth and intent. His expression was like an aphrodisiac to Bliss. Ailis Rogan, that was her real name. "Babe, our day is just starting to get good."

I wondered how much of what he was talking about had to do with his need to fight something. At the possibility of violence, he looked chipper and alert and ready to rumble. I felt tired and worn and ready for bed. If my new mattress had been delivered. I'd forgotten about that.

"No riding to be a hero, Batman, not right now," Alex said. "Now that we have a location to start from I need to ha—check out all the surveillance cameras nearby. So you and Catwoman get to take naps and I get to work."

"Without energy drinks," I said.

"Pretty much." His young face twisted up in what could have been sorrow or laughter. "I think I nearly killed our resident bloodsucker."

Yeah. Laughter. Kids think the weirdest things are funny.

Eli said, "I'm for bed. Ladies." He lifted two fingers to them in an abbreviated salute or maybe a half-connected hat tip, it was hard to tell, but he headed up to his bed, feet silent on the steps. Bliss' eyes followed him all the way to the top. He didn't look back. Eli had been present at the Witch Conclave. So had Bliss. Eli had an admirer.

"We'll leave you," Lachish said. "Call if you need me present when you enter the building." She placed a card in my hand: copper-colored, metallic coated, with raised lettering. It felt cool to my fingers, as if it had been in the fridge, and it didn't warm as I held it. Odd. I put it in my robe pocket and gave her a head-tilt/mouth-down-turning expression that meant, *I can do that.* Lachish opened the front door on the storm and left, Bliss trailing behind her. I realized the young witch had said only a single word while here and wondered if she was in training as Lachish's assistant. Which would be a cool gig if she got it.

I grabbed a towel and scrubbed my hair, my gold chain clinking softly against the nugget that kept me tied metaphysically to the location in the mountains where I relearned what it meant to be a skinwalker. I seldom thought about the necklace, but I touched it now. It was warm to my cold fingers. I couldn't remember when I'd been so cold, not even in the mountains in midwinter when a prolonged freeze would hit. It had to be the storm.

Satisfied that I had done all I could, I went to my room,

closed my door, stripped again, and crawled under the covers of my newly made, brand-new bed. The mattress supported, engulfed, and pampered my body. It was even better than the last one. Being the MOC's Enforcer had serious perks. I reached up and repositioned Bruiser's boxing gloves, his scent intensifying for a moment, soothing me.

As I rolled over, I caught sight of *le breloque*. It was resting on the table. My insides stilled. I had left it in the SUV, forgotten it even. Yet it was back here. It had followed me. Like a dog to a master. That seemed ominous. But not enough to keep me awake. I let sleep take me.

When I woke, I was human-shaped. The light through the windows was the dark of deep storm clouds and pre-dusk, and someone was knock, knock, knocking on my door, a little like the tall skinny guy on *The Big Bang Theory* TV show. Five hours had passed, and I rolled over for the first time to get off of the fabo dreamy (ha-ha) mattress. "Be out in a minute," I said, my voice rough with sleep. I pulled out old comfort clothes, warm sweats from my Appalachian-living days, and made myself decent if not fashion conscious. I smelled tea when I opened the door, a soothing chai made with piri-piri peppers and lots of whole clove. Someone had finished the laundry and there was a white basket loaded with folded clothes to the side. I scooted it inside. The house was mostly dark, lit by tablets and screens and lighted keyboards. I dragged myself to the kitchen.

In the shadows of the veiled sunset, I met Eli at the table, and of course he looked wide awake and well groomed, though he was nursing a small cup of espresso like it was the elixir of life. I sat in front of the soup mug of tea at my place and added a huge dollop of Cool Whip, stirred it with a soup spoon, and drank a quarter of it in a series of long slurps. Tea, the food of the gods, and I didn't care what coffee drinkers said about coffee. I wiped my mouth with a sweatshirt sleeve and spotted the cookies, two kinds: white chocolate macadamia nut and lemon-lavender. I took a lemon-lavender and it melted in my mouth. In a voice that was clogged by cookie and sleep, I asked, "Do you know why he waked us up? Woke us up? Whatever."

"No. I threatened to shoot him. He kept knocking."

"Three bursts?"

"Yeah. The knocking. Not the shooting. I'd only need one round."

"Ha-ha."

"You two awake yet?" Alex asked from the opening to the living room.

"No," we said together. I took another cookie.

He placed two tablets on the table, on stands, between us, positioned so we could both see the screens. There were images on them. Still shots plucked from security camera footage. The photos were of two vamps as they parked on a street, got out of the car, and vanished around a corner of a building. Sleepiness fell away from me like rain off a metal roof. The woman was exquisite, black-haired and dark-eyed, with alabaster skin and a swan neck. The man beside her, as always, looked cynical and bored and cruel. "Amitee and Fernand Marchand," I whispered, putting all the relationships in order. I knew, somehow, that all the pieces were on the board now. "The Marchands were brother and sister, formerly of the Rochefort clan in France, and they had been associated with the Damours. The Rocheforts were pals with the dog-fanged vamps in Europe. Leo's son met Amitee there, when she was still a blood-servant to the Rocheforts and she turned so she could marry him.

"Amitee hated Leo. From the very first moment she met him," I said. "And now we know why. She was part of layered plots by the Europeans, probably for decades."

"Trained up by Immanuel to hate him?" Eli suggested, draining his espresso and placing the small cup in the light of one screen.

That made sense. Long before I killed him, Immanuel had been replaced, eaten, by an *u'tlun'ta*, a skinwalker, a creature like me but one who had done deliberate black magic and taken the place of a living, breathing, sentient being. I had done a lot of bad things, but not that. Never that.

Alex said, "I haven't uncovered much in our own files, but your previous researcher had drawn some conclusions based on a series of parties thrown by the Rocheforts back in the 1960s. Parties attended by the elite of the world music scene and by the wealthy and the young royals of the time. Fernand was good friends with Lennon and Harrison before they died. Pete Townshend and Keith Moon. Keith Richards. Lotta rock-and-rollers."

I nodded. I recognized some of the names.

"Leo's son attended parties. He also socialized with the Damours when he came home to New Orleans," Alex said.

"Everything in this entire city and the vamp world seems to come back to the Damours." I muttered. But then, that was what the bloodsuckers' long game meant—the single inciting event that tied all the hatreds and deaths together in the vamp world.

The original Damour sire had weak vamp bloodlines that left their scions in the devoveo for decades, even centuries, mad, raving creatures referred to as the long-chained. Creatures that were supposed to be put down by the misericords, the Mercy Blades, like Gee DiMercy. Instead, the Damour clan guarded theirs and hid them away, using their slaves on Saint Domingue—before it was liberated in a bloody slave revolt—in breeding experiments to create a bloodline that might help bring the long-chained around. They also performed unspeakable experiments with blood sacrifice and magic, even after they came to the shores of the States. And then Tristan and Renee, brother and sister, married and added their inbred children to the list of the long-chained. And tried to use my BFF's children, my godchildren, in one such experiment to heal them. They, and their nameless sorcerer brother, were dead. I could almost hear Munchkins singing and celebrating even now.

"More than that," Alex said, bringing me back to the here and now. "The parties they gave were often well attended by the paparazzi. Get a look at the dudes in the background." He held out a tablet and widened a photo into a grainy close-up of a small group of people. "It's really fuzzy thanks to vamps not photographing well until the digital age, but I'm pretty sure this is Louis Seventh. And these guys"—he pointed—"might be the vamp emperor Titus Flavius Vespasianus with Le Bâtard. The three stooges of vamp hierarchy, in the same vicinity as Macario and Gualterio Cardona." He pointed at two humans in the photo. "You got thoughts about all this, bro?" Alex asked.

"Lots of thoughts," Eli said. He stood and went to the espresso machine. I heard him making a double shot, all without turning on a light. Gotta love muscle memory. "The Marchands are the European vamps' onshore liaisons."

Alex said, "Sleeper spies. Foresworn to Leo and all that. Yeah. I had time to download the vid collected from Adrianna's cage. The Marchands let Adrianna out of the crazy box. I have some security of them leading the way when HQ was attacked. They helped take Grégoire and the B and B twins."

Eli sat down with his oversized cuppa. He pointed to the screen with the sat map of the area where the witches said the storm witch was working. And he tapped the building with the lightning rod. "Our people may be in there. We need good intel, absolute one-hundred-percent intel about layout. A reconnaissance mission. And we need better shooters. I don't want dead local vamps or Onorios on our hands."

"There's more," Alex said, sounding grim.

"That's why you got cookies, isn't it?" I said. "To butter us up?"

"Hadda learn something from the suckheads. Give a present when you bring bad news. The Damours were clearly trying to set up NOLA for European vamp takeover, as far back as your arrival."

I scratched my fingers through my hair and pulled it over a shoulder, out of the way. "Agreed."

"Why? Why did they choose the Damours and the Rochefort clan and Peregrinus and the devil? Why did they chose the Rousseau clan?"

Because Adrianna—she of head-in-a-cooler fame—was originally a Rousseau, I thought. The rest of it . . . "This is tying my brain in knots," I said, thinking about Katie, on the inside, her sister a prisoner and a tool of Leo's enemies.

"The long-chained," Eli muttered.

"Amy Lynn Brown," I said fast, speaking of the vamp scion whose blood brought scions down from the devoveo in record time. There had been murmurs about her for years before the Shaddock clan in Asheville revealed her. "The

EVs planned all along to take over Leo's territory, but when the news about Amy leaked, they moved up the timetable." It all made sense. "We have to call—"

"Already called it in," Alex said. "Dacy and Leo have Amy under their wings and in a safe room. One that no one knows about. No one."

That meant us too. That meant our map of hidden passageways and staircases was still not complete. Dang vamps and their secrets. "Okay," I said. "Let's see the rest." Because Alex never showed all his cards on the first pass.

In footage from another security camera, we watched as Le Bâtard, Fernand, and his sister walked beneath a light, from another car, this time covered in blood. The date and time stamp were from the night Edmund was attacked with silver and nearly died. I remembered the unfamiliar scents from the night Beast had tracked Ed. The Marchands had a way to mask scent. I remembered the blood bottle. If they drank from that vile mixture, it would likely change them in all sorts of ways. *Crap.* I hated blood magic.

"Those sniveling *petits, mangeurs de morts.*"

I whirled to see Edmund standing behind Alex, the bookcase door opened to the sleeping nook/weapons room under the stairs. Eli relaxed and removed the mag from a weapon. He had drawn and aimed faster than I'd turned.

"Silver?" Edmund asked, casual, eyebrows raised at the mag.

"No, but they would have hurt," Eli said. Casually he added, "You were talking about sniveling eaters of the dead, I think? Cannibals? Which I understand is an insult of the worst sort for Mithrans."

"They were the ones who attacked you, weren't they?" I asked.

"I was never certain, but it now seems most likely. Their fighting forms were different from what I teach, and so I thought interlopers on these shores, not our own. But the Marchands came from France, so their styles would of necessity be different." A strange expression crossed Edmund's face, something cold and deadly, and was gone before I could place it. "My mistress, may I have permission to challenge the Marchands to Sangre Duello?" He meant blood duel, in the mishmash of languages the Mithrans used. It was a duel to the death.

"After we get our people back," I said, "I don't give a rat's hairy behind what you do."

"I'd take that as a yes," Eli murmured. "Gear up?"

"One more," Alex said, punching a tablet.

On-screen, we watched as Sabina was escorted inside a warehouse, her hands and arms bound by silver. A prisoner. "She let herself be taken," I said. "Why would she do that?"

Edmund's head swiveled on his neck in that eerie thing they do, that totally not-human, more bird or snakelike movement. "We are not alone."

Eli slid from his seat, weapons in both hands. He had one nine-mil pointed at the side door and another pointed at the front door. I'd left all mine in my room. Again. Eli grunted and stuck out a hip to reveal the hilt of a blade. I gripped the weapon in one hand and slid it from the Kydex holster with the softest of snaps. The hilt was crosshatched and a little too large for my grip but good enough. Way better than nothing.

A soft knock sounded at the front door. Eli and I slid toward it through the shadows. The house was dark, no lights except the glow of screens. On the front porch was Derek. And Rick. Eli looked to me, his eyes appraising my reaction even in the dark. He racked both slides, one at a time, and removed the rounds he had chambered. Holstered his guns and went back to the table. "You called them?" he asked his little brother back in the kitchen.

"Yeah. I did."

"Good. We need help for this one."

I stood in the doorway, hands on jamb and door, my arms outstretched blocking the way, staring at them through the dark. Thinking of my partners, *Traitors . . .*

CHAPTER 16

It's Called Method Acting

"What good are you to this SAR?" I demanded. A SAR was a search and rescue, what trained people did when a hiker or a kid was lost in the mountains and emergency crews had to go in and find them. We were going into unknown territory to search for and rescue our people. I didn't have to say it. Rick had known me long enough to understand.

Eli said softly, "This is likely to become a close-combat situation. What we have is a reconnaissance mission and an NAR. Nonconventional assisted recovery and exfil. Let's get the terminology right, people."

Exfil. Which was short for exfiltration. Got it.

"And Janie is right," Eli said, mockery in his tone. "You aren't particularly stable these days, Ricky-Bo. Maybe you should sit this one out."

I shot a look at my partner. He was being deliberately provocative, which made no sense. Unless he was testing Rick's ability to deal with the stress of a mission. Part of mission readiness. Yeah. That.

Rick's eyes began to glow, not the gorgeous black of his human days, but the green of his black wereleopard. "I don't have control of my leopard yet, but I have other were gifts. I can get inside without being seen and look around."

"We have cameras for that," Eli said. "Cameras don't cheat or lie."

"Ouch," Derek said. "Dude, that one went for the heart. Or the stones." He grabbed my wrist and twisted it, breaking my hold, pushing his way inside. His body was stronger since he had started drinking vamp blood. His scent had changed too. And tonight he smelled of Leo. The MOC himself had fed his part-time Enforcer. It occurred to me then that I had fed on vamps fairly often in the last months, for healing, and hadn't gotten noticeably stronger. Just healed. What was with that?

I quickly blocked the entrance again and felt Beast rising in my eyes but couldn't see her glowing in Rick's, not with his cat staring out. "PsyLED wants in on this operation? Why?"

"Jane," he said, the single word tender and soft as a breath, voice laced with what might have been pain. Or a really good con.

"Don't."

He looked away and back and ran one hand through his beautiful hair. Now that he had found his cat, his hair seemed to gleam in the night. "Okay. PsyLED has intel that will be helpful. Has resources that will be helpful. I'm offering them all. To you."

"I don't need your help. I don't want your help. I don't need or want you in my life."

"Okay. You don't *need* anything. Maybe your partners do. And I need something. Just one thing. To explain what happened with Paka when I walked away from you."

My heart clenched with remembered pain. But no new pain. No desire. No nothing. I said, "I already knew about your unfinished tattoos. Paka spelled your werecat and bound you with some kind of weird cat magic. You had no choice except to follow her off the dance floor. She spent the next months biting and clawing you on the full moon to bring about the shift into your wereleopard, all the time eating pieces of your soul and your magic. Torturing you. And then when you turned, she did something else, something magical to that tattooed spell, to keep you in werecat form."

"Who told—" He stopped. "*Nell.*" It was a growled, angry syllable. Nell worked for him. Nell and I were friends of a sort.

"Yeah." I narrowed my eyes at him, wondering if he was being mean to the little gardener. "The same Nell who fixed the damage Paka left spelled into your tat, your werecat-problem. *You owe her.*" I enunciated the last three words in case he was still as stupid about women as I remembered.

Rick frowned at me as if thinking that one over.

I smiled, or thought I did. My lower face didn't seem to be working properly. "And she's my friend, so you will *not* be mad at her."

Friend. That was interesting. With the exception of Molly Everhart, I'd been a total loner until I came to New Orleans. Now I had friends and family everywhere. "We talk every now and then," I added. "Mostly when she needs info she can't get through PsyLED databases."

Nell seemed to think I needed to be told how Rick was doing. Everyone seemed to think I needed to be told about him. I got that. Our parting was public and humiliating. It hurt.

Rick put my comments together and one side of his mouth went up in a broken smile. "I'm sorry, Jane. I can't fix what I was or what I did. But I can use my gifts to help you rescue your people."

Behind me, Alex said, "We might need him, Janie."

I wanted to snarl. Instead, I said, "Follow orders. Do what you're told. Stay out of my way." I gave him my back in a catty insult and went to my room. Shut the door and leaned against it, eyes closed in the dark. I wasn't grieving for losing him. I wasn't angry, not even at the public betrayal. I was more, just, empty. There was some tiny dark hole in my soul home, a place where Rick LaFleur had taken root, and that small dark place was still empty. Empty where those roots had been ripped away. I had healed around it, but the soil there hadn't regrown. Bruiser . . . he was rooted down inside me some-place else, had filled a different empty place. Bigger, stronger. Better. But Rick's empty place was still a void.

Time doesn't heal all emotional wounds. Often they scar over, leaving abnormal psychic tissue, faulty emotional patterns, sometimes with an absence of sensation at all. That was how I felt about Rick. Scarred and empty.

My soul home wasn't a green growing place, but a dark empty cavern where roots might grow. Roots, but nothing green. Nothing living. I wasn't sure what that might mean.

I took a deep breath and paused, taking in the scent of . . . werewolf. I flipped on the lights.

Brute was lying on my new bed. "You know better than to get on my bed," I growled. "This your way of telling me I haven't bought your fancy bed yet?"

Brute snapped at me, a doggie grin that said he had one-upped me. A glint of steel appeared between the white wolf's ears and Pea, or maybe Bean, pulled herself up to the crest of his head, her little nose wrinkled and sniffing. The neon green grindylow chittered in irritation, showing teeth.

I grunted. "I take it this isn't a coincidence. You're here to help hunt down the missing vamps." Brute just stared at me, though I knew he understood every word. I sighed and snapped my fingers, pointed at the floor. "Get off my new bed. Those sheets were clean." When neither moved, I raised my voice. "Now."

Brute rose to a crouch and stepped to the floor, Pea-or-Bean holding on with her steel claws. I opened the door. "There's a wereleopard in here," I said to the grindylow. "Don't bloody up my newly clean floors. If y'all decide to kill each other, take it outside." Brute trotted past and into the living space. I closed my door, stripped off the wolf-ie sheets, made the bed up with fresh ones, and took out both sets of my remaining Enforcer garb. I had gold and scarlet. I opted for the scarlet because it had been worn and would squeak less. Simple decisions. Easy to make. Not like letting Ricky-Bo LaFleur into my house. That one had been hard. I laid out the clothes and weapons and when I was calmer, I went back out into the living area.

The crew was bigger than I was used to. We had Eli, Edmund, Gee, Derek, Rick, Brute, a grindy, and now Bruiser. My honeybunch had arrived while I was hiding in my room. The guys were all sitting around the table drinking coffee. Gee had his wings out, which was new. The brilliant sapphire plumage with the band of scarlet at the shoulder was folded at his back, with the tips of flight feathers bent and splayed on the floor. Eli saw me first; he got up and poured hot tea into my soup mug and set it before my place. Chairs scooted back and away, leaving me a spot. I stood behind the chair, not sitting, not yet. Eli added Cool Whip from a tub on the table. Stirred. He'd been waiting for me with comfort food. I caught his eyes and gave him a head-tilt thank-you. He gave me one back. This was family.

The tension that had gathered across my shoulders at the first sight of Rick eased. Eli glanced at Gee's wings and raised his brows. I returned a minuscule agreement. The sight of the wings was an indication of how things had changed recently. Of the secrets that had been revealed for all of us.

Bruiser watched the exchange with a soft smile on his face, as if he knew how I felt about family, though we had never talked about the subject. That was a discussion for after the three-magical-words conversation. He crossed his legs and I realized he was wearing Enforcer garb, but his wasn't leather. It was some kind of water-wicking poly-nylon-plastic-something material.

I caught a fold of cloth between my finger and thumb and rubbed it. The crackle of magic snapped between the pads of my fingers. "Nice," I said.

Bruiser's smile widened. "Then you'll be happy with the package beneath your chair."

Trying not to grab it like a kid with a present, I reached under and pulled a brown grocery bag out. Inside was a folded block of charcoal-and-black cloth. I grinned at him. He laughed softly at me. I did not look at Rick. Not once. Until Bruiser said, "PsyLED provided us with their newest gear. Spelled and top of the line."

I remembered what Rick had said when I let him in. I set the uniform back into the bag and took my chair. To Rick I said, "Thank you." If my voice was a little cold, well, I forgave myself. The mug filled with comfort tea said, ME? CRAZY? I SHOULD GET DOWN OFF THIS UNICORN AND SLAP YOU. I hadn't seen it before. I liked. I said, "The warehouse on the videos. Is it in the circled section of the city provided by the local witches?"

Alex spun a tablet to me. "Here." He pointed. "Building was bought and paid for by the Marchands when they were consolidating their power base. It comes with a lightning rod, like a nice pretty bow."

I studied the maps, seeing the rod and the surrounding area. It was within two miles of the place where the car transporting Grégoire had been ditched. For the first time, a small flame of excitement blazed up in me. All the pieces had come together. "What do we know about the inside of the building?" I asked as I took my mug and drank.

Alex said, "Nothing on file anywhere since original construction. Building was designed and erected with the ability to move walls around and add drop ceilings, and it's been owned by seven companies since it was built, so the inside floor plans could look like anything." He pointed to the sat map of the block. The warehouse and its property took up most of the space, with a high metal gate around the parking area. One corner of the grounds was planted with dying banana trees and lemon trees. The lot was mostly broken pavement with weeds growing through. School buses and bread-truck-sized trucks were parked there.

"The building itself is U-shaped," he continued, "with the wider, longer body on the side street. The arm of the U on St. Louis Street seems to be the front, with a public entrance, connected with a metal-roofed, unwalled passageway to this other building at the side"—Alex tapped the screen—"which turns out to be a taqueria called Pepe's that sends food trucks into the city." He tapped still shots of the bread trucks and showed us photos of the restaurant's employees taken from security cameras along the nearby streets. They were all dressed in black jeans and black long-sleeved tees, with black hats with Pepe's logo: a bunch of red and green peppers. "The addresses are owned by the same privately held property company but are under different rental and lease agreements, with a shared parking area. Also, there's nothing to stop them from sharing internal space or entrances, though we only see the shared parking."

"So collateral damage concerns may have gone up," Eli

said. On the other tablet was a floor plan schematic with electrical and HVAC diagrams, showing the original plans for the warehouse site when it was built in the sixties. "Roof supports are here, here, here, and here." Eli tapped the screen. "Walls could be up anywhere between, in any configuration."

Derek pointed, indicating the arms and body of the U. "Front arm on St. Louis is alpha, side is beta, back is gamma. St. Louis entrance is six. This door"—he pointed to a narrow door off the parking area, one on the entrance arm of the U that faced the front of the building—"is five. Probably was originally an employee entrance and check-in office." He was assigning Greek alphabet names to the parts of the building and clock-face numbers to entrances. Even I could follow that. "Side entrance near the taco joint and parking lot is three." He pointed to a garage door inside the parking area on the small, back side of the U-arm. "Let's call it two o'clock. Odd location. Can't see a reason for it to be here. No way for trucks to back up to it easily for offloading. Along the back side of the property." He pointed. "Gated entrance for the trucks. Twelve."

Rick said, "These are old plans, but they seem to line up with the sat maps, except the garage door entrance at two. Entrances may be compromised or relocated. Brute and I could jog around the block and see how many scents we pick up."

"Yeah, that's real stealthy," Eli said. "Like no one's going to get suspicious of a man and a white wolf out jogging at night. In a winter storm." His voice added, *You idiot*, but he didn't say it.

I finished off my tea with a final slurp. "If a couple goes in together in the middle of a fight, they can make a scene, a big one, in the corner away from the door. Rick can get in and scoot around back."

Rick blinked once, almost methodically. Eli's eyes lit up with laughter. He said, "I get to insult you."

"When insulted, some women hit first and ask questions later," Bruiser said, a teasing glint in his eyes.

"So, typecasting," Alex said, tapping on a tablet.

"Ha-ha," I said. "Not."

"Once before I used simple radio communication signals," Gee said. "I can fly above the site and provide overhead camera angles. I can also receive orders and suggestions. I'll need a waterproof and magicproof system."

Eli said, "I'm guessing your magic would short out anything ultra-high-tech."

"It is always possible. Now would not be the time to test it."

"Okay." Eli opened the weapons room, studying his gear. The guys all followed him, the lure of toys too much to pass up. I stayed at my place, sipping tea, watching. Eli gave out communications gear consisting of earbuds and tiny mics, all attached to small boxes via curly wires that went down the back of the neck. The box went on a belt at the back. It wasn't military or Secret Service quality, but it was okay. While they checked the devices, I took the new armor back to my room and gathered my weapons into a gear bag big enough to hold them and towels and a change of street clothes. I repacked my gobag and added three oversized plastic bags with zippered closures for wet gear.

I tried on the new armor. The two-piece armored uniform was unpleasant on my skin even with silk-knit long underwear. The magic was crackly-feeling, but it would breathe, it would shed water, it had built-in armor, it was spelled to resist attack spells, it was warm, and it was dry. Mostly that. I peeled it and the long underwear off, rolled them up together, and tossed them into the gobag. Once I stomped into the expandable boots made of similar water-wicking material, I reassessed my wardrobe looking for something eye-catching. I pulled on a dancing skirt and rolled the waistband down, making it into a short hoochie-coochie skirt; pulled on a thin top; then added a belt and a beat-up leather moto jacket. I looked at myself in a mirror. Only the boots were a practical fashion choice in the winter storm. The rest of me looked trashy, which was sorta the goal. *Score!* I smeared on scarlet lipstick, braided my hair, and went into the foyer, where I could hear the boys chatting about weapons and gear. No one gave a wolf whistle or made a comment about the outfit, though I had to admit their reticence might be due to the nine-mil I was carrying, and my glare.

The rain had eased and we headed out. I was almost in the SUV when I remembered one more important thing. I tossed the oversized gobag to Eli and raced back inside, where I grabbed the cooler from the laundry room. It was starting to stink, even with the excellent rubber seals. Two rotting vamp heads and a rotten rev head might come in handy. Who knew what the night would bring.

I stopped at the living room entrance, watching the Kid. "Your guards will be here in a bit. Keep the shotgun handy until they check in and prove to be ours."

"Yes, Mooooom," he said, without looking up. But there was a gun on the floor at his feet.

"While we're gone see if you can find a link between Adrianna, Titus, Louis, Bethany, Katie, and Bâtard, or any combination of the above. Something that would tie them all together for hundreds of years." I thought about the painting in Leo's office. Yeah. There could be something in historical records.

Alex looked up at that one, his young face pulled tight in thought. "Adrianna is British. Maybe Celtic? The Romans conquered the British Isles before the first Mithran was created. If a Roman took servants and slaves back to Rome, Adrianna could have been one. Then when Titus came back from the holy lands a vamp, he might have bought her. Ended up with her somehow. Turned her himself?" He shrugged. "Too many variables."

"She didn't have Celtic or tribal tattoos that I noticed. But if you're right, then that would make her as old as the priestesses. A first- or second-generation vamp." I remembered the first time I saw her, as she attacked me at a party. Cold power had flowed from her like icy air from a glacier; her red hair, curly and wild, fanned out around her; and her blue eyes were not quite sane. Adrianna was powerful enough to be a master of a blood family, but in New Orleans she had only risen to the position of first scion of St. Martin. If she was a sleeper agent, planted in Clan Pellissier decades, even centuries before . . .

"And you killed her." Alex's eyes held mine. "And Immanuel."

Both of us were thinking about how that might affect everything relating to all that was going on. None of it felt good. I'd been trying to kill Adrianna from the first moment I saw her. Now I had succeeded. And I had to wonder if I had messed up monumentally.

"I'll see what I can find out," he said into the silence. "You should take some of your magical stuff. Just in case. Lock it into the weapons cache in the back of the SUV."

"Are you worried they'll attack here and take it?"

"I'm worried that you need more weapons than we think. Take a few of them. Keep my brother alive."

I stepped into my room and picked up *le breloque*. It vibrated against my fingertips as I slipped my arm through the circle to carry it. A shock of power rammed up my arm and I nearly dropped it. "Stop that!" I said to it.

Alex laughed in the other room. "You talking to inanimate objects?"

"Maybe. Maybe not," I muttered, too low to hear. I left the small box of magical trinkets, except for the former blood diamond, now called the Glob, a weapon designed with my blood, body, lightning, and magic. A weapon I had no idea how to use. I wasn't worried about it falling into the wrong hands. The only hands that could use it were mine. And I had a bad feeling that an angel had plans for it.

At the thought, my cell rang. Molly's number. Molly, who should be at the bottom of a gorge with no cell reception, camping. I answered, knowing who it was, who it had to be. "Angie?"

"Aunt Jane. My angel is watching over you."

My eyes teared up. I found it hard to speak for a moment. "Thank you, Angie Baby," I managed. The call ended. I had a feeling that if I called back, the call wouldn't go through, to the bottom of a gorge. I was pretty sure that Angie's magic had made the call happen. I looked around the room for Hayyel, who wasn't there. "Okay. I'll take any help you might want to give."

I carried out the cooler and the magical stuff. The former blood diamond I tucked into my gobag when I got to the SUV. The others went into the weapons cache as the Kid suggested. Ordered. Whatever. I did as I was told.

*   *   *

New Orleans was old. Like hundreds of years old, one of the first port cities, back when the land was colonial and run by the . . . European monarchs. *Right*. There were parts of New Orleans that had burned and not been restored, where buildings had been demolished or had fallen down and hadn't been rebuilt. Other sections hadn't been fully restored from Katrina. Still other areas had been upgraded and spiffed up to look pretty nifty. The Greenway fell into both categories. Currently, parts of it were muddy, weedy, eroded chunks of real estate, surrounded and segmented by walkways and ill-kept streets, sections of which hadn't been paved since the days of the Kingfish, Huey Long, and his huge modernization and reform of Louisiana. Long had possibly been a demagogue, but he had built roads and bridges and infrastructure and he had believed in and worked for the people. Not much good had happened in the state since he was assassinated at age forty-two. The greenway upgrades were an attempt to correct that.

The Lafitte Greenway had been created in 2016 on land that had, until that point, been ignored. The bicycle and pedestrian path was a twelve-foot-wide multiuse trail along the linear park, a nearly three-mile stretch connecting the French Quarter to Bayou St. John. The greenway also linked to the neighborhoods on either side via St. Louis Street and Lafitte Avenue. Counting the houses and businesses and warehouses along the length of the park-in-progress, it was a heck of a big place to hide enemies, especially in the rain and the dark.

We thought we knew where the vamps and their prisoners were hiding, but it never hurt to be careful. Eli and Derek, in separate armored SUVs, took different streets along the greenway; Derek was on Lafitte, with Rick, Brute, and Gee, checking out the neighborhoods for anything that felt or looked wrong; and Eli, Edmund, Bruiser, and I toured the St. Louis side. We drove slowly, in meandering circles, the storm runoff abated just in time for more rainfall. Three blocks from the warehouse, Eli spun the wheel, taking us along a side street to circle each of the blocks, studying every house, empty lot, business.

The wind and rain again increased, almost as if the storm had spotted us and worsened on purpose. I checked my cell and followed the progress of the spiral arms of the storm on weather radar. No, something was, for once, coincidence. The newest wave of rain and lightning was right on time. The weather map showed red blobs within the storm band where dangerous wind and hail were, and pink bands where sleet was falling. It was cold for New Orleans, temps now hovering well below freezing. Not normal.

I closed my cell and took in the industrial buildings, many marked with mixed gang signs and some really artistic graffiti. We passed little empty lots, a few two-story Creole town houses, and lots of Creole cottages. The residences were painted vibrant shades of purple and yellow and rusty red, most with small gardens anywhere soil could be found, along the sidewalks and between the houses in the narrow pass-throughs. There were also pots everywhere, most pulled up close to the houses and under front porches, many covered with plastic against the cold.

One house, painted a rich green and white that I could make out even in the dark, in the flash of headlights, sported a claw-footed bathtub on the ground in front of the front porch. On the porch itself were several huge planters and an honest-to-God urinal all planted with winter veggies and winter flowers. Everything was beneath plastic shower curtains printed with flying tropical birds. Because—New Orleans.

We circled slower as we neared the warehouse, the suspected lair of our enemies, windows down, Bruiser and Eli in front, comparing notes on tactics for getting inside, me behind the driver's seat, my nose out the window, sniffing. I caught the smell of blood at one house, but there were people sitting in the front window, watching TV, so I figured it wasn't a dead body. And I caught the smell of vamps, unknown vamps, powerful and deadly, the herbal scent of lemon verbena and anise and the rich scent of leather. Had to be Le Bâtard, Louis Seven, and the strangers from the dinghies. I smelled the Marchands, the little traitors, and a faint trace of Sabina. Riding above the scents was the tingle of magic, though that might be from the storm, which was gathering strength. Wind pummeled the SUV, gusts rocking the heavy vehicle.

Overhead, the clouds danced with lightning, and when I pulled on Beast-vision, I spotted *arcenciels* pirouetting in the flashes of power. Soul, Opal, and two others. Now there were four of them: one in blues and greens and crystal brightness, one copper tones and flashing brass, one in opal shades of fire and stone, and the last one in silvers and grays and glimpses of moonlight. They were stunning. But no one except Gee and I could see them. To the others they were simply lightning flashing cloud-to-cloud. And I worried. Why were they still here? Why were they not outside of time? Were they stuck in the clouds? *Arcenciels* could be trapped in crystal and ridden, their magic stolen by the person who rode them. Their time-altering abilities used. It was telling that they were here, in real time, not in their own little bubble of time, and that my time magics were malfunctioning.

Unknown magic skittered across my flesh and was gone.

Over the coms, Derek said, "Big Bird has flown the coop." It wasn't code, but if someone was listening in, they wouldn't know what had happened. Gee DiMercy had shifted shape and flown. A black-and-white image appeared on the screen on the backseat, the view from overhead.

My earbud hissed and then I heard Eli say, "Copy. We have visual. Initiating Operation Insertion. George will drive our vehicle. Give us until I mention my mama and then the big cat can come in. That'll mean the way is clear."

Big cat had to mean Rick.

"Roger that," Rick said.

The smell of Tex-Mex food grew on the air, chicken and beef, lots of spices, ears of corn roasted over an open flame, hot grease. Pepe's taqueria appeared at the end of the block, lights from inside spilling into the rain, making the lights flow like luminous liquid. Eli pulled over and shoved the SUV into park. In a street-tough, faintly Cajun accent I had never heard before, he said, "You ready?"

"I'm always ready." It was a silly line, but I liked it.

We both exited on the driver's side as Bruiser slid across the seat, put his foot on the brake, and shifted into drive. "Be careful," he said. Because vamps might have a lookout

inside. Right. Eli held out his hand. I took it and we raced
through the storm and under the awning, where we brushed
rain off us as we looked through the storefront window.

Eli said, "It's smaller in there than we thought. We'll have
to put on a real show to keep their attention from the door."

"Long as they don't call the cops," I said. "We don't have
time for the cops.

"Call the cops? In New Orleans? How long have you
been living in this city?"

He had a point. Unless there were ambulances and near
death, or rich people involved, cops didn't come to domestics
or bar fights. "Okay by me," I said, with that same evil grin.

Eli leaned and caught my jacket in one hand, pulling me
back. In that surprisingly good Cajun accent he said, loudly,
"You don' cheat on me. You hear?"

"You ass!" I shouted.

Eli twitched at my cussing. Just a tiny twitch, but it was
enough. Inside I thought, *Score!* He shoved open the door
of Pepe's and yanked me behind him. He shouted, "You
trying to tell me you din be makin' eyes at Jimmy Ray?"
He walked into Pepe's with all the machismo of a street
thug. Dragging me behind him by the jacket.

"I hadda look at him," I yelled back. "He was passing
me a beer. You want I should *guess* where it is?" I covered
my eyes, stretched out my other arm, and made a dramatic
waving motion. "You're stupid, you know that? Now lemme
go or things'll get nasty."

"You got a mouth on you, you do."

I yanked my clothes free, fisted my free hand, and took
a long step for momentum.

To the three people inside, he said, "You see what I gotta
put up with this li'l bit—"

I shoved Eli across the room, into the corner. Holding
back. The breath blasted out of him. "I was careful, so I didn't
hurt you. Much," I yelled. "I ain't no cheater, you ass."

This time Eli didn't twitch. He slapped the back of my
head. Not hard but it stung. And it was on, as I kicked his
shins. Like a grade school child. I charged him clumsily and
we spun around together. Maneuvering us toward the corner farthest from the door. We splashed though a wet spot

on the floor. My feet flew and I nearly fell. I screeched, kicked over four chairs and a small table, sending them crashing. A chair tripped Eli. We both went down.

As I fell I realized we had all three employees, a man and two women, racing to us, away from the entrance. *Perfect.* Except that I hit the floor, landing hard on my elbow. Pain sparked through me. My left hand went numb. A wounded breath whistled out of me.

Eli roared with fake fury. "You sleeping with Jimmy Ray!"

"I'm not, but if I did, his dick would be bigger than yours. Your mama told me so!"

"You bes' be leaving my mama outta dis!"

The helpful employees were trying to separate us and pull us to our feet. I screamed, keeping their attention on me as Rick dashed in from the storm and raced around the counter, into the kitchen. He vanished into the back.

"Lemme go!" I shouted, standing up. "You can take your silly insecurities and shove 'em where the sun don't shine!" I elbowed my way out of the group and out the door. Into the shadows and the freezing rain. Rubbing my elbow and my scalp and muttering, "Ow-ow-ow-ow-ow," as freezing rain blasted into my collar and down my back. My legs froze in the icy wet wind. Stupid girly clothes.

"Janie said *dick*," Alex said into my earbud. "And *ass*."

"Shut up," I said, breathing hard, laughing and wheezing in pain under my breath. "Holy crap, this hurts. And it's called Method acting."

"It's called foul language," he countered. "I get pizza."

"Whatever."

The SUV's lights flashed. I dashed to it and inside, into the amazing warmth of the heater and the towel Bruiser held out to me. I stripped, dried off, and wrapped up in a blanket, unfolding the new armor as my arm regained some painful sensation and movement. We listened to the angry banter between Eli and the store employees as I changed into the dry long underwear and the new armored uniform. Eli ordered a dozen tacos of various different kinds, putting down the now ex-girlfriend. It was colorful and Eli managed to sound like a total . . . well, a total dick. His ex-girlfriend had been a smart chick when she left him. A good ten minutes later Eli raced through the rain and got into the back-seat.

"Dude," Alex said over the headphones. "I am like, totally awestruck. Can I have your autograph?"

"What about me?" I asked. "You don't want my autograph?"

"Only if I can have it on a naked picture of one of the Kardashians."

Eli passed out tacos. "The cook said the shredded chicken is the best, but the two chicks said the pork is worth dying for."

I got one of each and we chowed down, me wrapped in a blanket, listening to Rick, following his progress via softly spoken bursts of comments. His voice deepened, growing scratchy as he narrated his passage, which showed up on the SUV's screen, and I realized he was wearing an IR monocular. And he was fighting going catty with the stress, even though it wasn't the full moon. I wasn't sure how much control Rick had over his wereleopard. If he lost control, this could get rough. "Walkway into parking area between buildings," he murmured. "Five vehicles. Three food trucks. Two limos. One of the limos is still hot." Which meant it had pulled in recently. Which meant people inside the warehouse somewhere. "I smell DBs."

Dead bodies. Got it. I tensed all over and the taco curdled in my stomach. Brian and Brandon were likely inside the warehouse somewhere. So was Grégoire. Hopefully still alive. I wrapped the rest of the food and put it back in the bag.

"No visible security cams," Rick said. "No lights on. Moving from the back of Pepe's around each of the trucks."

Eli murmured to us, "We have new visual from Gee on tablet." Black-and-white video shifted to low-light images from overhead. I could see Rick, barely, in between two food trucks, near the edge of the warehouse's narrow roof.

Derek said softly, "Pulling around the block. Positioned a hundred feet from the vehicle entrance at twelve."

Rick half growled, "Approaching alpha five. No cams noted. Door is open. Repeat, door is not locked. Entering."

I heard a door open and close and thought for a moment about Rick being a cop. Needing probable cause or a judge's signature on a warrant to enter private property. He had neither. Yet he was going in. Because paranormal creatures—like me, like the vamps we were going after—had no legal rights. None. Our law-keeping was done in the trenches, with blades and guns and no mercy. Something cold and hard formed in my heart. But now was not the time to look at that. Now was the time to get my people back.

The ambient noise in my earbud changed, the shushing sound vanishing. The sleet had been left outside. The images on the screen were now split, one side overhead, low light, the other attached to Rick's monocular IR camera. In it I saw a small room with a table and too many chairs, all dark. No residual heat from a watchman or a guard who might have ducked out. I watched as Rick moved through the cramped space like a cat, in a sinuous path to the door at the end. He leaned in and I heard him sniff at the crack where door met jamb. He rolled to the floor and looked under the door, sniffing again. "I smell fangheads," he snarled.

"Rick," I said. "Stop." Eli and Bruiser swiveled their heads to me in surprise. "Your cat is close to the surface. I want you to stand and move into a corner so your back is covered from two sides. *Now*. Move *now*, Rick."

He growled, the sound soft and menacing. The camera view repositioned as Rick backed into a corner.

"Breathe," I said. "In. Hold it. And out, slowly. Again, in. Hold it. And out, slowly. Again. Do it. That's good. One more time."

"Thanks," he said, a few breaths later, sounding more human. "Meditation stuff. I'll remember that. Going through the door now."

The door opened and Rick slid through, closing it behind him. On the camera, we saw an angle of the interior of the beta arm of the warehouse. What I could see of it suggested that it was a huge space, with the support beams exactly where they had been originally, but affixed with some kind of metal ties that indicated walls had once been secured in various arrangements. The floor around the outside walls was piled with office furniture, a few couches, and myriad tools including a forklift and barrels and shovels. My heart clenched when I focused on what might be a saw with an adjustable overhead arm and huge blade, a model number in big letters on one side. But the blade wasn't bloody and I relaxed. Just a bit.

"I smell blood," he said. "A lot of blood. And witches and suckheads and . . . other creatures."

Rick moved silently, his breathing steady and smooth, along the wall. Clockwise, I thought, a witch direction, not heading widdershins as humans might do. I could make out the barrel of a weapon from time to time, but he kept it down, out of sight of the camera, beside his thigh.

As he moved, more of the room came into focus. The floor looked like concrete, smooth and stained with oil or . . . "Bloodstains on the floor?" I asked softly. "Cold and dry?"

"Yes," he breathed back. "Human blood." He took three more steps and the rest of the room came into focus on the IR lens camera. The remainder of the building had been walled off, the parts with the odd garage-sized door shut away. I didn't see a door leading into the sealed section anywhere.

CHAPTER 17

Pawpawpaw. Silent. Beast Was Best Ambush Hunter.

The only other opening was a barn-type door on a rail, which Rick slid open about three inches. Beyond the door was a room fit for a king with a bed that looked as if it had come out of a porn movie. It was big enough to comfortably sleep six people, and the frame was carved into curlicues and swirls at the posts, the header, and the footer; the entire thing had been gilded. The gold caught the lights, two candles in hurricane-style glass lanterns that glared out the view several times as Rick examined the room. The bed was made up with shimmery linens, probably silk, with fluffy comforters and an electric blanket that was glowing warm. One pillow was stained dark with dried blood. In the corner was a table and four chairs, natch on the gilded stuff, and a steamer trunk big enough to cage a baby elephant. From here, there was a door that led into the walled-off portion.

Rick moved there and listened, his nose pressed to the crack, sniffing softly like a cat. I wondered what he heard but nothing came through the mic. He tried the door, but it was locked from the other side. He spent another ten minutes moving around the bedroom, looking into a wardrobe, and peering into the trunk. Then, the rest of the building sealed off and unavailable to him, he moved silently back the way he had come and outside into the sleet. He slipped past a food truck with a dead human at the wheel and another on the ground in the accumulating sleet. They had been there long enough that they were the same frozen temps as the asphalt beneath them. He moved to the corner of the fenced property, where he paused and holstered his weapon. I followed his progress on Gee's cam as, one-handed, he swung up the dying banana tree and over the high metal wall. It wasn't something a human could have done easily, but a demonstration of his newfound were-strength. He landed with cat-grace on the sidewalk outside and trotted to the SUV he had been in originally.

"I smelled some things I couldn't ID," he said as the door closed on the downpour and the ambient noise changed. "Something that smelled like electricity sparking, and heated metal. Something mineral. I also caught a whiff of sweat and blood from Brian, Brandon, and Grégoire. They're inside somewhere I couldn't get, and they're in trouble."

I pulled the Benelli M4 shotgun and reached for the door handle. Edmund, who had been so silent I hadn't even thought about him, grabbed my arm. "Let go of me," I said evenly.

"No, my mistress. I will not. This is a trap."

"Of course it's a trap. Eli and I already had this convo."

"We must not rush in where your angel might fear to tread." Something inside me slowed at the word *angel*. I hadn't told Ed about the angel Hayyel or that a celestial being had appeared and altered almost everything in my life. But Ed was sworn to Angie Baby. Had she called him too? Something in his eyes suggested so. "Not without more information," he went on.

"Yeah? How're we gonna get that?" I asked, hearing the derision in my tone.

Edmund lifted a shoulder easily and suggested, "Think as a cat?"

I knew what he was telling me. I was an ambush hunter. Any cat would want intel on the sealed room before rushing in. And that same cat would strike from the least likely place. "Okay. I'll bite. Cats go high. How do we get into the roof system?"

Edmund smiled and I might have sworn he was part cat himself. He tapped his coms mic. "Gee DiMercy. Would you be so gracious as to fly slowly and low, around the bottom of the roof system, around the entire block. We search for an unanticipated entrance point."

The black-and-white camera tilted, showing a swath of lightning-bright clouds and the underside of a pale wing. Gee was the only Mercy Blade out of the closet. I didn't think it was an accident that he had revealed himself as an Anzu just before Le Bâtard and Louis—the Deadly Duo—showed up. The camera angled back to level and circled the block. Edmund said, "Here," and tapped the screen. "Alex, will you make some still photographs of the apex of the gable? I do believe I spotted a vent. And here"—he pointed again—"another vent?" I didn't see anything, but I wasn't going to argue with a vamp.

Moments later still shots captured from the video appeared in black and white on the smaller tablets. And indeed there were vents, two of them in gables, one on each shorter arm of the U-shaped building. I thought about Rick's video. The ceiling was the dropped kind; that meant I could lift a panel and drop down. If I could get over the room. But the roof was pitched too low to stand, and in human form I'd have to crawl. Beast shoved her way through my mind and said, *Shift! Beast is best ambush hunter.*

"If I can get into the roof system," I said, "I can crawl over the sealed room. Drop in. Make a distraction."

"What I was thinking," Rick agreed, his voice casual. Too casual. I knew that tone and I narrowed my eyes at it. "Two cats dropping from the ceiling would give the others time to take down the walls and come through."

"No," I said, before I thought. "I don't mind flying by the seat of my pants, but I have to know my backup is dependable."

The silence on the coms channel was palpable. I wasn't sorry. I wasn't.

Rick enunciated carefully, "What you want, or do not

want, is of no concern to me. This is now an official PsyLED investigation. You go in with me or you go home."

Again the silence. Suddenly I laughed and said, "Hey, Big Bird. Can you rip off the vents?" Even as I spoke, the altitude and attitude of the Anzu's flight altered. He changed pitch and landed on the top of the roof. One foot was caught in the camera as Gee grasped the fascia and the metal of the roof, piercing it with his talons as he hung upside down. Using the talons of the other foot, he reached out and ripped off the vent. It was still falling to the ground when he launched off the roof, righted himself, and flapped hard to regain altitude. He came perilously close to the sidewalk before he managed that feat. Lightning brightened the night. Again. Magic whipped through the air, a burning tingle that even the humans felt.

"Ricky-Bo, you slimy piece of pond scum," I said, laughter in my tone, "you're on." I started tearing off clothes. Edmund's eyes went wide and he politely turned his head, giving me privacy. Not that he hadn't seen me naked, but I'd been nearly dead at the time. I shoved out of the boots just as Beast tore through the Gray Between and we shifted.

Beast growled, shaking pelt. *Like new bigness of Jane muscles. Like being big. But hunger. Need food.* Jane did not answer.

Stared at bag of food on floor. Taco. Beast never hunted taco. Did not know if taco was bird or alligator or pig. Was too stinky to be fish. Edmund opened bag and Beast sniffed. Was stinky. But Beast ate, swallowing fast. Taco was meat and bean-stuff and corn-stuff. Had man-spices in it. Taco meat would be better raw. But did not want to hunt taco. Stinky animal. Swallowed last of taco. Lifted head and sniffed air. Smelled stinky head of vampires. Could eat them. Would not be hungry if ate Adrianna head or other vampire head. But Jane would be mad.

"Janie," Eli said. "You okay? That was the fastest shift I've ever seen."

Looked at littermate, letting glow of skinwalker energies into eyes. Growled again. *Not Jane. Am Beast.* Batted gobag at Edmund. Snarled. *Stupid humans.* Batted bag again.

"I don't think that's Jane," Eli said. "I think that's a 'Timmy fell down the well' move."

"What happened?" Rick asked.

Sound came from dark snake-thing on floor. Thing Jane called coms and earbud. Snarled. Rick-mate left with black wereleopard Paka. *Hate Paka*. But Beast and Jane found other mate. Better mate. Batted gobag. Snarled, showing killing teeth.

"I think she wants her gobag on," Eli said.

Beast lay on seat and chuffed. Eli reached around and found small gobag. Strapped it on neck near gold from sacred place of first Jane-shift. Neck lace. Neck was good. Beast had strong neck. Lace was spiderweb humans wore, but not on neck. Was confusing.

"Is that okay, Janie?" Eli tugged on gobag.

Butted Eli hand. *Not Jane. Am Beast.*

"Okay," he said. "I think I'm talking to Beast."

Chuffed again. *Am Beast.*

"Do you wish to have an earbud?" Edmund asked. "It is possible to—"

Chuffed with sound that meant was stupid question. Shook head side to side in Jane-talk. *No. Vampire might hear. Vampire have best ears like Beast. Are predators.* But littermates did not understand.

"You ready?" Eli asked, patting Jane's gobag. "You have a nine, loaded with silver-lead rounds and three full mags. The gray one is standard ammo if you need to switch out. You have the new armor and a thigh rig. Your boots are not in here." Eli patted gobag. "Understand? No boots. You'll be in flops."

Eli was good littermate. Beast chuffed with sound that meant okay.

"We'll wait exactly five minutes from the time the SUV door closes. Then we're after you, through the doors."

"Ten minutes," Rick said. Was growl to his voice. His cat-growl. Liked cat-growl. Did not like Rick.

"Fine. Ten. Take your time, Janie," Eli said. "You'll hear us enter the bedroom where Rick ended up. As soon as you hear us breaking down the wall into the sealed room, you drop into the room."

Chuffed. Lifted head, dropped head, lifted head, in Jane-nod. Tapped door handle with paw.

Before Edmund reached around, earbud made noise. Like limb breaking.

"Wrassler to Jane Yellowrock. Wrassler to Jane Yellowrock. Do you copy?"

Eli said, "Eli Younger here. Yellowrock is with me. Over."

"The Council Chambers building is under attack again. The lower entry level has been breached. Repeat, lower entry level has been breached. Stairwells are still secure. Enemy combatants are humans and European suckheads as well as local gangs. And you need to know, Amy Lynn Brown went missing four hours past."

Eli made snarl face. "Leo?"

"Leo is secure at this time. Requesting backup."

Eli said, "We are not, repeat *not*, able to respond at this time."

Wrassler said word for sex and earbud made sound again.

Eli looked into Beast eyes. "Amy Lynn Brown is missing. The EVs are attacking HQ. So what do they want this time that they didn't manage to get in the last attack? Has to be the Son of Darkness. And we have to assume they took Amy. It's gonna be a long night, Babe." He opened door.

Beast stepped into cold and rain and falling ice. *Sleet. Hate sleet.* Raced along sidewalk to corner where building roof was low. Gathered self. Pushed off ground. Leaped high. Stretched hard, claws out. Gobag banged on neck and chest. Landed on roof. Slid on ice-slick metal. Scratched and pulled self to top of roof. Like top of tree. Top of mountain. Could see steel pole called lightning rod in middle of roof. Looked other way. Could see far. Could see magic in other *ess-u-vee*. Ricky-Bo was shifting into cat. Liked bigcat, but not Ricky-Bo. Ricky-Bo was slow to shift. Was new to his cat-self. Beast was better. Faster.

Looked up in clouds. Much lightning and rainbow dragons, flying. Much magic. Much danger. Anzu was flying there too. Watching dragons. Calling bird calls. Saw Anzu dive at dragon. Bit dragon! Was fighting dragons! Did not understand. Wanted to fight dragons but could not fly.

Wanted to watch, but sleet was hitting eyes. Snarled. Wanted many things but could not have.

Crept on belly to edge of roof and looked down. Hole in top part of pointy wall Jane called gable was like small window. Big enough for Beast. Placed paw and claws into holes left by Anzu. Tightened into metal like into tree bark. Swung down and around and caught lip of window with back claw. Hung. Wind hit, shoving Beast. *Might fall.*

Looked at ground. Not far. Could try again. But Ricky-Bo could be ready by then. Did not want to hunt with Ricky-Bo. Pushed with other back leg and swiveled large tail to twist body. Pulled with claw on roof. Head ducked inside. Then body. Darkness surrounded like good den in mountainside. Sleet and wind went away. Inside was cold and musky with snake smell and rat smell. And human blood smell. Vampire den was close. Shook rain and ice from pelt, hearing it patter into dark. Shook again. Pelt was good predator pelt. Nearly dry except where sleet penetrated deep to melt on skin. *Hate sleet.*

Found wood limb, shaped flat. Easy to walk. White man liked limbs made flat. Remembered sound of machine. Sawmill. In hunger times. And white man killing trees. Hated white man. But liked Edmund. And Bruiser. Was strange to like white man. But was time to hunt. Hunger cramped into Beast-belly like Anzu claws. Tacos had been small crunch and gone.

Walked along limb into building. Sleet on metal roof was loud. Covering all other sounds. Hunting was easy in dark place with flat limbs and sleet on roof. Caught spiderwebs with face. Like neck lace but with crawly things that raced across ears. Neck lace of web. White man words were confusing.

Smell of human blood was stronger. So was smell of Onorio. And witch. And death.

Pawpawpaw. Shaking crawly things off of body. Pawpawpaw. Silent. Beast was best ambush hunter. Reached place on flat limb above room that Ricky-Bo had not seen. Looked for light and found place where light came through ceiling below. Gathered self and leaped to flat limb, then to flat limb. Flat was easy to leap.

Settled to limb over hole in ceiling and watched through into sealed room. Could see . . . magic. Much magic. Sparking green, black, and many, many silvers. Gold like Beast eyes. Pulled on Jane eyes and saw also red—color of blood as seen with human eyes. Color of Damours magics. Color of evil magics. Color of magic in Jane that had not been there when we hunted in mountains. Wanted to go home.

Pawpawpaw to better place. Through new hole saw Brandon and Brian. Brother-littermate-Onorios were tied to posts in floor by leather straps with metal barbs. Metal pierced flesh and blood ran down. Brothers had been bitten many times. Vampires had not closed wounds. Left prey to bleed, like cat playing with mouse. Vampires were playing with meat. Was toy, not food. Wanted to keep toys alive. Did not know how vampires had trapped Onorios. Magic? Or bait. Grégoire was bait. Beast wanted to growl. Wanted to kill vampires.

Breathed in air. Quiet *scree* of sound, no louder than sleet on roof. Pulling air over tongue and roof of mouth and scent sacs there. Smelled vampires Jane knew, Amitee and Fernand vampires. Would put their heads in box with stinky head of Adrianna. Smelled Sabina and Sabina blood. Smelled witch-vampire did not know. Smelled Amy Lynn Brown. Smelled more-than-five sick vampires. Smelled more-than-five dead humans.

Heard Onorio brothers make sounds like hurt kits.

Did not have way to tell littermate about Onorios in danger.

Beast?

I/we are in building. Ricky-Bo is coming through other door in . . . in pointy roof. But Ricky-Bo is slow to find his cat.

What's the go word?

Beast thought. Remembered. *When noise comes from bedroom that Ricky-Bo was in. Before he was cat.*

Got it. Anything else that needs my attention?

Leo's den is attacked by predators.

Okay. Ordinarily I'd say, Not good, *but that means fewer Big Bad Uglies in the room below.*

Amy Lynn Brown vampire is prey, below in room.
Okay. So we have more problems to resolve. Ducky.
Want to eat Adrianna vampire head.
Ewww.

Snorted softly. Crouched onto paws. Wrapped big tail around paws. Twisted ear tabs, listening. Yawned, tongue curling. Waited. Outside, sleet got harder. Pounded onto metal roof like many, many rat claws. Saw in darkness of head many rats pouring from sky instead of sleet.

Again, ewww.

Beast snorted softly. Heard noise far off. Heard woman in room below flat limb say, "They're here. How did they find us so soon?"

"*Ce n'est pas possible*," a man said. "They can't find us."

"*Je les entends!* What do we do?"

"*Je . . . Je . . .*"

Beast heard sound in bedroom where Ricky-Bo had last been human. Beast placed paw on ceiling with hole in it and shifted weight onto paw. Roof piece gave way. Fell. Beast leaped through hole, screaming with rage. *Hunt. Kill vampires. I/we hunger!*

Ceiling piece landed. Beast hit floor with one paw. Shoved off and up. Snarling. Mouth open with killing fangs. Ripped into face of man vampire. Fangs sank into forehead and eye. Into mouth and jaw. Bit down with crunch of bones and flesh. Blood shot into mouth. *Good vampire blood.* Flesh tore with strange noise as front paws hit vampire chest. Bit. Twisted. Ripped off face of man vampire. Was still in air, still taking vampire to floor. Back paws hit hips. Man fell. Screaming. Landed. Body bumped. Head bumped. Heard screaming. Beast ate face whole. Whirled.

Saw woman vampire. Pushed off prey. Leaped at woman. *Amitee.* Was in midair when wall knocked in. Beast landed on woman vampire. Hit hard with all paws. Knocked her to floor. Heard gunshots loud. Felt pain in hip. Was shot. Did not like to be shot. Snapped fangs into woman neck. Dragged her into corner of room. Prey moved. Shook her. Pain in hip grew bigger. Curled in corner with prey in front. More gunshots.

Looked around room. Saw humans crawling through crack in large door. Not door Jane's littermates should come through. This door opened from ground.

Garage door, Jane thought. *Don't eat Amitee.*

Will eat prey. Woman vampire smells like Brian and Brandon. Woman vampire has been drinking of them.

Oh . . . Jane stopped thinking. Started smelling.

More humans entered. Firing guns.

Amitee raised hands to Beast face. Vampire claws tore into Beast. Trying to find Beast eyes. Beast shook her. Hard. Heard neck break. Vampire hands fell. *Vampire woman has been using claws on Onorios. Playing with Onorios like mice.*

Take out her throat. Leave her head attached. How bad are you hit? Jane asked.

Beast is shot. Need to shift. Blood is leaving Beast body. Could die.

Crap. Drink her blood to heal. Look at the room. I need to see. Jane shoved Beast aside and took over eyesight.

Fifteen humans had come under the door, into the room. Where had they been? The taco truck with the dead humans. The bodies had released bowels. The smell of spices and the stench of the dead probably covered up the living humans.

Beast has better nose than Ricky-Bo. Beast has nose from ugly dog.

She was right. Rick should not have done the recon. Beast and I should have. This was a trap for real.

Need food. Beast ripped out Amitee's throat and ate it. Lapped at the blood that spouted from the severed carotids at her chest.

I tried not to gag and watched the fight. The battle was fast and furious. The humans were all wearing unfamiliar black-and-gray patterned camo, dull black boots. They each carried a sword and a nine-millimeter handgun, make and model also unfamiliar. They were using both weapons.

Edmund dispatched five of the humans, leaving them bleeding or in dead heaps on the floor. One had been disemboweled. The smells were awful. Beast licked her jaws. I tasted Amitee's and Fernand's blood; it was delicious. Powerful. And *ick*.

Eli was behind a massive metal trunk in the corner across from me/us. He glanced at us and took in the room, acquired a target. Fired. Aimed and fired. Fired. Fired. Each round found its target. But no one fell. These humans were hyped up on vamp blood.

Good vampire blood, Beast thought, still drinking. And sounding maybe a little drunk.

Three humans were firing at Edmund, but if they hit him I couldn't see it. Several rounds hit Amitee, her humans less concerned about friendly fire. Her body jumped lightly with each shot, not that the round would do her harm. I didn't smell silver in contact with vamp blood.

Good vampire blood, Beast thought again.

On the floor some twelve feet away, Fernand was feeling around with one hand and touching his facial bones with the other. There was nothing left from ear to ear and from eyebrows to the top of his neck.

He was making little sounds like, "Ih ih. Ieeee." I was pretty sure part of his tongue was gone as well his face. But he was still moving and it looked as if the flesh of his face was starting to heal. Near us, Amitee's throat was starting to regrow. They had been drinking from an *old* vamp to be this strong. Or . . . Or they were more powerful than they appeared. Just how old was the Rochefort clan in France? Was it possible to hide vampire power when a master vamp, Leo, drank from them? And how long had they been planning Leo's overthrow? And . . . Immanuel, Leo's supposed son, had been a crazy skinwalker. It was all tied together, but I was missing something. Who had the power and the time to do all this? Plan all this? Set it all in motion? Le Bâtard? Louis? Or was there someone else on shore with the power here? I remembered the vamps in the photos, the ones where vamps were coming ashore in dinghies. Who would be smart enough to make all this happen? *Crap, crap, crap.* What was I missing? The wigged-up woman. The vamp with her. Were they the ones attacking HQ?

Eli fired. Fired. Shouted, "Jane! How bad are you hurt?"

Chuffed. *Stupid human. I am Beast. Am hurt bad or would be fighting.* Tore vampire flesh and drank more vampire blood. *Goooood vampire blood.* Eli cursed. Fired. Fired.

Inside Beast, I worried. Even after drinking healing vamp blood, I/we could feel Beast weaken. The round must have taken out something important, a major blood vessel. I/we dropped down, flatter, and pulled the body closer, over us. We were lying in a pool of cooling *Puma concolor* blood. The unmoving undead body was both food and protection. Beast was eating. I concentrated on the fight and on trying not to gag.

I smelled Sabina but she wasn't in sight. Her blood-scent came from near the garage door at a chair, one with a length of chain across the seat, near a small rod with an electric cord attached, an instrument like an electrician might use, a soldering iron. I caught a whiff of burned vamp-flesh. They had tortured her.

I took in Brandon and Brian. They were secured back to back. The only evidence I had they were alive was . . . nothing. No evidence at all. Until one took a faint, shallow breath and mewled again.

In the corner was a large silver cage. Inside was a vamp in rags. He was sitting on a three-legged stool, hunched over a rounded boulder, tangled hair trailing down over it. It was hard to be sure, with the degree of emaciation and scraggly beard and hair, but I thought it was the man from the mural, Adan Bouvier, the male witch-vamp who could call storms. Which he was doing, but clearly not by choice. He was mostly skeleton, his feet bare, burned where they touched the silver cage, his hands like bird claws. His talons were buried in the stone.

No. Not just a huge stone, but a massive geode. One end had been cut open and the inside was filled with crystals of pure, clear quartz. I remembered the saw outside. And the forklift. They'd have needed both to maneuver all this equipment. This wasn't a room that had been quickly thrown together. This room, this scenario, had been in planning for a long time. Fernand and Amitee had been busy.

Eli fired. Fired. He raced from the protection of the trunk, toward us. He took cover behind the silvered cage, which on first thought was foolish, but then I realized it had to be warded. That was part of the glow on the bars. Eli was standing near the door to the cage. He was trying to get it open. I wasn't sure that was wise, but I wasn't in a position to do anything about it. Beast ripped part of Amitee's upper arm away and chewed it. I remembered a time when the thought of Beast eating from a human had made me ill. Now she was eating a vamp who was still alive (undead) and all I could wonder was how long it would take the vamp to regrow the musculature and wonder if Beast would throw up the vamp flesh.

Around and within the silvered cage, surrounding the vamp, a nimbus of power bloomed, a burning, spitting corona in a shade of yellow like Beast's eyes. Outside, lightning cracked, hitting nearby. The silver cage lit up with power. Tilting Beast's head up, I followed the cage walls high. They weren't sterling, they were plated with a heavy coating of the stuff, but underneath the coating and above the cage, they were steel. Which would conduct power really well. The cage rose to the top like the spines of an umbrella, to the center, where they met and formed into a rod that went straight up into the roof. The lightning rod up top was attached to the steel and silver cage. *Oh crap.* The cage itself was a spell. With a witch-vamp inside it. With the quartz geode. In a storm that was affecting time magic.

Quartz was the best crystal to catch and trap *arcenciel*. And with a such a massive amount of quartz crystals, vamps could imprison the rainbow dragons easily. They wanted to ride the rainbow dragons and move through time, changing the future, and maybe the past.

I felt it before I heard it. Before I saw it. That hair-raising moment before lightning strikes. The instant between life and death by Mother Nature, when everything stands still. And then lightning struck the rod atop the roof. In less than a heartbeat of time it raced into the building and exploded down the silver cage. Lightning so hot it melted the silver off the steel in places, in an acrid sizzle of molten metal. And into the body and hands of the imprisoned vampire-witch. His head arched back, hair flinging and standing high, back warped in unbearable pain. Mouth open, he screamed in what sounded like an orgasmic moment. The nimbus of magics around him glowed and went white.

Beast took back over and turned our eyes away to protect our vision.

Outside, in the storm, I heard a scream, a sound I had never heard before but instinctively knew. Magic was calling *arcenciels*, trying to trap them in the crystals within the geode. To take them as slaves for use in stopping and altering time. *Lightning transformed into magic*, I thought. *In the hands of Leo's enemies. Oh crap. We're in so much trouble.*

A weak growl vibrated through me/us. Pain shuddered through with it.

Beast dropped her head and tore out the shoulder of the vamp she clutched in her claws. She lapped up Amitee's blood. The agony in my/our hip and side decreased. I/we were healing. But too slowly.

In the room before us, Edmund took a bullet in the face. Went down to one knee. Bruiser swept through the opening in the wall at the bedroom, swords flashing as he mowed down the humans. Three fell, one to the left and two to the right, dead at the hand of Leo's former primo, former Enforcer. Bruiser was a source of death, like the Reaper's darker evil twin. He was laughing softly as he moved. Laughing as he carved and cut and brought death to the humans in the strange camo clothing.

The remaining attacking humans gathered around him, swords glinting, flickering. They were fast for humans, slicing and advancing, using a form of La Destreza that was different from the one I was learning. Within moments the Onorio was bleeding from dozens of cuts and stabs. He staggered. I/we stood. Screamed out a challenge. *Mate!*

Gee stepped through the broken doorway. His sword cut so fast I couldn't focus on it. He engaged the humans, all at once. In moments they were on the floor. A bleeding, groaning mass of humanity.

Fernand rose to his knees. Pulled a gun. Took aim with his one eye. He shot Bruiser.

CHAPTER 18

Yada Yada, Physics, Yada Yada

Bruiser dropped to knees. Fell face-first into blood and gore on floor.

Bruiser? Jane thought, trying to take over Beast body.

Beast held Jane down. *Bruiser is Onorio. Is not dead. Is not meat.*

Bruiser rolled over, groaning.

Gee rounded on Fernand and cut him across belly and chest and down one side in move that Jane called *Zorro.* Fernand shot Gee.

Beast laughed, chuffing sound. Pulled paws beneath. Tight. Balanced. I/we launched across room.

A hundred forty-five pounds of Beast–mass and momentum, Jane thought. *This one is meat.*

Hit Fernand in stomach with front paws. Claws extruded. Caught flesh. Landed on top of Fernand. Vamp bounced on floor. Face was not healed. Tore out his throat too. Ate it. Tasted good. *Like vampire meat. Like vampire blood. Want more!* Screamed challenge.

Gee got back to feet. Took down the rest of humans in cutting arcs of silvered-steel death. Fight was over.

Scent of big-cat alerted me/us. Ricky-Bo dropped from flat limbs in ceiling. Landed beside us. Looked at Ricky-Bo. Snarled. Pulled vampire close. *Mine. Will not share.*

Rick looked at me/us. At meat in claws. Turned away. Like black shadow, he moved into darkness and out beneath garage door into sleet.

The entire fight took maybe three minutes, Jane thought. *A long time for a firefight.*

Eli squatted in front of us. "Babe. You're freaking out the natives. You gotta stop chewing on the dead."

Beast stood over body of prey. Raised bloodied paw and tapped body of Fernand. Shook head side to side like Jane talking without mouth.

"What? Not natives?" His face fell. "Not dead?" Eli leaned in and looked at wounds on vampire face and throat. Vampire caws rose, slicing faster-than-eye for Eli's throat. *Fernand.* Eli wrenched back. Beast lunged. Almost fast enough. Snatched hand/wrist into killing teeth. Yanked talons out of Eli skin. Eli and Beast met eye to eye. He put his hand to the bleeding place on his throat. Calmly, he said, "That might need a stitch or two."

Beast chuffed.

"Want me to finish this one for you?" Eli pulled vamp-killer from thigh-rig.

Beast backed away. With one swipe, Eli took head from Fernand. Blade tapped concrete of floor. Beast lapped blood at edge of neck. *Good vampire blood. I/we are healed, but blood is good. Beast likes.*

Padded to mate on floor. Was breathing. Heart was beating. Onorio was healing.

Thank God, Jane thought.

Eli stalked like predator to Amitee. Brought down blade on her too. Head rolled.

Beast trotted. Picked up head and carried it to mate. Pressed neck to mate's lips and blood spilled inside. Bruiser swallowed. Dropped head close by and went back to body. Drank last of blood. Then lay down and groomed blood and meat off pelt. Watched as Edmund stood to feet. Wavered like kit learning to walk. "I may need . . ." He swallowed. "I may require blood to heal."

"Find a blood-servant, dude," Eli said. "I'm not on the menu. There is no quid pro quo here." He toed one of the humans. "This one is still alive. So is that one. Heal them and drink. We'll have someone to question and you'll have dinner. Two birds." To me he said, "Janie, we need to get this guy out of the cage. Suggestions?"

Am Beast. Not Jane.

What am I? Chopped liver?

Do not need liver chopped. Have fangs and claws to chop liver.

Beast trotted to door in cage. Was locked with magical lock. Would need magic key to open. Snorted and lay on floor. Started to groom pelt again. Vampire blood was going bad faster than other prey blood. Tasted bad. Did not understand.

"Jane!"

Jerked to feet. Was command tone from Eli. Alpha roar. Cocked head. Waiting. Jane was inside, thinking. Not listening to Eli. Put head against Eli leg, panting. Littermate rubbed head with hand. Looked tired. "Shift back, Babe. We got work to do. And you need vocal cords and opposable thumbs for it." Eli went back to puzzle of silver cage.

Beast snorted.

Inside of head, Jane laughed. Sound was catlike. Mocking. *At least you got to drink vamp blood. You ate my tacos. What'll I do for calories to pay for the shift?*

Beast snorted again. Trotted to corner where gobag had come off. Picked up gobag in teeth and carried into darkness. Found shadowed place under bed in bedroom. Lowered belly to floor and pulled with paws under bed, pushing gobag in front with paws.

No! Do not! Do not *shift under this bed. Dang cat—*

Outside, thunder rumbled. Beast chuffed. Shifted.

"I'll kill you, you dang cat." I was staring at the bottom of the bed, which was an old-fashioned metal mesh, about a quarter of an inch from my nose. The mattress sat atop it and it smelled musty. A spider had built a web in the corner and the spider, a strange yellow and golden creature with a bulbous abdomen, raced away to the far edge and turned to face me, mandibles waggling back and forth. I wasn't scared of spiders, but that didn't mean I wanted to wake up with one.

The shift had been fast, like lightning. My entire body ached. My gobag had somehow gotten back around my neck and it was twisted, holding me in place, nearly choking. I shimmied slowly, wedging my fingers into the mesh with one hand, pulling the gobag with the other. The cement floor was cold and miserable. And I was naked on it. *Dang cat.*

I squirmed my way out, pulled the blanket off the bed, and wrapped it around me. It stank of vamp and blood and sex and fear, but that was moderately better than being naked and frozen and hungry. Now I was just hungry. I unzipped the gobag and dressed in the long underwear and the unfamiliar magicked cloth armor, feeling the tingly-scratchy on my skin even through the silk long johns. Strapped on the thigh rig, checked the nine-mil and snapped it into the holster. Same thing with the short-bladed vamp-killer. Slipped my feet into the flops. Stuck the Glob into a pocket. There was a box of four Clif bars in the bottom of the bag and I ripped open all four packages and ate them, swallowing faster than I could chew.

I had a sudden memory of the taste of vamp blood and vamp flesh and nearly lost my cookies. Pun intended. I forced the white chocolate macadamia nut down my throat. It tasted nothing like blood. Thank goodness.

I heard a knock at the door behind me, the one the boys had busted through. Eli's shadow lay across the floor at the foot of the bed, but he spoke from behind the smashed opening, giving me privacy. "You okay?"

Without looking his way I said, "Dressed. And not really. My Beast ate vamp flesh."

From the corner of my eye I saw him enter and shrug, one of the minuscule gestures that meant way more than a regular person's shrug. "Why waste protein?"

I looked at him quickly. His face was closed and distant, and I suddenly didn't want to know what he might have done to stay alive. Instead I reached and gave him a hug. Both arms around him. Both hands, on his back. At the same time. And then I didn't know what to do. Should I let go? Should I back away? Should I keep waiting for him to hug me back? How many Mississippis did I hug for?

Eli's chest shook. Again. "Babe?" His voice was quivering and strained. I realized he was laughing. "You frozen in horror? Trying to figure out what to do now that you got me in a strangle move?"

"Pretty much."

Eli touched my back, his hand slicking down my hair in a single tender gesture. Which somehow allowed me to step away.

"Thanks," I said.

Unexpectedly, Eli was still laughing, face pulled up in unfamiliar lines. Showing teeth and everything. "That felt really weird," he said.

"Think I'll ever do that again?" I asked, uncomfortable, and so glad he had let me step away.

"God, I hope not," he said. "It's so girly."

"I know, right?"

Chuckling, we walked back into the battle room and up to the cage. Adan was sitting on his chair, bent over the geode. His hair was standing up with static electricity, oily, slick, and charged all at once. My eyes traced the silvered bars of the cage up again, to the lightning rod, and back to the geode. I had been right. It collected power. It was a lightning battery of some sort. Adan was totally unaware of us, his attention riveted on the geode and the magic he was working.

I spotted something I hadn't noted last time. Copper wires ran from the base of the lightning rod to the cage, where they draped across the metal framework of the dropped ceiling. They passed from the cage to the chair where Sabina had been tortured. I hoped she had been fed. She was scary dangerous when injured, even more than most vamps.

Copper wires also ran to the pole the twins were still tied to. I pulled on Beast's vision and saw a magical haze, some kind of spell, covering Brandon and Brian. They were out like drunks on a Sunday morning. I looked back to the cage. The geode was glimmering, a soft golden glow shot through with red and black motes of power. If I knew vamps, it had more purposes than just the obvious. The crystals in the center of the stone were not only a trap for *arcenciels*, they were also possibly a battery powering the spells and keeping the prisoners in place. I was getting pretty good at figuring out magic.

Gee pranced in through the garage door, which was half-open. He was uninjured, dressed in black from head to toe: boots, black jeans, black shirt, and black peacoat. No weapons, but then if he could glamour his wings he could glamour his weapons.

"Have you found Grégoire?" he asked.

"No," I said. We had thought that Louis and Le Bâtard had set up this place, and that the missing would all be together. But, despite the scent patterns, there were no European vamps, no Sabina, no Amy Lynn Brown, and no Grégoire.

I looked back at the geode battery. "What's the weather like outside?" I asked.

"Nasty," Eli said. "No one in his right mind would be out in it."

Lighting boomed a few blocks over, lighting up the rod and the geode. I moved so I could see inside the open end of the hollow rock. The geode had a single massive crystal of quartz across the inside and thousands of smaller crystals attached to the outer walls. Something moved in the center crystal. An *arcenciel*. A rainbow dragon was already trapped, but not one I recognized. I stepped to the garage door and examined the clouds, bright with lightning and four *arcenciels*. They moved with agitated speed, ducking their heads, frilled necks billowing out like crowns and capes, bodies dancing with energy. Despite the apparent end of the battle, this wasn't over. Not all of the scent patterns had been accounted for.

I remembered the *arcenciel* saying something like, "Our sister must be set free." I had a bad feeling that I was supposed to do the dirty work. Saving a trapped *arcenciel* was a perilous undertaking. Not that it was difficult. All I had to do was break the crystal. But then the *arcenciel* might bite me, and I had no desire to experience that. The venom or saliva or blood or whatever they injected you with made paranormal beings crazy. Like, forever.

Arcenciels were shape-shifters, light dragons that could transform into other creatures, and do so outside the energy-mass ratio that bound my own shifting. Soul could become a three- or four-hundred-pound tiger, but in her human form she weighed about one twenty-five. She shifted without needing calories to pay for the energy used in the shift. I had wondered if she had a pocket of energy she could draw on as needed to change shape and mass.

I went back to the silvered cage and tried to get a better angle to see inside the geode. The *arcenciel* was blue, the color of bright sapphires, vibrant in the colorless quartz. There was plenty of room inside the crystals to capture additional *arcenciels*. I had no idea what Le Bâtard and Louis Seven might do with several of the time-altering, time-bending dragons, except that I wouldn't like it.

Eli had been staring at the lock for the last few seconds while I wool-gathered. He said, "Two things. It's fuzzy. It buzzes when I touch it. I don't have the tools I need to get this open. The rock inside might be calling something. Summoning something. As my gramma might say, I feel a vibration in my molars."

I put aside for the moment that Eli felt a summoning in his molars. And that he had a gramma. "Calling *arcenciels*," I said. "They've been acting weird, dancing in the magically charged clouds."

"Your hair is standing up. We might be about to get struck by lightning." He said it casually, the way he would say *It's sleeting outside*, or *Eating a dozen beignets in one sitting is bad for you*, or *Tea is no substitute for espresso*.

As he spoke, several things began to come together. The trapped *arcenciel*. The missing Sabina. The missing Grégoire. And time . . . "So if they have a time-shifting *arcenciel*, why haven't they— Holy crap!"

"Jane?" Eli asked.

I had stopped dead still, thinking. "They intended to go back in time and take over Louisiana. Reshape history to their own choosing. That could be the only reason to devise a trap for so many *arcenciels*. This is the purpose of the Europeans' visit to the United States." I knew it, deep in my bones.

"They could do that?"

"Pretty sure."

The silvered cage began to glow, brighter than the sun. Brighter than the last time by far. Lightning. Striking. A massive bolt was coming. Fear shocked through me like the lightning that had nearly killed me. Electric. Behind us, a door opened.

I grabbed Eli by the shoulder, my hands and claws sinking into the muscles and tendons and around the ball of his humerus. I leaped away from the cage in a move worthy of a mountain lion. Lifting his body as I jumped. Around me, the Gray Between opened, but it was not my own Gray Between, but the place of the Between that was all *arcenciel*, a bowing of space and time and energy that simply wasn't a skinwalker place. I held it away, watching it bloom, thinking. Trying to make sense of it all. I landed, touching down to my toes and knees and one hand. Eli dropped beside me, knees flexed, taking his weight. In time outside of time. An *arcenciel* time bubble, one that was blue and golden all at once.

"Janie? What—?" Eli slapped his hand atop mine, as if to make sure it stayed in place.

"Lightning was striking," I said. And my voice sounded odd. Empty. No echo, like the one in the warehouse. I hadn't even noted it until it was gone.

Eli looked around us. Everything was stopped, frozen in time. Tonelessly, he said, "We're in the GB, aren't we? The Gray Between." He was totally expressionless. Battle face.

"Yeah." The GB. That was funny. The initials made me smile, but it didn't last long.

My stomach heaved and I felt queasy. I watched as Eli acclimatized to the place outside of time, but he looked fine, not a hint of nausea. Maybe nausea is trained out of Army Rangers.

He took in the room and the movement of power down the lightning rod, the position of all the combatants, his hand holding mine down on his shoulder as if he understood that the moment we weren't touching he'd be back in real time. "Sound is weird here, Babe. My ears hurt."

"It's the air pressure. Light moves fast, so we can still see. But sound through air molecules can move only at certain speeds."

He stretched his jaw, trying to equalize the pressure in his ears. His gaze landed on the door. "Who's coming through? And from where?"

"A closet? A small space in the wall?" I asked. "I'm guessing Grégoire and his old master, to kill us all."

"Grégoire to kill—? Oh." He looked around again. "Because Le Bâtard has the twins. The Royal Bastard has leverage, and you think he'll use it to force Grégoire to kill us."

"That's what I'm thinking. Or not. Le Bâtard and Louis may be at HQ. We could have another unknown witch behind door number three, the wigged-up vampire female, or a unicorn, or a leprechaun. I hear they're mean little buggers." I changed the subject. "You need to let go. I don't know what being outside of time might do to your cells or your DNA. It might warp them."

"No." He patted my hand. "You look and sound not quite right. For the moment I have a strategical advantage. Hang tight." Eli released my hand and drew his weapon, switching out the mag for a fresh one loaded with frangible silver rounds.

"I smell vamps on the other side of the door. They'll be moving vamp-fast. They might be masters, old as the race. They might not die from silver," I said.

"True, but silver direct to the brain box will slow them down enough for us to take back the field of battle. And take a few heads. We should start a collection. Mount 'em at HQ on the fence." That was my partner. Always thinking about the high ground and how best to secure it.

But the image cleared my head and I shoved my reaction to the lightning down and away. I said, "*Ick* and *ewww*. The stink of vamp head in NOLA heat? No thanks."

Eli grunted, this one more like snorting laughter. "Okay. Let's move. Together."

We stood straight and shuffled to the doorway, close enough that we touched, sorta like a three-legged race but without the grain bags or the messy amputation. Eli reached forward and pushed the door. It didn't move. "Jane?"

"Laws of physics change some when we remove time from the equation. Things we have to reposition are more difficult. Sometimes. Not always."

He released the door. "When I fire my weapon?"

"It probably won't fire. If it does, the moment the round leaves Gray Between and enters real time, it just kinda hangs there," I said.

Eli grunted. It sounded a lot like me. He holstered the weapon and drew two silvered knives, turning them blades-back in his fists. The steel edges were honed so fine it hurt to try to focus on them. "Hang on tight," he said, and put muscle to opening the door. It moved two inches. His booted feet slid on the concrete floor. "You could lend a hand," he said.

"Could. Learning stuff."

"Glad I can be of help." He sounded snarky. Put his free shoulder against the door and shoved again. I kept my hand steady on him.

"For instance," I said, "I figured out why the whole door doesn't enter the Gray Between with me when I touch it. In fact, the part I'm touching, or, in this case, you're touching, does enter the GB. Makes me wonder what's happening to the structure of the wood itself at the boundary."

"You think too much. Yada yada, physics, yada yada."

"Or lack of physics." It also made me wonder what it was doing to my own cellular structure, as I entered it over and over. I knew it was changing me. But that was a problem for another day. For now, I was just glad I wasn't vomiting blood, thanks to the pentagram-shaped magics inside me.

With a lot of effort, the door slowly shoved open, the hinges emitting a low-pitched hum that was probably a high-pitched squeal in real time.

As the door opened, I smelled vamps and their power, a bloody scent full of death and sex, the blood of the old and powerful ones. Sabina. Maybe another nearly as old. There were a few of the first- and second-generation vamps in NOLA: Sabina and Bethany and the Son of Darkness. Who was a skin-bag of bones and gelatinous goo.

I remembered the painting on the wall in Leo's office. The eyes in the shadowed face, the woman watching Katie and the king in the bed. Bethany. Bethany's eyes. They had

Bethany, or Bethany was a spy for the Europeans in Leo's city. Had Katie hung the painting as a warning? A way to get us to notice the power structure and the old relationships that might be affecting the current EuroVamp political climate? Bethany had healed me and tasted my blood the first time we met. She knew what I was. She had to. And Bethany was certifiably insane. Or was she? What if she had been faking the crazies? God only knew what she was up to. They had Sabina prisoner. And maybe Katie was now a double agent. I wanted to bang my head at all the possibilities.

It would be best to consider and plan for the worst-case scenario and hope for something better. Worst case? They may have killed Sabina for her blood. Bethany and Katie were behind door number one. Or, Le Bâtard, Louis, and Grégoire were. I sniffed the air, but the scents hadn't reached us yet and the air just smelled stale.

I looked down at myself and my star-shaped magic. The silver and red motes were different. Moving slower, the speed uneven. The motes were zipping a bit and slowing, zipping a bit and slowing. It was as if there was some kind of interference. As if something was attacking and breaking, or worse, deciphering, my own magic. That couldn't be good. I needed to get out of the *arcenciels'* time bubble. "I need to let you go," I said.

"Not yet," Eli said.

He had the door open, and I wasn't surprised to see Grégoire just behind the door, his body positioned as if running, one hand out to shove the door open, the other holding a sword. Behind and to his sides were two other vamps. I got a good look at Le Bâtard and Louis le Jeune, king of France. Louis was as pretty as his portrait, with soft curling brown hair and a delicate face. He also looked cold and totally without emotion, a serial killer of humans, intent on his work. Le Bâtard was a man full of hate, his mouth pulled back in a snarl, fangs exposed, vamped out. There was also something excited in his eyes. Fever pitched. I'd seen that look before once. *Feeding frenzy.* He was looking forward to killing prey. A lot of prey.

They were wearing modern clothes. I had subconsciously been expecting pantaloons and waistcoats and big buckled shoes. Maybe powdered wigs. Instead, the Big Bad Uglies were wearing dark fighting leathers spelled with a geometric pattern, the energies looking like herringbone. Each carried two swords. *Dang*.

Le Bâtard wore a gold chain around his neck with trinkets on it: a red heart, an old key, a small stoppered glass vial that might have held blood. The necklace was flying in the air. His partner in murder wore earrings in each ear and a good dozen rings on his fingers, each one bright with gems and worth a fortune.

The pretty vamp—Louis le Jeune—had the point of a foil, a dueling sword, buried in the middle of Grégoire's back. There was blood on Grégoire's clothes. I didn't know if Louis was killing Grégoire for running away or herding Grégoire into the room to kill us, but I was betting on the latter.

Grégoire was wearing dark slacks and a dark wool sweater that clung to his boyish frame. He was crying, blue eyes brimming with tears. More tears glittered on his cheeks, streaked back across his face. He wasn't vamped out. He looked . . . afraid. In the V of his sweater, I could see burns and unhealed fang marks, some still bleeding. Grégoire's old master and sire had resorted to torture to get his scion to do his dirty work.

"Jane." Eli pointed to Grégoire's other hand. It was holding a small black instrument. "Switchblade," he said, "blade placed to penetrate his own chest."

"Blondie's planning to kill himself before he does whatever they want him to do." That was the epitome of sacrifice. I wanted to hug Grégoire.

Le Bâtard and Louis were Naturaleza vamps, and Naturalezas wanted power, power of all kinds. So . . . My mind kicked into gear. They wanted Sabina to drink from, Grégoire to fight for them, and for Le Bâtard to have bloody kinky sex with him, sexual torture—trying to make Grégoire fight to win. They wanted Leo for his land. The SOD for power. The *arcenciels* for time bending, and, if I was right, to carry them into the past so they could change history.

They wanted to own the world. And they needed the storm to call and capture the rainbow dragons to get it all. The European emperor had sent them ashore for a first strike, suggesting that Adan Bouvier couldn't do big magic on a boat. He needed dry land under him for anything major.

Grégoire was the linchpin. It was possible that Grégoire could defeat Gee DiMercy. And Edmund. And Leo. All the EuroVamps needed was to get him to fight his own people, and that alone would throw any defensive plans to the winds. They needed motivation.

They had the twins to force Grégoire to do what they demanded, hurting the boys until he complied. I looked back at the twins. The spell over them was a strangely geometric haze. The motes that were present in most magics were random. This working was regular, evenly spaced, and . . . herringbone, like the magics on the Deadly Duo's clothing. "Brandon and Brian are behind some kind of weird ward. I have no idea how to *break* it."

"Okay, so we do the next best thing. Stay close." He edged in behind Grégoire and beneath the sword in the vamp's back. Feet scuffling, I followed. With a flick of his hand and blade, Eli cut Louis' wrist. The blade, though sharp, barely sliced the flesh.

"That 'yada yada, physics,' thing?" I questioned. "You have to press hard. Things in the Gray Between appear to be more dense." Eli repositioned his grip and shoved the tip against the wrist. This time it penetrated and Eli rocked the blade back and forth, widening the wound. Blood appeared at the edges of the gash and I leaned to sniff. The blood smelled of fear and Grégoire and Sabina. And the stink of vamp blood meeting silver—acrid, burned, and vile.

My stomach rolled, sick.

Inside me, Beast thought, *Half-shift. Fighting form. Now. Not till Eli's done*, I thought back.

She snarled but didn't insist.

Eli patted my hand as if reminding me to grip harder and applied more pressure to the tendons beneath the skin. After a few nonmoments we both realized that incapacitating them was not going to happen fast enough. Bile rose up my throat. I gagged. I needed to half-shift. "Oh to heck with it. This is taking too long." I pulled a vamp-killer, handed it to Eli, and pointed at Louis' throat. "Cut deep. He'll heal faster than we want, but we've bought ourselves some time."

"You want it off?" He meant the vamp's head.

"Not until we know where all the prisoners are."

"Look at you, being all 'Think first and kill later.'" Eli hefted the blade and turned it to a backhand. He swung. Cut an inch or so into the neck on one side, into Louis' jugular and his carotid artery. The blade stuck in the time-hardened flesh. Eli waggled the blade, yanking it at the same time. The tissue parted and blood appeared. Not spurting yet, but that would come. However, Louis was Naturaleza and had fed well on blood. He was capable of healing most anything. Eli took another backswing and hacked into the cut, widening it. Removed his blade and gripped my hand with one of his, holding it on his shoulder. His hand was cold. Too cold.

"Eli?"

"Not yet."

He maneuvered back under the sword in Grégoire's spine and did the same thing to Le Bâtard's head. Then he went to Grégoire. With the smaller blade he cut into the flesh around Grégoire's thumb, the one holding the switchblade against his stomach, the weapon Grégoire intended to kill himself with. "Maybe he'll feel it and know he isn't alone," Eli said.

He looked back at me. "You're pale. Sweating." He touched my face. "Clammy. Bleeding?"

I shook my head, the motion jerky. "You're cold. You okay?" I asked.

"Not really. The GB is a onetime deal. But let's finish it. We need to free the twins and the caged witch."

CHAPTER 19

Hung in the Sleet like a Sad Sack of Potatoes

I looked at my own hand to make sure it was empty. I vaguely remembered drawing a weapon. Or three. I had no idea where the weapons were. I patted my rigs and discovered I'd replaced them without even noticing my own actions. Muscle memory was a good thing. I was feeling woozy and put an arm around Eli to hold us together. "Okay. Let's do this." In our three-legged walk, we moved back into the larger room and up to Brandon and Brian. "We have a herringbone magical pattern. I don't remember seeing that before, but at the moment my memory isn't so great. Can you see magic?" I asked. "Can you see the pattern?"

"Babe. Human here."

"Yeah. Right. I've seen a lot of funky magic." I lifted my eyes to the wires that originated at the lightning rod. "This is all geometric. I think I need to. . . ." I looked at Eli. He was so close it was hard to focus. "I think we need to cut the wires to the lightning rod."

He looked up. "We have multiple wires. Which ones do we cut?"

"All. Why not."

Eli was holding my vamp-killer. I wasn't sure when I'd given it to him. I was losing bits of time. *Not good.* "Hang on, Babe." He positioned his feet for a stable balance, took two test swings like a batter at the plate. And swung at the wires. Unlike vamp tendons, the copper wires parted. And nothing happened. "Hunh," Eli grunted. "Babe, you strong enough to take the twins into GB with us?"

"Maybe. Maybe not." I shrugged and the gesture hurt, a sick muscle ache, like after a major beating. "We could die."

"That would suck. You got a better idea?"

"We need them away from the pole."

We inspected the wires Eli had sliced through. As we talked, the wires separated a quarter of an inch, leaving a stationary light connecting the space between the ends. The herringbone pattern on the boys had begun to thin. "Wait," I said. I dropped to one knee and eased the blade of a vamp-killer through a space in the magical mesh pattern. The blade sparked on the working, throwing light even Eli could see. I sawed through the straps holding the boys to the pole. It took a bit of no-time, but the blade eventually worked through.

"Plan B," Eli said. "They get away by themselves."

We three-legged it over to the silvered cage. In the Gray Between I could see how the magical lock worked. It was tied to the security of the cage, the twins' bindings, and the lightning rod. It was slightly out of sequence with both real time and Gray Between time, making it fuzzy and hard to see. "It's slightly out of sync with real time." I looked at the crystal inside the geode.

"Brilliant security measure," Eli said, sounding fascinated.

"Unh." I pulled the former blood diamond out of my gobag. Hefted it in my fist. Reached over and tapped the lock. Nothing happened. "I figured that would be too easy." I took the tip of the vamp-killer. Pricked my left little finger. A single drop of blood welled. Skinwalker blood. Blood capable of bending, bubbling time. I smeared the tip of the gem into the blood and tapped the lock.

The lock fell open. Which said something about my blood. Something else to think about later. On that tropical vacation, while sipping a drink with an umbrella in it.

I used the tip of the vamp-killer to lift the lock away and tossed it to the side. It hit real time and dangled, suspended in the air. Eli opened the door. We eased inside. Adan was a skeletal mess of sallow skin over bone, lank hair that was lifting into the air with static electricity, and fangs that looked brittle. Power was wrapped around his hands, thick as taffy, coating his arms and his upper body. He was vamped out, but the sclera of his eyes was pale pink, not red, proving that he hadn't been fed recently. The vamp was starving. Starving meant insane and uncontrolled. I wasn't real excited at the thought of freeing him or drawing his attention.

I bent and looked into the geode. The rainbow dragon, the *arcenciel* trapped in the large central crystal, tilted up her head. She spread her brilliant blue frill and hissed at me. "Well. That's a surprise. But I guess you can see bubbled *arcenciel* time even when you're being ridden."

The *arcenciel* drew her head in, arching her neck. I might interpret the motion as surprise. Or not. Dragon body language was unfamiliar to me. "Yes, I see you," I said to her. "And I know you're being ridden. If I set you free, will you promise not to bite me?"

The dragon hissed and darted toward me as if she were free, biting inside the crystal quartz with her pearled fangs. She had a lot of teeth. Dozens. All of them finely serrated on the inside edges and curved in for tearing flesh. I rubbed my stomach. "Okay. So much for trust." And I couldn't risk setting her free while Eli was with me, couldn't risk him being bitten. I said to Eli, "Back to the hallway. Just in case our damage to Louis's and Bâtard's necks heal too fast, you take position with guns ready and I'll get back here and take care of the dragon. And we'll hope for the best."

"This Gray Between, bending-time stuff sounded like a superpower until I got inside it," he said, his voice too soft, his breathing fast and unsteady. "I have to say, it's got a lot of kryptonite."

We shuffled out of the cage. My stomach twisted and saliva filled my mouth, nausea reaching a peak. I didn't think I could speak without vomiting, so I just nodded and followed Eli beneath the sword in Grégoire's back. He drew

his weapon and placed it at Louis' temple. "Go!" he said. I
stepped away. Dropped my hand from his shoulder. Eli slid
out of the Gray Between. His lips were pursed as if he were
speaking, mouth tight, teeth together, the way he might say
the first letter of my name. "J—" The Gray Between sliced
through me, a slow, cutting change. Noise blasted my ears.
Eli's finger started to squeeze the trigger. Time bubbled
back, the sound died, the shot didn't come. Yet.

I slipped into the cage. I reached around Adan's arms,
threading my fingers through the striations of his magics
and into the geode. I got my hands on either end of the
quartz crystal that spanned the center of the hollow stone.
The dragon inside was in a frenzy, darting in the confined
space, banging on the crystal. I had never seen one active
inside stone, only frozen in place. I had a feeling that this
magic and this time bubble were different from anything
I'd previously encountered. And that what I was doing was
more dangerous.

Hands comfortably positioned on the crystal, the way I
might situate them on free weights before beginning a dead
lift, I got my knees under me, back straight, and took a slow
breath, which did nothing to halt the nausea. I stood up fast.
The crystal snapped cleanly away. But the *arcenciel* didn't
fly out either broken end. Not sure why she was still inside,
I retraced my steps from the cage, set the crystal on the
floor, and took more breaths. I was light-headed. The taste
of acid on the back of my tongue. The dragon was bashing
herself silly on the crystal walls. "Stop, you stupid flying
lizard. I'll set you free outside in a minute or two. Or whatever that amounts to in this no-time."

She stopped and looked up at me, her pale blue lids blinking once.

"You understand English."

She nodded, her frill wavering oddly, as if in a breeze,
though she was still trapped in stone.

I chuckled softly. "I don't trust you not to bite me or I'd
set you free now. The moment I'm ready to reenter time,
I'll go outside and break the crystal. Four of your sisters are
up in the clouds. You can fly straight up and get to them.
Make them go away with you."

The tiny dragon's wings furled shut and her body shifted in a blur I could see. She lifted minuscule human-shaped hands to place them on the crystal, hands that hadn't been there a moment past. Her head shifted to human shaped too, though she stayed blue, vaguely like a creature from the film *Avatar*, except in miniature and with exotic lustrous scales that cast back the light. She ducked her head, looking strangely suppliant, and there was a fine tremble along her body, back, lizard legs, and tail. She looked at her right hand and folded down her thumb, holding up fingers, spread.

"Four. Yeah. Four of your sisters. Two I recognize. We're friends. Of sorts."

Nausea rose in me like a tsunami. My balance failed and I slipped to the side, retching, but nothing came up, and at least I didn't taste blood. My pentagram magics were still working. When I could stand again, I gulped breaths.

I was reaching the end of what I could do in this form. It was half-shift or die. But I needed to finish what I had started. I walked back into the cage. Pulled the small vamp-killer. And placed the eight-inch blade at Adan's waist. Moving Beast-fast, I stepped behind the witch-vamp. Grabbed him in a sleeper hold. Stood upright, carrying his weight up with me, putting my back into the move.

Adan gasped, a sound that was instantly strangled off. His taloned hands gripped my arm. Feet kicked my shins.

"I don't want to kill you," I said, "but I will."

With the vamp not needing to breathe and not dependent on a heart-rate, the headlock wasn't a deadly move, but it did hold him in place. He tucked his chin and saw the blade at his liver. Or whatever vampish organ was on the right side at the rib cage. His eyes darted around the room and down at the geode. His body slumped. He hadn't bathed in a long time, and though vamps usually smelled like herbs and blood, he smelled of rot and bad breath and desperation.

"I have the *arcenciel*. Your buddies Louis and Le Bâtard are being disabled. We don't have long to chat. If I ease off the pressure on your windpipe and let you talk, will you promise to be a good little boy and not try to get away? Because, you know, circling back to that whole 'I don't want to kill you, but I will' thing."

Adan nodded, the pressure of his jaw on my forearm jerky.

"Your conversational gambits are between two words. Yes and no. Anything else and I'll cut you off. Literally. Understood?" I poked gently at his side with the point of the blade. I smelled the stink of vamp and silver instantly. Adan's starvation had left him no immunity against the metal.

Adan nodded again.

I was getting good at this interrogating stuff. I eased off his neck and said, "Are you here and working with them of your own free will?"

"No."

"Have you been working at optimum speed?"

"No."

"Are you here because the vamps have someone you care about hostage?"

"Yes."

"If I set you free, will they kill him or her?"

"Yes."

"So you want to stay here and work?"

"Yes."

I wasn't sure what to do about it. I needed to get Adan to stop working on the storm magic, and to do that I had to save his whoever. "Is the hostage on the ship in the waters offshore?"

"No."

"In Europe?"

"No."

A frisson of excitement sluiced through me. "Here in New Orleans?"

"Yes."

I realized the last word was nearly sobbed. "You just earned yourself some new words. How many hostages are we talking? Do you know where they are?"

"Two. Yes." A pale pinkish tear trickled down his cheek.

What was it with people crying lately? "If I can save them, will you stop the magic?"

"Yes. If you will pledge on your honor to save them I will end the working now."

Honor. That was a weighty word among vamps. It came with repercussions. The way he had phrased it meant that I couldn't fail. If I failed, my own life would be forfeit. "Provided you give me accurate locations, and they're on land, and not among a nest of hungry vamps, and not already dead when I get there."

"And you will feed me."

"I will take you, in shackles, to Leo Pellissier, and the Master of the City of New Orleans will provide food."

"You bargain like a Mithran, but you are not." Adan drew in a long slow breath, the air whistling against the pressure of my arm on his trachea. "Oh. Oh, yes," he said.

I knew he hadn't just been hanging in my arms. He had been drawing conclusions and sniffing with each breath.

"You are Jane Yellowrock. Leo's Enforcer."

"Got it in one."

"I have not been fed. I will not have my usual control. Which is impeccable."

"We're not finished bargaining. I want to know everything about Ka Nvista. Everything you know. Every story she told, every single thing."

Adan thrashed and I eased up more on the pressure. "She was my blood-servant," he whispered. "Was my primo before I was stripped of my power and placed in this cage. I will tell you what you desire to hear."

I wasn't sure that he had agreed to tell me the truth, but I said, "Done," before I thought it through.

"Done," he agreed. "I lift my hands, say one phrase, and the storm will begin to diminish. It will begin to follow normal weather patterns and not the artificially created one of my making."

"Go for it." Adan didn't respond and I figured he didn't understand the modern cant. "Make it happen," I revised.

Adan extended one taloned hand in front of us. *"Et tempestate mortis."*

I waited, watching the magics on the cage, over the twins, across the ceiling to Sabina's chair, still empty. It took what would have been a dozen breaths in real time, before I saw a flicker. An almost insubstantial alteration in the flow of magics happening outside of bubbled time.

"Your part of the bargain is satisfied," I said.

Adan made a sound that might have been laughter. Took a breath. "I thirst. I smell human blood." His fangs *schnicked* down.

"About that lack of control you mentioned?" I dropped the blade and it started to fall, hitting real time and hanging about two inches from my hand.

"You must—"

I placed my hands on Adan's head and twisted it with a ferocious jerk. His neck snapped. Adan went limp. I said into his ear, "Leo will heal you, never fear." I tossed him over my shoulder, reacquired my blade, and carried him beneath the open garage door and out of the warehouse. Outside, the weather was frightful, which had a Christmas song meandering its way through my head. *Dang it.* Sleet had piled up in corners, in crevices, and partially covered the face of the cold dead guy beside a food truck. Not one of ours so I didn't linger. I brushed through the sleet hanging in the air and up to the fence near the banana trees. Bending my knees, I tossed Adan up into the air. As he left my touch he entered real time and hung in the sleet like a sad sack of potatoes. His trajectory should take him over the fence to crash-land on the sidewalk. Derek would know what to do.

I raced back into the building and knelt near the crystal of quartz. I placed my hands on the cold concrete floor and said to the dragon, "I haven't forgotten you." To Beast, I said, "Okay. Now."

The transformation was fast and more painful. My spine snapped. Hips shifted, becoming more narrow. Knuckles and elbows and ankles swelled. The bones in my fingers elongated. I blacked out. Came to, still in bubbled time, something shoving up into my ribs. I rolled over, catching a glimpse of my body—half-form—and the crystal that had been sticking into me. "Oh," I moaned. "Owww."

I was furry but at least I wasn't quite so sick to my stomach now. And this was *my* Gray Between, a place where magic looked like it should, silver, gray, and sparkly. I rolled to my feet, feeling powerful and lithe, all the things that Beast liked about her own form but with opposable thumbs.

I picked up the crystal and carried it to the garage door. Standing in the halted sleet, I stared down at the dragon sprite inside. She was back in her winged lizard form, a look of what I might describe as hunger on her face as she pressed on the stone. She stared into the cold night, her entire body shaking with need. "I'm setting you free," I said, my voice now a scratchy hoarse sound, half-growl. "You bite me and I'll get Adan back here to call you into the geode. We clear on that?"

She swiveled her head and hissed at me.

I chuckled, the sound nasty. "I asked you a question," I ground out.

The dragon nodded, her frill wafting back and forth.

"Good. Your sisters are up in the clouds. Get them away from here. To a safe place. Maybe underwater in the Gulf, someplace deep. There's a rift below Cuba that's supposed to be deep. Stay away from here for a while." With that last bit of advice I slammed the quartz crystal onto the ground. The quartz busted into thousands of shards. The blue *arcenciel* leaped free. She was stuck in real time, a shimmering bit of legend, catching all the light, her scales iridescent, wings unexpectedly feathered. I looked at the clouds and saw that all the *arcenciels* were still stuck in real time, still caught in the magical storm. Shouldn't it have dissipated by now? That worry wriggled in the back of my mind like a worm on a hook.

Before I dunked myself back into normal time, I needed to see where the vamps had been hiding. And what and who else were at the other end of the hallway.

I passed the four combatants and scooted along the wall into the shadows. In the back was a small room, maybe ten by ten. The space had been constructed differently from the outer rooms, which were made of traditional wallboard and studs. This space had been bricked up, each wall two bricks deep. Rebar poked up along the top of the brick wall, showing that it had been reinforced. The bricks themselves were level, but the mortar between them was rough and had been left to dry in coarse clumps. There were iron rings in the brick, holding narrow metal frames to the walls, bed frames stacked three high, bunk bed style. Six beds, each with a prisoner on it. Vampires. Four of them were raging, faces contorted, vamped out, fangs snapped down on the little hinges in their mouths, some just needle-teeth, others longer, wider, thicker. They were hungry mad things. *The long-chained.*

But two of the six were aware, alert, sharing a glance across the distance of their beds. They had been healed. Recently, if the iron shackles on their arms were an indication. I'd bet good money they had drunk from Amy Lynn Brown. Eli would have said that early sorties were often for multiple purposes—to create destruction and lay groundwork, test the defenses, and take what they wanted. Because that was surely all this was, from the revs rising, the magical storm, the kidnappings of Sabina and Amy and Grégoire, everything. To lay the groundwork for a precipitate arrival of the full contingent of the EuroVamps.

Unless Del was right and there were factions among the EVs? And maybe the Deadly Duo had decided to jump ship early and take over before Titus Flavius Vespasianus landed? Or Titus had sent them on a sortie and they decided to take over instead? A double cross? Attempt a coup over Leo *and* Titus?

Holy crap. That was it. And Leo had to have known it from the very first, because he was good at the political mumbo jumbo. And that meant he had intended for me to deal with it from the very beginning. All by myself. While he cavorted in his office with his lovers. *"We are not doomed,"* Leo had said, with that faint smile, his eyes on me. *"We are quite safe. All is according to plan."* A bitter taste laced through me, dark and harsh. I was Leo's secret weapon.

Leo needed a good lesson in manners, but I had to survive this situation first.

I returned my attention to the bricked-up room. Sabina was slumped in a chair in the corner, her habit slashed, her olive skin exposed. She was chained with silver. Bites were everywhere, as if they had blood-drained her and then left her body wrapped in chains, silver chains tight and burning against her flesh. Sabina didn't drink often, holding to a lifestyle of self-restraint and iron discipline, the epitome of the Mithran vampire. Her age gave her a natural resistance to silver, but she had been drained, left weak; the silver had inflamed and blacked her skin. Some of the fang marks were tiny. At some point, they had turned the long-chained loose on her, and the vamps had attacked her. The outclan priest-ess had also been burned, her torso, neck, and face. Hun-dreds of tiny pinpoint burns were weeping vampire blood or were burned black.

Her glove was missing, her burned hand exposed. The hand she had nearly lost handling the Blood Cross to save lives. So much history in this woman. So much pain and promise. Yet even so weakened, Sabina was protecting an-other. Behind her, in the corner against the wall, was Amy Lynn Brown. The young vampire was crouched, her face full of terror, tears streaking her cheeks. She was under a *hedge of thorns* working. Somehow, Sabina had put Amy under a ward, protecting her.

I had to break Sabina's chains. If she was free, Sabina could drink from the still-crazy long-chained and find her strength. Get away. And take Amy with her. But the chains would be much stronger, harder to break in bubbled time. I bent over and examined them, following the largest chain around to the back. It was held in place with a lock, the old-fashioned ver-sion of a keyed padlock, the outer case corroded green metal, the hasp steel. It had a keyhole in the middle.

Le Bâtard's necklace had been strung with a key. I spun back into the hallway and lifted the necklace off over the vamp's head without touching him. Carried it back to the bricked room and opened the old lock. "*Et voilà!*" I said. And stopped. I didn't speak French, but I understood a lot more than I had once upon a time. I'd even picked up a few phrases, it seemed.

It took effort to peel the chains off Sabina, and they moved with a hollow, dull clanking noise, the sound waves slowed and deep. I dropped them and they hung in midair. I put the necklace from her tormenter in her lap. Maybe she could make good use of the other trinkets on it.

I went back into the main room and got a feel for where everyone was, all the combatants, even Gee, whom I had ig-nored while outside of real time. He looked as he always did, except his magics were more pronounced, his glamour less effective. I could see feathers on his arms, which was freaky.

I got into position, drew two vamp-killers, and dropped time.

Clamor and screams battered my ears. Blood spurted across the walls and into the main room. Gunshots sounded from the hallway—Eli shooting the vamps. Grégoire stumbled through the doorway. A steel foil swinging in the air behind him. The silver-plated point of the sword was buried in Blondie's back. No one was holding it. But at least he hadn't stuck himself with the switchblade.

He whipped his head back, saw whatever was happening in the hallway, and tripped. Caught his fall. Pushed off the floor with one hand, took three steps and reached back. He ripped the sword out of his body. Blood flew. Grégoire saw me and vamped out, a snarl on his mouth. *"Putain t'étais où, bordel!"*

That one I hadn't heard before. Pretty sure it was cussing in some form. Before I could reply, lightning hit the building.

The flash was massive. So bright I went blind. Was thrown across the room, my skin burning as if it were being flayed off me. Time bubbled, bubbled, bubbled. Lightning shocked through me in a colossal thrust of energy.

And then it was gone. I landed hard. Skidded. Rolled. The pain vanished. My sight returned. I heaved breaths. Heat burned through my pocket. The pocket where I'd stashed the weapon made from my flesh. The Glob had protected me from lightning and magic. The weapon was branding my skin and burning my pelt, but I'd take that over a lightning strike.

Grégoire, however, was down, as was Gee, both blinded by the light. I raced to the hallway to see two vamps with partially severed heads, evidence of multiple gunshots, and my partner blinking against the booming brilliance. Lightning blind and probably temporarily deaf. "You okay, my brother?" I shouted in New Orleans' lingo.

Blinking hard, he turned in my general direction and shouted back. "Yeah. Are they down?"

"Yes. Excellent work!"

I spun back to the room. Gee was getting up off the floor, half his glamour gone, iridescent feathers visible, in shades of sapphire and scarlet, the stink of singed feathers hot and acrid on the air. He looked punch-drunk, blinking against the too-bright light.

Grégoire crawled upright in one of those not-human movements the fangheads do when they're hurt or not aping human, elbows and hips high, body low, hands splayed on the concrete, a sword in one, a switchblade in the other.

I heard a hum from the side. From the cage. Where the lightning had been drawn by the rod. Right. Red motes of power were buzzing around the geode. The magic looked wrong, out of sequence, just zapping here and there, like sparklers in the hands of a three-year-old child. Adan was out cold on the floor by the geode. His hands were scorched to the bone.

Soul walked in through the open garage door. Behind her was a woman in blue. Or a blue woman wearing blue. Both were staring at the geode in the cage. "All *arcenciels* are in your debt," Soul said. "You are accumulating a large repository of boons and debt favors that gift you with much power."

"Whatever. This is not a good time," I said, sheathing vamp-killers and pulling weapons of more modern heritage, working both slides as I did. "Grégoire." I pointed both barrels at him. "Stop. I'll fill you with silver if you don't."

"Putain de merde, t'étais où, bordel?" he snarled at me. *"On attendaient que tu arrives, pendant qu'ils nous torturaient!"*

I wasn't sure what I had done, but it sounded awful. The blue woman spun to him, insubstantial gauzy skirts billowing out. "No! Not her!" She pointed to me. "The message you received was not from this one! It was a ruse."

Soul held up a hand and Grégoire stopped. Blue Girl took Soul's gauzy skirts in her hands and slipped close, wrapping the skirts around her legs, as if sliding under a wing. Her bright blue eyes were on me. Soul said, "Cerulean tells me that you are betrayed. By one you do not expect."

Grégoire stopped his crawl. Got to his feet. "Put away your weapons," he said to me, as if they were toys not to be bothered with. To Soul he said, "Who has betrayed us?"

Soul turned to me instead of answering him. "You have a problem that we might solve."

"Yeah?" I challenged.

"That"—she pointed at the cage and the sparkling geode—"is a time trap. It calls to us. If it takes us in, broken as it is now, it becomes a weapon. If it detonates, the explosion will wipe out most of New Orleans. You can deactivate it while in a bubble of time."

"What?" I said. "How? It comes with an instruction manual?"

Soul didn't even smile. "It isn't difficult. It is vibrational, a drumming magic."

Which I had never heard of. Drumming magic? "Why not you? Or him?" I pointed at Gee, who dropped to a knee at the side of Louis.

"All other time-benders will be imprisoned," she said. "Only you have the skills and the ability to move through time that is neither *arcenciel* time nor Anzu time. But you must hurry."

"Well, crap. Of *course* I have to deactivate a bomb that's going to wipe out the city. Why not?" I leaned to her and snarled, "I don't believe you. I think you just want me to destroy a trap that scares you silly." Soul didn't blink, but Little Girl Blue twitched. *Gotcha.*

"Yeah. That's what I thought," I said. "There's problems at HQ. I'll deactivate your bomb. But in return, the *arcenciels*, all of you, will agree to support Leo and the city against the rest of the European vampires. You will make a fast parley, agree to terms within one hour of the onset of negotiations, to begin at dawn, and you will support him and us against them."

"Done," Soul said. "Bomb first."

"Whatever."

Soul gave me instructions. I shoulda refused.

CHAPTER 20

Your Faith Has Waned and All but Disappeared

First, I bubbled time, which was a lot easier than once before. I wasn't sure if that was a good thing or a bad thing, but I pulled in the Gray Between and folded it around me like a cloak. No nausea. Weird. But then, the Glob in my pocket seemed to warm even more, as if the lightning had activated it this time. Maybe a lot of the changes in my magic were the result of its power.

I took a single, solid sterling silver stake and entered the silvered gate, stepping over the vamp. Sat on the floor near the sparkling geode, not touching it, not bringing it into the bubble of time with me. I crossed my legs like a yoga position. My feet were pawed, big as dinner plates with retractile claws, so it wasn't graceful. I hadn't even noticed that I'd been barefooted. Bare-pawed? Whatever. The puma pads were resistant to the cold and the rough surfaces. I began to tap on the geode's coarse outside. Soul had said to tap on the stone with a specific beat, a rhythm that reminded me of one of Aggie's drums. Soul had said, *"This is a ceremony, outside of time, in the midst of battle. But it is a ceremony that has no rules, one that you must feel your way through, as you feel your way through a dance, each step the result of the previous."* What she meant was that I'd be flying by the seat of my pants. As always.

I tapped, a slow steady pace. The sound waves, initiated in the Gray Between, entered the geode in regular time, supposedly setting up a vibration. What would have been long minutes, outside the time bubble, passed. The sparklies inside the geode didn't alter. More time passed. I settled into the rhythm: hard, soft, soft, soft. Hard, soft, soft, soft. A tribal drumming.

I crossed my legs, relaxing into it. *TAP, tap, tap, tap. TAP, tap, tap, tap. TAP, tap, tap, tap.* My heart rate settled into the beat, old as tribe. Old as time. The beat slowed. *TAP, tap, tap, tap. . . . TAP, tap, tap, tap. . . . TAP, tap, tap, tap.* And slowed again.

The magics gathered in the geode began to mutate. To form a single throb in counterpoint. To spark in time to the tapping, to quiver outside the pulsation. I softened the beat. *Tap, tap, tap, tap . . . tap, tap, tap, tap . . . tap, tap, tap, tap . . .* The magics in the crystals, a soft, glowing, golden light, dropped from the mouth of the cut stone, ragged and tempestuous, and climbed up to twist around my stake, like a snake made of glowing barbed wire. Up the stake. Around my fingers. My hand. Wrist. My arm. Prickling and faintly stabbing. Across my body with a spiteful, tingling sensation like electrified water and heated metal. And down to the Glob in my pocket. The Glob absorbed it. Absorbed it all.

The weapon lay hot against my blistered leg. It contained so much energy that it glowed through the cloth of my pants. And still I tapped, though the rhythm was so slow, so soft, that my wrist barely felt the drop and bounce of the silver stake. The geode glowed palely, the energies sliding elsewhere. Or maybe elsewhen. The crystals grew darker, vacant.

In the corner of the parking area, I saw motes of power dancing, the motes moving in time with my own rhythm. Then growing closer together. In the halted sleet, a pale glow began to coalesce. Brightening. *Tap, tap, tap, tap . . . tap, tap, tap, tap . . . tap, tap, tap, tap . . .*

A man stepped out of the glow. A man with wings. I knew him. *Hayyel.* Angie Baby's angel. I had seen him before, for an instant that was seared into my brain. He had changed everything and everyone around him in that instant of time . . .

But no. Time wasn't a factor or a boundary for whatever this being might choose to do. I wasn't sure if he *had* any boundaries. Did any angel, beyond the will of God?

Hayyel ducked under the partially open garage door, and I smiled at the thought of him having to duck beneath anything merely matter, merely physical. This was the first time I had seen Hayyel in person for more than just an eye blink of time. He was beautiful, his skin darker than Eli's, and glowing from within. Wings he folded as he moved, all in teal and charcoal and iridescent black. And who knew angels wore jeans and T-shirts?

Hayyel wove his way through the room, pausing a moment to look into the faces of Soul and Blue Girl—Cerulean. Then down to me, where I sat on the floor of the cage, tapping. He said, "You have disturbed the direction of time. The texture of time. The intent of time."

"How does time have intent?" I asked. "Does that mean it has free will? Or that it's bound to the will of another?" *Tap, tap, tap, tap . . . Tap, tap, tap, tap . . . Tap, tap, tap, tap . . .*

Hayyel didn't reply. "You have saved lives," he said, as if finishing a monologue.

"Yeah? How many?" I looked around the room. "Counting the humans outside and the vamps inside, maybe twenty? That many are dead at my hands in the last few days."

Hayyel smiled, and I swear if I hadn't been covered in blood and gore, exhausted, and beating on a rock I'd have melted into a puddle. The man—the being—was gorgeous, even in the aftermath of a battle. "No, *Dalonige'i Digadoli.* You have saved three hundred eighty-nine thousand, six hundred twenty-seven humans and Mithrans and many more of Yahweh's assorted creatures."

Shock shut me up. Beast took over, pressing down on my brain. I continued to tap, but she spoke, her English halting. "The I/we of Beast. Is better hunter than Jane or big-cat alone. Our broken soul, it is healed. You offered us strength and power. I/we ate it. I/we became all that is Beast. We are *more*

than Jane or big-cat. You made us so." *Tap, tap, tap, tap . . .
Tap, tap, tap, tap . . . Tap, tap, tap, tap . . .*

Hayyel's smile widened. "Yes. Much more. But there has
been a price. Death seeks you outside of time. There has
been pain, temporary bondage, loss of love. Injury. Wounds
so deep they have scarred your soul. Your faith has waned
and all but disappeared."

That last part was for me. I wanted to argue about the
statement. I still had faith. Didn't I? *Tap, tap, tap, tap . . .
Tap, tap, tap, tap . . . Tap, tap, tap, tap . . .*

"Has it been worth the price?" the angel asked me.

I answered, "My family and my friends are still alive. So
yes."

"The drinkers of blood, predators in human form from
across the seas, bring more pain. More suffering. You will
have to sacrifice much to keep those you love alive and safe."

"Nothing new there."

"No. Nothing new beneath the hand of God." Hayyel
pointed to the middle of my/our chest. "The new configuration of energies is yet another strength."

"Ducky."

The angel shook his head, either amused or exasperated.
"It too comes with a price and with limits and with temp-
tation. Use it with discretion. With wisdom. And, Jane Yellowrock, love wisely."

"Right. Totally, dude."

Hayyel laughed. It was a musical sound, like bells and
harps and gypsy violins. "I have healed your soul home.
You are welcome." Before I could reply, the angel Hayyel
disappeared in a trail of golden sparks.

I stopped drumming. The sound of the tapping, deeper
than I remembered, hung on the air, multiple echoes all out
of sequence. I set down the stake. Pulled a small throwing
knife and pricked my finger. I replaced the small blade and
stuck the bleeding hand in my pocket, wrapped my fist
around the Glob. Drew it out. Centered myself with a single
deep breath. And slammed it down on the trap of the *arcenciels*.

Which really *was* a bomb.

As if my eyes were faster than the no-time of the Gray

Between, I saw my fist hit it. The geode cracked. Shattered. Power blasted out, a shock wave, a deadly concussive force. The Glob went hot, a scalding might. And it sucked all the power back into itself.

My fist busted through, smashed the geode into a bazillion pieces. Everything within shattered. Every single quartz crystal inside the rough exterior split and crushed and fell into a sparkling ruin. And the Glob pulled it in, absorbing it all.

As I watched the destruction, I realized that the specific vibration of the tapping, inside and outside of time, had weakened the geode's skin and prepared it for destruction.

The silvered cage tremored. Cracks began to run down the bars. Spreading like the veins in a bolt of lightning. Slow, but in neither real time nor Gray Between time. Something outside of both. Something created by the power of the rhythm.

I leaped to my feet and raced to the hallway. I grabbed Eli and yanked him into the Gray Between with me. I tossed him over my shoulder, raced out the garage door. He shouted something, but I ignored it. Sprinting through the sleet, my claws gripping the asphalt for stability. I leaped over the fence. Landed on the roof of a car parked in the street. Slid off. Hit the ground hard, knees buckling, paws sliding. Eli lost all breath. I skidded across the road's ice-hardened surface, caught my balance. Set Eli down and raced back inside. Leaving him alive. Back in time.

In the Gray Between, I sprinted to the bricked room. Sabina was draining a woman on one of the beds, one of the long-chained. I remembered Eli's comment about wasted protein. Beside her stood Gee DiMercy, the Mercy Blade of the NOLA vamps. There was a knife in his hand, the misericord, the blade of mercy. It was blooded. On the upper bunk was the body of a dead man, his head removed and hanging from the fingers of Gee's other hand. When Sabina was healed, Gee would kill all the scions who had not recovered from the devoveo. It was his job. It was his nature. I gathered the silver chains and left them to it.

In the hallway, I chained Louis le Jeune. He had drunk enough ancient blood that his wounds were almost healed, all but the silver head wound administered by Eli's guns. That might take a while. I stuck a silver stake into the head wound to impede the healing and made sure the silver chains were too tight to break, even if he had an immunity to the poison. Now that Louis was stable and out of commission, I needed to take him to the SUV, but first things first.

I looked down at my chest. The star of energies was a slow-moving pattern of red and silver. Controlled by or controlling my half-form. The lowest angles of the star bracketed my abdomen, passing through my hips and to my feet. I had a feeling that the magics were currently protecting me from blood loss and nausea. Woo-woo stuff.

In the main room, I positioned an arm around Grégoire's neck. I jerked back, bringing him into no-time with me. He gasped and kicked, struggling. Into his ear, I said, "We're gonna bargain, you and me. Do you want to kill your sire?" His struggles stopped. I eased off on the throat pressure. "Yes or no?"

"Yes. What bargain do we strike?"

"You will tell not one single person what I can do. Not in spoken language, not in written language, not in paintings, not in music, not in pantomime, not in sign language. Not when you share blood with any other creature. If you can't promise me that, I'll let Le Bâtard go and hope to kill him some other time."

"That monster raped me for forty-two years." Grégoire stopped and just breathed for three tortured breaths, human breaths he no longer needed, except for the pain he had endured, the memories he carried. Softer, he continued. "Then he sold me to his friends. I would cut off my arms and give them to you for the chance you offer."

I didn't tell him that it would be hard to kill Le Bâtard without arms. Instead, because I knew vamps and how they thought, I said, "And?"

Grégoire laughed softly as if he had read my mind. "I offer my word and a boon."

"Done." I set the small man on his feet. "Hold my hand."

Grégoire placed one hand in mine. With his other, he drew his sword. We moved back into to the hallway, where Grégoire saw his tormentor, his sire. Grégoire vamped out so fast, if I'd blinked I would have missed it. In the small warrior such a fast transition wasn't a sign of loss of control, however. It was deliberate. Focused. A controlled speed.

"He has been wounded," Grégoire growled around his fangs.

"With silver. Like you. Eli cut his throat and shot him. Don't tell my partner, but the wound wouldn't have been lethal. It entered the temple, missed the brain, and came out the other side. It blinded Le Bâtard, but his optic nerves will probably heal in seconds. Throat too. He'll be hungry."

Grégoire laughed and the sound traced along my spine like jagged sleet from outside. A glacial hatred centuries in the making. "So long as he can see me when I kill him, I will be happy."

"I'm leaving you in *time*. I'll be slipping out. Don't play with your supper too long. Leo is under attack at HQ. We could use you and Sabina and Gee there."

"Attack? Our enemies are here."

"Factions?" I asked.

Grégoire snarled, "*Oui. And Titus would use them all.*"

I dropped Grégoire's hand, leaving him in real time, staring at his tormentor. I hefted Louis' body over my shoulder. I carried him through the warehouse, pausing for a moment over Bruiser, knowing he was alive, seeing how well he was healing, and then trotted into the night.

Back at the SUV, I spotted Eli, his legendary badass calm long gone. His mouth was contorted in fury as he shouted. Droplets of spittle hung on the air; his breath was a cloud of condensation in front of his face. I was pretty sure he was cursing me.

I dumped Louis on the ground and went to stand by Eli. I touched him and he whirled out of time, into the Gray Between. I caught his arm as he finished his scream, which was inventive and foul. "No pizza for you tonight," I said.

"Son of a bitch!"

"Neither." I opened the front door, which may have warped it in its frame as it pulled too fast through time, deposited him in the car, and slammed the door. Sometimes I loved the incredible strength of my half-form. Okay. All the time.

In back, I lifted the hatch, tossed Louis in and closed it. Letting the Gray Between go, I opened the passenger door and climbed in. Eli grabbed my hand. "Jane? What the fu—funny bone of Satan. You're okay?"

"I'm . . ." I stopped and touched my stomach. "I'm amazingly good." I touched my fangs and smoothed my pelted face. "Hunky dory." I pointed out at the weather. "Right as rain."

"Ha-ha. You ever carry me out of a fight again and I'll break your neck."

I play-socked his upper arm. "I love you too. Update on HQ?"

"Alex? You got that?" he asked his cell.

"I got it. You can break her neck tomorrow. For now, we got more problems at HQ. Unknown vamps came in through the side entrance again but disappeared. Seems there's a hidden stairway in the brick passageway leading from the side entrance, one you can see with a four-thousand-lumen flashlight. Once you're beneath the building."

"Another passageway we didn't know about," I hazarded.

"Yeah and it opens straight in Leo's bedroom. Macario and Gualterio Cardona knew about it. Just the two of them came in. They attacked Leo in a hidden lair, a tiny room off his bedroom, trying to take him away with them. He was better, but not healed. He was able to fight them off, but they hurt him bad."

My heart might have stopped, but he continued. "Wrassler was on guard on Leo's room and heard the commotion. He broke the door down."

"Get Wrassler on conference." I looked back at the metal fence around the compound, seeing lights moving in the parking lot. I needed to get back there. *Now.*

Alex said, "Wrassler, I have Jane and Eli on conference. I was telling them you got to Leo before the MOC took the shadow bridge to vampy hell. How is he now?"

Wrassler said, "Katie and Bethany are with him, healing him."

"What?" I said. "Wait. Did Leo feed and read Troll? Katie's primo?"

"No. His injuries weren't bad enough for Leo. He was passed off to a lesser Mithran."

"Crap!" I shouted. "Get someone in there. Katie's sister is a prisoner of Le Bâtard. He turned her against Leo!"

Wrassler cursed and a clatter came over the connection as he shouted for reinforcements. "On my way to the lair," he yelled back into the phone. "Janie! Are you one hundred percent sure of this? A false accusation against the heir of Clan Pellissier, who is also the heir of the Master of the City, is a certain death sentence." Wrassler sounded short of breath, a very big man, still in physical therapy, running on his prosthetic leg. "Janie? How sure?" he demanded.

I didn't know how to answer. If I was wrong . . . "Sure enough to kill both of them myself, not sure enough to risk you. So don't make an accusation. Just show up and stand there, unless Leo's in danger. We have video of the woman known as Madam Spy, Alesha Fonteneau, in chains, coming ashore with a small group of unknown vamps in the storm. Madam Spy is Katie's sister. She looked bad. Bethany, on the other hand, has probably been working with the Europeans, or a faction of them, for centuries. She always wanted the Blood Cross— Crap. Get someone to the vamp cemetery to guard Sabina's stash. If Leo's enemies get the Blood Cross—"

Wrassler interrupted with orders for a security unit to take motorcycles and back up the security team at the burial grounds.

I listened as he gave instructions to his crew and heard the sounds of wood splintering as they took down the door to Leo's room. "Alex. I need to know where the Deadly Duo, the Cardona brothers, are, right now."

"Working on it," he said. "They don't know the warehouse was taken, so they may be on the way there."

Hope shot into my throat, but I strangled it. "Right. Something's going to go our way. The bad guys are going to walk right up to us and I'm going to kill them. Really?"

"Okay. Snark away if it makes you feel better," Alex said, sounding more adult than I did. "Just stay put until I find them. I got three people at HQ working with me on traffic cams and security video. We'll find them."

"Where's Brute?" Eli asked.

"Haven't seen him or Pea. Or Bean," I said. "I'm going back in. I need to bring out Bruiser."

I left the uncertain warmth of the SUV and leaped the gate. On the other side I took the oversized padlock in my oversized hands and twisted it until the hasp broke off. I shoved open the swinging door and waggled my fingers at Eli. He started the SUV and drove into the compound. I trotted back for my team. Gee, Derek, and Edmund were standing in the parking lot, in the protection of a food truck awning they had let down. Bruiser and the two other Onorios were on the ground at their feet. The twins were still out cold, Bruiser was pale and bloody but breathing. More relief flooded through me and I dropped down to him. Took his hand. It was colder than normal, but still warmer than my own. "How you doin'?"

He squeezed my hand. Placed a chilled kiss on the back of it. "I'd steal a term from you and say *Ducky*, but I feel as if you could tell it was a lie, love, so I'll settle for no longer bleeding. Healing. Edmund fed me. I fed him."

"Eddie's a good guy."

"Edmund," my primo said distinctly. "Not. Eddie."

I grinned but had the good sense to hide it. Bruiser gestured with our clasped hands inside the warehouse, through the garage door, which now stood all the way open.

Still squatted down, I swiveled around until my back was to the truck's oversized wheel, and watched the wonder boy, Grégoire, with his toys. And his sire.

Sleet shushed down all around us, peppering onto the layer already deposited on the asphalt. The events inside were personally disturbing on multiple levels: visually, scentwise, and emotionally.

Le Bâtard's clothing was sliced and ripped and falling in shreds, exposing bloody flesh beneath. His face was slashed, one amputated ear on the ground at his feet. His swords were up and circling in the Spanish Circle fighting form, but he was gasping, sounding all too human. He reeked of blood, fear, fury, and desperation.

Grégoire stood with only one sword, against his sire's two. Leo's secundo heir was bleeding only slightly and not breathing at all so far as I could see. Even with only one sword, Grégoire was winning. His face was frozen in a ric-

tus of horrible delight as his sword circled and circled, in
La Destreza. Sword flashing, steel clashing, he stepped inside and then away, performed a swivel motion, and one of
Le Bâtard's weapons went flying. Grégoire cut his sire twice
more. They were using dueling flat-bladed swords, lighter
than vamp-killers, faster, but more brittle. He'd never be
able to behead an opponent with it. But that wasn't the
purpose of this fight.

Silently, slowly, Grégoire administered death to his sire,
a death sentence that I knew. The hairs on my pelted body
lifted in alarm. My hands began to ache as my claws extruded. I began to pant. Fear whispered through me.

"Jane?" Bruiser murmured, catching my scent change.

I shook my head. Grégoire was passing judgment on his
sire. The punishment of a thousand cuts. It was exactly as
it sounded, La Destreza taken to dark heights, bloody, painful, and because the sword was silvered, a slow and certain
death unless help came. It never would. Eli walked up carrying a small subgun in the crook of one arm and an automatic rifle over the other shoulder. He took up position,
ready to fire should more EuroVamps appear. No one was
stopping this fight. It would end only when Grégoire ended
it. As it had ended for me, when my grandmother had chosen so.

I had a flash vision of my fist, holding the cross-hatched
bone hilt, blood dripping down the blade, covering my small
hand. In memory, I looked down at the blood splattered
over my dress. Over my feet. Ground into the mud beneath
where I stood, my feet cold and bare and filthy. I blinked
and the memory vanished.

Grégoire slashed. Le Bâtard lost his other ear.

His nose.

All the fingers of his right hand. Le Bâtard switched the
sword to his left.

Grégoire took his left eye.

Delivered a series of slashes to Le Bâtard's forehead,
blinding him with his own blood.

Sabina appeared at the opening to the brick room and
stopped in the doorway. Gee DiMercy stood at her side.

Both were bloodied, faces cold as they watched the slow methodical dismemberment of an ancient enemy.

On the battleground, Le Bâtard whimpered. Grégoire laughed, the sound pitiless as death. I looked down at Bruiser's hand in mine. His flesh was too pale against my golden Cherokee glow, far cooler than normal. But Bruiser was alive. We were alive. His hand tightened on mine again. I looked at him from the corner of my eye to find him watching me, a look so tender, so gentle, that without even knowing why he felt so, tears gathered in my eyes. "What?" I murmured.

"Only that you still feel sympathy, mercy. If it were you who fought him, you would show forgiveness. Kindness. You would let him live."

I tilted my head farther away from the slow slaughter. "I killed a man with a death of a thousand cuts. Killed him for killing my father. I was five years old. You know that. How can you believe that I would show mercy to a serial rapist, sexual predator, Naturaleza blood drinker, and murderer for centuries?"

A corner of his mouth lifted. "Because you carry guilt in such great measure that you would do most anything to assuage it."

"But setting a predator free is not the way to assuage guilt." As the words left my mouth, I realized the truth of them. A mini revelation in the middle of battle and a sleet storm. "Has he begged?" I asked. "Asked for mercy that you say I would give?"

"No."

I nodded. "Good." I turned on my cell, set it to video, and handed it to him. "We'll need a witness. An official record." In one lithe motion I rose to my feet and pulled a vamp-killer, the blade fourteen inches of steel, silver-plated. Walking to the side, so the camera view was unobstructed, I crossed through the sleet to the entrance of the warehouse and up to the fight. Pulled on Beast-speed and caught Le Bâtard's sword in mine. Whipped it away. It spun, catching the lights in the torture room. Still moving fast, I blocked Grégoire's blade as it fell. It clanged onto mine. Grégoire slid his eyes from his tormentor, slowly to me. There was emptiness and confusion in his gaze. A blankness that went soul deep.

I drew on all the training in suckhead politics, stuff I hated, and discarded all insulting names, like Blondie, which totally would not do in this moment. I said, "Grégoire, Blood Master of Clan Arceneau, of the court of Charles the Wise, fifth of his line, of the Valois Dynasty. You have challenged your sire, François Le Bâtard, for control of his body, his house, and his line. Blood Challenge, Duel Sang, has been fought. You have won the challenge. Do you wish to dispatch your opponent or do you wish me to do so for you?"

At my side, Le Bâtard sank to the floor, a languid, boneless motion, like a dance move.

Grégoire blinked, his blue eyes still empty except for the tears that gathered there. He looked down at his sire, his eyes raking Bâtard from his slashed head to his boots, all bloody and torn and broken. A sound like a sob broke from Grégoire, so shattered, so torn, it might have been a scream. Or laughter. Or all three. It sliced into the memory of my hand, holding the knife, covered with blood. He shifted his gaze to me. "This is my right."

I swallowed against rising gorge. "Yes." I flipped the vamp-killer to him, hilt first. Extended my empty hand for his sword. Gingerly, hesitantly, Grégoire placed his weapon into my hand. The hilt was colder than the frigid air. He accepted the vamp-killer. Stared at his hand on the unfamiliar, warm hilt. I stepped back.

"Your reign is ended," I said to Bâtard.

Grégoire pulled his small frame upright and said, "All you possess is forfeit. All you owned is mine. I claim all you are and all you have, your titles, your position, your power, your people, your land and holdings." With a single massive swing, he took the head from his sire.

It flew toward Sabina and hit the floor and she picked it up by the hair—now confirmed to me as the official way to carry a severed head—and walked to us, the head dangling and dripping. The body of Grégoire's enemy and sire slumped flat to the concrete floor.

Grégoire knelt before the body of his maker and lifted the vamp's left little finger. From it he pulled a ring, gold beneath the blood that was drying on it. He slid the ring onto his own finger and even beneath the gore, it was a ring I recognized, a crest ring he often wore.

Le Bâtard's men had taken Grégoire to Arceneau Clan Home. Had this been what they were looking for? What they had retrieved? Was this the official seal of Clan Valois?

Grégoire spread his hand as he studied the ring, and his fangs retracted. His eyes bled back to human. "It is mine in truth. I am now *Le Valois. Le Orleans.*"

"So witnessed," Sabina said. "Do you still honor your vow to Leonard Pellissier, Master of the City of New Orleans and surrounding territories?"

Grégoire raised his eyes to hers. "I do so swear, surrendering any claim to the lands of the Louisiana territory, as purchased by the United States of America."

"I bow to *Le Valois.*" Sabina inclined her head. "Long live the undead ruler of the court of Charles the Wise."

I looked around and said, "I don't think there's room in the cooler for all the heads."

From a cell phone beneath the awning of the food truck, I heard Alex's voice. "I think we need a bigger cooler."

Eli laughed.

CHAPTER 21

The Shooter Fired a Last Shot

From out of the sleet storm and the darkness, I heard footsteps. Ricky-Bo LaFleur walked through the opened gate. His walk was all tracking cat, slinky and loose and intent. Beast perked up. I batted her down.

Rick was wearing postshift clothes, loose and cheap and thin, too thin for the weather except that he was were, and were-creatures could stand the cold better than humans. He said, "Dead bodies in the food truck, stacked up like cordwood. Car parked down the road pulled away, toward the Quarter and the river. We going after?"

I walked from Grégoire, who stood, sword down, blank eyes on the body at his feet, to the awning. I glanced at Bruiser and he shrugged slightly. "Not with you," I said to Rick. "I don't know where you were during the battle."

Rick didn't flinch, but his scent went hot and angry at the implication that he stayed away from fear and cowardice.

"The battle lasted a grand total of twenty minutes."

It was much longer in my subjective time.

He said, "I take twenty minutes to shift forms, forty minutes combined." He stopped beneath the awning and held me with hunting eyes, Frenchy-black and glowing green still, from his cat. "You shift fast. Faster than any werecat I know. Show me?"

"No. I'm not a were. We won't shift alike." I almost stopped there, but despite myself, I added, "Ask Paka."

"Hooah," Eli said softly, in a tone that meant *gotcha*.

"Paka's gone," Rick said. "Permanently." He looked away from whatever he saw on my face, taking in the dead bodies and the cage. He walked away from our small group and inside the garage door. For reasons I didn't understand I followed, though I stayed well back. Over his shoulder, Rick said, "This is now a PsyLED crime scene. I've called in PsyCSI and the local LEOs. Legally I should keep you here. But for old times' sake, your people and you need to get out."

I laughed and it was part growl. If I were a cussing woman I'd have started about now, because this "crime scene" existed only because we had found it and taken over and saved the hostages. And killed the bad guys. Our people had done this. Not Rick's. Instead, I laughed harder, took Le Bâtard's head from Sabina. and nodded to Bruiser, who had attained his feet and was leaning against the truck. "Let's go. We're needed at HQ." To Derek I said, "Gather up the heads and buy that bigger cooler. Take Amy Lynn Brown, Grégoire, the Robere twins, and Adan Bouvier and the others to safety." He nodded and I walked away.

Back in the SUV, Le Bâtard's disfigured head shoved into my cooler, Eli pulled away from the curb. Bruiser was riding shotgun; Edmund was in the backseat, passing my gear over to me. I was all the way in back with Louis, who still had a silver stake in his head and was bound in silver chains. He stank of poison and death, though he was marginally still undead.

With my feet, I shoved him against the over-full cooler to make room so I could strip and dress in my leathers, the formal ones Leo'd had made for my official presentation to the EuroVamps. I figured I had killed all the EVs I'd met except Louis and he wasn't long for this world, but looking spiffy couldn't hurt for the next meeting. Me in half-form and fancy leathers. I'd scare the devil himself. *Go me.*

I was more limber in this form and dressing wasn't as

difficult as it would be otherwise. I left off my boots in favor of paws and claws, and shrugged into my weapons rigs. I tightened some straps and loosened others—to better fit the rigs to my new shape—and I could feel water thudding onto the undercarriage as I worked. We rolled down St. Louis Street; the flooding was much worse, water up under the houses on raised foundations and stilts, inside others. We passed the green house with bathroom planters and the antique iron feet of the tub were underwater. The rainwater was rising.

We might have ended the curse that was keeping the storm systems in place, but they hadn't dispersed on their own yet, though the air temps had risen. Rain had begun to fall again, melting the icy slush. I reinserted my earbud and mic, clipped the coms unit to my pants, and braided my hair, tying it off with a bit of string I found on the floor.

Over the vehicle's coms, Alex said, "Patching Wrassler through."

"Wrassler to the Enforcer," a raspy voice said. "Do you copy?"

Dread filled me and I remembered the sound of splintering wood. "Wrassler? Copy. Go ahead."

"Katie and Bethany are gone. They fought us. They took Leo."

The scent of shock and fear filled the SUV. "Casualties?" Eli asked.

"Four . . . four wounded." Wrassler cleared his throat and I realized he had to be injured. "We have them with masters. Two might make it."

Gently, in a New Orleans' cant, Eli said, "Are you one who will survive, my brother?"

"It was touch and go. But I should survive."

"We'll find them," Eli said. "We'll bring Leo back." He was promising what he couldn't. Until I realized he hadn't said Leo would still have his head when we brought him back.

"Thank you," Wrassler said. "Out." The connection ended.

Over coms, Alex said, "I haven't found the group of EVs or Leo, but I have a visual of Brute staring at a surveillance camera outside Pat O'Brien's near the corner of St. Peter and Bourbon Streets."

"Staring at the camera?" I asked as I climbed over the seat and shoved Edmund across the center, behind Eli, stealing his position behind Bruiser. Ed gave a long-suffering sigh that also sounded amused. I just grinned, my oversized canines pulling at my lips.

"Directly at it," Alex said. "Wait. He moved. Okay, I got him again on a traffic cam, trotting down toward Royal Street, toward the river. Now staring at a camera near an antique shop. Water's up to his ankles. The river is over its banks, flooding over the railroad tracks. The storm is stalled north of us, dropping more rain, and temps are rising, melting all the sleet, which means runoff is higher. The drainage system is diverting it, but not fast enough."

"Best route?" Eli asked, punching in a street map and navigation of the city on the SUV's computer system.

"Traffic is minimal with the rain. Recommend you stay on St. Louis, to Chartres, and right onto St. Peter. Brute is speeding up. Dead run through the water, up past Jax to the top of the levee. Lost him."

Eli gunned the motor and the heavy vehicle shoved water out of the way as we sped downtown, river side. All of us checking weapons, silent but for the *click* and *schnick* and *clack* of guns. Edmund passed water to each of us and we hydrated. I pulled the Benelli and reloaded with silver fléchette rounds. Loaded the holder attached to the barrel.

Eli spun the wheel right and onto St. Peter Street. Muddy water from the river rushed down the street, flooding the lower level of buildings in the old Jax brewery. There were no lights in this part of town, the storm having unleashed its fury on the electrical grid. The night was thick and wet and threatening. Rain shattered through the darkness and pounded on the SUV like thousands of frenzied fists. We bumped over the railroad tracks and up across the grass to the top of the levee. Without waiting for the vehicle to stop, I shoved open the door and stepped into the rushing water, icy, above my ankles. My claws extended and pressed into the mushy, eroding soil. I pulled on Beast's night vision and spotted Brute, downstream, fighting the debris-filled current. Someone in his jaws. Another form stood over him, a handgun extended, firing at him. The gunfire was muted in the roar of pounding rain, rushing water, screams. Even in the darkness, it was clear the werewolf was badly wounded.

Close in, the mud-brown water was white-capped and boiling. I caught sight of a tree, moving in the current, faster than I could run, only a few feet out. It was bigger around than a whiskey barrel, its limbs broken and sharp. I raced through the overflowing river, slipping twice, knowing that if I fell in, I might be swept away.

About thirty feet out in the dangerous current, a small boat fought upstream. A familiar man was at the motor at the back, steering, muscling the boat against the current. Vamped out. Trying to get to shore but spinning in the flooded river. This was their getaway plan. Dumbasses.

The shooter aimed carefully at Brute's head. I gathered myself and leaped. Twisted in the air and shoved forward with my feet, back with my body. The shooter fired a last shot at Brute. The werewolf staggered and fell on top of the person in his teeth. I landed on the shooter with both paws. Screaming. Took him down. Removed his head with a single cut of the vamp-killer, seeing only afterward that I'd killed a human. One of the Cardonas, Macario or Gualterio.

I fell to the water, rolled up from my hip, and engaged his brother, slashing with pure, instinctive strength, no finesse. Cut off his hand, his sword and fist dropping into the Mississippi. Swept beneath the waves. Took his head too, his body falling.

Behind me, someone fired. In front of me, people fell. I took a shot to my upper arm. Eli was gonna be pissed off when he discovered he'd shot me.

Beast shut off the pain receptors and I engaged a vamp, the man from the still shots who had brought Madam Spy to shore in a dinghy. I felt two cuts, midchest, the force and the cutting power decreased by the leathers. He was good. His arms were long and his reach with the flat swords was longer. I was sneaky, which beat perfect form anytime. I threw a vamp-killer. The hilt slammed into his face before the blade spun into the night. I followed it up with a slash across his throat. And then I was inside his reach. Pulled a silver stake and shoved it between his ribs and into his heart. He fell. I went after another vamp. And another. None I knew.

I sliced the wigged-out woman's face, and she backpedaled into the river, where she fell beneath the muddy water. Where was Katie's sister? Where was Katie? And Leo?

And then I saw him. Unconscious or true-dead. I fought toward Leo, Bruiser at my side. I blocked a sword, ducking a second strike. Falling against my honeybunch. Bruiser pushed me back upright and took on two vamps. I kicked out. Struck a knee. Felt the bones snap. Saw my opponent fall away. Saw Leo's hand clench.

"Get Leo!" I shouted. "I'll cover!"

Bruiser ducked under two swords striking and rolled to Leo. I pulled the Benelli and fired twice. Point-blank. Two vamps dropped into the mud. I fired twice more as Bruiser hefted Leo to his shoulder and raced from the battle, into the night.

I spun, seeing forms moving in the dark and the rain. I took two steps toward them.

Bethany leaped onto my back, wrapped her arms around me, and said, distinctly, "You are mine, Skinwalker." She sank her huge fangs into my throat. I smelled Leo's blood on her breath. Her fangs ripped through my flesh. I fell. Toward the water. Toward a long limb that spun in a mini whirlpool.

Inside me, I heard Bethany's voice. *You are mine. I claimed you before my Leo did. I claimed you before the angel did. I claimed you long before the Cherokee woman showed you the place you call your soul home. I claimed you before my George chose you in my place. You are mine.*

"Jane!" Bruiser, screaming. He grabbed her hair and yanked her back. I twisted, her fangs ripping deeper into my flesh.

Everything happened fast, yet in that slowed battle time, where every detail is crystal clear.

Bruiser's blade sliced across Bethany's throat.

My feet slipped. Still twisting, I caught sight of Callan, in the dinghy only feet offshore. I landed hard on the slope. In the edge of the water. Bethany on top of me.

Lightning brightened the sky. My blood spurted into the night.

With her last strength. Bethany tore her fangs away, taking flesh with her. She pushed me. Down. I slid deeper.

The current caught me. Yanked me under. The water closed over me.

And then there was only darkness. Sucking me down.

I woke on a boat, lying in three inches of water. The sun was overhead.

My eyes were crusted with salt and gunk. I blinked but my vision got no better. I'd have wiped my face, but my hands were cuffed behind me. My shoulders, back, and butt ached.

I pushed to a sitting position. Remembered the fangs buried in my throat.

Looked around. I inspected my surroundings and myself. Storm clouds were on the northern horizon. The sun was setting in the west. Land was invisible. Around me was nothing. Water, water everywhere. I had been in a storm in the Mississippi. Now I guessed I was in the Gulf of Mexico. I had been bitten by a master, crazy, outclan priestess vamp. The water I was sitting in was red with my blood. I kicked the gas cans that were connected to the motor. Both rang hollowly, empty. *Not good.* I was still pelted, still fanged, and I was alone.

I tested the cuffs. The chain holding the wrist bracelets was the weak link. I chuffed out a laugh. *Weak link.* I braced my shoulders and spine, took a deep breath. And jerked. The cuffs abraded the flesh over my wrist bones, but nothing else happened. I tried again. Again. I smelled my blood; the pain in my wrists was terrible; my left fingers went numb. I tried it one last time and the metal gave way. I fell forward, into the bottom of the boat, taking in a mouthful of bloody, salty water. My arms dropped to my sides. I fought back to a sitting position and as quickly as I could, I started slow stretches to get my muscles moving and to get feeling back in my fingers. I started bailing out the boat.

Beneath the hull, something scratched, and my first thought was *sharks*. Then I thought, *fanghead*, hiding from the sun, instinctively reacting to the presence of blood in the water. I paused, remembering Callan in this very boat, in the river, trying to make it ashore. Good odds he was under the dinghy.

I touched my throat. It was heavily knotted and rippled with scar tissue. Healed. Not well, but well enough to not be dead. My skinwalker magics? Or the thing under the boat? I went back to bailing, ignoring the possible vamp under the boat, for now.

There was nothing useful with me in the boat. No cooler, no water, no food. I wasn't sure how I'd gotten aboard. I wasn't sure what day it was. I pulled my cell to find it was soaked and dead. I had a feeling that my people thought I was dead too. "Well, this sucks," I said, my voice hoarse. Thirst dragged through me. I desperately needed to pee, but I also needed to save the urine in case I needed to drink it. *Gag.* Fortunately or not, there was nothing to pee into. For the moment, holding it was the wiser choice. My clothes were ruined, the leather damaged by salt water, gray and crusty white and stiff. I kept bailing out the boat. It took a while, but the blood in it was starting to smell.

As I worked, I heard more scratching from the underside of the hull. Come nightfall, I'd have to fight him. I rechecked for my weapons. All were gone. Even the Benelli. I remembered carrying it at some point. If the suckhead under the boat had tossed my gun, I'd rip off his head with my bare hands. Then I wondered if he had my guns and blades with him. If he was smart, he would have taken everything I had overboard with him and come up shooting. He didn't need air, but by dusk, he'd be hungry, boiled, burned, and as salt damaged as my leathers.

I went through my pockets, finding a few trinkets: the Glob, of no use whatsoever since I had no idea how it worked or how to activate it, and a stone. It looked like black glass with bits of white in it. I didn't know what it was. And then I started laughing.

He had held out a closed fist. Dropped a small black stone, one with white inclusions in it, in my big-knuckled paw. *"It's called an Apache tear,"* he'd said. *"If you need me, you can crush it. I will come."*

I closed my fist around it and I squeezed. Nothing happened. Even in half-form I wasn't strong enough to crush it. I pulled out the Glob, set the Apache tear on the engine housing, and brought the Glob down on it, shattering the obsidian.

Gee DiMercy to the rescue, I thought. But he didn't come. And he didn't come.

The day went on. And on. Cold, with a brilliant sun, and lapping waves. Eventually, the sun began to set, the clouds picking up the red rays and casting the entire skyline in shades of scarlet and crimson and fuchsia. The moon rose. The first star peeked out. The sky began to darken. The vamp beneath began to scrabble on the boat bottom. Hull. Whatever. Vamp nails on wood.

The scratching on the bottom of the boat got stronger. This was not going to end well.

The clouds to the north boiled. Sparkled. Dragons. *Les Arcenciels.* Five of them, in all colors of the rainbow. Gee DiMercy darted among them, his blue and scarlet plumage catching the pale light. I came to my knees in the bottom of the boat. I was so thirsty that my throat ached. I'd never be able to yell at them, and in the light they wouldn't see me. But I was wrong. They dove down from the clouds, the dragons diving into the water near my boat, long and lean and glistening, erupting to play, creating huge waves that nearly capsized me. "Hey!" I yelled. "Watch it!" But it came out a scratchy croak and I was ignored.

Gee DiMercy alighted on the small seat of the dinghy. From a pocket he pulled a bottle of water, cold and wet with condensation. "You called, my mistress?"

I took the bottle, opened it and crushed the weak plastic, forcing the water into my mouth in a single long drink. I dropped it in the bottom of the boat. "Another."

"No. As your IT specialist says it, you will hurl."

I blinked. Laughed. "Yeah. That sounds like Alex." Out in the water, dragons played, dipping and splashing and trumpeting like elephants and cheeping like birds. Their scales caught the last rays of the sun and threw back the light. Their frills splashed and wings made waves big as buses. The dinghy rocked violently. Beneath the boat, the vampire had grown silent, unmoving as the dead. "I need a ride home. Can you help with that?"

"Of course, my mistress. Your people will be pleased. They think you are dead." He handed me a cell phone. "It is a satellite phone. It might save his life if you were to call George Dumas."

I punched in his number. It rang and rang. He finally answered, the single word raw and ragged. "What."

"Howdy, Bruiser."

A silence grew, too long, too vacant, a void, barren of life and hope. "J . . . Jane?" he whispered.

"Yeah. You okay? Leo okay? Did we win?"

"I'm . . . Leo is . . . fine. Jane?" he repeated, his tone still disbelieving.

"I have one last vamp to take care of. Then I'll be home."

"Dear God in heaven." He took a breath so tattered it groaned in pain. "Jane?"

"Yeah. I'm okay. Ish. I'll be home soon. I gotta take a swim."

"I love you," he whispered. "I was afraid . . . Afraid I would never get to say the words. I love you."

"I love you too," I said. "See you soon." I ended the call and gave the cell to Gee DiMercy. There was a weird pain and odd warmth in my chest, and I wondered if my heart was gonna explode or something. I blinked into the sunset, seeing a reverse image on the inside of my eyelids. *Bruiser loves me.* I took a breath. It felt cold and wonderful going down. I felt weightless and buoyed and . . . totally weird. Instead of saying any of the things I was thinking and feeling, I said, "There's a suckhead under the boat."

"I am aware. The *arcenciels* are teasing him much as cats tease mice."

Ten feet off the sidewall of the boat, the water rose in a liquid bowl and erupted. A dragon made of light had become flesh, pearled and glistening and leaping for the sky, a cerulean creature of myth made real. In her jaws was a vampire. She flew straight up and whipped her tail, flipped her body, and dove for the ocean. Carrying the vampire, she leaped and frolicked before leaping for the sky again, and diving back. Two feet above my fragile boat, she hovered and shook her prey. Guns and blades fell into the boat. My weapons. Callan looked like a rag doll in her dragon hands.

Another *arenciel* broached the water and leaned over the side of the boat, her face human and gorgeous, human hands holding her in place. Soul said, "We'll take him to your house. He may provide some intelligence that we don't yet have."

"Yeah. Okay. Thanks."

"You will ride me."

"Say what?"

"My little bird is fierce but too small for your mass. You will ride me, as recognition for saving our sister." She stretched out in the water, her hands disappearing, wings out, one under the boat, holding it steady. "This is not a boon offered to another since ancient times."

Gee seemed amused. "Ummm. Okay?" I gathered my gear, shoving the blades and other weapons in place, hearing the small snaps as they settled. I worked my left hand, happy that my fingers again had feeling. It had taken all day to get the sensation back. I accepted a second bottle of water from Gee. Drank it down, wished I had taken the time to pee. And stepped onto the back of a dragon made flesh.

I spent that night wrapped in Bruiser's arms. And a blanket. A heating pad at my feet. Riding an *arenciel* was freezing business. They fly high, in a nearly airless part of the Earth's atmosphere. I had nearly suffocated until Soul realized I was having problems staying alive and dove lower. I'd been so cold when she dropped me off on the boulders in my backyard, I could barely move. So exhausted I could hardly speak.

Bruiser had carried me into the shower, cut off my ruined black leathers, and held me there until I started to thaw. It had been nearly impossible to get him to leave me long enough to shift to fully human, and when it took too long, I'd had to resort to bribery to get him to go away—promises of a future date to last an entire day and through the night. On the gulf. On a boat. With umbrella drinks and music.

Shifting had been . . . hard. So hard I didn't want to think about it just yet. I hadn't made it directly from half-form into human, and finally resorted to shifting into Beast, and from *Puma concolor* into my human form. The pain had been incredible. The snake that resides in all things, the twisted strands of my DNA, were tangled and tripled and torn. Finding my form in the mess of genetics had been nearly impossible. I wasn't sure what it meant. And when the shift was completed, I had been too exhausted to eat. I had never been too exhausted to eat. Not ever.

Now it was night again and hunger rode me, a fierce, desperate need. I sliced into a full slab of very rare beef, a ribeye that had started out postlife as a sixteen pounder, before Eli rubbed it down and threw it on a grill to sear. He had cooked two, thank goodness, so the others had meat to eat. There were potatoes and beer and salad too, but I drank water and ate beef and listened as my partners and my clan filled me in, asking monosyllabic questions to get the info I wanted. The questions did not come out in an order I'd have expected. "Brute?" I asked first.

Eli straddled a chair and cut off a bite of cow. "Brute's at a local veterinary hospital, being attended to by a vampire and a witch and a vet who's scared shhh— witless of getting were-taint. She only agreed to help when Dacy Mooney of Asheville agreed to feed her father to help him heal from cancer."

"Werewolf? Dacy?"

"Yeah," he said, understanding what I wanted to know. "There's no record of a vamp ever sharing blood with a werewolf. But Brute seems to be special. And he saved Leo's life."

"On the levee?"

"Exactly. He pulled the Master of the City away from his captors. When the vamps were losing Leo, they decided no one could have him. Brute took the silver bullets meant for the MOC."

"Howee c'aaa," I said. *Holy crap,* through a mouthful of food.

Alex talked around a mouthful of potatoes. "He's like the king of all weres right now, owed a boon by Leo and every other vamp in the city."

Edmund said, "Leo declared Brute Friend of the Mithrans, which entitles him to anything he wants." Edmund was chuckling, but there were new scars on his throat where a powerful vamp had tried to drink him down. "Dacy, who showed up at the scene just after you were swept away by the flood—" Ed stopped. Took a drink of his red wine, as if he was thirsty, but there were pink tears in his eyes. The clink of cutlery was the only sound until he was able to continue.

"Dacy kept your Onorio from throwing himself into the waters to find you. Then she fed him to bring him to sanity."

"I was not without sanity," Bruiser said distinctly, his dinner untouched, sipping an aromatic tea. "I was grieving. There is a difference."

"Perhaps in theory, not in practice," Edmund said. "Dacy then fed the Master of the City and the wolf, at the same time."

"And Ed had to feed Dacy when she overextended," Alex said. "It was a regular blood-fest."

"You weren't there," Eli said.

"Coms were on. It's all recorded. I've listened to it about a dozen times now. Pretty much got it all down."

"Katie?" I asked.

"In Leo's lair, caged with her sister until Leo can pass judgment. He loves her, so she may not die as a traitor. But she could have come to Leo at any time with word of her sister and Leo would have forgiven them both. Now it isn't so certain that he will give pardon."

"There were sleepers in Leo's house. Still are, I expect. Katie knew that," I said. "She couldn't take the risk."

Edmund didn't reply to that. Rather, he poured himself more wine, poured Bruiser more tea, and brought me another slab of ribeye. The whole sixteen pounds wouldn't fit on my plate at once. Go figure. "Before dawn," he said as he transferred meat to my plate, "the heads of the European Mithrans you had collected, and all others in accordance with Leo's orders, were placed into three coolers and delivered to the ghost ship in Lake Borgne."

I started eating and Ed retook his seat. "They were accompanied by an envoy carrying a letter from Leonard Pellissier, Master of the City of New Orleans."

At the formal titles, I stopped shoving food into my mouth. Chewed. Waited.

"The envelope was addressed to Titus Flavius Vespasianus," he said, managing to sound ever so slightly bored. I kicked him under the table and he went on, a faint smile on his face. "Not to Emperor Titus Flavius Vespasianus. Just to Titus. A calculated insult. It was a challenge to blood duel. Leo has said there will be no further moves in this match. He will clear the board and challenge the dark king to blood duel. With a dark queen at his side, he will end the cold reign of the European Mithrans."

I had a bad feeling that the dark queen was me. I scowled at Ed. He smiled back, genial and unperturbed.

"The coolers?" Alex asked. "Derek said it was a stink worse than death by the time the Europeans agreed to drop the *obfuscation* spell and accept them."

Alex chortled, all amused disdain. It was a very grown up, cynical sound.

Eli finished his meal and cleaned away the dirty dishes, saying, "According to the Coast Guard, who were keeping watch, when the *obfuscation* working around the ship fell, Leo's enemies took the coolers aboard, along with their remaining people—all in silver chains and well drained, though still undead."

"Wait," I said. "You weren't there?"

"No," Eli said, his voice bland. "We were grieving."

"Oh." *For me. Right.* I thought about that for a while, started eating again.

As I finished the last bite of beef, Ed picked up the narrative. "The envoy's delivery of challenge to Sangre Duello was accepted, with assurances that it would be delivered to Titus Flavius Vespasianus, and the ship motored out, deep into international waters in the gulf."

Eli added, "The Coast Guard's keeping an eye on their progress, though if they reapply the *obfuscation* working we'll lose them."

"Bethany?" I asked, smelling dishwashing detergent and hearing water filling the sink.

"Her head went with the others," Bruiser said shortly.

I grunted.

"Outclan priestesses are banned from intervening in international Mithran politics," Edmund said, his eyes on my honeybunch, "so there will be no repercussions for George Dumas taking her head."

Bethany had been a special project of Bruiser's from the time he was a boy. I shot him a glance, taking in his face, his eyes. Ravaged and grieving and still terrified. I swallowed down a chunk of half-chewed beef and touched his hand. "I'm sorry. I know she meant a lot to you."

His eyes softened and he gripped my hand. "I made the choice for happiness a long time ago. For you."

And my heart melted. I pulled my hand away and went back to eating. There was still a couple pounds of meat left. Between chatter, the guys were watching me eat, and during those moments, it was cutlery against stoneware and the sound of chewing. Not much else.

"There's a shindig at Royal Mojo Blues tonight," Alex said. "Eli and Ed and I are going. You two interested? Or are you gonna be too busy bumping uglies?" There was a thump under the table. "Ow! What? You know that's what they do, right? They're not asexual. Dang, bro. Just because you and Syl broke up you don't hafta kick me."

I stopped, fork halfway to my mouth. "You and Syl?"

Eli shrugged. "Long-distance stuff. That stupid cruise. It had stopped working three months ago. I just hadn't ended it."

"Sorry," I said, knowing it wasn't enough, but not knowing what to say. My social skills were excellent at the fist-bumping stage and were getting better at the vamp-protocol stage, but the stuff in between, where most humans live, was nonexistent.

"Happens." Eli shrugged. A real shrug, and not one of his tiny things. And I realized he was moving like a normal person, not like the controlled version gifted back to him by Uncle Sam when the government was finished using him. I remembered the Choctaw water ceremony. The emotional break in the limo. The tears. Maybe he was beginning to heal. I stuffed more meat in and chewed. Swallowed. "I could do some dancing." I looked down at my rounded belly. It looked like a volleyball had been strapped to me. Or a sixteen-pound ribeye. "If I can get into clothes."

"Whoop!" Alex said. "Bro, I promise I will get up early

and wash all the dishes and clean the kitchen if you let me skip it for tonight." Eli lifted his eyebrows and said nothing. "Okay. I'll clean the grill too."

"Deal," Eli said. "Let's get pretty, bro."

That left Edmund and Bruiser and me at the table. I put down my fork and knife and sighed. "I feel better. So. What else do I need to know?"

Edmund stood and took the rest of the dishes to the sink, where he swished them in sudsy water. "While you healed last night and today, Eli went into the attic space and discovered that it's open and livable. Nothing but rough wood studs, but they are beautiful wood, and the flooring is cypress. He thinks he can board up the windows and make it safe for me. And for Brute. If you are willing for us to move."

He meant move into the house proper and not behind the wall of shelving that protected my family and guests from them both.

I rubbed my overfull belly and thought. "Stairs?"

"He'll hire a contractor to open up the space and put a stairway in the wide part of the second-floor hallway. He suggested a circular one. We'll get bids on both and you would make the final decision, of course."

"Gee's my Enforcer now. Where would he sleep?"

"I assume a bed could be found. There's quite a bit of square footage up there."

"Okay. Good by me. It's cheaper than buying a bigger house."

Edmund gave me a small smile and finished his wine. "I took it upon myself to purchase Brute a new mattress, memory foam, with a lining and white cotton sheets so they could be bleached easily. Wolves are often dirty. He should be back by morning. One assumes he will be cranky, and the bed may ease that."

A cranky werewolf would be dangerous. "Thank you," I said.

Edmund nodded and stood. "I'll dress. My mistress shall require proper attendants at the soiree." He glanced at Bruiser. "Someone who will focus on threats and not simply dancing."

Bruiser's brown eyes warmed. "What we do is not *simply dancing*."

Edmund's eyes rolled.

"Seriously?" I asked. "You did an eye roll?"

Edmund said, "You would prefer me to suggest that you get a room?"

Bruiser chuckled, the low burr of sound that slid along my nerves like heated velvet, and pulled me to my feet and into his arms. "Let's get dressed and go 'simply dancing.'"

I managed a nod, feeling again that odd warmth and fullness in my chest, as if my heart was expanding, too big for my rib cage. Bruiser wrapped my hand in his and led me from the kitchen.

In my room, on my bed, was a box all wrapped up in shiny silver paper, with a bow big enough to hide a small car. I opened the card. It was plain white, with Bruiser's distinctive scrawl on the inside. *Jane, love*, it read. *This was a gift for a future evening, but nothing will be more important than celebrating your return to me. Madame Melisende claims to have created the perfect dancing dress for you. I hope she is correct and that you adore it. I'll call for you at the designated time. Love, Bruiser.*

I touched the last line, a small smile on my face. Sat on the bed and opened the box. Inside was a dress, a black dancing creation with spaghetti straps, a tight bodice, and a flared, split skirt to my calves. It came with a loose shawl in a dark shade of gold that matched my eyes, swirled through with blue, the color of a midnight sky. In its own velvet box was a gold necklace with a matching blue faceted stone. I kissed my Onorio and he kissed me back. Things happened. Hot, hard, and fast. We ended up having to take our own vehicle to the dance club.

In some cities, a major flood might mean closing up shop and waiting out the cleanup. In New Orleans, in parts of the French Quarter, especially, flood cleanup was down to an art, and nowhere so advanced than at Royal Mojo Blues Company, Leo Pellissier's bar and grill and dance hall. If wallboard had been reapplied to the walls after Katrina, the cleanup would have been longer, stinkier, moldier, and messier, but the walls had been left with the raw brick exposed. The recent flood had meant pulling out the pressure washer and blasting the walls and concrete floors, cleaning out the bathrooms and the appliances, and letting it all dry before bringing in a ton or two of food and liquor. And New Orleans, after a day and night of miserable hard work, wanted to party, so every open bar and dance joint in the city was bursting to capacity.

Half an hour after arriving, I was sweaty and tired and utterly satisfied, ready to take a table reserved by Bruiser for our crowd, one just off the dance floor. We had been boogieing to Roddy Rockwell, the band having driven in from Mobile to entertain the city, and the mix of music from the last seventy years was perfect for dancing. They had ended the set with a Bro-country version of their eighties hit "Blindsided," and we had whooped it up with a country line dance created on the spot by Eli. My partner could dance, especially with a stunning witch encouraging him. Bliss, who would forever after be called Ailis, was swinging her booty and stepping high. Eli was entranced with the black-haired, pale-skinned witch. Unlike Sylvia, Ailis didn't use guns, but then, as a witch, she didn't need them. I hoped neither one would get hurt from the rebound attraction.

After the set, we all gathered around two tables, my clan and Leo's vamps, drinking and laughing and telling stories from the last few days, filling each other in, and bragging about head count. Vamp head count. So far, I seemed to be in the lead. Go me. Or not.

We shared baskets of wings, bruschetta with a half dozen kinds of toppings, hummus with flatbread, spinach dip and chips, small burger sliders, house-made Parmesan cheese with hot peppers, and little pizzas. I wasn't too full to enjoy, my metabolism still high and my appetite higher.

And when the band returned to the stage, I took the opportunity to go to the ladies' room—not something I'd take for granted again. I heard the song start, the music piped into the restroom, the lead singer's raspy voice singing, "I used to be the spark. I could always start a fire in your heart."

I smoothed my hair back into the French braid. Tucked the blue stone into my cleavage—what there was of it—with the gold nugget. I looked good and for once I knew it. I stretched my lips and reapplied scarlet lipstick.

Over the speakers, the singer crooned, "Our love was so hot, so hot . . ." In the background, over the speakers, a saxophone started playing. The notes low, plaintive. Familiar.

My hand, holding the lipstick, froze. Dropped away from my face. The tube fell and clattered to the countertop. I pushed through the door and out into the poorly lit hallway. And around to the dance floor.

"Didn't think you would ever stop, carrying my flame, but baby, something's changed."

The saxophone player was wearing black, a long-sleeved, nearly see-through T-shirt and black jeans. Black hair hung over his face. Too long. Unkempt. Frenchy-black eyes closed.

"Where's the fire that was in your eyes whenever you were close to me," the lead singer sang. "Where's the fire? don't you realize, just how much you mean to me?"

Rick's eyes opened above the sax and found me, instantly, standing in the shadows, his eyes gleaming the green of his cat. "Where's the fire, baby? Why are you so cold? Where's the fire, baby . . ."

The song. Had been written for me? For us? The look in his eyes said yes. "Don't try to tell me everything's all right. Just tell me. Where's the fire tonight?"

Eli appeared at my side. "He knows what he did, Babe. I think this is an apology. As public as he could make it."

Bruiser stepped out from behind my partner. He held out his hand. "May I have this dance, love?" I put my hand into his heated one. His palm and strength centered me. I let him lead me to the dance floor. He enfolded me, holding me close, my face pressed into his shoulder, arms around me, keeping me safe. All the while, the lyrics of love lost sang into the bar.

"Where's the fire that was in your eyes whenever you were close to me? Where's the fire? Don't you realize, just how much you mean to me?"

Bruiser and I danced to the song of heartbreak and lost love. When it was over, I looked up. Rick LaFleur was gone.

CHAPTER 22

Shove It Up Your Royal Ass

We were called to vamp HQ just before dawn, with orders to run by the house first and pick up a few items. Leo offered assurances that we would be allowed to leave with everything we brought, so I agreed, though with misgivings. Bruiser was now wearing all his weapons. I was weaponed up and also carrying two magical items, the Glob hidden in a pocket and *le breloque* in my hand. Laden with the belongings we had been ordered to bring, Bruiser and I stood before Leo's office like supplicants or children at the principal's office. Scrappy, who had led us in, as if we needed to be shown the way, knocked and opened the door.

We entered.

The smell of Leo—papyrus and ink and black pepper—hung strong on the air. We heard a tapping, as if on a laptop, soft but unsteady, and I remembered the damage to Leo's hand. The furniture was back in its place, businesslike instead of raunchy-orgy-ménage à trois–like. Leo was sitting behind his desk, dressed in casual clothes, things I thought he probably slept in when he wasn't doing sex and blood—

thin knit black pants with a loose long-sleeved shirt. His hair was back in a short queue, looking as if it had been trimmed again. The Master of the City was pale and was wearing slippers, but he was upright and working.

He stopped typing and indicated the two wingback chairs, his fingers still taped in place where they were reattaching. Bruiser and I sat, the magical crown on my lap, out in clear view. It felt weird to have it exposed this way, but Leo didn't even glance at it.

It wasn't silent in the office. Soft instrumental music, piano and violin, Vivaldi maybe, played on the speakers in each corner, surround sound rising and falling to low ebbs. Leo leaned across the table he used as a desk and rested his chin in his hands, studying us over the short distance. One piece ended and another began before he spoke. "I did not know if you would come," he said to Bruiser.

"You are no longer my master, but you are the master of this city," Bruiser said, formally. But then he added, "And you are the best master I could imagine. You always have been. Even in the midst of madness and misery and pain, you have put your people first. I honor that now and always."

Leo looked down, but I thought I caught a hint of surprise and tenderness in his eyes before they were shuttered. He tilted his head in acknowledgment. His lips curled up slightly. "You may wish otherwise soon. My plans are all for naught," he admitted. "Two centuries of moves and countermoves, wasted." He lifted his eyes to me. "You took Adrianna's head?"

"I did."

"She was the favorite of Titus Flavius Vespasianus. There were those who said she would be Titus' queen one day. She was my bargaining chip. My last checkmate move in a match that would clear the board without war and death."

"Cry me a river," I said.

Leo burst out laughing and sat upright in his chair, dropping his arms to the desktop.

"This isn't a game," I said, over his laughter, leaning in. I placed a palm on his desk and rested my weight on it. "It's only a game when you play."

Leo's laughter slid away, and he sat back, creating distance between us again. "It takes two to play? Perhaps. But a game is better than a war, my Jane."

"Are we at war?" I asked.

"I do not know. Titus Flavius Vespasianus, the emperor of the European Mithrans, has accepted my offer of Sangre Duello. It is now a *new* game, with new rules." Leo held Bruiser with his eyes for a moment, something in the depths I couldn't read. Then he looked back at me. "Will you stand with me, becoming more than my Enforcer? Will you become my dark queen, to fight beside me?"

Bruiser tensed, the reaction more a scent than a movement.

A queen was a king's wife, right? Was this some kind of funky proposal? Or was a queen something else in the vampire world? I wasn't sure what to answer, whether this required a special Mithran-politics reply or something more crude on my part, like blowing raspberries. There was something too thoughtful about Leo tonight, something that felt wrong, something too planned, too devious. It made me edgy. I decided to walk a careful track between the two responses. Being terribly obvious about it, I stood to my full height and set my hand on a silver stake at my side. "I would be a pitiful second in a duel. And no way am I anyone's queen. So, no. No queen stuff."

Wisely I didn't add that I was a War Woman and a skinwalker and Bruiser's love. I didn't need anything at all from Leo Pellissier, Master of the City of New Orleans. But there was no reason to rub his face in it.

Leo inclined his head, as if my answer didn't surprise him. "Grégoire, *Le Valois, Le Orleans,* is my secundo in the duel against Titus' primo or his secundo, should the emperor choose to make that move on this new board we play. If you will not be my queen, then will you be my Enforcer in truth? You would be the first Enforcer of such power and position in the long history of Mithrans." He added, "If you still honor that position."

Bruiser said, carefully, "Jane, according to Mithran precedent, this negotiation, this proposal and the position of Enforcer, and the primo Leo gifted you with . . ." He stopped, as if turning lots of things over his mind and memory. With a hint of laughter in his voice, he finished with, "In many ways, this makes you a queen in your own right, beneath the heel of no king."

I hesitated, feeling that something in all this chitchat was still wrong, but the blood challenge with the emperor might be the only thing that would keep Angie Baby and her family from being held in vamp cages, slaves of the EVs, or worse, dead. It might prevent a vamp war, a major vamp war, with the resulting death of hundreds of vamps and other paranormals, maybe thousands of humans. And . . . *a queen in your own right, beneath the heel of no king*. Ahhh. This wasn't chess. It was five-card stud. I couldn't be blood-bound. I was Leo's wild card. I was between a rock and hard place, flying by the seat of my pants, as always. There was really no choice. "Sure," I said, putting as much snark as I could into it. "Why not."

Leo's smile teased out again before he shifted his eyes to Bruiser. "And you, my Onorio. Will you stand by me?"

"I will. As will the Roberes."

"Three Onorios," Leo mused. "Perhaps it will be enough, now that you have come into the first of your powers."

Bruiser held the eyes of his former master, unblinking. I wondered if Leo had learned that Bruiser had drained a vamp. Leo answered my unspoken question with his own.

"And your Mithran scion?" he asked, his tone silky. "The one you bound?"

Bruiser frowned unhappily. "I have gifted her to Edmund."

Leo's eyebrow quirked up in surprise, calculation flashing through his eyes. "Indeed? Ahhh . . . *Indeed*."

Bruiser didn't reply, and I didn't know what the emphasis on the last word meant. Bruiser did, however, and he glanced at me and away. I was missing something.

"Katherine and Alesha have been restored. Alesha offered much intelligence about the plans and preparations of our enemies. They are being fed as we speak."

"Completely restored?" Bruiser asked. "In all ways?"

"Katie is no longer my heir. I could not allow her that position without great loss of face."

"And your heir?" Bruiser asked, his voice going hard.
"You will not saddle one of us with that."

Leo looked at me wryly. "That gift belongs to Edmund
Hartley."

Bruiser sucked in a breath, his eyes going wide.

I started to rear back at the alarm pumping through him.
"What—"

Before I could get the word out, Leo *moved*. Popping to
my side faster than I could see. He jerked *le breloque* out
of my hand and placed it on my head.

The sizzle of power shocked through me, the same sensation I had felt when I'd looped the wreath around my arm.

Bruiser dove for Leo, but the Master of the City was
faster and popped back behind his desk. They grappled
across the expanse, sending the laptop crashing to the floor.
A lamp. The music went silent. The sound of blows landed.
Grunts and curses. The smell of blood. I sat through it all,
feeling what had just happened. I had been crowned. With
le breloque. A magical item that controlled the weather.
That collected power to be used for magic. That vamps and
witches had fought over.

Fear coursed through me as the tingle of magics slid
around me, to tangle onto my bones. I dropped deep into
my soul home, the cavern dark and chilled, a fire burning
in the center, the air tinged with hickory smoke. There was
strange light glowing in the cavern, centered in the ceiling
overhead. I looked up to the doomed ceiling, seeing the
center, above the fire. Light spread out from that center
height like the plumage of a bird, like angel wings, feather-
ing down. The light was growing brighter, illuminating my
soul home.

From the base of the stone walls, a golden fire rose, cold
blaze licking up the damp rock. The flame tips were shaped
like the leaves of *le breloque*. The power of the magical
device was trying to take over my soul home. Was trying to
take over *me*. Giving me some new power, some new responsibility. Heavy. Onerous and oppressive. In the vision
of my home, my knees buckled. I fell to the ground near the
fire.

Leo had asked me to be his queen. I had said no. He had

seemed fine with my reply. He hadn't been. *That sneaky little suckhead.*

Beast padded close, her golden pelt shining in the odd lights. *Leo is good ambush hunter. Crown is making Jane different. Do not like what crown is making Jane.*

She was right. *Le breloque* was making me . . . making me . . . something. I didn't know what.

Jane has choice, Beast thought at me.

I remembered the words Hayyel had spoken about me making good choices. This was surely one. "No," I said. "I refuse."

Beast chuffed in approval.

Above me, the wings fluttered. Lifted. Resettled. Covering the dome of my soul. The light from them spread. The licking flames of the corona's power died down. Flickered. Vanished.

The Glob in my pocket warmed. Sparked with electricity. I pulled it free and lifted it. Held it high. "I will not accept the magic. I have my own."

Swiftly, the Glob drained *le breloque*. The vision of my soul home, shot through with brilliance, dimmed and disappeared. I was back in Leo's office, holding the Glob over my head. Over the sound of the scuffle I thought I heard the whisper of angel wings.

I reached up and took the wreath off my head, looked it over, and said simply, "Stop."

The fight stopped. Bruiser was bleeding and Leo's severed and reattaching fingers were at an odd angle. "It didn't work." I hooked the crown over my arm. "I don't know what you intended to happen, but it didn't take." I *thunked* the crown with a fingernail. The sound reverberated in the room.

Leo looked horrified. Bruiser looked relieved, the kind of desperate relief he might have expressed when I called him from the boat to say I was alive. "I'm not a queen." I *thunked* the corona again. "I'm leaving now. And if you ever try to crown me again, I'll cut off your head and shove it up your royal ass." I looked at Bruiser and added, "You coming?"

Bruiser remembered to breathe. Leo started laughing.

I grinned at them both. A Beastly grin, all teeth and violence.

Without another word, I left the Mithran Council Chambers, a crown over my arm, my honeybunch at my side.

Due to a twist in diplomacy and an aggressive move on Leo's chessboard of vamp politics, the invasion of New Orleans was over, but the danger wasn't past. A blood challenge might be worse than anything we had faced to date. But I had my team and my love by my side. And I still had myself, my own soul—both of them. Together we could survive.

We might, just maybe, even win a challenge to the death.

Read on for an excerpt from the first book
in Faith Hunter's Soulwood series,

BLOOD OF THE EARTH

Available now from Roc.

Edgy and not sure why, I carried the basket of laundry off the back porch. I hung my T-shirts and overalls on the front line of my old-fashioned solar clothes dryer, two long skirts on the outer line, and what my mama called my intimate attire on the line between, where no one could see them from the driveway. I didn't want another visit by Brother Ephraim or Elder Ebenezer about my wanton ways. Or even another courting attempt from Joshua Purdy. Or worse, a visit from Ernest Jackson Jr., the preacher. So far I'd kept him out of my house, but there would come a time when he'd bring help and try to force his way in. It was getting tiresome having to chase churchmen off my land at the business end of a shotgun, and at some point God's Cloud of Glory Church would bring enough reinforcements that I couldn't stand against them. It was a battle I was preparing for, one I knew I'd likely lose, but I would go down fighting, one way or another.

The breeze freshened, sending my wet skirts rippling as if alive, on the line where they hung. Red, gold, and brown leaves skittered across the three acres of newly cut grass.

Branches overhead cracked, clacked, and groaned with the wind, leaves rustling as if whispering some dread tiding. The chill fall air had been perfect for birdsong; squirrels had been racing up and down the trees, stealing nuts and hiding them for the coming winter. I'd seen a big black bear this morning, chewing on nuts and acorns, halfway up the hill.

Standing in the cool breeze, I studied my woods, listening, feeling, tasting the unease that had prickled at my flesh for the last few months, ever since Jane Yellowrock had come visiting and turned my life upside down. She was the one responsible for the repeated recent visits by the churchmen. The Cherokee vampire hunter was the one who had brought all the changes, even if it wasn't intentional. She had come hunting a missing vampire and, because she was good at her job—maybe the best ever—she had succeeded. She had also managed to save more than a hundred children from God's Cloud.

Maybe it had been worth it all—helping all the children—but I was the one paying the price, not her. She was long gone and I was alone in the fight for my life. Even the woods knew things were different.

Sunlight dappled the earth; cabbages, gourds, pumpkins, and winter squash were bursting with color in the garden. A muscadine vine running up the nearest tree, tangling in the branches, was dropping the last of the ripe fruit. I smelled my wood fire on the air, and hints of that apple-crisp chill that meant a change of seasons, the sliding toward a hard, cold autumn. I tilted my head, listening to the wind, smelling the breeze, feeling the forest through the soles of my bare feet. There was no one on my property except the wild critters, creatures who belonged on Soulwood land, nothing else that I could sense. But the hundred fifty acres of woods bordering the flatland around the house, up the steep hill and down into the gorge, had been whispering all day. Something was not right.

In the distance, I heard a crow call a warning, sharp with distress. The squirrels ducked into hiding, suddenly invisible. The feral cat I had been feeding darted under the shrubs, her black head and multicolored body fading into the shadows. The trees murmured restlessly.

I didn't know what it meant, but I listened anyway. I always listened to my woods, and the gnawing, whispering sense of *danger, injury, damage* was like sandpaper abrading my skin, making me jumpy, disturbing my sleep, even if I didn't know what it was.

I reached out to it, to the woods, reached with my mind, with my magic. Silently I asked it, *What? What is it?*

There was no answer. There never was. But as if the forest knew that it had my attention, the wind died and the whispering leaves fell still. I caught my breath at the strange hush, not daring even to blink. But nothing happened. No sound, no movement. After an uncomfortable length of time, I lifted the empty wash basket and stepped away from the clotheslines, turning and turning, my feet on the cool grass, looking up and inward, but I could sense no direct threat, despite the chill bumps rising on my skin. *What?* I asked. An eerie fear grew in me, racing up my spine like spiders with sharp, tiny claws. Something was coming. Something that reminded me of Jane, but subtly different. Something was coming that might hurt me. Again. My woods knew.

From down the hill I heard the sound of a vehicle climbing the mountain's narrow, single-lane, rutted road. It wasn't the *clang* of Ebenezer's rattletrap Ford truck, or the steady drone of Joshua's newer, Toyota long-bed. It wasn't the high-pitched motor of a hunter's all-terrain vehicle. It was a car, straining up the twisty Deer Creek mountain.

My house was the last one, just below the crest of the hill. The wind whooshed down again, icy and cutting, a downdraft that bowed the trees. They swayed in the wind, branches scrubbing. Sighing. Muttering, too low to hear.

It could be a customer making the drive to Soulwood for my teas or veggies or herbal mixes. Or it could be some kind of conflict. The woods said it was the latter. I trusted my woods.

I raced back inside my house, dropping the empty basket, placing John's old single-shot, bolt-action shotgun near the refrigerator under a pile of folded blankets. His lever-action carbine .30-30 Winchester went near the front window. I shoved the small Smith & Wesson .32 into the bib of my coveralls, hoping I didn't shoot myself if I had to draw it fast.

I picked up the double-barrel break-action shotgun and checked the ammo. Both barrels held three-inch shells. The contact area of the latch was worn and needed to be replaced, but at close range I wasn't going to miss. I might dislocate my shoulder, but if I hit them, the trespassers would be a while in healing too.

I debated for a second on switching out the standard shot shells for salt or birdshot, but the woods' disharmony seemed to be growing, a particular and abrasive itch under my skin. I snapped the gun closed and pulled back my long hair into an elastic to keep it out of my way.

Peeking out the blinds, I saw a four-door sedan coming to a stop beside John's old Chevy C10 truck. Two people inside, a man and a woman. *Strangers,* I thought. Not from God's Cloud of Glory, the church I'd grown up in. Not a local vehicle. And no dogs anymore to check them out for me with noses and senses humans no longer had. Just three small graves at the edge of the woods and a month of grief buried with them.

A man stepped out of the driver's side, black-haired, dark-eyed. Maybe Cherokee or Creek if he was a mountain native, though his features didn't seem tribal. I'd never seen a Frenchman or a Spaniard, so maybe from one of those Mediterranean countries. He was tall, maybe six feet, but not dressed like a farmer. More citified, in black pants, starched shirt, tie, and jacket. He had a cell phone in his pocket, sticking out just a little. Western boots, old and well cared for. There was something about the way he moved, feline and graceful. Not a farmer or a God's Cloud preacher. Not enough bulk for the first one, not enough righteous determination in his expression or bearing for the other. But something said he wasn't a customer here to buy my herbal teas or fresh vegetables.

He opened the passenger door for the other occupant and a woman stepped out. Petite, with black skin and wildly curly, long black hair. Her clothes billowed in the cool breeze and she put her face into the wind as if sniffing. Like the man, her movements were nimble, like a dancer's, and somehow feral, as if she had never been tamed, though I couldn't have said why I got that impression.

Around the house, my woods moaned in the sharp wind, branches clattering like old bones, anxious, but I could see nothing about the couple that would say danger. They looked like any other city folk who might come looking for Soulwood Farm, and yet . . . not. Different. As they approached the house, they passed the tall length of flagpole in the middle of the raised beds of the front yard, and started up the seven steps to the porch. And then I realized why they moved and felt all wrong. There was a weapon bulge at the man's shoulder, beneath his jacket. In a single smooth motion, I braced the shotgun against my shoulder, rammed open the door, and pointed the business end of the gun at the trespassers.

"Whadda ya want?" I demanded, drawing on my childhood God's Cloud dialect. They came to a halt at the third step, too close for me to miss, too far away for them to disarm me safely. The man raised his hands like he was asking for peace, but the little woman hissed. She drew back her lips in a snarl and growled at me. I knew cats. This was a cat. A cat in human form—a werecat of some kind. A devil, according to the church. I trained the barrel on her, midcenter, just like John had showed me the first time he put the gun in my hands. As I aimed, I took a single step so my back was against the doorjamb to keep me from getting bowled over or from breaking a shoulder when I fired.

"Paka, no," the man said. The words were gentle, the touch to her arm tender. I had never seen a man touch a woman like that, and my hands jiggled the shotgun in surprise before I caught myself. The woman's snarl subsided and she leaned in to the man, just like one of my cats might. His arm went around her, and he smoothed her hair back, watching me as I watched them. Alert, taking in everything about me and my home, the man lifted his nose in the air to sniff the scents of my land, the delicate nasal folds widening and contracting. Alien. So alien, these two.

"What do you want?" I asked again, this time with no church accent, and with the grammar I'd learned from the city folk customers at the vegetable stand and from reading my once-forbidden and much-loved library books.

"I'm Special Agent Rick LaFleur, with PsyLED, and

this is Paka. Jane Yellowrock sent us to you, Ms. Ingram," the man said.

Of *course* this new problem was related to Jane. Nothing in my whole life had gone right since she'd darkened my door. She might as well have brought a curse on my land and a pox on my home. She had a curious job, wore clothes and guns and knives like a man, and I had known from the beginning that she would bring nothing but strife to me. But in spite of that, I had liked her. So had my woods. She moved like these two, willowy and slinky. Alert.

She had come to my house asking about God's Cloud of Glory. She had wanted a way onto the church's property, which bordered mine, to rescue a blood-sucker. Because there was documentation in the probate court, the civil court system, and the local news, that John and I had left the church, Jane had figured that I'd be willing to help her. And God help me, I had. I'd paid the price for helping her and, sometimes, I wished that I'd left well enough alone.

"Prove it," I said, resettling the gun against my shoulder. The man slowly lowered his hand and removed a wallet from his jacket pocket, displaying an identification card and badge. But I knew that badges can be bought online for pennies and IDs could be made on computers. "Not good enough," I said. "Tell me something about Jane that no one but her knows."

"Jane is not human, though she apes it better than some," Paka said, her words strangely accented, her voice scratchy and hoarse. "She was once mated to my mate." Paka placed a covetous hand on Rick's arm, an inexplicable sort of claiming. The man frowned harder, deep grooves in his face. I had a feeling that he didn't like being owned like a piece of meat. I'd seen that unhappy look on the faces of women before. Seeing the expression on the face of a man was unexpected and, for some reason, unsettling. "He is mine now," Paka said.

When Jane told me about the man she would send, she said that he would break my heart if I let him, like he'd broken Jane's. This Rick was what the few romance novels I'd read called tall, dark, and handsome, a grim, distant man with a closed face and too many secrets. A heartbreaker for sure. "That's a start," I said. In their car, a small catlike form jumped to the dash, crouched low, and peered out the windshield through the daylight glare. I ignored it, all my attention on the pair on my land, moving slowly. Rick pulled out his cell phone and thumb-punched and swiped it a few times. He paraphrased from whatever was on the screen, "Jane said you told her you'd been in trouble from God's Cloud of Glory and the man who used to lead it ever since you turned twelve and he tried to marry you. She also said Nell Nicholson Ingram makes the best chicken and dumplings she ever tasted. That about right?"

I scowled. Around me the forest rustled, expectant and uneasy, tied to my magic. Tied to me. "Yeah. That sums it up." I draped the shotgun over my arm and backed into my home, standing aside as they mounted the last of the steps. Wondering what the church spies in the deer stand on the next property would think about the standoff.

They thought I didn't know that they kept watch on me all the time from the neighbor's land, but I knew. Just like I knew that they wanted me back under their thumbs and my land back in the church, to be used for their benefit. I'd known ever since I had beaten them in court, proving that John and I were legally married and that his will had given the land to me. The church elders didn't like me having legal rights, and they didn't like me. The feeling was mutual.

My black cat Jezzie raced out of the house and Paka caught her and picked her up. The tiny woman laughed, the sound as peculiar and scratchy as her words. And the oddest thing happened. Jezzie rolled over, lay belly-up in Paka's arms, and closed her eyes. Instantly she was asleep. Jezzie didn't like people; she barely tolerated me in her house, letting me live here because I brought cat kibble. Jezzie had ignored the man, just the way she ignored humans. And me. It told me something about the woman. She wasn't just a werecat. She had magic.

I backed farther inside, and they crossed the porch. *Nonhumans. In my house.* I didn't like this at all, but I didn't know how to stop it. Around the property, the woods quieted, as if waiting for a storm that would break soon, bringing the trees rain to feed their roots. I reached out to the woods, as uneasy as they were, but there was no way to calm them.

I didn't know fully what kind of magic I had, except that I could help seeds sprout, make plants grow stronger, heal them when they got sick and tried to die off. My magics had always been part of me, and now, since I had fed the forest once, my gifts were tied to the woods and the earth of Soulwood Farm. I had been told that my magic was similar to the Cherokee *yinehi*. Similar to the fairies of European lore, the little people, or even wood nymphs. But in my recent, intense Internet research I hadn't found an exact correlation with the magics I possessed, and I had an instinct, a feeling, that there might be more I could do, if I was willing to pay the price. I had once been told that there was always a price for magic.

"Come on in," I said, backing farther inside.

I watched the two strangers enter, wondering what was about to happen to my once sheltered and isolated life. I wondered what the churchmen watching my house with binoculars would have to say about it. What they would do about it. Maybe this time they'd kill my cats too—more graves to feed the earth. Grief welled up in me, and I tamped it down where no one could see it, concentrating on what I could discern and what I already knew about the couple.

Paka seemed less human than anything I'd ever seen before, not necessarily unstable, but all claws and instinct with a taste for games and blood. Rick was with PsyLED, a branch of law enforcement, which meant he'd have a certain amount of self-control.

The Constitution, the different branches of government, citizens' rights, and law enforcement were all taught from the cradle up in the church school, so all the church members would know how to debate the illegality of any incursion or line of questioning. But PsyLED was an organization that had been formed after I had left the church. Instead of learning about the quasi-secret agency at my husband's or my father's knee, I had made a trip to the local library, where I had looked up the paranormal department and discovered that PsyLED stood for Psychometry Law Enforcement Division of Homeland Security. PsyLED units, which were still being formed, investigated and solved paranormal crimes—crimes involving magic and magic-using creatures: bloodsuckers, were-creatures, and such. They had unusual and broad law enforcement and investigatory powers. They worked at the request of local or state law enforcement, and took over cases that were being improperly handled or ignored by local law. Officially the head of PsyLED reported directly to two organizations, the National Security Agency/Central Security Service, and Homeland Security, and by request to the CIA, the chief of the Department of Defense, the Secret Service, and the FBI. They were a crossover branch of law enforcement, one created just for magic.

In the back of my mind flitted conspiracy reports, urban legends, government machinations, and treachery. Things left over from a life lived in the church. Even John and his first wife, Leah, had believed that the government was evil, and living in Knoxville, near Secret City (where the US government has its ultra–top secret research facilities, the ones that made the first atomic bombs and contributed to every other major military creation since) only made the stories more plausible.

Warily, keeping my body turned toward them, I backed into the main room of the house, sliding my bare feet on the wood floor into the great room that was living room, the eating area, and the kitchen at the back. I jutted my chin to the far end of the old table and mismatched chairs that had been John's maw-maw's. He'd been dead and gone for years now, but in my mind it was still his and Leah's. Leah had been sister and mother and friend. I had loved her, and watching her wither away and die had broken me in ways I still hadn't dealt with. When I walked through her house, I still missed her. "Set a spell. I got some hot tea on the Waterford."

The man waited until the woman sat to take his own seat. *Solicitous*—that's what the romance books called it. Stupid books that had nothing to do with the life of a mountain woman. City women, maybe. But never the wives and women of God's Cloud of Glory Church. I moved to the far side of

the table. When I was sure we were all in positions that
would require them to make two or three moves before they
could reach me, I set the shotgun on the table and got out
three pottery mugs. I wasn't using John's maw-maw's good
china for outsiders whom I might have to shoot later. That
seemed deceitful.

With a hot pad, I moved the teapot to the side of the
woodstove, where the hob was cooler, and removed the tea
strainer. I could have made some coffee—the man looked
like a coffee-drinking type—but I didn't want to encourage
them to stay. I poured the spice tea into the mugs, smelling
cloves and allspice, with a hint of cinnamon and cardamom.
It was my own recipe, made with a trace of real ground
vanilla bean, precious and expensive. I put the mugs on an
old carved oak tray, with cloth napkins and fresh cream and
sugar. I added three spoons and placed the tea tray on the
table in front of the sofa. I took my mug and backed away
again, behind the long table, to where I could reach the
shotgun.

"Welcome to my home," I said, hearing the reluctance
in my tone. "Hospitality and safety while you're here." It
was an old God's Cloud saying, and though the church and
I had parted ways a long time ago, some things stayed with
a woman. Guests should be safe so long as they acted right.

The nonhumans took the tea, the woman adding an inch
of the real cream to the top and wrapping her hands around
the mug as though she felt the chill of winter coming.

With a start, I realized my cats, Jezzie and Cello, were
both on the woman's lap. I tried not to let my guests see my
reaction. My cats were mousers, working cats, not lap cats.
They didn't like people. Annoyed at the disloyal cats, I pulled
out a chair and sat.

The man held his mug one-handed, shooting surrepti-
tious glances at my stuff, concentrating on the twenty-eight-
gauge, four-barreled, break-action Rombo shotgun hanging
over the steps to the second floor. It was made by Famars
in Italy and had been John's prize position. I narrowed my
eyes at him. "See something you want?" I asked, an edge
in my voice.

Instead of answering, Rick asked a question again, as if

that was a built-in response. "You cook and heat this whole place with a woodstove?"

I nodded once, sipping my tea. The man didn't go on and for some reason I felt obliged to offer, "I can heat most of my water too, eight months of the year. Long as I don't mind picking up branches, splitting wood, and cleaning the stove."

"You are strong," Paka said, Jezzie on her lap and Cello now climbing to her shoulders to curl around her neck. "You use an ax as my people use our claws, with ease and . . . what is the English word? Ah." She smiled at Rick. "Ef-fort-less-ness. That is a good word."

She sniffed the air, dainty and delicate. "Your magic is different from all others I have smelled. I like it." Her lips curled up, she kicked off her heels, and shifted her feet up under her body, moving like a ballerina. She drank the tea in little sips—sip-sip-sip, her lips and throat moving fast.

I wasn't sure what she might know about my magic, so I didn't respond. Instead I watched the man as he looked around, holding his tea mug, one hand free to draw his weapon. He had noted the placement of the other guns at the windows, the worn rug in front of the sofa, the few electronic devices plugged into the main outlet at the big old desk. Upstairs on the south side of the house, farthest from the road and any sniper attack, was the inverter and batteries. Rick looked that way, as if he could see through the ceiling to the system that kept me self-sufficient. Or he could hear the hum of the inverter, maybe. I was so used to it that I seldom noticed unless I was up there working.

He looked to the window unit air conditioner, which was still in place for the last of the summer heat, and up to the ceiling fans, thinking. "The rest of the year, the solar panels on the dormer roofs meet all your needs, I guess," he said. I didn't reply. Few people knew about the solar panels, which were situated on the downslope, south side of the dormers. John had paid cash for them to keep anyone from knowing our plans. I didn't like the government knowing my business and wondered if Rick had been looking at satellite maps or had a camera-mounted drone fly over. I didn't usually ascribe to the churchmen's paranoid conspiracy theories, but maybe they had a few facts right. I glared at the government cop and let my tone go gruff. "What's your point?"

He said, almost as if musing, "Solar is great except in snowfall or prolonged cloudy days. They run the fans overhead?" He gestured with his mug to the ten-foot ceiling. "The refrigerator?"

It felt as if he was goading me about my lifestyle, and I didn't know why. Maybe it was a police thing, the kind of things the churchmen said the law always did, trying to provoke an action that would allow them to make an arrest. But there were ways to combat that. I set my mug on the smooth wood table, the finish long gone and now kept in good repair with a coating of lemon oil. I spoke slowly, spacing my words. "What. Do. You. Want? Make it fast. I'm busy."

"I understand you have good intel on God's Cloud of Glory Church. We need your help."

"No."

"They killed your dogs, yes?" Paka said, her shining eyes piercing. To Rick, she said, "I smell dogs in the house; their scent"—she extended her thumb and index finger and brought them closer together, as if pinching something, making it smaller—"is doing this. And there were piles of stones at the edge of the front grass." To me she said, "Graves?"

My lips went tight and my eyes went achy and dry. I'd come home from the Knoxville main library to find my two beagles and the old bird dog dead on my porch, like presents. They had been shot in the yard and dragged by their back legs to my front door. I still hadn't gotten the blood out of the porch wood. I'd buried the dogs across the lawn and piled rocks on top of the graves. And I still grieved.

I gave Paka a stilted nod, my hair slipping from the elastic, swinging forward, across my shoulders and veiling my face, hiding my emotions.

Paka nodded absently, her eyes distant, the way some people look when thinking about math or music. "I also smelled three men. Outside. They . . ." She paused as if seeking words. ". . . urinated on your garden as if marking territory. This is strange, yes? They are only human, not were-kind." Peeing on my garden sounded like some of the men of the church, childish and mean, to kill my plants, to urinate on my dinner. "My people do not keep dogs," she said, "but I understand that humans like them as pets, like family. There was dog blood on your porch. The men should not have killed your pets."

Rick said, "That was what I smelled coming in."

Without turning her head, Paka shifted sharp eyes to me. "Do you want me to track and kill the killer of your dogs?"

"Paka," the man said, warning in his tone.

A suspicious part of me wondered why she was being so kind, while another part heard a murderous vengeance in the words, and yet a third part wanted to say, *Yes. Make them hurt.* But vengeance would only make the churchmen come back meaner, and this time they'd kill me for sure, or make me wish for my own death. The churchmen were good at keeping their women pliant and obedient, or hurting them until they submitted. I didn't plan on doing either, and I didn't plan on leaving, not until I could get my sisters and their young'uns to come with me, to freedom and safety. I shook my head and said, "No," to make sure they understood. "Leave them be."

"Is that why won't you help us with intel on the church?" Rick asked, his voice gentle. "The dogs? You're afraid of their killers coming back and hurting you?"

My mouth opened and I said words that had been bubbling in my blood since I saw them in my yard. "You were supposed to be here months ago. Jane said you'd help me stay safe. Instead, the churchmen have come on my land— *my land*," I added fiercely, "three times and they done bad things. Threatened me. Shed blood." I lowered my voice and clenched my fists tightly on the tabletop to keep the rising energies knotted inside or maybe to keep from picking up the gun and shooting them. "And then *you* come here and want more favors instead of the help she promised."

Rick started to move. I whipped to the side, one hand grabbing the shotgun, aiming. Fast as I was, the man was faster. He had drawn a fancy handgun in a single motion, so quick I hadn't even seen him move. It was a big gun. Maybe a ten-millimeter. And it was aimed at my head.

Beside him, Paka draped an arm across the sofa back and watched him. And she purred. The sound was like a bobcat, but louder.

"Get outta my house," I said. "You might shoot me, but I'll put a hurting on you'uns too." But they just stayed there as if they were rooted to my furniture. Cello crawled around Paka's neck and nestled with Jezzie on her lap, her nose lifting close to the werecat's face. *Traitor.* Something that might have been jealousy settled firmly in my chest like a weight. I scowled. Paka blinked, the motion slow and lazy.

"Mexican standoff," Rick said, his voice soft. "Unless you have silver shot, we'll heal from anything you can do to us. You won't heal from a three tap to the chest."

I laughed, the sound not like me. It was a nasty laugh. I set the shotgun back down and placed one hand flat on the table. Paka raised her head. "I smell her magics," she said. "They are rising. Your gun might not hurt her as it would a human." She petted Cello and she smiled again, her eyes tight on me. "This woman is dangerous, my mate. I like her. Her magic smells green, like the woods that surround the house. And it smells of decay, like prey that has gone back into the earth."

"You're like Paka, aren't you?" I asked Rick, reaching through the wood table and floor, down into the ground, into the stone foundations and the dirt below the house, into the roots of the woods that gave the farm its name, roots tangled through the soil in the backyard, deep into the earth. "Werecat." I placed my other hand on the table too, flat and steady.

"We are African black were-leopards," Paka said, watching me in fascination, her nostrils almost fluttering as she sniffed the air.

"Not exactly the same, though," Rick said, his weapon aimed steadily at me, even though I'd put down my shotgun. "I was infected when I was bitten. She was born this way."

"Why do you tell our secrets?" Paka asked, not as if in disagreement, but as if she was mildly curious while being bored.

"Because we need her help," Rick said. "We need to know about the Human Speakers of Truth and any possible connection to the church. Nell's the only one who might be willing to talk to me. To us," he added, including his mate.

"Who are the Human Speakers of Truth?" I asked, letting the power and safety of the woods wrap around me like crawling snakes, like vines, growing in place. All I needed was one drop of his blood and I could take his life. It was my best protection; it was my magic and the magic of my land. His blood on my land, on Soulwood, put his life into my hands. "What do you want to know? The federal and state raid on the compound told most folks all there was to know about the church."

"Do you still have family ties to God's Cloud?" Rick asked, again not answering my question. It was probably a police tactic, but it set my teeth on edge. "Someone you could go to, or talk to, safely, but not get into more trouble with the people who killed your dogs?"

"I have family there," I said, using the time to gather as much of the woods' energy as I could. "We run into one another from time to time. Farmers' market. Yard sales. Why you asking?" I said, my tone challenging, deliberately accented by years in the church.

"The FBI, state police, and PsyLED have reason to believe that a group calling themselves the Human Speakers of Truth, on the run from the authorities, stopped in Knoxville. But HST disappeared. They don't have a home base here, so they may have joined forces with a local group. We want to rule out that the HST allied with God's Cloud of Glory Church."

"Never heard of HST," I said.

"They're a homegrown terrorist, anti anyone nonhuman, militant group," Rick said, "investigated by PsyLED for years. Our unit's been tracking their financial trail, but it went cold five days ago here in Knoxville."

"What kind of reason?" I asked. When he looked confused I said, "You said you had *reason to believe* that Human Speakers of Truth may have holed up in Knoxville. What kind of reason?"

"HST needed a place to regroup after the arrests of three high-ranking members and the freezing of the group's financial accounts. We tracked them here and then lost the trail.

"God's Cloud of Glory Church—your old cult—was in trouble with the Tennessee child services department, after the state arrested some of their leaders and placed the children in foster care. Both groups are ultra–right wing paranormal-haters, and both are in trouble with the law and financially. It makes sense for them to join up, but we can't find anything electronically that supports that possibility."

"Guesswork," I said, but I couldn't help my small smile. I'd helped damage the church. Me losing my peaceful life had meant getting one hundred thirty-eight children, some of them sexually abused, out of the clutches of God's Cloud. I had helped, even if only passively, by letting the team have access to the church's compound through my property. But I knew a fishing expedition when I heard it. There was no evidence in Rick's statements, just supposition and wishful thinking.

Rick LaFleur acknowledged my smile with a tight one of his own. "HST stopped here, we know that, so it's possible that they might have joined forces with the church, even if just temporarily. And if that's true, then HST and God's Cloud merging was a match made in, well, not heaven. Maybe in the boardroom."

"Huntin'," I said. "The menfolk would have made a deal with rifles or shotguns and dead meat for the dinner table."

Something in my tone made Rick holster his gun. I tapped off the energies from the woods, holding the gathered power under my palms, flat against the table. The wood of the table had been cut from my forest, over a hundred years ago. I could use it. "So, yes. I got family there. Some will still speak to me at market. If I choose to talk to them."

Watching my posture, Rick said, "Can you ask your family a few questions? For instance, if any new people have been admitted onto the compound?"

"That's it?" I asked. "Information?"

"That's one reason why we came up here today," Rick said.

There was a lot of wiggle room in his answer, but there was also no threat. This was a negotiation.

Realizing that, I started to let the power I had gathered

trickle back through the table, into the floor, and into the ground beneath the house. I took a slow breath. "Jane Yellowrock asked for help to save a captured vampire, and in return, she got the children out of there. My life is in danger because of her, but, if I'm honest, I think it was a fair trade. And she paid me. You ask for help with nothing in return. Why would I be so stupid?"

"Because helping us might make the church leave you alone. For good," Rick said.

"I can't see how that might even be possible." But it sounded like heaven. They had done research on me, enough to know what buttons to push to make me do what they wanted.

"You could come to work with PsyLED, on a consultant basis."

And there it was, the carrot Jane Yellowrock had suggested so long ago. A way to be safe, finally and completely, from the church, because they might walk away if I worked for law enforcement, especially one of the shadow organizations like PsyLED. I would have a different lifestyle, a different place to live . . . assuming I could leave the land, which was in doubt, but wasn't something I could say to strangers. To anyone, for that matter. I set a thoughtful expression on my face, as if their offer was okay, but not all that great. "I'll consider talking to my family." I stood straight and rubbed my palms on my thighs. "I'll think about consulting. If the money's good enough. For now, though, you gotta go."

Without replying, my guests watched as I shook open a used plastic grocery bag, filled it with late fall squash, a small plastic baggie of an herbal air-freshener mixture that contained catnip, and a bottle of local honey. I put it on the table between them. "Twenty-five bucks. Cash. And make sure the bag is visible when you go to your car. The men watching my place need to see you with it. If they stand in the road as you leave, you have two choices: run through them, which I recommend, or stop. If you run through them, be prepared to be shot at and for the local law to do next to nothing. If you stop, don't let them know you're a cop. Just act like honeymooners and tell them you bought my Blue Pill Herbal Tea and Aromatherapy."

"Blue pill?" Rick asked.

"Some men need a little help in the bedroom. They come to me for my herbal Blue Pill Blend."

He frowned. Paka smiled. I said, "Git."

"Thank you for your time." Rick placed a small stack of five-dollar bills on the side table, beside his nearly full mug. He touched Paka's shoulder and she stood, still holding my cats. The cop moved to the door without ever quite turning his back to me. He paused at the small table beside the door, one laden with library books and DVDs. He set a business card on top. "I know you don't have a cell signal here or a landline phone, but if you need me and can get to one, call the number on that card. I'll get here as quick as I can. Tomorrow is Tuesday, and the farmers' market is going all week in honor of the Brewer's Jam fall festival." When I looked surprised that he knew that, he added, "We do our homework. In case you decide to help us, call when you get to town. We can be at Market Square early in the day. We'll find you."

They'd find me. Yeah. That was plain. No matter what I did or where I went, someone would find me. "Git," I said again, this time with a little heat, letting the power of the land writhe around my hands and into my flesh.

Paka scented the air with her lips drawn back, sucking air over her tongue, then set my cats on the floor just inside the door and followed her mate out, closing the door behind her. I grabbed up the gun and raced to the window, watching them as they entered the car, Rick carrying the bag prominently and placing it on the floor of the backseat. The small catlike creature that had run around in the car was gone from the dash. The car made a three-point turn and wheeled sedately down the drive for the road.

As I watched, Jezzie walked up to me and sat, her front feet together, posing as only a house cat can, and mewled. I bent down hesitantly and picked her up. Jezzie wasn't fond of people, but this time, she snuggled against me, purring, and scrubbed her head on my chest. Cello walked up and wound her body around my feet, and she had never done that before.

Paka had done this.

I glowered at the sight of the retreating rental car. I hadn't given them my little blue pill mixture, but on cats, the catnip mixture might work the same way. If so, Rick would probably have a fair number of scratches on him by morning and Paka would be smiling and purring. She looked like the kind of female who liked a lot of sex a lot of the time. Some women did, not that I ever understood that sentiment. It was mean of me to give them my catnip blend, and had I known that Paka was mesmerizing and taming my cats for me, I might not have. But at the time, I hadn't been able to help myself. It had seemed the least they deserved for the trouble that would follow their visit.

I stayed at the window, petting Jezzie, watching, waiting. Maybe ten minutes later, I saw a form move down the drive, keeping to the shadows. Two others followed it. The churchmen were here, and they were sneaking in along the east side of the property, not coming openly down the drive, which meant nothing good. The only good thing was that there weren't enough of them to surround the house, which meant they were likely here to threaten, not to burn me out. Looked like I'd get to use the energies I had been gathering from the forest after all. I set Jezzie on the floor and scooted the cats up the stairs, where they liked to watch birds from the dormer windows.

THE JANE YELLOWROCK SERIES

BY FAITH HUNTER

Shape-shifting skinwalker Jane Yellowrock fights vampires, demons, and everything in between in the city of New Orleans.

Find more books by Faith Hunter
by visiting prh.com/nextread

"Faith Hunter has created one of my favorite characters, ever . . . Highly recommended."
—Fresh Fiction

"Hunter's very professionally executed, tasty blend of dark fantasy, mystery, and romance should please fans of all three genres."—*Booklist*

faithhunter.net
⬛ official.faith.hunter
🐦 hunterfaith

Penguin
Random
House